D1539927

St Antony's Series

General Editor: **Jan Zielonka** (2004–), Fellow of St Antony's College, Oxford

Recent titles include:

Valpy FitzGerald and Rosemary Thorp (*editors*)
ECONOMIC DOCTRINES IN LATIN AMERICA
Origins, Embedding and Evolution

Victoria D. Alexander and Marilyn Rueschemeyer
ART AND THE STATE
The Visual Arts in Comparative Perspective

Ailish Johnson
EUROPEAN WELFARE STATES AND SUPRANATIONAL GOVERNANCE OF SOCIAL
POLICY

Archie Brown (*editor*)
THE DEMISE OF MARXISM-LENINISM IN RUSSIA

Thomas Boghardt
SPIES OF THE KAISER
German Covert Operations in Great Britain during the First World War Era

Ulf Schmidt
JUSTICE AT NUREMBERG
Leo Alexander and the Nazi Doctors' Trial

Steve Tsang (*editor*)
PEACE AND SECURITY ACROSS THE TAIWAN STRAIT

C. W. Braddick
JAPAN AND THE SINO–SOVIET ALLIANCE, 1950–1964
In the Shadow of the Monolith

Isao Miyaoka
LEGITIMACY IN INTERNATIONAL SOCIETY
Japan's Reaction to Global Wildlife Preservation

Neil J. Melvin
SOVIET POWER AND THE COUNTRYSIDE
Policy Innovation and Institutional Decay

Julie M. Newton
RUSSIA, FRANCE AND THE IDEA OF EUROPE

Juhana Aunesluoma
BRITAIN, SWEDEN AND THE COLD WAR, 1945–54
Understanding Neutrality

George Pagoulatos
GREECE'S NEW POLITICAL ECONOMY
State, Finance and Growth from Postwar to EMU

Tiffany A. Troxel
PARLIAMENTARY POWER IN RUSSIA, 1994–2001
A New Era

Elvira María Restrepo
COLOMBIAN CRIMINAL JUSTICE IN CRISIS
Fear and Distrust

Ilaria Favretto
THE LONG SEARCH FOR A THIRD WAY
The British Labour Party and the Italian Left Since 1945

Lawrence Tal
POLITICS, THE MILITARY AND NATIONAL SECURITY IN JORDAN,
1955–1967

Louise Haagh and Camilla Helgø (editors)
SOCIAL POLICY REFORM AND MARKET GOVERNANCE IN LATIN
AMERICA

Gayil Talshir
THE POLITICAL IDEOLOGY OF GREEN PARTIES
From the Politics of Nature to Redefining the Nature of Politics

E. K. Dosmukhamedov
FOREIGN DIRECT INVESTMENT IN KAZAKHSTAN
Politico-Legal Aspects of Post-Communist Transition

Felix Patrikeeff
RUSSIAN POLITICS IN EXILE
The Northeast Asian Balance of Power, 1924–1931

He Ping
CHINA'S SEARCH FOR MODERNITY
Cultural Discourse in the Late 20th Century

Mariana Llanos
PRIVATIZATION AND DEMOCRACY IN ARGENTINA
An Analysis of President–Congress Relations

St Antony's Series
Series Standing Order ISBN 0–333–71109–2
(outside North America only)

You can receive future titles in this series as they are published by placing a standing order. Please contact your bookseller or, in case of difficulty, write to us at the address below with your name and address, the title of the series and the ISBN quoted above.

Customer Services Department, Macmillan Distribution Ltd, Houndmills, Basingstoke, Hampshire RG21 6XS, England

Economic Doctrines in Latin America

Origins, Embedding and Evolution

Edited by

Valpy FitzGerald

and

Rosemary Thorp

in association with
St Antony's College, Oxford

First published in 2005 by
PALGRAVE MACMILLAN
Houndmills, Basingstoke, Hampshire RG21 6XS and
175 Fifth Avenue, New York, N.Y. 10010
Companies and representatives throughout the world.

PALGRAVE MACMILLAN is the global academic imprint of the Palgrave
Macmillan division of St. Martin's Press, LLC and of Palgrave Macmillan Ltd.
Macmillan® is a registered trademark in the United States, United Kingdom
and other countries. Palgrave is a registered trademark in the European
Union and other countries.

ISBN-13: 978–1–4039–9749–4
ISBN-10: 1–4039–9749–7

This book is printed on paper suitable for recycling and made from fully
managed and sustained forest sources.

A catalogue record for this book is available from the British Library.

Library of Congress Cataloging-in-Publication Data
    Economic doctrines in Latin America : origins, embedding, and
evolution / editors, Valpy FitzGerald, Rosemary Thorp.
        p. cm.—(St. Antony's series)
    "In association with St. Antony's College."
    Includes bibliographical references and index.
    ISBN 1–4039–9749–7
    1. Latin America—Economic policy. 2. Economics—Latin America—Foreign
influences. 3. Free enterprise—Latin America. I. FitzGerald, E. V. K.
(Edmund Valpy Knox), 1947–. II. Thorp, Rosemary. III. St. Antony's series
(Palgrave Macmillan (Firm))
HC125.E37355 2005
338.98'009—dc22   2005047295

10 9 8 7 6 5 4 3 2 1
14 13 12 11 10 09 08 07 06 05

Printed and bound in Great Britain by
Antony Rowe Ltd, Chippenham and Eastbourne

Contents

List of Figures and Tables

List of Abbreviations

BANCOMEXT	Banco Nacional de Comercio Exterior
CANACINTRA	Cámara Nacional de la Industria de Transformación
CEMLA	Centro de Estudios Monetarios Latinoamericanos
CENDES	Centro de Estudios de Desarrollo
CEPAL	Comisión Económica para América Latina y el Caribe, also ECLAC
CFCE	Consejo Federal de Comercio Exterior
CONCAMIN	Confederación de Cámaras Industriales de los Estados Unidos Mexicanos
ECLA	Economic Commission for Latin America and the Caribbean, also CEPAL
ESCOLATINA	Escuela de Graduados en Economía para América Latina
FAO	Food and Agriculture Organization
FGV	Fundação Getulio Vargas
FTAA	Free Trade Area of the Americas
GATT	General Agreement on Tariffs and Trade
IADB	Inter-American Development Bank
ILO	International Labour Organization
ILPES	Instituto Latinoamericano de Planificación Económica y Social
ISI	Import-substitution industrialisation
ITAM	Instituto Tecnológico Autónomo de México
MERCOSUR	Mercado Común del Sur
NAFINSA	Nacional Financiera, SA
NAFTA	North American Free Trade Agreement
NGO	Non-governmental organization
OAS	Organization of American States
ODEPLAN	Oficina de Planificación Nacional
OECD	Organisation for Economic Co-operation and Development
PAN	Patrido de Acción Nacional
PEMEX	Petróleos Mexicanos
PRI	Partido Revolucionario Institutional
RBE	*Revista Brasileira de Economia*
RCE	*Revista de Ciencias Económicas*
SEPAFIN	Secretaría de Patrimonio y Fomento Industrial
SUMOC	Superintendência da Moeda e do Crédito
TE	*Trimestre Económico*
UN	United Nations

UNAM	Universidad Nacional Autónoma de Médico
UNCTAD	United Nations Conference on Trade and Development
UNDP	United Nations Development Programme
UNESCO	United Nations Economic, Scientific and Cultural Organization
UNIANDES	Universidad de los Andes
UNICEF	United Nations Children's Fund
UNIDO	United Nations Industrial Development Organization
USAID	United States Agency for International Development
USP	University of São Paolo
WTO	World Trade Organization

Notes on the Contributors

Paul W. Drake is Dean of the Division of Social Science and Professor of Political Science at the University of California, San Diego. He specializes in Chilean politics and, more generally, in Latin American political economy.

Valpy FitzGerald is University Reader in International Economics and Finance at the University of Oxford, a Fellow of St Antony's College, and Director of the Finance and Trade Policy Research Centre at the university's Queen Elizabeth House Department for International Development. His research focuses on global capital markets, open-economy macroeconomics of developing countries, and the history of economic thought, with an area focus on Latin America and Spain.

Peter Gourevitch is Professor of Political Science at the University of California, San Diego. He specializes in political economy with a particular focus on international trade and economic globalization, trade disputes, and regulatory systems.

Nils Jacobsen is Professor of History at the University of Illinois at Urbana-Champaign. He has worked especially on the Andes and on comparative rural history, with his current research focusing on politics and society in nineteenth-century Peru, Indian communities, and land in Latin American history.

Joseph L. Love is Professor of History at the University of Illinois at Urbana-Champaign and Director of the university's Center for Latin American and Caribbean Studies. He concentrates particularly on Brazil, the history of Latin American economies and economic ideas. His current research focuses on the history of economic development and economic theory in Latin America.

Marco Palacios is Rector of the National University of Colombia, and a historian specializing in the political history of Colombia in the nineteenth and twentieth centuries. Based at the Universidad Nacional de Colombia, his recent work includes a general history of Colombia and a detailed study of the history of coffee in the country between 1850 and 1970.

Frances Stewart is University Professor in Development Economics at the University of Oxford and Director of the Centre for Research on Inequality, Human Security and Ethnicity at the university's Department for International Development, Queen Elizabeth House. Her main research interests include horizontal inequalities, poverty and human development, group behaviour, and the causes and consequences of conflict.

Rosemary Thorp is Reader in Latin American Economics at the University of Oxford, and a Fellow of St Antony's College. She works on issues of inequality and conflict, the role of institutions, and the economic history of Latin America.

Laurence Whitehead is Official Fellow in Politics at Nuffield College, University of Oxford, and Director of the University's Mexican Studies Centre. He works mainly on international aspects of democratization, and on the relationship between democratization and economic liberalization, with a principal focus on Latin America.

Ngaire Woods is Lecturer in Politics and International Relations and Director of Global Economic Governance Programme, University College, University of Oxford. She specializes in governance and accountability in the world economy, and the political economy of developing countries in the international economy.

Preface

For a number of years, we have been intrigued by how difficult it is for liberal *economic* ideas to become generally accepted (that is, socially 'embedded') in Latin America despite the universal support for liberal *political* ideas and recognition of the logic of the global market system. This seems to be an issue common to other industrializing regions: particularly the process of economic liberalization that occurred in Southern Europe in the 1980s, then in Russia and Eastern Europe in the 1990s and is now spreading to Asia. In all these cases, economic reform has been initiated 'from above' with reference to external precedents (in the case of Eastern Europe this was often Latin America itself). Just how these ideas are accepted, resisted or transformed by civil society and the role of international institutions in their transmission is widely discussed in practice but does not yet have a scholarly literature.

This volume responds to the determination of a group of scholars in Oxford with colleagues from the Latin America, the United States and Europe to deepen our understanding of how ideas are not just transmitted but *embedded* with varying degrees of solidity, and how that process of embedding is conditioned by local contexts and history, so that what reaches the stage of implementation may be quite distinct from what is transmitted at some other level. The context of our curiosity was the to-be-proven embedding of the neo-liberal paradigm in Latin America. Indeed, as the project has developed, the rise of radical governments such as that of Chávez in Venezuela, Kirschner in Argentina and Lula in Brazil on the one hand, and the rapid decline in popularity of conservative 'liberal' leaders such as Fox in Mexico and Toledo in Peru on the other, seemed to underline the need to understand this process better.

We felt that the topic was so demanding of interdisciplinary as well as comparative skills, and so intangible analytically, that the most appropriate methodology would be a workshop of diverse and very experienced researchers who could interact, challenge and encourage each other in the rewriting of draft chapters. This took place in Oxford with funding from the Hewlett Foundation, which we warmly acknowledge. Institutional support was provided by the Latin American Centre and St Antony's College. All chapters were then reworked, some several times. The inclusion of a historical perspective was important in the dynamics of the project – both in providing a background of previous shifts towards (and away from) economic liberalism, and in imposing a necessary academic rigour on a diverse group of social scientists.

Although it is not customary to do so, we wish to thank our authors in this case for their patience. Researching at the interdisciplinary boundary – in this case several at once – is always hard work, and even more so when attempting to combine the comparative analysis of contemporary events with a rigorous historical perspective. The gestation period of this volume has thus been protracted by the need to revise the various contributions in order to produce a whole that we believe to be considerably more than the sum of its parts. Last, but not least, we are extremely grateful to Emma Samman for providing both research and editorial assistance with exceptional efficiency and good humour.

VALPY FITZGERALD
ROSEMARY THORP

1
Introduction: The Acceptance of Economic Doctrine in Latin America

Valpy FitzGerald and Rosemary Thorp

The power of economic ideas

A crucial shift in the dominant economic doctrine – in the sense of a consistent set of ideas about how the economy should be organized and policy be conducted – undoubtedly took place in Latin America during the 1980s. This shift was characterized by a move away from state-led industrialization, domestic market expansion and public welfare provision as the basis for national economic development. In fact, the transition towards trade liberalization, fiscal consolidation and private social provision had already begun in most of the region during the 1970s and it was still being consolidated and modified in the 1990s. However, the doctrinal change itself was most evident in the 1980s, and was expressed as an explicit move from 'developmentalism'[1] towards 'neo-liberalism' as the intellectual foundation of economic strategy throughout the region.

This shift in economic doctrine is usually regarded as matching the new dominance of liberal political theory that underpinned the re-establishment of democracy in the region on the one hand, and the spread of market institutions in the world economy ('globalization') in the wake of the cold war on the other. According to most observers the dominance of neo-liberal economic doctrine was largely complete in Latin America by the end of the twentieth century – becoming almost universally accepted by political leaders and policy-makers as well as by businessmen and scholars. The process by which this transformation in ideas took place and how far the shift is irreversible form the central themes of this volume.

Intense debate continued (and still continues) as to the best way to conduct privatization and structural adjustment, on how to respond to the endemic instability of global capital markets and on the consequences of economic stagnation for the large and increasing number of poor families in the region. Moreover, the unexpected political events and new political leaders in Argentina, Brazil and Venezuela that have occurred in the opening years of the twenty-first century might be expected to bring the dominance

1

of a single doctrine into question once again. However, despite the 'lost decade' of the 1980s and the 'boom and bust' of the 1990s in Latin America, even radical critics of the present state of affairs appear to lack an alternative economic doctrine on which to base domestic policy. While criticizing the social consequences of economic globalization and attacking the inequitable representation of developing countries in global institutions such as the IMF and the WTO, these critics are unlikely to suggest autarky as an alternative development strategy and certainly would not question the virtues of liberal democracy as a form of political organization.

A gradual process of structural change in the Latin American economy accompanied the development of these economic ideas during the twentieth century – or more precisely the shift from liberalism through developmentalism to neo-liberalism.[2] The arguments presented in this volume suggest that we should observe some relationship between the two – although the direction of causality is complex, for doctrines emerge from the economic experience of the past, while these doctrines affect economic strategies in the future. The periodization of economic policy 'episodes' in the region can be seen in Figure 1.1, which illustrates income level, educational spread, trade openness and government size for the six largest economies in the region: Argentina, Brazil, Chile, Colombia, Mexico and Venezuela.[3]

Levels of per capita income grew slowly over the first three decades of the century, and were also very volatile – so that the interest in a more purposive economic development model was not surprising, particularly after the exogenous shocks of the Great Depression and World War II forcibly reduced the region's trade openness. This shift in both doctrine and practice was followed by some four decades of rapid and steady growth (from about 1937 to 1977) associated with protectionism in the region and then world economic recovery after World War II. This period came to an end by the early 1980s under the combined shocks of fiscal insolvency and external debt, coinciding unsurprisingly with the shift in dominant economic doctrine towards liberalism. However, despite the expectations of the reformers the closing decades of the century did not display a recovery of growth, and in fact were remarkably unstable as the region suffered a series of financial shocks. In this context the success of the new doctrine in gaining political support requires some explanation, as does the absence of a widespread questioning – let alone abandonment – of the liberal economic model. Indeed, the periods of slower growth and greater volatility in the region during the twentieth century clearly correspond to those where neo-liberal ideas have had *most* influence on policy.

Meanwhile, the educational level of the population was steadily rising, particularly in the middle part of the century, with the proportion of the population enrolled in primary school rising from a twentieth towards a fifth near the end; this was accompanied by rising literacy rates and falling child mortality. In combination with urbanization itself, this educational

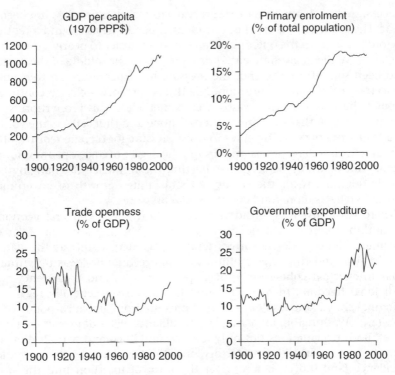

Figure 1.1 Economic progress and liberalization in Latin America during the twentieth century

Source: OxLAD, http://oxlad.qeh.ox.ac.uk

process undoubtedly led to a more active and educated population that could increasingly express its own ideas – on economic organization in particular – through social movements and the electoral process. The emerging role of civil society and the pressures of mass politics in determining the way economic doctrine is embedded in Latin America form another strand which runs through this volume.

We would expect that the shifts in dominant economic doctrine – from liberalism through developmentalism to neo-liberalism – during the twentieth century would be most clearly expressed in economic policy variables such as trade openness and government expenditure. In Figure 1.1 the first process is very clear, with the decline in the ratio of trade to total output from a quarter to a tenth between 1900 and 1950 reflecting the effective closure of the regional economy. The subsequent rise of this ratio from the 1970s onwards reflects in turn the process of import liberalization (the replacement of quotas by tariffs and steady tariff reductions) so that by the end of the century Latin America was basically a 'free-trader'. The second process, that of changing state size relative to the economy, has not been so clear. The broad shift is from government expenditure as around a tenth of regional product in the opening decades of the century to nearly a quarter by the close. While many state enterprises created in the middle of the century had been sold off by the end, the pressure for expenditure on the central concerns of the state – education, health and defence – clearly continued, though the rate of growth was slower. Nonetheless, this proportion is still less than half of that in (say) southern Europe and thus reflects the continued ability of liberal ruling elites to resist pressure for income redistribution through fiscal welfare provision. In sum, the degree of trade openness for the region can plausibly be seen as reflecting the influence of changing economic doctrine, while the steady but still limited growth of government probably reflects more fundamental social pressures.

There exist two widespread notions of how the neo-liberal economic revolution occurred as it did in Latin America in the last quarter of the twentieth century. Conservatives tend to regard this shift as the natural dominance (and thus inevitability) of sound economic ideas by virtue of their intellectual coherence, proven policy record, and consistency with individual freedom. In marked contrast, progressives generally regard the doctrinal shift as the result of external pressure from global corporate interests (and Washington in particular) in alliance with domestic economic elites. Both explanations not only are oversimplified and partial; they also ignore the long historical trajectory of Latin American debate since independence (and indeed before) over the form of insertion into the world economy and the appropriate relationship between state and markets. Moreover, they overlook the fact that contested economic doctrine tends to reflect domestic political conflict as much as professional disagreement between experts. Indeed the use of the technical 'objectivity' of economists to legitimate particular political positions on the social order dates back at least to the Enlightenment.

A number of recent studies explore how this new economic doctrine was created, transmitted and transformed in individual Latin American countries.[4] Yet there is apparently no comparative study for the region as a whole. This is the gap we hope to begin to fill with the present volume, by focusing on economic ideas – as opposed to focusing on the outcome of political and social conflict, or even on the policy consequences of these new ideas. The national and international institutional context of economic doctrines is clearly crucial. In particular, it is essential to understand the interactions between domestic institutions ranging from central banks and universities on the one hand, and international institutions ranging from CEPAL to the IMF on the other. Clearly, this is not only – or even primarily – an issue of the intrinsic merits of the economic doctrine itself in terms of either its theoretical adequacy or its practical efficacy. Therefore, the skills of political scientists, social theorists and historians of ideas have to be combined with those of economists in order to evaluate this process. Above all, we felt that comparative work would generate new insights by permitting individual national factors to be distinguished from common external influences on the one hand, and by allowing some differentiation between domestic political factors and the shared regional socio-economic structure on the other.

In an effort to address this agenda a research workshop was held at St Antony's College, Oxford, in September 2000, with the generous support of the Hewlett Foundation. The conference brought together some 40 Latin Americanist historians, political scientists and economists along with scholars of the history of thought. The central focus of the workshop was the shift in economic doctrine during the last quarter of the twentieth century in Latin America, which we examined in terms both of broad external and internal influences and of specific institutional transmitters. In order to provide an appropriate historical context, papers were presented on the role of economic ideas in other industrializing regions and on their role in earlier stages of liberalism and developmentalism in Latin America itself. The robust and constructive critique of the draft papers by colleagues at the workshop required a further round of extensive research that is reflected in their final versions as the individual chapters of this volume. The task of this introductory chapter is to summarize the arguments and distil some overall conclusions.

Analytical approaches to the influence of economic doctrines in Latin America

The book opens with four chapters that offer very different yet complementary analytical interpretations of how economic doctrines have shifted in the last half of the twentieth century. The differences arise from distinct disciplinary perspectives and research viewpoints. Two leading authorities in the history of ideas and economic development respectively contribute Chapters 2 and 3, in order to provide a wider framework for our focus on Latin America. Chapter 2 presents an initial conceptual framework for considering how economic ideas accumulate influence and become dominant: this framework distinguishes between the transmitters of the doctrine itself (the 'epistemic community') on the one hand and the domestic and external political influences on this process on the other. Chapter 3 establishes the background of the way ideas on economic development have changed since World War II, and proposes a way of understanding the continued conflict between the neo-liberal economic doctrine espoused by increasingly powerful international financial institutions and the evolution of an alternative model based on 'human development' from the earlier tradition of state-led industrialization.

Chapter 4 also examines this doctrinal conflict but takes a contrasting 'view from below', presenting a taxonomy of the domestic institutional context in which the evolutionary process is embedded in Latin America.

Social and political conflicts mean that economic doctrines are inevitably contested on the basis of the economic interests involved, and the chapter argues that the hegemony of the international epistemic community identified in Chapter 2 is not as complete as it may appear from the outside or 'above'. Finally, the nature and dynamics of the external pressures on the region to adopt a particular economic doctrine – essentially that dominant in the United States – is analysed in Chapter 5, fleshing out the notion of a 'northern' blocking mechanism to autonomous models of national development posited in Chapter 3.

We now present these chapters in more detail. In Chapter 2, Peter Gourevitch synthesizes the recent theoretical and empirical literature on the role and power of ideas, drawing on European and North American experience in order to apply three explanatory factors – which act as 'drivers' of change – to Latin America. These are first, the influence of 'epistemic communities', or key intellectual elites within a particular discipline, in this case economics; second, the extent of external pressures from the international community, in this case the United States in particular and foreign capital in general; and third, the role of internal political actors – especially those to whom decision-makers listen. This schema is enormously helpful in clarifying the processes involved, even if the other authors do not apply it systematically to their own material. In contrast to models of the diffusion of new economic ideas in industrialized countries, Gourevitch's approach emphasizes that in constructing a model for Latin America, international pressures need to be considered as an active force (rather than as a mere 'constraint') and that economics training needs to be taken into account as a crucial transmission mechanism.

Gourevitch first considers the events that cause the established beliefs of professional economists throughout the world to shift in the closing decades of the twentieth century. The apparent success of East Asian industrialization, the consequences of the debt crisis and the collapse of the Soviet economic model are clear examples of such events with an immediate impact on the Latin American economic debate. He also identifies a growing professional concern with micro-institutional issues such as corporate organization and contract law, expressed in the debate on the relative merits of the 'US–UK' and 'German–Japanese' models of economic organization. The historical example of the widespread shift to Keynesianism after World War II is used to illustrate the importance of the shifting weight of political interests in the changing influence of different schools of thought within the epistemic community.

Gourevitch's interpretation of the absorption of a new economic doctrine has thus a somewhat different schema from that previously established by Hall (1989), who suggests that a new system of economic ideas will take hold in a society when there is a clear need for them, as well as a clear and congruent political dimension. Hall uses the concepts of 'viabilities' (economic, political and administrative) to explain the same case of the reception of Keynesian ideas in the postwar decades. This theme of the administrative influence of Latin American economists is taken up by FitzGerald in Chapter 5 and by Palacios in Chapter 9, who also emphasize the contested and heterogeneous nature of this epistemic community.

Gourevitch then develops the second driver – external leverage – under four headings: the US administration, the international financial institutions such as the IMF, multilateral treaties such as the WTO and NAFTA, and private market actors such as multinationals and banks. Gourevitch argues that their ideological influence can be considered as part of that of the epistemic community of economists: the leverage arises from their ability to influence economic outcomes through access to finance and markets. He points out, but does not resolve, the difficulty of separating the leverage exercised by institutions such as the IMF from that of the United States itself. This theme is taken up in more detail by Drake in Chapter 4 and by Woods in Chapter 10 – although both give rather more weight to the direct geostrategic interests of the regional hegemon than to the influence of the epistemic community of economists as such.

The final section of Chapter 2 addresses internal political determinants, which Gourevitch sees as conditioned by institutional structures as well as class and sectoral interests. The political sociology of policy preferences suggests that who supports or opposes a particular reform, and with what resources, will condition change. The role of institutions determines how the political system influences the likelihood that one or other coalition will prevail. On preferences, Gourevitch argues that both class interests and sectoral interests may apply at different historical moments. On political institutions, he is opposed to any necessary correlation between economic liberalization and either authoritarian or democratic regimes. His conclusion is that the third factor – domestic politics – predominates. Although 'ideas matter', they need power to be effective. While international influences are also important, they too need power within a country to become translated into policy. This view of the overall balance is taken up – albeit with different conclusions – by FitzGerald in Chapter 5 and again by Whitehead in Chapter 11, as well as being reflected in the historical interpretations by Jacobsen and Love in Chapters 6, 7 and 8.

In Chapter 3, Frances Stewart also focuses on the extent to which alternative sets of ideas from the orthodox doctrine *do* develop – but cannot penetrate social and political structures sufficiently to have a significant or prolonged effect on policy-making. She describes how the strongly statist view of development which prevailed among development economists, international institutions and national governments in the first three decades after World War II was subsequently replaced by a neo-liberal market-oriented doctrine. Nonetheless, in terms of objectives, the general focus on maximizing GDP growth as the major objective of development was at least partially displaced by an emphasis on human goals. The official aid community and major policy establishments in the 'North' advocate human development policies only in so far as they do not conflict with the liberal agenda. Her explanation is that doctrine and policies evolve as a product of a cycle in which events lead to new thinking and new policies the consequences of which, in turn, often reveal new problems, thereby giving rise to further developments in thinking and policies. But both thinking and policies are heavily influenced by powerful interest groups, themselves shaped by the consequences of policy.

In particular the international financial institutions acquired a huge amount of influence, pushing policy in the direction they favoured in country after country. Some governments resisted, or tried to shape the policies to their own agendas, but all moved in a similar direction. Ironically, in the import-substitution era, governments were relatively free to pick their own policy mix. Yet it was this era that gave rise to the dependency school, which pointed to excessive dependence of Southern countries on the North, but had little real influence because autarchy did not appear to be a viable option in a globalizing world. Stewart argues that the recent focus on human development in accepted development doctrine – reflected through the United Nations – evolved as a result of the failures of both state-led forced industrialization and neo-liberal structural adjustment. Human development has been accepted in principle by international financial institutions and developing country governments as a *social* objective, but has not been implemented in practice, being overridden by the logic of neo-liberal economic strategy. However, Stewart concludes that the process of globalization itself – mobile capital and technology – means that national ability to compete globally is now based on labour skills and public infrastructure, and thus on eventual adoption of human development as an *economic* strategy. This argument finds a striking parallel in that of Chapter 11, the closing chapter of this volume, where Laurence Whitehead suggests that the democratic heart of the neo-liberal project will inevitably lead to social change in Latin America.

In Chapter 5, Valpy FitzGerald questions the notion that by the end of the century neo-liberal economic doctrine had in fact achieved the hegemony of ideas (as opposed to power) that current writing by both supporters and critics might suggest was the case. 'Sound economic fundamentals' are of course associated with the current hegemony of central banks, finance ministries and international institutions over state policy: indeed, monetary orthodoxy flourished even at the height of structuralism during the middle decades of the twentieth century, sustained by central banks and the IMF. Nonetheless, the 'old' doctrine of developmentalism is still widely held within ministries of industry and agriculture, while local administrations and regional governments still engage in economic planning. Social service institutions in the public sector still follow 'human development' strategies, supported by UN agencies and international NGOs. Epistemic institutions such as university departments and international agencies thus continue to serve as contested spaces as well as transmission mechanisms.

FitzGerald also argues that the notion of a single, professional epistemic community of economists that shifts its doctrinal position in unison (as natural scientists are purported to do) does not correspond to reality. 'Popular economics' based on radical social ideas, while not always forming a formally consistent body of doctrine, does clearly influence non-state actors ranging from trades unions to business associations. The content of this latter doctrine is extremely diverse, ranging from mercantilism to socialism, but shares a common commitment to public action in order to overcome market failures. 'Left' popular discourse itself in Latin America owes much to liberation theology, and is mainly focused on income distribution, employment and poverty reduction, based in a strong critique of capitalism. 'Right' popular discourse is that of the small business sector – against the state and for the market in principle, but also distrustful of globalization and confusingly mixed with scholastic notions of a 'just price' and 'unfair competition'.

He suggests not only that alternative economic ideas persist in the region, and thus that there are many epistemic communities rather than one, but also that the shifting *balance* of the influence of particular doctrines may matter as much as changes in the doctrines themselves. This shift in turn reflects changes in the relative power of the institutions that carry these ideas and in that of the interests behind them, although the relative efficacy of the doctrines themselves as a basis for successful economic policy is also relevant to their political acceptance. This may help locate the Latin American experience within a wider debate on the way in which economic doctrines such as Keynesianism are accepted (and later rejected) on the one hand, and the persistence of a systematic gap between the ideas of professional economists (which inform official doctrine) and those of the general public on the other.

In Chapter 4 Paul Drake takes a view of the doctrinal shift that emphasizes external leverage above domestic or ideological factors, contrasting with Gourevitch's model of the primacy of local politics but also, by suggesting the dominance of a single model, contrasting with FitzGerald's vision of contested doctrines. Drake argues that the rise to dominance of the neoliberal paradigm in Latin America during the 1980s was the result of a conscious US 'offensive', which resulted in a rapid capitulation of almost all the governments in the region. The United States has long been the hegemonic power in the region,[5] but the factor that altered the balance of influence on economic policy in the 1980s was the debt crisis. That exogenous shock interacted with a number of other trends such as the Reagan administration's commitment to the restoration of democracy, the end of the cold war and the apparent benefits of openness in a global economy.

Local forces do enter Drake's interpretation: the decision to collaborate with rather than resist Washington depends on domestic politics. The coalition of vested interests behind import-substitution and large government is important in explaining why many Latin American countries held out so long – until the debt crisis – against multilateral criticism and the US. The coincidence of neo-liberalism with what some rulers and their supporters wanted to do anyway, the conceptual strength of the remedies, the logic of calling for government to do less when it had few resources in any case and the value of reassuring market signals to nervous investors were all strong influences on policy-makers. Moreover, the policies themselves weakened, often fatally, the very actors likely to oppose them, such as the labour unions. Nonetheless, Drake argues that these internal factors are secondary compared to the strength of external leverage. As he points out, even the apparent 'deviation' of import-substitution in Latin America is only a regional version of the no less radical Keynesian and interventionist economic policies that both the United States and Europe had adopted at the same time.

The historical trajectory of economic ideas in Latin America

The second part of the volume comprises three chapters that explore the historical background to the central themes raised in the first. Chapter 6 places the debate on the growing influence of neo-liberal economic doctrine in Latin America during the second half of the twentieth century within the comparative historical context of the forces propelling economic liberalism during the nineteenth century. Chapter 7 traces the development of an indigenous economics profession in the region during the early twentieth century, which was central to the emergence of an authentically Latin American economic doctrine during the middle of the century. The emergence of this endogenous economic doctrine after World War II, and its influence on the emerging institutions of public intervention in the economies of the region, is the theme of Chapter 8: this is the emblematic case of the emergence of an autochthonous epistemic community not only distinct from but also influencing in its turn the global profession of development economics – as Stewart points out in Chapter 3.[6]

In Chapter 6, Nils Jacobsen explores the spread of liberal ideas in the nineteenth century. He argues that the established theoretical models that seek to explain the spread of ideas – the infectious diseases model, information-theory-based models focusing on transmission mechanisms ('encoding and decoding'), or the 'marketplace of ideas' approach (where the best ideas win out) – give insufficient weight to the recipients of these ideas. They also ignore the multiple iterations by journalists, academics and politicians between periphery and metropolis. He shows that economic liberalism became dominant in the region only after the mid-nineteenth century and then far from completely: economic interests had to mesh with liberal doctrine for the idea to become socially embedded.[7] Until the middle of the nineteenth century, Jacobsen argues, policy-makers in most countries frequently perceived free trade, let alone free labour and property markets, as potentially ruinous. Thus, after the general financial and commercial crisis of 1825–6 in Europe, the 1830s and 1840s saw the decline of the influence of merchants in Latin America, and although European governments continued to pressure for trade access they were not always successful.

In contrast, Jacobsen describes the period 1849–90 as one of 'liberalism triumphant'. The doctrine became more powerful as its success in Europe made it more credible in Latin America. Although it is often suggested that the adoption of liberal ideas in this period was a response to the failure of other options – a suggestive parallel with the 1980s – Jacobsen argues that growth had already recovered beforehand in countries such as Peru and Bolivia. Rather it may be that better economic performance and the resulting realignment of sectoral interests opened the way for and created confidence in liberal ideas – another possible parallel with the late twentieth century. The importance of domestic political drivers is underlined by the fact that legislation based on sound and universal liberal principles, such as the guarantee of private property rights, turned out in practice (by real intention or poor design) to be a vehicle for local landowners to further increase their power.

Joseph Love documents the growth and consolidation of the Latin American economics profession in Chapter 7. Such a profession – let alone an epistemic community – did not exist as such in 1915. Love shows how the gradual development of the economic institutions of a modern state gave rise to a demand for economists who could deal in the language and concepts of modern administration. Such institutions also provided channels for diffusion of North American and European economic ideas into the region. Key centres of training and research – such as the Colegio de México, ESCOLATINA in Chile, the Getúlio Vargas Foundation and the Instituto de Economía in Brazil, the Economics Faculty of the University of Buenos Aires in Argentina – were established and spread their ideas through training of local economists and students from the region, supported by flourishing professional economics journals.

In this way the Latin American economics profession was transformed between the 1930s and the 1950s. However, broader cultural and institutional obstacles impeded the development of social science in Latin America. Love points out that 'the intellectual traditions of the region ... largely revolved around the *pensador* (lit., thinker), a man who prided himself on his broad culture and who eschewed specialization ... [His] vehicle was the essay.' The *pensador* gave way to experts, but only slowly – and indeed is still alive in TV round tables, newspaper op-ed pages and even privately published pamphlets, as FitzGerald records in Chapter 5.

In Chapter 8 Love focuses on the spread of an economic doctrine explicitly opposed to neo-liberal ideas. He describes the spread of structuralism, protectionism and public intervention between the 1920s and 1960s in the region. For Love, the important agents in the spread of ideas are institutions and key founding figures within them, such as Prebisch. The central institutional development from the point of view of economic thought in this period was that of the state itself, and the closely associated expansion of public sector central and development banks. Most economists developed as *practical* professionals within this growing public sector, while the recognition of economics as a distinct professional discipline with its own authority came slowly in the 1930s and 1940s. The diffusion of ideas occurred mainly through the journals and research institutes established from the 1920s to the 1940s, as described in Chapter 7.

The key innovator – Prebisch – based his innovative ideas on practical experience, moving from market research for the Sociedad Rural (the stockbreeders' association) in the 1920s, through Argentine central banking in the 1930s to leadership of the UN Economic Commission for Latin America (ECLA) in the 1950s. ECLA used civil service training and government policy advice throughout Latin America as an extremely effective means of spreading its doctrine. It also helped establish and support planning ministries and research institutes throughout the region, as well as influencing international agencies ranging from the IADB to the ILO. However, the influence of US universities – and US-dominated institutions such as the World Bank and IMF – grew from the 1970s onwards as successive generations of young economists were trained abroad to become the technocrats charged with liberal reform, as Drake outlines in Chapter 5.

The embedding of liberal economic doctrine in Latin America

The third and last part of the volume addresses the 'embedding' of neo-liberal doctrine within Latin American public institutions and wider civil society. Chapters 9 and 10 contain detailed case studies of those institutions identified in previous chapters as key interface locations for epistemic communities, external leverage and local politics – university economics faculties and international financial agencies, respectively. Chapter 11 draws together the main threads of argument in the volume by arguing that the political roots of liberalism are so now deep in Latin America that the durability of neo-liberal economic doctrine does not seem to be in question, despite the poor economic and social outcomes – although the process of democratization itself may well lead to much greater social demands on the taxpayer than has been the case so far.

In his detailed study of the training of the epistemic community of economists in Colombia in Chapter 9, Marco Palacios provides a penetrating account of the interplay of conflicting ideas, domestic politics and external influences in transmitting economic doctrine. An elite of economic experts developed over several decades under the influence of aid programmes, development plans and university faculties. Early foreign advisers (such as the Kemmerer missions of the 1920s and 1930s) established a group of local experts, who came to effectively replace parties and even the legislature in economic decision-making. The influential multilateral aid agencies further reinforced the authority of economic experts in the postwar period, who became largely unaccountable in political terms. By the 1950s, the Colombian universities had started to train economists, but one school (the Universidad de los Andes) established itself as the key provider of access to both doctoral study in the US and public office at home. This was achieved not only by access to local and foreign funding, but also by discrediting its nearest rival (the Universidad Nacional) as 'politicized' rather than 'technical'. The majority of professional economists in Colombia continued to be trained by the Universidad Nacional, but this epistemic community was excluded from the leadership of policy-making agencies even though it provided most of the professionals within them.

However, Palacios argues that the ostensible power of these elite economists was significantly moderated by the way the Colombian political system works in practice. The relatively weak state and the absence of any populist period strengthened the close relationship between public officials and the business elite, thus grounding the *técnicos* in the pragmatism of private enterprise. This significantly moderated the power of neo-liberal economic doctrine and helps explain the comparative brevity and superficiality of Colombia's reform period during the early 1990s before the resurgence of pragmatism, in marked contrast to the more permanent shifts in Chile and Mexico.

In Chapter 10, Ngaire Woods provides an insightful description of the complex intertwining of domestic politics and external influences in the change of official economic doctrine in Mexico. Mexican economic management since the 1981 debt default is often presented as a straightforward story of crisis caused by government mismanagement leading to the acceptance of rational and technically sound policies. Woods shows how, in fact, the initial victory for neo-classical ideas came as economic conditions were *improving* in 1984, albeit amid violent debate within the civil service and vociferous contestation from civil society. She traces the evolution from protection to a strong neo-liberal position through three distinct political moments, and documents how the World Bank and the IMF worked with a small group of Mexican state managers, principally within the Ministry of Finance and Banco de México, who were themselves able to advance their career by developing a relation of trust and confidence with these global institutions.

The Bretton Woods agencies were also able to strengthen the policy-making position of their counterpart institutions within the Mexican government by making them the privileged interlocutors in debt negotiations with the US Treasury. They also developed particular (and discreet) relations with individuals to whom they could offer financial incentives and intellectual support. The penetration and diffusion of the new economic doctrine was also driven by the fact that while previous economic crises had led to debate and the discussion of alternatives, by the mid 1990s there were virtually no policy alternatives to those endorsed by the IMF and the World Bank. Woods thus sees the Mexican *técnicos* operating pragmatically to their own advantage just as much as Colombia's elite of economic experts. While Colombian pragmatism was based on close relationships with the business sector in a weak democracy, the Mexican propensity for economic ideology was driven by career prospects in a relatively autonomous one-party state – until the 2000 presidential elections that signalled its collapse.

In Chapter 11, Laurence Whitehead draws together many of the preoccupations of the other authors – in particular, the concern with the deep historical-political roots of liberalism in Latin America, which he adduces as a powerful reason for the solidity of its hegemony today. He suggests that the political power of the doctrine is in part a result of the increased degree of agreement and intellectual coherence of the epistemic community itself. However, the lack of an alternative feasible economic strategy is also important, as Gourevitch emphasizes in Chapter 2. The defeat of communism and the declining role of the Catholic Church both allowed the projection of neo-liberalism as 'values of universal applicability', once socialism and corporativism had been consigned to the past. Above all the wide practical application of neo-liberal economic doctrine and its apparent challenge to privilege and corruption generate internal political support for the idea and its policy implications beyond that of the immediate beneficiaries. Domestic political backing is also helped by the surprising degree of political pluralism within the hegemonic economic idea in Latin America during recent decades.

In view of the robust intellectual foundations, varied practical applications, relative pluralism, broad basis of support and weakened sources of resistance to global liberalism, Whitehead's conclusion that the 1990s represented a substantial break with the past is incontestable. Moreover, contemporary liberalism offers a series of ambitious and wide-ranging projects of transformation, catch-up and 'modernity', which even if they have originated 'from above and without' may be anchored in the collective institutions and memories of the region to a far greater extent then earlier initiatives. Those politicians and parties ideologically and emotionally out of sympathy with economic liberalism must now claim a commitment to 'responsible' economic policies in order to reassure markets of their reliability. Thus the opponents of neo-liberalism are reduced to relying on moral exhortation alone, rather than on economic arguments or some analytical framework that aims to contest dominant ideas on their own terrain.

In synthesis: modelling the adoption of a new economic doctrine

The key drivers identified in the literature to explain how ideas come to shift the behaviour of decision-makers are, as Gourevitch states in Chapter 2 (p. 23): 'epistemic communities, US hegemony and the power of international capital, and domestic politics and interest groups.' The evidence of our cases and our debate has reinforced the centrality of these considerations to the initial shift in doctrine or paradigm, although our authors differ as to their relative weight. What the contributors to this volume have revealed in addition is the importance of distinguishing the initial acceptance of a new idea from the embedding of the doctrine in policy – what Hall calls its viability.[8] It is in this embedding process that country differences become more evident than in the generation or even the content of the doctrine; and the complex role of internal social and political structures and institutions is revealed.

As we move from acceptance of a doctrine to its embedding, the role of the epistemic community remains important, but the way in which the ideas then penetrate the policy-making community and eventually civil society is far less direct and more ambiguous. Here Palacios's account in Chapter 9 of the evolution of a corps of professional economists in Colombia is illuminating in showing how an elite group of neo-classical economists emerged with a privileged policy-making position through the access of one university to scholarships abroad and job opportunities. The epistemic community of Colombian economists is not united, a very different doctrinal line being taught at the second leading university, but that more radical group is marginalized from power. The diversity of the epistemic community is also developed in Chapter 5 by FitzGerald, who shows the strength of various currents of economic ideas varying over time, rather than one simply replacing another. He moves from the centrality of particular state institutions in establishing the dominant doctrine emphasized by Palacios and other authors in this volume, to the way that changes in the relative power of a wide range of social organizations affect the fate of the economic doctrines associated with them.

Within this context, the political influence of particular sectional and regional interests comes into play – influencing the political potential of economic doctrines insofar as they imply support for a particular sector (such as export agriculture), social group (such as labour market flexibility) or geographical region (such as development banking). It is this political dissonance between general principles and particular influences that often underlies difficulties in implementation and thus of the *adoption of*, as opposed to the *acquiescence in*, a new economic doctrine.[9] Last but not least, the formation of a common set of economic ideas among politicians is clearly essential if ideas are to be translated into practice. This kind of epistemic community should be distinguished from its professional equivalent: it is not just a question of transmission of scientific truth from economic theorists, through economics education, to administrators and then to politicians. Rather politicians and journalists form their own view on economic doctrine from the success or failure of previous governments and above all from comparison with other countries – where academic theory is probably only a subordinate component compared with international perceptions of national success.

The second driver – the influence of external economic and political factors – is clearly crucial, and various authors stress this, above all Drake in Chapter 4, as we have shown. Generally, the form of economic insertion into the world economy will affect the dominant economic doctrine in positive and negative senses. On the one hand, a doctrine which promises (or above all has secured in another country) export success or industrial competitiveness will clearly be more attractive to policy-makers and civil society. On the other hand, an exogenous obstacle to international trade – whether market access or essential supplies – will increase enthusiasm for a doctrine that purports to explain or overcome such obstacles. By extension, the existence of international trade agreements limits the scope for doctrinal variance, both in the positive sense of committing the government to particular principles and in the negative one of excluding others as unrealistic. Good examples of this are the commitment to import-substitution and industrial planning in the Andean Pact, and the locking in of tariff reduction and market liberalization under NAFTA.

More pressing perhaps is the direct influence on economic policy of aid donors, international creditors and foreign investors. This is not just a question of adopting particular policy decisions in their favour, which would not in itself constitute a doctrine.[10] Rather the desire to attract further external funds and to retain domestic capital in an age of global capital mobility means that governments must adopt a particular economic doctrine that guarantees both the return on and the security of such funds. However, to convince capital markets (and aid donors) that this will hold true for the future, the new doctrine must be seen to be institutionally embedded in some permanent form. By extension, as in the case of trade arrangements, this situation in turn removes legitimacy from any economic doctrine that might upset capital markets.

Moreover, neo-liberalism was not really a new economic theory but rather a return to an older tradition in the region. Although the technical apparatus had been improved meanwhile by economic theorists, this was not the reason for its being taken up. Indeed a whole range of technical theories have been tried and discarded (for example, fixed versus variable exchange rates) without the doctrine as such being undermined. However, the nature of the national economy does matter, particularly the role of natural resource exports (which sustain a traditional view on openness) versus industrial interests (which insist on a more protective economy); and also the degree to which there is a large enough domestic market for demand management to be effective. This may be why only the larger economies (Brazil and Mexico) could to some extent hold out for a more heterodox approach.[11]

The influence of the US on economic doctrine in Latin America is evident, but it is not entirely consciously directed. In fact, changing economic doctrine within the US itself – the rise and fall of Keynesian policy or the university economics curriculum for instance – is probably more important than explicit Washington policies in influencing economic ideas within Latin America. Nonetheless, the exertion of leverage in specific areas such as the privatization of state enterprises, tariff reform or investor protection clearly affects economic doctrine in the ways outlined above. Only one of our authors considers external leverage to be the overriding determinant of economic doctrine in the region, but in Chapter 4 Drake does make a detailed and convincing case for this being an explicitly designed process involving a wide range of US institutions.

Moreover, Love's two chapters (7 and 8) demonstrate that an internally led shift of doctrine is likely to occur only when that external power is *not* exercised. In the early postwar years the hold of the great powers over the region was necessarily relaxed by the depression and the war, so that export competitiveness seemed less important, debt could be repudiated and Washington did not oppose nationalist regimes. But again, as with the epistemic community, the ability of the external agent to penetrate the domestic policy-making environment is institutionally and socially determined. Here Chapter 10 by Woods contributes an insight from the Mexican case. It was the way the Bretton Woods institutions were able to work with key state managers, and those managers were able to advance their own careers in so collaborating that was the key to the embedding of neo-liberal economic doctrine in the Mexican case.

Our third driver – the forces of internal politics and group interest – becomes more important as we move from the issue of shifts to that of embedding. The political resonance of the idea is vital to its viability. This aspect needs far more elaboration and expansion than is possible in this volume. This resonance comprises both characteristics of the formal political process (whose preferences are expressed and with what consequences) and the nature of civil society – albeit in the negative sense of a space for autonomous political action by an elite in the absence of a fully articulated civil society. Indeed, in Latin America at least, the more important changes in economic regime have been associated with major political upheavals that can be termed 'constitutional' in the sense that they go far beyond the alternation of political parties in power. The adoption of an economic doctrine will thus reflect its congruence with a major political doctrine such as nationalism, liberalism or socialism. As the constitutional project goes beyond purely political concepts such as democracy and free speech to encompass property rights and welfare provision, economic doctrine has a strong political content, which may be as significant as the issue of its efficacy. Moreover, the association of a particular economic doctrine with a rejected political regime clearly reduces its political attractiveness and increases that of an alternative.

Finally, all our authors recognize the complexity of the relationship between the three drivers. This interaction is also a central aspect of Hall's model of the Keynesian revolution. We would want to emphasize that the *interaction* between the three drivers is essential for successful adoption of an economic doctrine. In this context we understand by 'adoption', as Hall does, not just acceptance in principle but also implementation and thus agreement (or at the very least, acquiescence) by civil society as a whole. Adoption requires more than adding up the three drivers, but rather the three reinforcing each other – and it seems that all three are necessary. In terms of the rise (and fall) of the developmentalist model between the 1930s and (say) the 1960s in Latin America, it is clear that initially the conditions were met. First, the epistemic community was warming to ideas of economic nationalism. Second, politically, urban voters had become a majority and the concept of 'nation building' was popular, socialist ideas of planning and state enterprise were current if not respectable, and the previous experience of primary export booms had been insufficient to create employment for the new urban majority. Third, the depression and the war led to a period of relative isolation from external pressures.

The downfall of these developmentalist ideas occurred once these three conditions were no longer met. Indeed a theme of Whitehead's in Chapter 11 is that the confluence of the failure of the previous economic regime (leading to inflation and debt), the pressures for democracy and a more open society, and international pressure from Washington explain both the rise of neo-liberalism and the decline of developmentalism. In the specific case of Chile, which so far at least is the most successful economic example of the effectiveness of neo-liberal reforms in the region, the confluence of these three factors in the reform period is notable but not coincidental – it had to be purposefully integrated over three decades.

However, it is also true to say that when the three drivers are not integrated properly, then the new doctrine does not take root successfully. Although the governing elite may acquiesce in the doctrine it may not implement the corresponding policies fully; or the political class may adopt a doctrine that does not permeate civil society. This is well illustrated by the somewhat extreme cases of Peru under Fujimori and Chile under Pinochet.[12] Fujimori had two alternative economic projects prepared for his consideration when he ran for president in 1990. His option for the neo-liberal project once elected was a consequence not of any internal set of considerations, but rather of his realization that the choice would bring him external funding.

The result was a period of neo-liberal policy-making that neglected the institutions necessary to make the policies work, and required increasing resort to repression and corruption, which eventually defeated the experiment. In contrast, the neo-liberal strategy adopted by the Pinochet regime from 1975, although initially mismanaged and unacceptably repressive, did correspond to the long-term requirements of Chile's business classes. Indeed, so embedded had the doctrine become that the return to democracy was based on the retention of much the same economic model, albeit moderated by a greater commitment to social welfare.

If there is little internal political resonance in response to a new economic doctrine, for whatever reason, then the power of the external can be expressed in a way that undermines the viability of that doctrine as the basis for a sustainable policy shift. Peru in 1990 had weak political structures and given the absence of a broad internal political base to digest, robustly select from, and mobilize support for the model and its necessary institutions, resulting polices were extreme and out of touch with the realities of the economy and society. This differs sharply from the Chilean case, where a robust internal political choice was made at the same point in time, but to continue the neo-liberal model buttressed by more welfare support for those disadvantaged by it.

Further, an internally generated doctrine is as subject to the interplay between domestic economic and political structures as an externally transmitted doctrine. State-led industrialization as espoused by ECLA ultimately failed in part because in contrast to East Asia, its political support base remained narrow and unable to sustain the domestic adjustments necessary to overcome external shocks and fiscal constraints without abandoning the model itself.[13] There *was* broad political support for the crude notion of *national* capitalism based on government intervention and employment creation, but the key actors in the public sector lacked the training and sophistication – and many, the political will – to construct a broad coalition of domestic interests in support of their project. Interestingly, this was in part a result of weaknesses in the doctrine itself, in its view of the state and government as comprising an autonomous public sector fully able to put into practice its theory of industrialization, and its neglect of the implications for fiscal solvency and private investment.[14]

Conclusion

Returning to the conflicting interpretations as to how the neo-liberal economic revolution occurred as it did in Latin America in the last quarter of the twentieth century that opened this chapter, we find that economic doctrines are not transmitted uniquely by their inherent intellectual 'truth'[15] or by external leverage, or by the interests of powerful domestic groups. Rather, internal political structures respond to and modify ideas: so that it is the *interaction* between external leverage and internal agendas that determines how ideas play out through a complex and contested process of social decoding, feedback and redefinition.

These perceptions should condition the often-heard observation – in both praise and criticism – of the 'victory' of the neo-liberal model. Indeed, many even go so far as to argue that there is no place for national or even regional economic doctrine in a global economy. This seems too bleak a conclusion, and on the basis of the findings of this book, even a dangerous one. For it incites us to the neglect of the internal factors that in fact make all the difference in the way the model plays out – and to the decoding and feedback. Where external leverage is less strong, the role of the domestic epistemic community becomes more prominent – and we suggest, internal political structures and responses remain equally significant. The contrast between Latin American and Asian responses to recent economic crises is illustrative here. The acceptance in East and South Asia of neo-liberal economic doctrine has been far less enthusiastic than in Latin America: in part, because the state sector itself was solvent and better able to manage response to financial shocks, but also because political support for economic nationalism and state intervention was much stronger. Moreover, although the epistemic community of professional economists in Asia has received very similar influences from the United States, the strategy and power of the regional hegemons has created a greater space for heterodox policy formation and implementation.

In fact, there are now signs of an increased willingness to engage in public action to correct market failure in Latin America – ranging from social entitlements and environmental protection, through consumer protection and technology transfer to customs unions and transborder regulation – all within the dominant economic model. Meanwhile, the longstanding debate between the principles of individual liberty and commutative justice on the one hand, and those of social responsibility and distributive justice on the other, continues at all levels in Latin America – and indeed in the world as a whole. The ultimate democratic challenge to *any* economic doctrine is its ability to reduce this contradiction of principle in the arena of practice.

Notes

1. Terms such as structuralism and Keynesianism are often used by external observers of the region, but not by Latin Americans themselves – where the most widely employed descriptor is perhaps '*desarrollismo*'. We are indebted for this point to José Antonio Ocampo.
2. For a full discussion of economic growth and social progress during the twentieth century in Latin America, see Thorp (1998).
3. The graphs show the population-weighted mean of the variable for the six economies. In 2000 these six accounted for some four-fifths of production and

three-quarters of population in Latin America and the Caribbean. We are indebted to Ame Berges for compiling them from the OxLAD database.

4. See, for instance, Babb (2001) on the case of Mexico, Conaghan (1997) on Peru, Hunneus (1997) on Argentina, and Silva (1996) and Valdés (1995) on Chile.

5. Although US direction of Latin American monetary reform in the inter-war decades appears to have been directed towards the much more limited objective of protecting the interests of foreign investors (Drake 1989).

6. The subsequent fate of these ideas is taken up by Palacios in Chapter 9, in the context of institutional barriers to the spread of ECLA doctrine from Colombian universities into state management, and by Woods, in her account of the countervailing force of World Bank training for senior civil servants in Mexico, in Chapter 10.

7. The Chilean Minister of Finance expressed it neatly in 1822: 'we are liberals in all that does not tend to ruin us' (cited in Will 1964:6–7).

8. Hall's seminal analysis of the penetration of Keynesian ideas is carried out in terms of their economic, political and administrative viability. His analysis was developed for and is appropriate for the developed economies and societies of Europe and the US; as we turn to peripheral countries, the importance of external constraints and leverage (for him a subset of economic viability) rises, while the independent role of a professional civil service is considerably reduced.

9. This is not of course peculiarly Latin American – as the vicissitudes of free-trade doctrine in the US demonstrate.

10. No more than the commitment to central planning in the USSR prevented particular concessions to foreign investors.

11. Though note that their size also makes them better able to negotiate heterodox deals with creditors.

12. See Thorp (1998:ch. 8) for further development of these ideas.

13. The case of Brazil is perhaps an exception in Latin America, but if so, it is the example that proves the rule.

14. See FitzGerald (2000) for further discussion.

15. As should be clear by now, this is why the Kuhnian notion of 'paradigm shift' in the sciences is inappropriate in the analysis of economic ideas.

References

Babb, S., *Managing Mexico: Economists from Nationalism to Neoliberalism* (Princeton University Press, 2001).

Conaghan, C. M., 'Las Estrellas de la Crisis: El Ascenso de los Economistas en la Vida Publica Peruana', *Pensamiento Iberoamericano*, 30 (1997) 177–206.

Drake, P. W., *The Money Doctor in the Andes: The Kemmerer Missions 1923–33* (Durham: Duke University Press, 1989).

FitzGerald, E. V. K., 'ECLA and the Theory of Import-Substituting Industrialisation in Latin America', in E. Cardenas, J. A. Ocampo and R. Thorp (eds), *Industrialisation and the State in Latin America: The Post-war Years* (London: Macmillan, 2000).

Hall, P. A. (ed.), *The Political Power of Economic Ideas: Keynesianism Across Nations* (Princeton University Press, 1989).

Huneeus, C., 'Tecnócratas y Políticos en la Política Democrática en la Argentina (1983–1995)', *Pensamiento Iberoamericano*, 30 (1997) 207–28.

Silva, E., *The State and Capital in Chile: Business Elites, Technocrats, and Market Economics* (Boulder, CO: Westview, 1996).

Thorp, R., *Progress, Poverty and Exclusion: An Economic History of Latin America in the XXth Century* (Baltimore: Johns Hopkins University Press for the Inter-American Development Bank, 1998).

Valdés, J. G., *Pinochet's Economists: The Chicago School in Chile* (New York: Cambridge University Press, 1995).

Will, R. M., 'The Introduction of Classical Economics in Chile', *Hispanic American Historical Review*, 44/1 (February 1964) 1–21.

2
Economic Ideas, International Influences and Domestic Politics: A Comparative Perspective

Peter A. Gourevitch

Introduction

Why has economic policy shifted in Latin America from the statism of the left and right to the more market-oriented neo-liberal approaches of recent years? It is not hard to think of possible reasons: US hegemony, economic conditions, the cogency of the ideas themselves, the political power of the idea-holders, interest group preferences in each country, communication technology, the movement of peoples, examples from other regions of the world such as East Asia, and the collapse of the Soviet model. More difficult is sorting through the abundance of possible explanations to evaluate their relative impact. It is not possible to do this perfectly, but one way to begin could be to focus on the mechanisms through which the various arguments are thought to work.

To have an impact, Max Weber argued, ideas need to have advocates with the power to make them felt. He wrote about 'idea-bearing classes', groups whose position in society meant their ideas could be translated into practice, as opposed to groups with ideas but no power (Weber 1946). In contrast to reductionist arguments about ideology, Weber thought ideas really did matter. They were the switchmen of history. At the same time, to matter, ideas had to have the support of power; people with leverage had to support them. Where would the Chicago Boys in Chile be without Pinochet's guns?

To show how 'speaking truth to power' works, one must explain the mechanisms of influence: the way ideas shape the behaviour of decision-makers with the power to produce policy outcomes. Three such mechanisms appear to predominate in the literature on economic ideas and policy choices: epistemic communities, US hegemony and the power of international capital, and domestic politics and interest groups. In various forms, these arguments have been applied to cases all over the world in both contemporary and historical episodes (Gourevitch 1978, 1986). It is useful for the Latin America discussion to examine the character of these arguments, the mechanisms of influence they contain, and the types of empirical evidence that they require. We do not have in each case the research material these arguments would require, but it is nonetheless useful to explore what it would mean to operationalize the arguments and see what would constitute evidence for or against them.

Mechanisms of influence and change

Epistemic communities

'Latin American policy has changed because the ideas of elites have changed.' The logic of this argument is as follows. Economic policy derives from the ideas of key decision-makers, or policy elites, who have the requisite training and expertise. These elites form part of an international community of intellectuals, of experts on economic policy, that is, an epistemic community (Haas 1992a, 1992b). The predominant thinking about economics among the economics epistemic community has changed in favour of neo-liberalism. As the perspectives of that community have evolved, so has the thinking of key elites in Latin America.

The central mechanism of change in an argument of this kind is the culture of the epistemic community in which these elites participate. Economic knowledge is specialized. It is a set of ideas with some esoteric qualities that lie beyond the reach of people who are not specially trained. Those who are trained form part of a community of experts with their own ways of thinking. They have their own criteria for what is good or bad, their own standards, and modes of evaluation and reasoning. Ideas operate within this community. As the community's ideas change, so do those of its members; they contribute to the change, and also reflect it. It has a hierarchy of leaders and followers. As the leaders change, the members of the epistemic community evolve with it. At some point, a 'norms cascade' takes place, a kind of tipping point argument (Lohmann 1994; Fearon and Laitin 1996; Keck and Sikkink 1998; Laitin 1998). Members of the group go along with the dominant mode of thinking; some risk-takers start to shift their perspective; and at a certain moment, enough have done so to alter the risk calculations of the rest so that a massive shift takes place around a new consensus. A new norm or dominant ideology takes hold in the epistemic community.

This sort of reasoning about epistemic communities and the evolution of ideas can be found in the history and sociology of science, in the study of specialized bodies of knowledge, such as biology and physics, or in the arts, in architecture. It is a way of thinking about cultural change. It has been applied to earlier periods of economic policy change, notably the spread of Keynesian ideas. Researchers traced the evolution of demand for Keynes's own writings, by focusing on where these were published, when they were translated into other languages, who studied with him, who published work drawing on his ideas, where his work was taught, what pupils picked them up – in short, the formation of the intelligentsia of an epistemic community around Keynesian ideas. They then examined the connection between that community and policy by looking at who from that community was appointed to key positions, or how policy-makers interacted with them (Drake 1989; Hall 1989).

Applied to our case, the logic of this kind of reasoning calls attention to the ideas of the key technically trained people in Latin America – the *técnicos*, broadly conceived. It is the change in their ways of thinking which is critical. It is they who have moved from the statism of ISI, dependency theory and nationalized industry toward a neo-liberal perspective. They have done so because the epistemic community of which they are a part has turned against these ideas.

To research this approach empirically would involve exploring several components: the education and training of the members of the epistemic community; 'testing the conceptual priors about what works' – tracing the development of the new ideas in contrast to the existing ones, looking at what information and development challenged the older ways of thinking, opening thought in new ways; the composition of the group; and the political sociology of its power. Each of these is examined in turn.

Education and training

To measure education, training and other modes of socialization, several sorts of evidence can be traced:

- The location of education. Where did the elites receive their training? The role of US universities in economics and business schools is frequently noted: the Chicago Boys, Harvard's Kennedy School, Stanford and Berkeley, and so on. This could be quantified, along the lines of such work as Peter Smith's book on Mexican elites (Smith 1979).
- Training and jobs in institutions and think tanks. Often the *técnicos* in the making go from advanced degrees to first jobs at the IMF, World Bank, or other prestigious institutions in the United States. These continue the socialization. Some become faculty members for a time at leading universities before returning to their home countries to take vital jobs.
- Research and publications in journals. Some *técnicos* publish in major research journals or policy journals, and read them.
- Advising and consulting. Major institutions inside the epistemic community of economic elites provide advice by providing consulting services to governments and business. For instance, IMF missions, advisers from the US Treasury and Federal Reserve, and consulting firms all provide a flow of ideas and information from a particular point of view.

By building up a rich database on members of a community, their education, their jobs, their careers, their publications and subscriptions, one could map out the empirical correlates of an epistemic community argument. It would not prove influence, but it would establish whether such a group exists.

'Testing the conceptual priors about what works'

Another empirical dimension to an epistemic analysis would be 'process tracing' of the evolution of the new ideas in contrast to the old. To learn a new way of thinking, old ones must be challenged. We all have a set of ideas about how the world works, a set of 'priors' or expectations and assumptions about how the facts relate to each other. Events are fitted into the framework of our priors. To change in a deep way how we think, those priors have to be shaken loose. Events must happen that do not fit, uncomfortable facts which cannot be integrated into the existing paradigm (Kuhn 1962).

In the Latin American case, this would lead us to examine what events and facts challenged existing opinions. One could examine the evolution of these conflicts between events and priors through discussions within the epistemic community. Some possible events in such an analysis include (1) the East Asian case, (2) the collapse of the Soviet Union and Eastern bloc, and (3) the Latin American debt crisis.

The success in the 1980s and 1990s of the East Asian newly industrializing countries (NICS) may have undermined dependency theory and the ISI policies that drew upon such thinking for inspiration (Gereffi and Wyman 1990; Haggard 1990; Wade 1990). The world systems logic of that approach suggested that countries were stuck in their peripheral placement in the global division of labour, and that market forces alone would never let them escape (Cardoso and Faletto 1979). State intervention was thus necessary to shield countries from the costs of that position and to help move them out of it. The success of the East Asian NICs suggested that countries could indeed escape the 'core-periphery trap', and that they could do it with policies other than ISI.

It would be interesting to trace the debate over East Asia in Latin American policy circles as economic thinking in that region has become more liberal. Two contradictory tendencies appear to have taken place. One response was to reject East Asia as non-comparable to Latin America, for reasons of culture, ethnicity, history and geography. Another response was to see in East Asia an alternative not only to the failing patterns of ISI but also to the neo-liberal model put forth by the United States.

The East Asian model was not neo-liberal. It had a strong statist cast to it. The Japanese experience on which it drew was itself statist (Johnson 1982), and Japan in turn followed the German model, what Gerschenkron (1962) called the late development model, of centralized banks and an active state. East Asian states played an active role in their national economies with restrictions on imports; subsidies for exports; restrictions on foreign owner-ship of national production capacity; capital controls; state support for training, investment and research; and many other activities (Wade 1990;

Haggard 2000; Simmons and Elkins 2000). It is possible that after some hostility to the Asian examples, some elites saw it as an alternative to the more completely neo-liberal US ideas. Salinas at first turned to Japan for aid and a model; then, when little help was forthcoming, he turned to the United States and NAFTA.

Indeed, for much of the 1980s and 1990s, the East Asian case was held up in intellectual circles as an alternative to the Anglo-American model. As the US economy seemed to be faltering, while Japan and Germany boomed, the intellectual tide held the American model up to inspection and found it wanting. Japanese advisers were telling developing countries that their model was superior. They encouraged the adoption of Japanese modes of corporate organization, relationships to banks, supplier systems, and government activism through ministries like the Ministries of International Trade and Industry (MITI) and of Finance, to encourage economic growth. There was certainly, as with the Americans and their model today, a desire to promote patterns that would benefit their own, Japanese, model. Having the Asian economies look like Japan would facilitate Japanese corporate penetration and the development of a yen trade bloc.

Japan encouraged the development of a rival epistemic community, built around ideas that modelled the distinctive features of its economy. It pushed the World Bank to write a report on the East Asian miracle and to make sure that the report reflected Japanese thinking about how development worked, rather than reflecting only American ideas. *The East Asian Miracle* (World Bank 1993) shows rather stiffly this blend of rival models of growth: an American one which encourages *laissez-faire* and a Japanese one which assigns an important role to state action.

Thus, it is possible that East Asia provided an important transitional linkage in the emergence of neo-liberal thinking. On the one hand, East Asian success undermined the logic of dependency analysis and strengthened a belief in the efficacy of markets. On the other hand, East Asia supported for a time a 'developmental' version of statism.

That debate on East Asia resonates with two other developments in the epistemic community of political economy in recent years: the shift from 'macro' to 'micro' in economic theory, and the resurgence of comparative capitalism analyses following the collapse of the Soviet model. These two developments reshape the meaning of 'neo-liberalism' vs. 'market intervention' as they highlight some important differences in the ways market economies can operate.

Policy discussions in response to Latin America have tended to focus on macro issues such as inflation, stabilization, budget balancing, taxes, trade and cutting government deficits. These are of course extremely important, as without stable macro policies it is difficult to 'get prices right'. But that approach obscures important microeconomic issues: forms of corporate organization, bank–business relations, instruments of financial accounting and monitoring, shareholder rights, contract law, rules on discharging works, rights of unions, regulatory structures, and so on.

Along these dimensions, there are substantial differences among market economies. The literature on European economies pays considerable attention to differences in corporate organization, namely the way in which authority relations are structured within firms, which links together their owners, managers, employees, and contractors. The starkest contrast is between the liberal market economy (LME) version of the US–UK model and the organized market economy (OME) model of Germany and Japan (Hall and Soskice 2001). The LME model is arm's length and external shareholder driven; the OME model is networked and internal relationship driven. The first type sees the core managerial problem as agency, and solves it by stressing the monitoring powers of external shareholders; the second type sees the core managerial problem in terms of transaction costs, and solves it with strong internal linkages (Kester 1992; Gourevitch 1996, 2001).

In the 1980s and 1990s, when Japan and Germany were doing well, and the United States was stumbling, the OME model seemed to have its attractions. In the late 1990s, the balance has shifted. Japan's sluggish performance, and then the East Asian financial crisis of 1997, have raised severe doubts about the moral hazard of 'crony capitalism' (MacIntyre 2001). These developments brought home very forcefully the importance of microstructures and regulatory systems, as it became understood how these could undermine macro policy. As Latin America debates its future, one of the major dimensions of policy choice for each country has to do with its micro-institutions – whether it picks the LME or the OME mode (Woodruff 1998).

The demise of the Soviet Union, the disintegration of the Soviet bloc, and the abandonment of the planning/nationalization model in Eastern Europe was another major event that challenged the thinking of the Latin American epistemic community. It removed a major alternative to neo-liberalism and the US model. However sceptical about communism many elites in Latin America were, or had become, the Soviet model still represented an alternative which in some version or another loomed large in the cultural imagination. Communists, social democrats, christian democrats and social corporatists of various kinds all held some deeply critical feelings about the market model and took seriously the effort to think of alternatives, at a minimum the 'third way' of the Scandinavian social democracies. These views were weakened by the collapse of the 'second way'.

In the 1980s, the debt crisis and economic turmoil faced by Latin America was certainly a major force in shaking belief in the economic policy approach of previous decades. As this has been substantially analysed by experts on the region, I will do no more than to say it must surely have had an effect in shaking attachment to the economic 'orthodoxies' then prevalent in that region.

In sum, a set of events developed in recent years that provided the grounds to challenge previous modes of thinking about the economy in

Latin America: the growth of East Asia confronted dependency ways of reasoning; the collapse of the USSR undermined the notion of a 'second way' alternative to capitalism; the success of Japan and East Asia provided an alternative to ISI which was nonetheless not fully neo-liberal, providing an intellectual transitional bridge; the debt crisis of Latin America shook faith in ISI policies; and the growth of the United States in the 1990s shifted the balance from the East Asian model toward the American version of neo-liberalism.

All of these ideas could be traced in Latin American discussions – but how were they interpreted and how did they come to challenge the orthodoxy? Exploring this element of the epistemic community argument would constitute a research agenda.

Who are the people?

A third dimension of epistemic communities deals with their actual composition: who is in it and who is not? This is important for tracing hard data such as education, socialization, and publication and other writings. At its core, the concept requires the definition of a group of people with specialized knowledge unavailable to those not specially trained, that is a group of people literate in economic ideas. The narrowest view would include only those with advanced education in economics, masters or doctorates. A broader view might include those with business training, such as MBAs or their equivalent. One could then track who had this kind of training, from what places, and with what ideas and debates. One could track the positions that members of the community held in situations of decision-making: ministries, bureaucratic positions, and places in business and economic journalism. (One must be careful not to do the reverse: define the group by the jobholders. This would mix the issue of decision-making with that of ideology, leading to circularity.)

It may be that policy change in Latin America has to do not simply with the intellectual orientation of the epistemic community, but with other attributes of its composition. Education levels may have risen and spread. As the community broadens, so may its exposure to ideas, and its connection to other aspects of the economy.

It is important to sort out the issue of composition from the next point, the question of power. It may be that the change is due not to a change in intellectual outlook of a defined group, the epistemic community, but a shift in the relationship of ideas to power. That brings the discussion to the next point.

The political sociology of power

The most serious weakness with the epistemic community argument arises in linking ideas to power. What gives a particular set of ideas the means to become policy? Neo-liberal ideas have existed for the whole past century.

Why then in the 1990s did they become adopted for policy? After all, there are always policy alternatives around, and there are generally sophisticated concepts available to support them. For policy to change, one set of ideas has to defeat another in the political arena.

Indeed, it is possible that politics can generate policy without very sophisticated economic rationales behind them. When American farmers were unhappy with tight money and gold standard policies in the late nineteenth century, they did not need formal training in economics to support the free coinage of silver and loose money. Latin American economic history provides plenty of examples of politics shaping the choice among alternative ideas.

So how do ideas get power? The strictest of epistemic community notions might postulate that non-specialist laypersons (interest groups and politicians) lack the expertise to make decisions without specialized knowledge, and that therein lies their power. However, it is not hard to find examples of people ignoring expertise: Stalin and Lysenko biology is one infamous example; the school board of Kansas and creationism is another.

In the case of Keynesianism, demand stimulus policies were taken up not when people read *The General Theory*, but when political shifts altered the power balance in relationship to orthodoxy (Hall 1989). Under the pressure of high unemployment in the 1930s, in the United States and much of Europe, governing coalitions collapsed (Gourevitch 1986). New political alliances supported policy change. In Britain, this meant going off the gold standard and walking away from free trade toward imperial preference. In Sweden, it meant high employment compensation, abandoning gold, and deficit spending. In Germany, it brought corporatist regulation into the economy and a willingness to run deficits. In the United States, it also brought economic experiments of various kinds and some deficit spending. Economists were listened to or ignored, as the political forces in play wanted. When the United States was debating the highest tariff in decades, virtually the entire economics profession of the day signed a petition against it; nonetheless, one of the most protectionist pieces of legislation ever, the Smoot–Hawley Tariff Act, was passed by Congress by a large margin.

Having defined the epistemic community by training and knowledge, it is thus possible to examine what positions it holds in the society – thereby inferring something about its political power. Does it increasingly dominate key positions in government and finance? But this too requires some political analysis: what is it about the changing balance of political forces that enables them to make sure that key positions are occupied by people with a particular policy outlook? We shall return to these issues in the last section of the chapter.

International system pressures

The previous section explored the notion that economic policy changed in Latin America because ideas changed. While this is literally true, this approach leaves open the problem of linking ideas to power. This section looks at an interpretation which does just that. It examines the argument that what causes policy to change in Latin America is the ability of international power, the United States in particular, and foreign capital more generally, to impose its views on Latin America. The character of this argument is familiar. Like the argument about epistemic communities, the international pressure argument has been used to explore a variety of cases around the world and in different historical periods (Drake 1989, this volume).

The core of the argument has to do with instruments of pressure. A power external to the country or region is able to impose its views on that country and obtain policy compliance. What exactly are those instruments of leverage? Upon whom do they operate and how?

United States pressures

The United States has several mechanisms of influence:

- *Access to its markets.* This is a powerful instrument of interest to exporters in Latin America. Trade treaties impose some limits on both sides: they force Latin American countries to open their markets, but they also constrain the United States from closing its markets. Indeed some observers argue this is a major motive for Canada and Mexico in supporting NAFTA: to prevent the elephant from rolling over the smaller animals, or put more formally, to constrain the opportunism of the larger country which faces fewer costs from breaking a trade agreement.
- *Access to its capital.* Such access is extremely important to domestic interests who could receive it and to the various social groups that would benefit from greater US investment.
- *Military and economic foreign aid.* This includes disaster relief and the fight against drug interests.
- *Debt relief.* Debt rescheduling or relief is an important form of aid, to be given or withheld.
- *Military assistance.* Aid to the police and military is of interest to specific groups in society, but a matter of controversy and hostility to others. Does the United States provide a security blanket for Latin America? It is no longer clear from whom. Police assistance helps domestic order, but as this has been used in different ways, it is controversial – it takes us to the point examined in the next section, that the domestic response to pressure from the outside has to be examined as analytically separate from the external pressure itself.

The mechanisms of influence can be operationalized by measuring these different types of leverage: the degree of trade dependence of the various countries as measured by the percentage of trade with the United States, and the GNP of each country in relationship to that trade dependence; the degree of capital flows, as a percentage of total capital formation; and the type and amount of military assistance and foreign aid.

Showing these data is important to an influence argument. It does not by itself prove the point. Analytically, it is possible to have some kind of dependence without being able to show that the dominant country obliges the dependent country to conform to a policy behaviour. Each has to be established, then shown to correlate, then shown to be causally connected.[1]

International agencies

A second tier of pressure lies with the international agencies that provide assistance to the countries of the region, namely the IMF and World Bank. These agencies have power as a function of the aid they provide for stabilization programs and debt relief; this is different from their ideological influence, which belongs in the previous category of mechanisms. Thus, their power is in direct proportion to a country's dependence on that aid. They have little influence on countries that are big enough or stable enough to do without them.

The content of the leverage turns on what the agencies demand as conditions for their assistance. By and large, the major international agencies provide classical neo-liberal advice: balance the budget, get prices right, stabilize the currency, cut back spending, give up government controls, privatize, and open the economies to trade.

The East Asian financial crisis has brought this advice under attack. The countries of the region were seen as having relatively stable, productive economies. Why, critics of the IMF charge, treat them as if they were classic stabilization cases with hyperinflation and unproductive economies? The so-called Washington consensus held that the problem in Asia was crony capitalism and the solution was thorough neo-liberal reforms. However, critics argue that these ideas were not appropriate to the Asian cases. The problem there was more similar to a classic liquidity crisis and a bank run, for which the solution was more money, not less, and liquidity, not deflation (Stiglitz 2000). The controversy resonates with the comparative capitalism debate noted in the previous section. Is there more than one way to run a market economy, or must all countries look like the Anglo-Americans?

It is not clear how this debate launched by the Asian financial crisis affects the approach to Latin America. Towards Peru, the traditional IMF approach seems relevant. Is it for Mexico? Will the IMF and World Bank adjust their analyses and policies to fit new conditions in industrializing countries?

For our discussion here, there seems little doubt the international agencies took a neo-liberal approach in their dealings with Latin America and thus contributed to that change there. How to measure it as leverage, rather than ideology? That would turn on evaluating the degree of dependence of each country on the agencies. The more dependent, the more conformity – one could measure the timing and rate of change, and then see if it correlates with degrees of dependence. There may be some contradictions: countries in trouble may be the most dependent, and these may be the ones which had been the most anti-neo-liberal in the first place.

Are the international agencies separate from the United States, or an extension of US influence? A common charge is that they are tools of the United States. How could this be proved, or more accurately, disproved? That is, how can one tell whether the international agencies reflect a consensus of which the United States is part, or whether they reflect the ability of the United States to impose its views on other countries, thus defining the consensus. There are many analytic issues of agency involved. The IMF and World Bank are agents (the epistemic community view requires them to be principals in part – that they are the high-priests of the epistemic community and thus have an independent role). Of whom are they the agents? Of the United States or of a community of major nations? If there is tension between the United States and the other countries, as happened in connection with the Asian financial crisis, these two models can be differentiated. If there is no conflict, it is harder to separate them. If there are disputes, but the United States always wins them, it is also harder to show the institutions are more than US puppets.

One would have to reason in a different way: if the United States were simply the whole principal here, what need would there be of the agencies – what do they do that the United States cannot do directly? Were they just puppets, they would be wasted. They 'must' therefore do something the US cannot do by itself. They provide resources (the contributions of the other countries) – but even that can be argued to be 'imposed'. Do they also provide legitimacy? Only if the United States does not always win.

Thus to provide legitimacy, there has to be something beyond US pressure – there must be some autonomy of the other countries, some ability on their part to withhold approval. If the agencies are direct puppets, they lose any ability to play a legitimating role. This is proving the point by reasoning rather than by empirical evidence – but that is an analytic problem that arises in the principal–agent reasoning: if the principals dislike something the agent does they could complain. If they do not, this is taken as *prima facie* evidence of approval. These discussions could be extended to include various hemispheric institutions, such as the IADB, ECLA, and so on.

Markets themselves

A third line of reasoning involving international pressure looks at the global market itself. Rather than focus on the United States or international agencies, it emphasizes the role of capital and trade more generally. Latin American countries seek prosperity. To attain it, they have to trade, attract capital, and/or hold domestic capital. Accordingly, they have to pursue economic policies which are attractive to investors, which typically means neo-liberalism.

The mechanisms in this argument are clear enough: the need for markets and capital give leverage to external buyers and suppliers of capital. One can measure dependence on markets and capital without much difficulty, and there is substantial research of this kind. Countries with low savings rates are clearly more dependent than those who generate capital internally – thus Japan and East Asia are markedly different from Latin America, and the rest of the world for that matter. The United States, by this indicator, would be heavily dependent as it is a major importer of capital. The American market exerts an immense pull around the world, on Asia and everywhere else. Indeed this is certainly one of the most powerful levers the United States has – but that is an indicator of the argument advanced above under 'United States pressures', not the more general one here.

In this regard, the liberalization of trade and capital (see 'International trade treaties' below) has a powerful magnet effect on countries. As trade opportunities grow, so do rewards for participating in the system. It was the collapse of world trade in the 1930s that sent Latin American countries away from neo-liberal approaches in the first place. Its revival has a powerful pull effect. In Latin American countries, this argument can be measured using degrees of involvement in trade, for example export/import balances.

The mechanism of this influence at first seems clear: countries adjust their policies to conform to the demands of foreign capital and markets. When countries do not like what this implies, they complain: Malaysian Prime Minister Mahatir's comments in 1997 are notorious – he blamed the collapse of markets that year on foreign speculators, particularly Jews like Soros. This did not please capital markets, and Malaysia paid for Mahatir's remarks.

Does capital want neo-liberalism? This argument assumes a uniform preference function for economic policy. This is not likely to be the case. Markets of different kinds provide various sorts of rewards to different investors. Some countries have done quite well under interventionist states, authoritarian rulers and crony capitalism. Investors have different discount rates for risk, favouritism, political certainty and predictability. A study of investment during the Suharto years shows this well: stocks in the Indonesian exchange were classified according to proximity to Suharto's power and their prices were then tracked against various events in the Suharto regime. When Suharto was sick, those stocks closest to him fell, while those distant from his favours rose; when news was good, the returns reversed (Fisman 1998; Fisman and Gatti 2000; Fisman and Svensson 2000). Investors do not necessarily stay away from non-liberal regimes; rather the nature of the regime causes them to target their investments. The countries of East Asia attracted a lot of capital and had high savings rates without the full-fledged neo-liberalism of the United States (MacIntyre 2001). So has much of Europe for much of its history.

Certainly some policies can clearly cause capital flight, and these we can see are sanctioned strongly by world markets. However, there is some range in the attitude of markets. Different sorts of capital will place a different risk premium on government action of various kinds. It will certainly prefer a predictable and stable intervening government to an arbitrary or chaotic one.

International trade treaties

A fourth type of external influence on the countries of Latin America involves the impact of various international treaties and institutions on trade, for example, MERCOSUR, NAFTA, WTO. These institutions commit their members to a trade regime which, for the protectionist countries of Latin America, are neo-liberal in their impact. By signing these treaties, the countries are committed to renouncing various practices that cut them off from the open flow of goods and capital. As such, these are again mechanisms of influence on national policy, pushing the countries in a neo-liberal direction.

Are these mechanisms different from the others mentioned so far? They raise the same issues discussed concerning the World Bank and IMF above. The institutions are 'agents' of international capital and the countries that seek to encourage open trade. At the same time, the institutions play a role that needs to be modelled for itself. The counterfactual is: Where would trade be without these institutions? Those countries and interests who seek free trade realize that there are obstacles in national and international regulation that need treatment. Trade poses classic collective action problems: only a very powerful hegemon can renounce protectionism unilaterally, and even there, the other countries will seek limits on the hegemon's opportunist behaviour. Most countries will lower their trade barriers only if others do the same. Bilateral reciprocal trade treaties are one instrument. Generalizing these into a comprehensive treaty is a more developed version of the same goal. Institutions are able to provide partial solutions to collective action problems: they reduce transaction costs, provide incentives to trade concessions, create mechanisms for dispute resolution, facilitate information sharing, supply processes for making decisions, and through multiple interactions, build trust (Keohane and Martin 1995). Institutions may provide mechanisms for dispute resolution, such as ways of shifting conflict from direct political confrontation to mediated 'legalization' processes (Goldstein *et al.* 2000).

The institutions of trade are broadly neo-liberal. They ask countries to lower tariffs and other trade barriers, and to harmonize regulations, in effect to create uniform markets that deepen the division of labour and extend mutual interdependence. As such, they transform the societies to which they belong. As countries participate, their economies change; the inefficient are driven out while effective participants grow. So long as that happens, majorities in favour of free trade grow. If it does not, hostility rises, prompting a backlash.

This last point – regarding support and opposition to free trade – brings the discussion to the third major type of interpretation of the neo-liberalizing trend: internal politics and debates within the countries of Latin America.

Internal factors

Countries make choices. Some range of policy alternatives exists, from which countries select their course of action. Certainly, there are limits and pressures. The world provides only so much choice, but it does provide some. Liberalism is one of several possible policy options. Adopting those policies requires decisions by members of a national government. To make that decision, such governments require some domestic support. If countries shift from one policy to another, we must find some basis of domestic support for that policy shift.

The importance of this variable has emerged at several points in the previous discussion. In examining epistemic communities, we faced the problem of linking ideas to power. If thinking among experts changed, how do we explain the ability of the experts to get support for their policies? Experts are not always listened to, indeed often they are not. Political decision-makers 'choose' to listen to them, or to ignore them. We need some understanding of the politics behind that decision.

Similarly, external pressures are certainly real, but they can elicit different responses. Foreign influences can be listened to or ignored. For those pressures to translate into national policy, there have to be some domestic advocates of the policy choices international actors desire. Research on Japan, for example, shows that US pressure, 'giatsu', works when there are important lobbies in Japan that support the direction of the US pressure; when there is no or little support at home, US pressure has little impact (Schoppa 1993, 1997). If foreign pressure desires neo-liberalism, that means costly policy changes – cutting spending, compressing the economy to stop inflation, raising the price of goods and taxes – which are politically difficult. Some support for them must be found. Foreign 'pressure' requires governments to construct coalitions between foreign and domestic supporters.

Some countries do choose to reject neo-liberal economics – North Korea and Burma come readily to mind, as do many countries of the Middle East and Africa. There is a price to be paid in that these countries will surely have less economic growth. However, that is a price some 'countries' – or those who hold power in certain countries – are willing to pay. We cannot therefore take for granted that the 'functionalist' imperative of the world economy 'compels' countries to respond. Need does not necessarily impose itself in policy. It may be of macro advantage to GNP, but to the micro disadvantage of various key political figures to pay that cost. Suharto in Indonesia, Marcos in the Philippines and many other authoritarian rulers in Latin America, Africa, Asia and Europe have sought to bolster their Swiss bank accounts at the expense of GNP. The disadvantage to the nation of their doing so does not provide an explanation for the shift to liberalism. It may provide the motive for efforts within the nation to throw them out, but a political account of why such efforts succeed or fail is necessary (Bates 1981).

International pressure needs to be given human agency – specific individuals who have a motive to accept that pressure, and a process whereby they are able to translate that preference into policy. To have an effect, globalization has to be internalized.

Each step in the shift to neo-liberal policies involves an important policy change, which involves benefits and costs, and thus will surely provoke into action its own coalition of supporters and opponents. To understand the choice among policy alternatives, we need a way of explaining why one coalition prevails and alternatives fail. For that, we need a theory of policy outcomes.

Two modes of analysis predominate in the study of policy, often in conflict with each other, sometimes together. One line of reasoning looks at the political sociology of policy preferences. It asks who supported or opposed a particular policy reform and what resources they had with which to advance their cause. The other line of reasoning stresses institutions or mechanisms of aggregation. It asks how the political system in a given country influences the chances that one or another coalition will prevail. Each of these has something important to say.

Arguing from preferences

The general logic of a preferences argument is familiar to everyone. The interests of particular groups within a country are differentially affected by policy according to their competitive position in the national and world economy. At the same time, interest groups lobby the government to get the policies that fit their preferences (Frieden 1999). For example, in explaining the adoption of Keynesian policies, support for breaking with the liberal orthodoxy of the day can be found among disgruntled farmers, unhappy workers and parts of the business community such as export industries in Sweden and the United States, and domestic industry in Nazi Germany (Gourevitch 1986; Hall 1989).

In Latin America, this sort of argument is quite familiar (Smith 1969; Evans 1979). Indeed, it has been the dominant line of reasoning among researchers. Political institutions have been seen as weak, as the pawns of powerful forces in society. To understand what happens, one needs to find who supported this or that government, this coup, or that shift to political liberalization. Strong landowners, natural resource producers, landless labourers, urban workers, the liberal professions, and shopkeepers are the raw ingredients of politics in analysis of the region. The combinations among these groups provide the driver for policy choice and policy analysis. In this tradition of research, political institutions are seen as instruments of the winners, the tools by which powerful groups create structures to attain their ends. O'Donnell's (1973) famous essay on bureaucratic authoritarianism had this character to it, as do interpretations of Pinochet and other coups in the region.

To understand the politics of liberalization from the preferences approach requires that we specify what incentives the situation provides for one policy direction or another. Liberalization involves two policy arenas. The first involves liberalization of the economy in a direct way: in relationship to foreign markets, free movement of goods and capital; in relationship to domestic markets, less regulation. These are not identical, but they do overlap. Much of the literature on liberalization refers to trade, so with that caveat, the two forms can be treated as analytically similar and often politically in substantial overlap. The second policy arena has to do with the provision of 'public goods' within a national economy, to include education, health, public works and the efficient delivery of services, all of which are essential for a well-run economy. Although related, the two are not identical, and generate somewhat different politics.

Liberalizers see benefits from trade while protectionists see costs. Who is situated on each side? To predict that, endogenous macro theory calls for situating interest groups in their economic situation, be it domestic or foreign (Magee *et al.* 1989). Two contrasting logics can be found, one based on class, the other on factor endowments. Rogowski (1989) uses Stolper–Samuelson models of trade to predict that those whose factor endowment was scarce within their country would prefer protectionism, while those whose factor endowment was abundant would support free trade. This produces economic conflict along class lines, between owners of capital, landowners and labourers.

The sectors argument draws on Ricardo–Viner trade theory to stress factor specificity (Frieden 1991). Where some force (for example technology or geography) inhibits the mobility of factors of production, these become tied to a particular industry. All the participants of that industry then have an interest in its preservation and growth, and will ally despite the difference in their class position. Thus, workers in the Argentine meat-packing industry might ally with their bosses to protect the industry as a whole, as steel workers might do in the face of foreign competition. Hiscox (1999, 2001) argues that the two theories should be read as empirical alternatives. Both are deductively valid, but apply to different historical moments.

These concepts help clarify coalition patterns in Latin America. At times policy conflict has had sharp class elements to it: workers fighting their employers, agricultural labourers against great landowners. At other times, the cleavages cut across class lines, pitting agriculture against industry, city against country, and the exporters of raw materials against the manufacturers of finished products. Smith (1969), writing on meat and grain in Argentina, shows these relationships quite vividly.

In broad historical terms, liberalization can be explained as the result of changing incentives to interest groups within Latin American countries. The spread of statist policies in the past was a response to collapse and instability in the world economy. The advanced industrial countries experienced substantial contraction and all responded with protectionism in their policy mix. The resulting environment provided reduced opportunities for export and specialization in the world economy. The result was a policy mix that reflected the behaviour of the United States, Europe and Japan.

The late part of the twentieth century provided quite a different set of incentives. World trade has grown substantially, eventually exceeding its pre-World-War-I levels. The advanced industrial countries have liberalized their economies substantially in most areas (though not in agriculture, to the detriment of developing-country farmers). Manufacturers have globalized production in new ways, disaggregating final products into components, each of which is then located in different countries seeking optimal conditions (Gourevitch *et al.* 2000; McKendrick *et al.* 2000). Global production networks have become very skilful at breaking the components of a final product into distinct pieces, sending these pieces around the world to the optimal production setting in cost/skill ratios, and then reconnecting the pieces for final assembly. Huge sums of capital have been invested in developing countries. In Latin America, Mexico and Brazil are particularly important targets of this process.

These processes increase quite substantially the incentives for liberalization. Economic gain can be reaped by exporting and by attracting investments. Both require economic policies that make the country more attractive to foreigners. Countries tend not to import without some kind of trade-liberalizing treaty, while investors tend not to come without some evidence of market-promoting policies. Therefore, in general terms, economic liberalization of the world economy provides powerful incentives towards an outward economic orientation in Latin America.

Saying that in general terms countries could benefit from trade does not, however, tell us whether a country will actually pursue liberalization. This is a flaw in efficiency arguments: it may be efficient for the country as a whole to liberalize, but it may not be advantageous to some powerful interests. General welfare arguments do not tell us who in each country actively supports taking advantage of those benefits. There are always losers in trade, as well as gainers – how else to understand the conflicts so readily observable about trade policy? Within a country, some groups will benefit substantially more than others, and some groups will be hurt substantially more than others. Opportunity can cause conflict. Who supports each side?

The beneficiaries from trade are those whose skills or resources are rewarded in the international economy, and who have the capacity to adjust to new situations. Historically in Latin America, these have been extractive industries based on natural resources or agriculture. These groups are able to sell far more in world markets than they could in those that are domestic and sheltered. As consumers of manufactured products, they have been supporters of free trade. The opponents of free trade have been the reverse: manufacturers seeking shelter in a national economy from more efficient competitors in 'advanced' countries.

These cleavage lines remain significant in Latin America, but there are also strong sectoral tensions which cut across class lines. Trade theory tells us unskilled workers could benefit from open markets if they have a comparative advantage there. This can put them into conflict with skilled workers employed in manufacturing industries which are sheltered, and with the middle- and upper-level managers and technicians of such industries. Manufacturing industries in turn are becoming fragmented in their interests by the globalization of production. As firms locate component manufacturing or final assembly around the world, those employed and investing in that process acquire an interest in keeping trade flows open, while in other places lobbyists may seek to attract foreign capital through protectionist national-content legislation. Globalization processes thus, as expected, produce cleavages along both class (factor) and sectoral (specific assets) lines.

While this discussion of preferences has looked primarily at the relationship to foreign markets (protection vs. free trade), similar reasoning applies to the issues of regulation in domestic markets. Regulation produces winners and losers, so that the former will seek to preserve regulations, while the latter may support change. The same kind of interest group process develops as with trade. The two coalitions may overlap. Regulation can be a form of protection from world markets; deregulation at home may be supported by those who wish to compete abroad.

Another set of economic interest questions concerning liberalization has to do with public-goods provision (Nielson 1997; Shugart and Haggard 2001). As economies develop, indeed in order to develop, they need a variety of services more or less effectively performed: education, transportation, health, communication and financial regulation. These can be provided in more or less efficient ways, and with greater or less waste, or corruption. Goods can be distributed by generalized or particularized principles – 'pork-barrel', as part of a system of patronage, or general, in response to universal criteria. The fights over liberalization in Latin America are intermingled with conflicts over this process. Liberalizers in the economy overlap substantially with those who seek 'reform' in domestic services, so that the cleavage preferences are likely to overlap. At the same time, it is possible that protectionists (those who fear foreign competition) may at the same time prefer 'efficient' services and government at home.

Thus, various factors may increase preferences within Latin American countries for economic liberalism: greater opportunities in the world economy, foreign investment, and internal demand for efficient government services. As incentives strengthen these preferences, we may observe a linkage mechanism at work, a 'spillover' process. Haas used this label to analyse European integration: as integration proceeds, it generates interests which support it, which then interact to generate more support, thereby creating a spiral toward expansion. Once a process of liberalization starts, it creates its own lobbies, the way a downward spiral would do the reverse. Policies over time remove their opponents and strengthen their supporters.

At the same time, there is certainly a backlash process: those who suffer from the adjustments to liberalization fight its development. As the pain of adjustment deepens, it generates opposition. This has happened in many countries, both in the current period and in each historical period of rapid economic change and globalizing trends, in the highly industrialized countries as well as the newly emerging ones. In many countries, some kind of political policy bargain is struck to accommodate the conflicting forces at work. In Europe and North America, this was an 'historical compromise', formed in the 1930s and the years after 1945. It combined a market economy with extensive social insurance systems (unemployment compensation, retirement, health, education benefits); this helped to shield citizens from the shocks of trade and to spread the benefits as well as the costs (Cameron 1978; Katzenstein 1985; Gourevitch 1986; Iversen and Wren 1998; Iversen 1998, 1999; Iversen *et al.* 1999). Over time, it will be interesting to see whether bargains of this kind are formed in Latin America (Haggard and Kauffman 1992, 1995).

Institutions

So far, the discussion has focused on the political sociology of liberalization and economic reform processes. Governments cannot operate without support, so specific groups provide the underpinnings for that support. It is often insufficient, however, to look only the sociology of support. How preferences are aggregated into policy outputs can be strongly influenced by the structure of institutions. For any set of preferences, a different institution can produce a different result. The preferences approach explores the obverse: different institutions produce similar results, because they have a common social profile pressing against them (Rogowski 1999).

Liberalizing coalitions can be inhibited or enhanced by specific institutional arrangements. The period of liberalization in Latin America corresponds roughly to a period of growing democratization. Is this an accident or is there a strong relationship, and if so, which way do the causal arrows run?

An authoritarian regime can skew considerably the relative power of various social actors. However, it is not so clear in which direction that power will be used. The Pinochet regime used its powers often to liberalize. The causal mechanism assumed that repression was the only way to contain opposition to neo-liberal policies from labour and business groups with too much to lose. This is an old argument in the modernization literature: economic change runs up against entrenched interests which have to be blocked for change to occur; this has been used to justify authoritarian rule from Soviet Russia to modern Singapore and the East Asian NICs. Certainly, the military regime's insulation from popular protest gave it the autonomy to move quickly in restructuring the economy. It was possible for the people with power to listen to a particular epistemic community (in the case of Chile, the Chicago Boys) and to follow their lead.

Yet, it is not so clear why the military chose to hear the Chicago Boys rather than other economists or advisers. Authoritarian rulers, military or other, have in other places and at other times behaved quite differently. Many authoritarian rulers in Latin America have applied corporatist doctrines, of a regulated society and economy, and in some cases have supported a kind of military socialism. Authoritarianism allows some range of choice which the institution itself does not fully explain.

Indeed, in several cases, it is the collapse or weakening of the authoritarian model which correlates with neo-liberalism. In Argentina, a turn away from state policies followed the collapse of the military government. In Mexico, it correlates with political liberalization more broadly. The older political structures of one-party rule and military dominance seem linked to older economic approaches. The decline of one opened up a new game for the other. At the same time, 'democratic models' do not by any means guarantee liberal policies, or efficiency in a liberal economy. Democratic politics is vulnerable to capture by special interests, which may be interventionist in various ways.

The authoritarian/democratic dichotomy does not capture adequately the issues raised by Institutionalist analysis. Democratic and authoritarian institutions can vary quite substantially in their specific arrangements in ways which may have a considerable impact on policy outputs.

The theory of institutional variation is most advanced in research on democratic systems. Researchers have been examining carefully the impact on policy of institutional variance in electoral laws, the structure of the executive (presidency, prime minister/cabinet), the powers of the legislature, and the degree of federalism (Haggard and McCubbins 2001). These arrangements interact to shape the number, range, and impact of 'veto gates', or structures which provide opportunities to influence an outcome. These arrangements are held to influence several dimensions of policy, for example resoluteness vs. decisiveness, private-regarding or pork-barrel policies vs. public or public-goods provision.

The complexity of the relationship arises in connecting constitutional forms to changing policies. Political pressure can cut in different directions; it can sustain vested interests and pork-barrel politics, or it can sustain majorities that want reform, more honest government, and comprehensive rather than particularistic policies. Work on Japan, for example, argues that the voting system in effect for most of the postwar period encourages pork-barrel, particularistic, specialized clientelistic politics. Each legislative district elected several members of parliament, often from the same party; this encouraged candidates to differentiate themselves from their party brethren by targeting specific clienteles within each district, thereby rewarding the particularistic targeting of benefits. By contrast, a single-member, winner-take-all system encourages coalition formation by the party at a broad national aggregate level, and thus approaches that are more public-goods-oriented than particularistic (Cox *et al.* 2000). Specialists on Latin America are applying this kind of reasoning to Latin America. They examine voting systems, presidential powers in relationship to the legislature, federalism and other such formal structures to see which encourage particularism, and which encourage more general appeals (Shugart and Carey 1992; Ames 1995). Brazil is an interesting case. The reformers are quite severely handicapped in their efforts by the institutional rewards to particularism. Politicians have little incentive to play a cooperative national game, but rather maintain their fiefs. Reformers thus seek to change the rules of the game in order to shift the incentives and produce reformist politics. There is naturally a contradictory quality to this: those who oppose the substance of reform also oppose changing the institutions that would make it easier for policy reforms to pass. When the institutions are stacked against reform, the coalition seeking it has thereby a tough mountain to climb.

Mexico provides a good case-study of the interaction of economic reform coalitions and political reform processes. Salinas started a process of economic liberalization, putting Mexico into NAFTA and accepting greater liberalization. He seemed cautious on institutional reform, though some groundwork was laid even before Zedillo in allowing opposition governors in various provinces. The two mechanisms interacted: economic change enlarged the coalition for economic reform, while political change gave more voice to the discontented. Mexico seems a case where the timing matters: support for political liberalization, cleaner government and less connection to the old boss system seems correlated with support for economic liberalization, but the two are not identical. The connection is historical and situational: the two arise at the same moment in Mexican history, and so are linked. In Chile, by contrast, economic liberalization began as an authoritarian project.

The internal politics line of reasoning stresses national choices in the face of both international pressures and epistemic communities. Countries face pressures, which in turn are linked to opportunities. What countries do with these turns on their own internal political choices. It is a decision to accede to foreign pressures or resist them; to decide for economic growth as opposed to other values; and to pick neo-liberalism as a motor for growth, as some countries have not done so and have done well. Whatever strategy is picked for managing relations to the world economy, these require domestic foundations. That, in turn, means political support coalitions for the policies involved, and having the political institutions that enable such coalitions to win and govern. Institutions influence the ways in which various support coalitions and oppositions express themselves politically, whether they turn to authoritarianism or work through constitutional means.

Conclusion

Each argument raised to explain the shift to neo-liberalism in Latin America points to a different line of research and evidence. It will be difficult to construct tests that would allow us cleanly to select one argument over another, and of course it is likely that more than one process is at work. However, it is possible to test some portion of each argument, to see whether the available evidence can be found to confirm or disconfirm it. Moreover, it is also possible to clarify the role each variable makes in an outcome. My emphasis here has been to structure the argument in ways that privilege domestic politics: ideas matter, but ideas need power. International influences matter, but they too need power within a country to become translated into policy. Domestic politics is the switchboard, or prism, through which these influences are refracted.

Note

1. Hirschman's (1945) *National Power and the Structure of Foreign Trade* is a pioneer book of this kind, in looking at the way Nazi Germany promoted the dependence of the east European countries in the 1930s on it, in order then to force their compliance with German foreign policy.

References

Ames, B., 'Electoral Rules, Constituency Pressures, and Pork Barrel: Bases of Voting in the Brazilian Congress', *Journal of Politics* 57/2 (May 1995) 324–43.
Bates, R. H., *Markets and States in Tropical Africa: The Political Basis of Agricultural Policies* (Berkeley: University of California Press, 1981).
Cameron, D. R., 'The Expansion of the Public Economy: A Comparative Analysis', *American Political Science Review* 72/4 (1978) 1243–61.
Cardoso, F. H. and E. Faletto, *Dependency and Development in Latin America* (Berkeley: University of California Press, 1979).
Cox, G. W., F. M. Rosenbluth and M. F. Thies, 'Electoral Rules, Career Ambitions, and Party Structure: Comparing Factions in Japan's Upper and Lower Houses', *American Journal of Political Science* 44/1 (January 2000) 115–22.
Drake, P. W., *The Money Doctor in the Andes: The Kemmerer Missions, 1923–1933* (Durham, NC: Duke University Press, 1989).
Evans, P. B., *Dependent Development: The Alliance of Multinational, State, and Local Capital in Brazil* (Princeton University Press, 1979).
Fearon, J. D. and D. D. Laitin, 'Explaining Interethnic Cooperation', *American Political Science Review* 90/4 (December 1996) 715–35.
Fisman, R., 'The Organization of Productive Activities in Developing Countries: The Role of Diversified Business Groups', PhD thesis, Harvard University, 1998.
Fisman, R. and R. Gatti, *Decentralization and Corruption: Evidence across Countries*, Policy Research Working Paper no. 2290 (Washington, DC: World Bank, February 2000).
Fisman, R. and J. Svensson, *Are Corruption and Taxation Really Harmful to Growth? Firm-Level Evidence*, Policy Research Working Paper no. 2485 (Washington, DC: World Bank, November 2000).

Frieden, J. A., *Debt, Development, and Democracy: Modern Political Economy and Latin America, 1965–1985* (Princeton University Press, 1991).

Frieden, J. A., 'Actors and Preferences in International Relations', in D. A. Lake and R. Powell (eds), *Strategic Choice and International Relations* (Princeton University Press, 1999).

Gereffi, G. and D. Wyman (eds), *Manufacturing Miracles: Paths of Industrialization in Latin America and East Asia* (Princeton University Press, 1990).

Gerschenkron, A., *Economic Backwardness in Historical Perspective* (Cambridge, MA: Harvard University Press, 1962).

Goldstein, J., M. Kahler, R. O. Keohane and A. Slaughter, 'Introduction: Legalization and World Politics', *International Organization* 54/3 (Summer 2000) 385–99.

Gourevitch, P. A., 'The Second Image Reversed: International Sources of Domestic Politics', *International Organization* 32/4 (1978) 881–911.

Gourevitch, P. A., *Politics in Hard Times: Comparative Responses to International Economic Crises* (Ithaca, NY: Cornell University Press, 1986).

Gourevitch, P. A., 'The Macropolitics of Microinstitutional Differences in the Analysis of Comparative Capitalism', in S. Berger and R. Dore (eds), *National Diversity and Global Capitalism* (Ithaca, NY: Cornell University Press, 1996).

Gourevitch, P. A., *Comparative Capitalism in the Globalized Economy: Understanding National Production Systems* (mimeo) (University of California at San Diego, 2001).

Gourevitch, P. A., R. Bohn and D. McKendrick, 'Globalization of Production: Insights from the Hard Disk Drive Industry', *World Development* 28/2 (February 2000) 301–17.

Haas, P. M., 'Introduction: Epistemic Communities and International Policy Coordination', *International Organization* 46/1 (1992a) 1–35.

Haas, P. M. (ed.), 'Knowledge, Power, and International Policy Coordination', *International Organization* 46/1 Special issue (1992b).

Haggard, S. *Pathways from the Periphery: The Politics of Growth in the Newly Industrializing Countries* (Ithaca, NY: Cornell University Press, 1990).

Haggard, S., *The Political Economy of the Asian Financial Crisis* (Washington, DC: Institute for International Economics, 2000).

Haggard, S. and R. R. Kaufman (eds), *The Politics of Economic Adjustment* (Princeton University Press, 1992).

Haggard, S. and R. R. Kaufman, *The Political Economy of Democratic Transitions* (Princeton University Press, 1995).

Haggard S. and M. D. McCubbins (eds), *Structure and Policy in Presidential Democracies* (New York: Cambridge University Press, 2001).

Hall, P. A., *The Political Power of Economic Ideas: Keynesianism Across Nations* (Princeton University Press, 1989).

Hall, P. A. and Soskice, D., *Varieties of Capitalism: The Institutional Foundations of Comparative Capitalism* (Oxford University Press, 2001).

Hirschman, A. O., *National Power and the Structure of Foreign Trade* (Berkeley: University of California Press, 1945).

Hiscox, M. J., 'The Magic Bullet? The RTAA, Institutional Reform, and Trade Liberalization', *International Organization* 53/4 (1999) 669–98.

Hiscox, M., 'Class versus Industry Cleavages: Inter-industry Factor Mobility and the Politics of Trade', *International Organization* 55/1 (Winter 2001) 1–46.

Iversen, T., 'Wage Bargaining, Central Bank Independence, and the Real Effects of Money', *International Organization* 52/3 (Summer 1998) 469–504.

Iversen, T., *Contested Economic Institutions: The Politics of Macroeconomics and Wage Bargaining in Advanced Democracies* (Cambridge University Press, 1999).

Iversen, T. and A. Wren, 'Equality, Employment, and Budgetary Restraint: The Trilemma of the Service Economy', *World Politics* 50/4 (July 1998) 507–46.

Iversen, T., J. Pontusson and D. Soskice (eds), *Unions, Employers and Central Banks* (New York: Cambridge University Press, 1999).

Johnson, C. A., *MITI and the Japanese Miracle: The Growth of Industrial Policy, 1925–1975* (Stanford University Press, 1982).

Katzenstein, P. J., *Small States in World Markets: Industrial Policy in Europe* (Ithaca, NY: Cornell University Press, 1985).

Keck, M. E. and K. Sikkink, *Activists Beyond Borders: Advocacy Networks in International Politics* (Ithaca, NY: Cornell University Press, 1998).

Keohane, R. O. and L. L. Martin, 'The Promise of Institutionalist Theory', *International Security* 20/1 (1995) 39–51.

Kester, W. C., 'Industrial Group as System of Contractual Governance', *Oxford Review of Economic Policy* 8/3 (1992) 24–44.

Kuhn, T., *The Structure of Scientific Revolutions* (University of Chicago Press, 1962).

Laitin, D. D., *Identity in Formation: The Russian-Speaking Populations in the Near Abroad* (Ithaca, NY: Cornell University Press, 1998).

Lohmann, S., 'The Dynamics of Informational Cascades: The Monday Demonstrations in Leipzig, East Germany, 1989–91', *World Politics* 47/1 (1994) 42–101.

MacIntyre, A. J., 'Institutions and Investors: The Politics of the Economic Crisis in Southeast Asia', *International Organization* 55 /1 (2001) 81–122.

Magee, S. P., W. A. Brock and L. Young, *Black Hole Tariffs and Endogenous Policy Theory: Political Economy in General Equilibrium* (Cambridge University Press, 1989).

McCubbins, M., R. Noll and B. Weingast, 'Structure and Process, Politics and Policy: Administrative Arrangements and the Political Control of Agencies', *Virginia Law Review* 75 (March 1989) 431–82.

McKendrick, D., R. Doner and S. Haggard, *From Silicon Valley to Singapore: Location and Competitive Advantage in the Hard Disk Drive Industry* (Palo Alto, CA: Stanford University Press, 2000).

Nielson, D. L., 'The Development Shift: the Political Economy of Policy Adjustment and Institutional Reform', PhD thesis (University of California at San Diego, 1997).

O'Donnell, G. A., *Modernization and Bureaucratic-Authoritarianism: Studies in South American Politics* (Berkeley: University of California Press, 1973).

Rogowski, R., *Commerce and Coalitions: How Trade Affects Domestic Political Alignments* (Princeton University Press, 1989).

Rogowski, R., 'Institutions as Constraints on Strategic Choice', in D. A. Lake and R. Powell (eds), *Strategic Choice and International Relations* (Princeton University Press, 1999).

Schoppa, L. J., 'Two-Level Games and Bargaining Outcomes: Why *Gaiatsu* Succeeds in Japan in Some Cases but Not Others', *International Organization* 47/3 (Summer 1993) 353–86.

Schoppa, L. J., *Bargaining with Japan: What American Pressure Can and Cannot Do* (New York: Columbia University Press, 1997).

Shugart, M. and Carey, J., *Presidents and Assemblies: Constitutional Design and Electoral Dynamics* (New York: Cambridge University Press, 1992).

Shugart, M. S. and S. Haggard, 'Institutions and Public Policy in Presidential Systems', in S. Haggard and M. D. McCubbins (eds), *Structure and Policy in Presidential Democracies* (New York: Cambridge University Press, 2001).

Simmons, B. and Z. Elkins, 'Globalization and Policy Diffusion: Explaining Three Decades of Liberalization', paper presented to Conference on Globalization and Governance (University of California at San Diego, March 2000).

Smith, P. H., *Politics and Beef in Argentina: Patterns of Conflict and Change* (New York: Columbia University Press, 1969).

Smith, P. H., *Labyrinths of Power: Political Recruitment in Twentieth-Century Mexico* (Princeton University Press, 1979).

Stiglitz, J. E., 'The Insider: What I Learned at the World Economic Crisis', *New Republic*, (17 April 2000) 56.

Wade, R., *Governing the Market: Economic Theory and the Role of Government in East Asian Industrialization* (Princeton University Press, 1990).

Weber, M., 'Social Psychology of World Religions', in H. H. Gerth and C. Wright Mills (eds), *From Max Weber: Essays in Sociology* (New York: Oxford University Press, 1946).

Woodruff, C., 'Contract Enforcement and Trade Liberalization in Mexico's Footwear Industry', *World Development* 26/6 (June 1998) 979–91.

World Bank, *The East Asian Miracle: Economic Growth and Public Policy* (New York: Oxford University Press, 1993).

3
The Evolution of Economic Ideas: From Import Substitution to Human Development

Frances Stewart

Introduction

Over the course of the last half-century, there have been major changes in development thinking – in the assumed goals of development policy, the mechanisms at work and, consequently, the policy prescriptions. Presenting the changes in very broad terms, not allowing for the many exceptions, in terms of processes or mechanisms of development, a strongly statist view of development which held in the first part of the period was replaced by a neo-liberal, market-oriented view in the latter. At the same time, in terms of objectives, the general focus on maximizing GDP growth as the major objective of development was at least partially displaced by an emphasis on human goals.

The purpose of this chapter is to explore these changes and examine the factors responsible for them. The central premise here is that the changes were not arbitrary, but followed a logic – a complex, organic and interactive process which explains evolving development thinking. The next section describes the nature of the interactive cycle hypothesized. In the third, fourth and fifth sections, I will trace the evolution of the cycle in practice over the last half of the twentieth century. The final section will draw some conclusions.

The evolution of development thinking

It is possible to detect a complex, organic and cumulative process involving an interaction between development outcomes (or events in the world), thinking, policy-making and the consequences of those policies which in turn affect the way the world is perceived, leading to a new cycle of thought/ policy/ events.

In a cyclical process, there is no logical place to start because all elements interact and are changing. But let us start with a certain 'reality' in a particular economy (or rather reality as perceived by the main actors). This reality consists in perceptions about the structure of the economy (primary production/secondary/tertiary), achievements (in terms for example, of economic growth, income distribution, poverty, human development), and political and economic possibilities.

There are two components to development thinking: definition of the objectives or goals of development and identification of recommended mechanisms for achieving them. Perceptions about reality influence both, with considerable interaction among the two, since many apparently neutral 'mechanisms' (for example, the market system) are important objectives for some players.[1] Policy-makers try to guide the economy from where it is (that is, perceived reality) to where they would like it to be, the latter being affected by their own power, position and ideology as well as dominant thinking in the development community as a whole. The preferred mechanisms for achieving development goals are in turn influenced by experience with prior mechanisms, as well as by ideology.[2] Consequently reality influences the choice both of objectives and of mechanisms, that is, development thinking. Development thinking then feeds into policy-making.

Policy choices have consequences – foreseen and unforeseen – that is, they lead to a new 'reality'. Where the policy choices lead to unforeseen and undesired consequences, they cause a revision in development thinking – for example, if a growth-promoting policy has the consequence of an unsustainable level of debt, new thinking evolves to deal with the debt situation. New policies are then introduced, once again affecting reality, which in turn affects development thinking.

This view of a cyclical interactive process between reality, thought and policies is clearly too simple. One reason is that the cycle has been depicted as occurring in one place, without external influences. Yet thought in and about developing countries is heavily influenced by thought in and about developed countries; while the reality in developed countries is also conditioned by events outside (for example, terms of trade, market opportunities and so on). Developed countries and international institutions generally have a leading role in influencing development thinking, with the World Bank being particularly influential. Because of this and the fact that much of the study of development economics and the education of developing country economists is located in university departments in developed countries, changing thought in developed countries has a very strong influence over thinking about developing countries. Thus although our main focus is on the evolution of development thought, it is also necessary to take into account a parallel process of evolution of economic thought in and about the advanced countries.

Second, the causal nexus presented above omits developments arising from the scientific process, which would occur irrespective of changing events. The empirical testing of hypotheses and the development of new theoretical tools generates its own process of evolution. This sort of advance, however, which we term 'scientific' advance, generally occurs within particular topics rather than in the changing focus relating to 'the grand issues of the subject' as Stern (1989:598) describes them, which form our main focus here.

Third, particular interest groups can form a compelling influence on perceptions, thought and policies. This may occur directly, as various interest groups are incorporated in government, or indirectly, via lobbying, threats and so on. Such influences affect the policy and thinking of both Northern and Southern governments.

Fourth, there is rarely a unique and universally held view of development which feeds into policy, as implied by the view above. It is usually possible to detect a dominant strand of thought, but given the multitude of views, and uneven pace at which one view gives way to another, the dominant view at any particular time may often be a matter of controversy. Views often vary quite radically according to the perspective of the observer, between Northern and Southern thinkers and policy-makers, for example. Differences among countries, in political economy, stage of development and so on influence the pace and nature of paradigmatic changes in particular countries. The views espoused by the official donor community, however, typically led by the World Bank, are particularly influential in development thinking because the World Bank and other aid donors devote considerable resources to disseminating their message, and because they frequently use conditionality to enforce it. In the discussion below, we make the process of changing views more clear-cut than it was for the sake of clarity of exposition.

In the next section, we trace how this evolutionary process played out in the second half of the twentieth century.

The evolution of ideas on statism and interventionism from the 1950s to the 1970s

For most developing countries at the beginning of the 1950s, the overriding reality was a situation of underdevelopment, characterized by low incomes, a predominantly agrarian structure with a large subsistence subsector and heavy dependence on the advanced countries for all modern inputs. Before World War II, economic development in most countries of the South had focused on a small primary producing export sector, leaving the rest of the economy, which typically accounted for most of the population, outside the small 'modern' enclave. The production of primary products was owned and controlled by settlers, foreigners or colonialists. In many countries, the education and health levels of the majority of the population were very poor. Latin American performance was typically better than that of Africa or Asia, but the majority of countries had a life expectancy of below 50 years and quite a few below 40 years, while illiteracy rates of over 50 per cent were common. This was the reality confronting policy-makers in the early 1950s. To combat this situation, developing countries thinkers and policy-makers emphasized economic growth as their overriding economic objective, with industrialization seen as the most effective way of achieving higher incomes in the light of the experience of the more developed countries.

Developed countries, too, recognized the need for a new approach to the former colonial territories. Indeed, already in 1937, the governor of Nigeria announced that: 'The exploitation theory is dead ... and the development theory has come to take its place' (quoted in Cowen and Shenton 1995, p. 7). In a famous statement President Truman declared that:

> We must embark on a bold new program for making the benefits of our scientific advances and industrial progress available for the improvement and growth of underdeveloped areas. The old imperialism is dead – exploitation for foreign profit has no place in our plans. What we must envisage is a program of development based on the concepts of democratic fair dealing. (Inaugural address, 20 January 1949)

In the developed countries a quite strongly interventionist economic philosophy then prevailed. This was the result of the successful planning involving heavy state intervention in the economy in World War II, and the Keynesian revolution in economic thought, itself partly a reaction to the heavy unemployment that had accompanied the mainly *laisser-faire* policies of the 1930s. In some countries, a number of basic industries were taken into public ownership, for example, in the UK and France. This was also the era of apparently thriving socialism in the Russian empire. The statist interventionist philosophy resonated with the objectives, politics and philosophy of Latin American governments, which had already started to initiate active industrial policies in reaction to the fall in commodity prices in the 1930s. Newly independent countries elsewhere in the world adopted a similar policy stance in an attempt to overcome their state of underdevelopment and dependence.

The growth objective was overriding: it was assumed that if growth were achieved then other objectives would also be met, including employment expansion and poverty reduction, through what came to be known as a 'trickle-down' process. Economists' advice on how to achieve the growth objective had three main prongs:

- that industrialization was an essential element in the process of catching up developed countries;
- that surplus labour in agriculture provided a major potential resource;
- and that government intervention of various kinds was needed to tap this potential and promote industrialization, including support for investment and protection against industrial imports.

Economists from both North and South accepted this pro-government, pro-intervention and pro-industrialization stance, as well as the associated import controls. Prebisch, Mahalanobis and Lewis were the intellectual giants behind the strategy from the South. For the North, Nurkse, Rostow, Rodenstein-Rodan and Myrdal were prominent.

Not all economists placed equal emphasis on each of these elements. For example, Nurkse focused on the potential of unused labour in agriculture; Prebisch and Singer were strong proponents of the need for industrialization to counter the deteriorating terms of trade for primary products; Rosenstein-Rodan, considering development in Eastern Europe, particularly emphasized the need for government intervention to overcome externalities; while Mahalanobis stressed the need to develop capital goods production capacity to permit accelerated investment. The Lewis model incorporated the two key ideas mentioned above – the latent potential of surplus labour in agriculture and the key role of industrialization in development.

Interest groups in both North and South were united in supporting these policies. In the South, the elites saw opportunities for profits and power in developing industry and workers stood to gain from industrial expansion, while the poor in agricultural sector – most likely to lose from the policies – were generally not organized for political or economic lobbying. In the North, support for development offered both economic and political benefits – markets for their products, a role for their companies and a weapon in the cold war.

Policies in the 1950s and 1960s

The desirability of development planning was widely accepted by developed country observers as well as developing country theoreticians and practitioners.[3] On the ground, Mahalanobis in India, Prebisch in Latin America and visiting economists in many African economies, such as Seers and Lewis, introduced Development Plans (see for example, Killick 1976). The state was given a major role in determining economic priorities via price and import controls, investment planning and sometimes as a producer. Policies promoted savings and investment, through state investment, especially in the underdeveloped infrastructure, and the encouragement of foreign investment through a variety of tax incentives. Import-substitution industrialization (ISI) was adopted based on high tariffs and quantitative import restrictions. Although the focus was on economic growth based on industrialization, policies were also introduced to accelerate the development of the social sectors.

Consequences

The policies adopted were in some ways remarkably successful. Savings and investment rates rose dramatically from the mid 1950s and growth accelerated in most countries, while some, notably in East Asia, experienced spectacular growth rates. Social indicators, such as infant mortality and literacy rates, also improved (Figures 3.1 and 3.2 later). But other developments were less welcome. Population growth accelerated and growth in employment, especially in the industrial sector, lagged behind output. Un- and underemployment emerged as a serious problem. This was partly a consequence of the very success of the policies in expanding output and employment in the industrial sector. The growth of employment opportunities plus a rise in real wages in this sector (partly owing to the widespread introduction of minimum wages) increased workers' desire for formal sector employment, especially among those who had completed secondary education, but also among many primary school leavers. The Harris–Todaro migration model formalized the relationship between growth of the formal sector, with relatively high real wages in the sector, and growing urban unemployment. As opportunities and real wages in the modern sector expanded, rural–urban migration increased, as did open urban unemployment. Moreover, the incidence of poverty remained very high as a proportion of the population in most developing countries, while the absolute numbers of people falling below a given poverty line increased.

A dualistic pattern of development resulted, with a small, relatively privileged modern sector leaving the rest of the economy with low incomes and investment. The ILO summarized the position: '[I]t has become increasingly evident, particularly from the experience of the developing countries, that rapid growth at the national level does not automatically reduce poverty or inequality or provide sufficient productive employment' (ILO 1976:15). Put briefly, trickle-down from economic growth had been insufficient. Moreover, the economic independence sought was elusive, as dependence on developed countries for capital and technology increased.

Thinking in the late 1960s and 1970s

These consequences led to new thinking about development. Three distinct strands may be detected, each a reaction to different aspects of the development experience over the previous 20 years. First, there were those who became concerned with the lack of economic independence achieved. This gave rise to the dependency school of thought, some Marxist and some structuralist, by writers mostly from the South, such as Furtado, Sunkel, Amin and Frank (the last an American but working in Latin America). They focused on the problems arising from the heavy dependence on developed countries in peripheral economies – for markets, technology, finance and managers – and mostly advocated reduced links between rich and poor countries, although there were important differences within the dependency school (see reviews by Palma 1978; Oman and Wigneraja 1991:ch. 5). Some believed that the North–South relationship could be controlled by active policies; some that this was impossible because of the political consequences of dependency (for example, Leys 1975); while some thought that the North–South connection was ultimately progressive and would lead eventually to the emergence of a proletariat and revolution (Warren 1980). The dependency school was dominated by scholars from the South, and its views were in no way shared by the donor community.

A second reaction to the events of the 1950s and 1960s, initiated in the 1970s and becoming dominant in the 1980s, reflected the rising monetarist and neo-classical influence in the North. 'Lessons' were derived from the rapid and fairly egalitarian growth experienced in East Asia in contrast to the capital-intensive and elite-dominated pattern of growth observed in many other countries. It was argued that in the latter countries, the incentive system had been distorted by government interventions, while the role of the government in the economy was too large and that of the market too small (see for example, Little *et al.* 1970; Balassa 1971; Krueger 1974).[4] This criticism of the statist model came almost entirely from western-trained economists, sponsored by major western institutions – for example, OECD, the World Bank and the US government.

A third reaction was to the rising poverty and unemployment that had become evident in the 1960s. It was argued that countries had been pursuing the wrong objective: Seers pointed to the need to 'dethrone GNP' (see ILO (1970)). Candidates for replacing GNP as the main economic objective were successively employment, redistribution with growth and the fulfilment of basic needs (BN). This reaction came primarily from the developed countries and international institutions, eventually penetrating the World Bank. It was viewed less favourably by developing country governments.

The idea of taking employment as the major objective of development was initiated by Seers, who led an ILO employment mission to Colombia that made full employment its central objective and did not even include GNP projections in the main body of the Report.[5] However, analysis of the employment objective soon revealed that employment was generally not wanted in itself (indeed traditionally economics has regarded employment as involving *disutility* not *utility*), but rather for various benefits it conferred, especially generation of incomes for the poor, while some types of employment were not adequate in this respect because the associated incomes were at or below subsistence. Consequently, the second major ILO employment mission (to Kenya, led by Singer and Jolly) concentrated on productive employment, focusing on raising productivity and incomes of those already working (often in the informal sector) as much as providing new employment for the unemployed. The Report (ILO 1992) advocated 'redistribution from growth'. This theme was taken up and developed by Chenery and others as *Redistribution with Growth* (Chenery *et al.* 1974). The proposed strategy involved siphoning off the fruits of growth in the form of investment resources for the poor, thereby permitting continued growth while gradually increasing the incomes of the poor through income from additional assets.

The process of deconstructing objectives continued; incomes too, it was argued, were not wanted for themselves but for the way of life they made possible. The poor had basic needs that should be met; income was a means rather than an end, and often not a very efficient means since some of the basic needs were for goods or services that were best provided by the public sector. Hence a 'basic-needs' approach to development emerged, first in the ILO, then taken up by the World Bank (see ILO 1976; Streeten *et al.* 1981).

Each of these approaches was a reaction to the consequences of the previous development strategy: the dependency approach to the evident failure of developing countries to become economically independent or to achieve favourable terms of trade, market and technology access, despite industrialization and economic growth; the anti-planning reaction, to the perceived inefficiencies of the growth strategy; and the nexus of employment/redistribution/basic-needs approaches to the failure of the growth strategy to deliver in terms of human needs and distribution. These three approaches differed, however, in the interest groups which they served. *Dependencia* reflected the interests of the South, generally challenging those of the North, which benefited from the poor terms received by the South. The market-oriented strategy offered potential benefits to the private sector generally, especially in the North, but at the same time it challenged some existing private sector interests, especially in the South, such as those firms making profits through the protection offered as a result of the import-substituting policies. The basic-needs approach did not, on the whole, represent powerful interests in either North or South – being mainly intended to benefit the poor in developing countries who mostly lacked political power. Indeed elites in the South saw it as a way of perpetuating underdevelopment, by diverting the focus away from industrialization and from developing country demands for improved international terms with respect to trade and technology. However, the approach did gain support among the aid community (temporarily) and some progressive Southern governments.

Policies in the 1970s

In terms of changing policies over the 1970s, the *dependencia* approach was most effective, though its effects were short-lived. The neo-liberal philosophy only began to have major effect in the 1980s, as the ISI policies continued to work quite well in the 1970s, sustained by overseas borrowing, while strong interests supported their continuance. Most developing countries continued their previous inward-looking macroeconomic and interventionist policies over this period. The basic-needs approach had a strong, but short-lived, influence on donor philosophy, with limited impact on developing country policy, perhaps in part because of its short life in the donor community.

The underlying belief of the dependency school was of gross unfairness in the world's economy, with a bias against the South: this formed the background to OPEC and its successful efforts to raise oil prices, as well as to the New International Economic Order (NIEO) put forward by the G77 in 1974, which contained a number of demands for improved terms, extending to market access, terms of trade, terms of technology transfer and aid. Other policy manifestations of the dependency approach were developing-country restrictions on direct foreign investment and controls over technology transfer, adopted most comprehensively by the Andean Pact countries and India. A number of countries attempted to reduce pharmaceutical prices by introducing a generic drugs policy.

Neither the employment objective nor redistribution with growth significantly affected policy, the latter perhaps because of a basic political flaw in its reasoning: that once elites have secured large benefits from growth they were unlikely to allow these benefits to be taken away and redistributed to the less well off as required by the strategy. The BN approach was widely adopted by the international community, first the ILO, then by the World Bank under MacNamara as well as by major bilateral aid agencies and some of the special agencies of the United Nations which adopted a series of BN-style targets, such as universal primary healthcare and universal primary education. But in general, developing country governments were more impressed by the conclusions of the dependency school, regarding the BN-approach as an excuse by the advanced countries to avoid the demands of the New International Economic Order. Nonetheless, although few developing countries accepted the approach fully, evidence shows that there was some acceleration in improvements in human indicators over this decade (see Figures 3.1 and 3.2). Aid was also redirected towards agriculture and the social sectors, and away from support to industry.

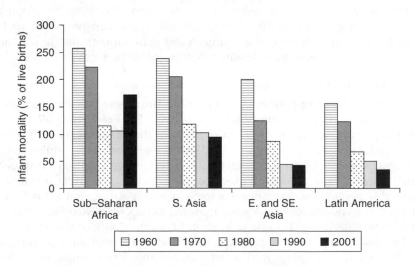

Figure 3.1 Infant mortality rates, 1960–2001

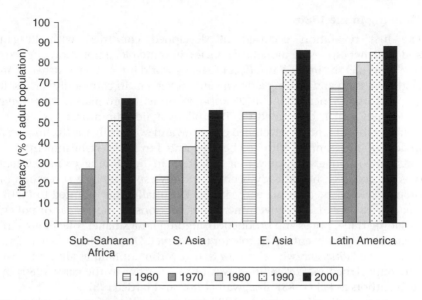

Figure 3.2   Adult literacy rates, 1960–2000

Consequences

In the sellers' market created by high world demand, the belligerent attitude of the oil producers, partly inspired by the dependency school, led to the oil price rise of 1972–3, creating large imbalances in the world economy and inflationary pressures in developed countries. Most oil-importing developing countries borrowed to finance the consequent trade deficits, resulting in a massive accumulation of debt as well as rising budgetary and trade imbalances, made worse by a further increase in oil prices in 1978–9. In developed countries, inflation rates accelerated. These changes were influential in generating a major turnaround in thinking in both developed and developing countries in the early 1980s.

Liberalization and globalization

The neo-liberal reaction to statist interventionism started in the early 1970s. But it had little effect until the 1980s when it received a powerful boost both from the monetary policies adopted in the UK and US and from the debt crisis which enabled the international financial institutions to impose pro-market and *laissez-faire* policies on borrowing countries. This era saw a sharp reversal from the short-lived focus on human objectives represented by the BN approach.

Thinking in the 1980s

The first revolution occurred in developed countries, with Reagan and Thatcher espousing monetary policies, in principle, if not always in practice.[6] This had the immediate effect of raising world interest rates, ushering in world recession and causing a downward movement in commodity prices. It also imparted a new monetarist, anti-government, pro-market *laisser-faire* philosophy which permeated the IFIs, bilateral aid administrations, educational establishments in developed countries and eventually the 'technocrats' in developing countries who had been educated in these establishments.

As noted above, the view that the state in developing countries had overreached itself had already been powerfully espoused by a succession of pro-market observers in the early 1970s. Essentially, they pointed to inefficiencies associated with government interventions in most areas of policy, including trade, prices and production, arguing for a smaller role for governments and a greatly enhanced role for the market. Discrediting of what came to be termed *dirigisme*, with the view that government failures almost invariably outweighed market failures, was carried further in the early 1980s by such authors as Lal (1983), Bhagwati (1982) and Little (1982).

The 'new political economy' (NPE) took the virtues of an all-embracing market for granted and focused on explaining why governments were almost universally prone to 'failure', including failing to 'liberalize' (that is, extend the realm of the market) despite the recommendations of neo-classical economists. Krueger's rent-seeking hypothesis providing a starting-point, while Bates, a political scientist, pointed to the underlying political economy of African states. Because these states tended to be captured by urban elites, he argued, governments chose sub-optimal policies (Bates 1981).[7] The basic neo-classical assumption of maximizing behaviour by all individual agents was subsequently applied to political and bureaucratic behaviour by economists such as Lal (1984), Conybeare (1982), Bhagwati (1982) and Srinivasan (1991), drawing on the work of Buchanan and Tullock.[8] This replaced 'the image of the benign state with its mirror opposite, the negative state' (Grindle 1991: 43). The maximizing actions of self-seeking individuals (bureaucrats and politicians), or groups of individuals, it was argued, led to individual rent-seeking, group short-termism and state predations, arguing for a minimalist state which would do least damage to social welfare.

Northern governments had been quite frightened by events of the 1970s – in particular by the success of OPEC, by the subsequent inflationary pressures and by the power of their own workers stemming from sustained full employment. They had no intention of giving way to the demands of the NIEO, which might adversely affect real standards of living in the North, especially in the short run.[9] The neo-classical/monetarist revolution in the North can be seen as an attempt by the old establishment there to regain control both within their own countries and internationally. They were supported by multinational companies aiming to reverse the rising restrictions on their activities. A stream of scholarships to Southerners to study economics in the North had trained a powerful cohort who would support the neo-classical philosophy, while the debt crisis provided the occasion to enforce it.

Policies

By 1980, the anti-state, pro-market philosophy had been adopted by the World Bank, whose power over policy-making in developing countries greatly increased with the onset of an acute debt crisis and the initiation of structural adjustment loans. While the World Bank emphasized deregulation, reduced price controls, subsidies, tariffs and the elimination of restrictions against direct foreign investment, the IMF promoted the monetarist view – that the prime objective of macro-economic policy should be to eliminate budgetary and trade imbalances through tight control over the budget and money supply, conveniently labelled by Williamson (1990) as 'the Washington consensus'. Considerations of poverty reduction or basic needs virtually disappeared from these institutions. The IFIs' growing control over policy-making in developing countries was one reason why monetarism and deregulation were adopted, in part at least, in the majority of developing countries over the course of the 1980s.[10] There was a massive switch in policies with some countries adopting the Washington consensus policies on their own, indicating that NPE theorists had been excessively determinist about policy-making.

Consequences

For the regions most subject to Washington tutelage – Africa and Latin America – the stabilization and adjustment policies were accompanied by falling GDP per capita for much of the 1980s, in many cases worsening income distribution, falling real expenditure per head on the social services, and a quite sharp rise in both private and social poverty. In many African countries, there was evidence of rising malnutrition. In a number of Latin America and African countries, educational enrolments and achievements fell off. Investment rates fell. Despite the strong efforts, the imbalances were often not eliminated, as falling commodity prices and continued accumulation of debt made the situation more difficult. It does not appear that economic performance was systematically worse in 'adjusting' than 'non-adjusting' countries – and may have been marginally better. There is more evidence that performance on human indicators was worse among adjusting countries, but again the differences were not large, and some observers came to the opposite conclusions (for Africa at least); in each case, the conclusions depended heavily on what was assumed about the 'counterfactual'.[11] Yet perceptions of policy consequences are generally affected by what is *actually* happening, rather than a comparison with some counterfactual, or what might have happened in the absence of the programmes. The actual large and widespread rise in absolute poverty in Latin America and Africa led many to question the apparent elimination of human concerns from the development agenda.[12]

New thinking in response to the adjustment era

The stabilization and adjustment policies of the 1980s were criticized both for their failures with respect to poverty and also for the simplistic economic model that underlay them. Concern with the rising poverty associated with the stabilization and adjustment policies was initiated in the mid 1980s by UNICEF and rapidly gained support under the rubric of *Adjustment with a Human Face* (Cornia *et al.* 1987). From 1987, World Bank staff guidelines required World Bank Policy Framework Papers for low income countries to include 'a brief description and assessment ... of the social impact of the government's intended adjustment program'. From 1990 poverty reduction became a central objective of the World Bank, starting with the poverty-focused *World Development Report*. World Bank President Lewis Preston declared that 'poverty is the benchmark against which we must be judged'. There were similar changes at the IMF. In 1990 Camdessus, managing director of the fund, acknowledged that

> macroeconomic policies can have strong effects on the distribution of income and on social equity and welfare. A responsible adjustment program must take these effects into account, particularly as they impinge on the most vulnerable or disadvantaged groups in society. (Speech to the US Chamber of Commerce, 26 March)

Each IMF country Mission was required to report on the poverty implications of country programmes. Williamson himself revised the proposed content of the 'Washington consensus' to include poverty reduction and investment in human resources (Williamson 1997).

The UNDP presented a more fundamental challenge to neo-liberal philosophy, questioning the basic objective of maximizing monetary income which economists generally accept as a proxy for utility and which underlies the model. The *Human Development Report*, first published in 1990, instead focused on the lives people may lead as the fundamental objective of development, not the resources they have. 'The basic objective of development is to create an enabling environment for people to live long, healthy and creative lives' (UNDP 1990:9). The quality of human lives, both as the central objective of development and as a critical development resource, became a central theme of development thinking.

Intellectually, the human development approach has its antecedents in the poverty and basic needs concerns of the 1970s, with many of the same people involved. In the 1970s, Jolly, Singer and Stewart participated in the ILO's Kenya mission; while ul Haq, Streeten, Ranis and Stewart participated in the World Bank basic-needs work. All were involved, in one way or another, with the new focus on poverty and human development. Meetings of the North–South Roundtable, organized by Mahbub ul Haq, Khadija Haq and Uner Kirdar, kept this group of people together and working on these issues throughout the 1980s, leading in 1986 to one of the first books explicitly using the term human development (Haq and Kirdar 1986).

However, the human-oriented approach represented by the ILO missions, the basic-needs approach and 'adjustment with a human face' was greatly enriched by A. K. Sen's work on capabilities, which challenged the theoretical foundations of the utilitarian approach to human well-being (Sen 1985, 1993). The capability approach constitutes an alternative way of conceptualizing individual behaviour, assessing well-being and identifying policy objectives, based on the rejection of utilitarianism as the measure of welfare and of utility maximization as a behavioural assumption (Sen 1977). It is rooted in a critique of the ethical foundations of utilitarianism. Sen argues that the only defensible basis for a utilitarian approach is to ground it in a concept of utility interpreted as 'desire fulfilment'. This implies that an individual's mental disposition dominates social evaluation while such aspects as their physical condition which greatly influence their quality of life may be neglected. Someone can be 'satisfied' with what is a very deprived state (for example, ill-health, termed 'physical condition neglect' by Sen), while their desires are constrained by what seems possible (described as 'valuation neglect'). Furthermore choices are influenced by the social context not only in terms of its influence on expectations but also through strategic interactions, making observed behaviour in the market of dubious value for social valuation.

In the capability approach, well-being is seen as the freedom of an individual to live a life that is valued (termed the capability of the individual), that is the realization of human potential. In the context of poverty, the focus is on the failure of some basic capability to function, where basic capabilities are 'intended to separate out the ability to satisfy certain elementary and crucially important functionings' (Sen 1992:45). Basic capabilities are very similar to basic needs, especially since they are typically assessed by actual outcomes or functionings, not by potentials or capabilities. This emphasis on the 'outcomes' characterizing the quality of life of an individual implies a shift away from monetary indicators (which at best can represent indirect measures of those outcomes) and a focus on non-monetary indicators for evaluating well-being or deprivation. Monetary resources are considered only as a means to enhancing well-being, rather than the actual outcome of interest. Moreover, they may not be a reliable indicator of capability outcomes because of differences an individual faces in transforming those resources into valuable achievements (functionings), differences which depend on different individual characteristics (for example, differences between individuals in terms of metabolic rates or differences between able-bodied and handicapped individuals) or differences in the contexts individuals live in (for example, differences between living in areas where basic public services are provided and areas where those services are absent). If the emphasis is on final outcomes, well-being (and poverty) assessments should take into account the fact that some people need more resources than others to obtain the same functioning achievements.

Probably the most important contribution of the human development approach, represented by successive human development reports, has been to draw attention away from monetary income and GNP per capita as the exclusive way of assessing outcomes. The Human Development Index (HDI), even though it is agreed by all including its initiators to be a very imperfect measure of human development, has come nearest to achieving Seers's objective of 'dethroning' GNP. Of course, this does not mean that monetary incomes and GNP can be neglected – economic resources provide a fundamental means to achieve human development, while human development in turn feeds into higher growth. But it does mean that well-being assessments should give priority to what happens to human lives, rather than what happens to the economy, and this has important implications for policy choice and sequencing.

The new focus on poverty (by the World Bank and bilateral donors) largely retained a money metric as its measure of poverty, and continued to rely on the neo-classical economic model, and conventional stabilization and adjustment policies for macro-policy prescriptions. UNDP's human development approach represented a more radical departure from the neo-liberal model, since it redefined objectives, abandoning the money metric. The approach has not taken a specific view on the appropriate economic model or macro-policy package, although the Human Development Reports and other writings on human development show an eclecticism, with frequent departures from the model and the macro prescriptions, often picking up concurrent theoretical criticisms of the model which are briefly reviewed below.

Over this period, there were a large number of criticisms of the validity of the neo-classical model – both from an empirical and a theoretical perspective. One criticism of the model was its failure to capture essential elements of the successful East Asian cases.[13] In both Taiwan and Korea, the governments were shown to have played a much more active role than allowed for in the market model, while high savings and investment – public as well as private – and high levels of human resources were also demonstrated to have been an essential feature. Moreover, the relatively weak economic performance of many of the 'adjusting' countries also led to doubts about its validity. The initial premise and promise of the neo-classical critique were that growth and equity would improve in a liberalized economy (for example, Little et al. 1970). Yet macro performance in the liberalized economies mostly did not live up to this promise. There was a fall in investment rates and per capita output in 'adjusting' regions during the 1980s. Despite some

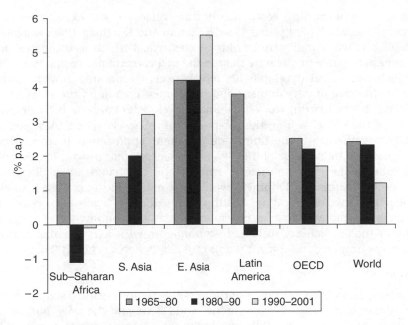

Figure 3.3   Growth in GDP per capita, 1965–2001 (% p.a)

recovery subsequently, economic growth in Africa and Latin America was sluggish in the following decade and did not again reach the rates of the 1960s and 1970s (see Figure 3.3). Only China and India – which each retained extensive government intervention in the economy – showed accelerated growth, but in each case accompanied by worsening income distribution. Destabilizing fluctuations in private capital flows in the 1990s, following the liberalization of capital markets – notably in Mexico and East Asia – also led to widespread questioning of this aspect of the model, and advocacy of capital controls and/or a tax on international capital transactions (Haq *et al.* 1996; FitzGerald 1998; Caprio *et al.* 2001).

Critiques of the underlying theoretical structure of the neo-liberal model were also advanced. The view of economic agents as exclusively and unavoidably short-term maximizers was questioned: long-term self-interest, altruism, a sense of identity and community were also shown to influence behaviour.[14] Moreover, cooperative behaviour has been shown to be an important element in the efficient operations of an exchange economy, which is costly to replace. Large firms in the private sector themselves emphasized the need for cooperative behaviour for efficient performance.[15] The model's assumptions about information, as well as individual motivation, were shown to be deficient (see Stiglitz and Weiss 1981; Stiglitz 1994); while new developments in growth and trade theories emphasized the importance of learning, economies of scale, oligopoly and externalities (for example, Lucas 1988; Roemer 1986; Helpman and Krugman 1986; Krugman 1986). The major policy thrust of these theoretical criticisms is the need for a more active role by the state than in the neo-classical prescriptions.

Such theoretical developments mostly accept economic growth as the basic objective of development and use money income as the measure of welfare, here departing from the human development approach. Their criticism of the model is from the perspective of *efficiency*. Where they tend to come together with the human-development approach is in the strong emphasis on human capabilities as a *source* of economic growth. This is most clear in the 'new growth theories' where technical change broadly depends on human capacities. Empirical evidence at macro and micro levels shows the importance of education, health and nutrition as *inputs* into economic growth.[16] Moreover, analysis of sequencing, at an economy-wide level, has shown that to achieve sustained economic growth, it is essential *first* to promote human development (Ranis *et al.* 2000; Boozer *et al.* 2003).

Policies

Some aspects of these critiques of the neo-liberal model gained support from the donor community (including the World Bank and the IMF), but others did not. At the macro level, the need to restore investment rates was quickly recognized. The Brady Plan, involving a series of debt write-offs and rescheduling in Latin America, was an important consequence. In sub-Saharan Africa, the highly indebted poor countries (HIPC) initiative made a small contribution to writing off multilateral debt. In addition, serious questioning of early capital market liberalization following the East Asian financial crisis of 1997 led to a revised timetable for this aspect of the liberalizing agenda. However, all other elements of the macro-policy prescriptions appear to have remained unchanged, including budgetary and monetary restraints, import liberalization, privatization (increasingly being extended to the social sectors) and, more generally, reductions in the role of the state in the economy.

As far as human development is concerned, donors and developing countries have accepted the need to advance human-resource investments, and these have formed an increasing proportion of much donor and developing country expenditure. The poverty agenda has also been strongly promoted by the World Bank and prominent bilateral donors (notably DFID). This led to considerable resources being devoted to poverty reduction strategy papers (PRSPs) – required for a good deal of World Bank and IMF lending to poor countries. For middle-income countries, the Comprehensive Development Framework – also emphasizing participatory mechanisms for reducing poverty – has played a similar role. Social funds, microfinance and social sector investments have been the main mechanisms advocated for reducing poverty.

While these processes and programmes increase support for human development to a greater extent than the unadulterated neo-liberal package of the 1980s, major progress on human development is limited by several constraints. First, neither PRSPs nor the CDF change the macro-policy package fundamentally.[17] Because this package remains basically unaltered, continued restrictions on government expenditure limit the total available for the social sectors. Further, income or asset redistribution form no part of the macro-policy package, while continued globalization and liberalization tends to make income distribution *more unequal* over time (see for example Morley 1995; Berry and Stewart 1999). At the same time exogenous or near-exogenous developments – notably HIV/AIDs, natural disasters and civil war – are having serious deleterious impacts on human development.

The donor community is thus giving mixed messages on human development and poverty. On the one hand, the general idea that human development should be promoted and poverty reduced has gained widespread support and a large number of programmes that promote human development have received support at a micro-level. But on the other hand, the pressures for more liberalization in the economy and for orthodox macroadjustment have continued unabated; these are not supportive of human development and can indeed threaten progress. Ironically, competitive pressures by the global economy have the same effect: there is downward pressure on taxation and expenditure so that economies remain competitive in the short term, yet in the longer run promoting human capacities through investment in education and health are essential for sustaining growth.

Developing countries themselves are, of course, filtering these contradictory messages though their own political systems. All are being pushed in a similar liberalizing direction, but the pace of change varies, and some countries with strong traditions of supporting human investments succeed better than others in continuing to promote human development. In Latin America, Chile, Costa Rica and Mexico are outstanding examples (Ranis and Stewart 2002).

The problem arises in part from a fundamental failure of the human development approach to make inroads into the basic neo-classical economic model in two respects. First, while human resources are regarded as important inputs in the revised model, they are still treated, like all other factors in the model, as *substitutable*, that is, inroads into human resource investments, the model implies, can be compensated for by other resources, such as extra foreign investment. Yet the evidence suggests this is not so, and without the human development, neither the foreign investment nor the long-term growth will ensue. Second, there is a failure to recognize the key sequencing issue which follows in part from the first point: that human development must come first for sustained growth, while conventional policy advice is to get the economy right first and then invest in human development. In practice this sequencing does not work and neither human development nor economic growth will be assured over the long run. Both these flaws would almost certainly be corrected if human development was recognized as the overriding objective and economic growth as the means: this, of course, is the fundamental premises of the human development approach.

Conclusion

This chapter has illustrated how doctrine and policies evolve as a product of a cycle in which events lead to new thinking and new policies the consequences of which, in turn, often reveal new problems, thereby giving rise to further developments in thinking and policies. But it must be emphasized that the developments over this period have underlined how both thinking and policies are heavily influenced by powerful interest groups, themselves shaped by the consequences of policy.

Over the 50-year period, the international financial institutions acquired a huge amount of influence, pushing policy in the direction they favoured in country after country. Some governments resisted or tried to shape the policies to their own agendas, but all moved in a similar direction. Ironically, in the import-substitution era, governments were relatively free to pick their own policy mix. Yet it was this era which gave rise to the dependency movement, which pointed to excessive dependence of Southern countries on the North. Subsequent developments led to much greater dependence at least in terms of policy formulation, with rather little changes in terms of technology and capital dependence. Nonetheless the dependency movement lost much of its influence, partly because autarchy did not appear to be a viable option in a globalizing world. Not only did the potential loss in access to world capital and markets seem too great a price to pay, but also many decision-makers in the South became converted to the neo-liberal doctrines.

The chapter has traced how an emphasis on human objectives evolved as a result of the too limited success in this arena, first of ISI policies and then of neo-liberal ones. This culminated in the UNDP's advocacy of human development. Nonetheless, the human development approach has been taken up only half-heartedly, both by the IFIs and by many developing country governments. Yet evidence suggests that giving priority to human development is essential for sustained success in both human development and economic growth. Pragmatic as well as moral reasons therefore legitimate the approach. Pragmatic reasons are likely to become even more compelling as globalization increases and competitive success at reasonable terms of trade can be achieved only through a productive, well-nourished and educated workforce.

Notes

1. For example, George W. Bush has stated: 'The case for trade is not just monetary, but moral' (Speech, 19 November 1999).

2. Ideology, of course, influences how prior experience is interpreted.
3. For example, although the policy prescriptions advocated by Fei and Ranis were not as strongly interventionist as many of the writings of the time, they accepted that: 'The need for development planning is well recognized' (Fei and Ranis 1964:199).
4. Deeper analysis of the East Asian experience suggested this was an incorrect interpretation, and that they too had intervened heavily in the economy, but in a more efficient way (see for example Amsden 1989; Wade 1990).
5. Though ironically an appendix showed that achievement of the full employment objective involved a substantial acceleration in growth of GNP (ILO 1970). In fact, there is generally not an inconsistency between employment and output growth (Stewart and Streeten 1971).
6. Thatcher did succeed in slowing down the growth in the money supply and securing a budgetary balance. Reagan pursued monetary policies to the point of generating high interest rates. But budgetary and trade imbalances exploded in a most Keynesian way.
7. Lipton (1977) had come to very similar conclusions.
8. The underlying assumption was that 'agents behave rationally; that is, they have a consistent set of preferences over the outcome of their actions, and they choose an action whose outcome is preferable given the constraints within which they act' (Srinivasan 1991:126).
9. Though in the long run, it was argued that a transfer to the South would be a positive sum game, benefiting the North as well as the South (see the 'Brandt Report': *The Independent Commission on International Development Issues*, 1980).
10. See for example, Williamson (ed.) (1990), World Bank and UNDP (1989) and Dean *et al.* (1994) for evidence of the advance of these policies in Latin America and Africa.
11. See Kakwani *et al.* (1995), who find that countries with adjustment programmes made less progress on some social indicators than countries without such programmes; but see also Sahn *et al.* (1977), who argue for Africa that adjustment programmes tend to benefit the poor. For criticisms of the latters' model, see De Maio *et al.* (1999).
12. There have been numerous studies of the macro effects of stabilization and adjustment policies, both by the IFIs themselves and by academics. The assessments of the IMF tend to suggest somewhat negative effects on growth, while those of World Bank slight positive effects compared with an estimated 'counterfactual'. Effects on investment were negative. See, for example, Khan and Knight (1985), Khan (1990), Killick *et al.* (1991), World Bank (1990) and Mosley *et al.* (1991). Most studies have been unable to find significant positive effects in Africa.
13. For example, by Wade (1990), Amsden (1989), Lall (1994) and Pack and Westphal (1986).
14. For an overview, see Alkire and Deneulin (2002). Recent developments in behavioural economics endorse the view that most people are not short-term maximizers.
15. Some empirical evidence suggests that 'participation, communication, creativity and decentralization' within the firm is positively correlated with growth in sales and profits (Denison 1993:266). See also Kay (1998).
16. See summary in Ranis *et al.* (2000).
17. For example, the Honduran NGO network, *Interforos*, was told by government officials that 'the Fund's position with regard to macro-economic policies was not negotiable' (Knoke and Morazan 2002). See review of PRSPs in Stewart and Wang (2003).

References

Alkire, S. and S. Deneulin., 'Individual Motivation, Its Nature, Determinants and Consequences for within Group Behavior', in Judith Heyer, Frances Stewart and Rosemary Thorp (eds), *Group Behaviour and Development: Is the Market Destroying Cooperation?* (Oxford University Press, 2002).

Amin, S., 'Accumulation and Development: A Theoretical Model', *Journal of African Political Economy* 1 (1974) 9–26.

Amsden, A., *Asia's Next Giant: South Korea and Late Industrialisation* (New York: Oxford University Press, 1989).

Balassa, B., *The Structure of Protection in Developing Countries* (Baltimore, MD: Johns Hopkins University Press, 1971).

Bates, R. H., *Markets and States in Tropical Africa: the Political Basis of Agricultural Policies* (Berkeley: University of California Press, 1981).

Berry A. and F. Stewart, 'Globalization, Liberalization, and Inequality: Expectations and Experience', in A. Hurrell and N. Woods (eds), *Inequality, Globalization, and World Politics* (Oxford University Press, 1999).

Bhagwati, J. N., 'Directly Unproductive, Profit-Seeking Activities', *Journal of Political Economy* 190/5 (1982) 988–1002.

Boozer, M., G. Ranis, F. Stewart and T. Suri, 'Paths to Success: The Relationship between Human Development and Economic Growth' (New Haven, CT: Yale Center for International and Area Studies, 2003).

Buchanan, J. M. and G. Tullock, *The Calculus of Consent: Logical Foundations of Constitutional Democracy* (Ann Arbor: University of Michigan Press, 1962).

Caprio, G., P. Honohan and J. E. Stiglitz, *Financial Liberalization: How Far, How Fast?* (Cambridge University Press, 2001).

Chenery, H. *et al.*, *Redistribution with Growth* (Oxford University Press, 1974).

Conybeare, J., 'The Rent-seeking State and Revenue Diversification', *World Politics* 35/1 (1982) 25–42.

Cornia, G. A., R. Jolly and F. Stewart, *Adjustment with a Human Face* (Oxford University Press, 1987).

Cowen, M. P. and R. W. Shenton, *Doctrines of Development* (London: Routledge, 1995).

Dean, J., S. Desai and J. Riedel, 'Trade Policy Reform in Developing Countries Since 1985: A review of the Evidence', World Bank Discussion Paper no. 267 (Washington, DC, 1994).

Denison, D., 'Organisational Culture and Human Capital', in Etzioni, A. and P. Lawrence (eds), *Socio-Economics: Towards a New Synthesis* (Armonk, NY: Sharpe, 1993).

De Maio, L., F. Stewart and R. van der Hoeven, 'Computable General Equilibrium Models, Adjustment and the Poor in Africa', *World Development* 27/3 (1999) 453–70.

Fei, J. and G. Ranis, *Development of the Labor Surplus Economy* (New York: Richard Irwin, 1964).

FitzGerald, E. V. K., *Global Capital Market Volatility and the Developing Countries: Lessons from the East Asian Crisis*, Development Studies Working Paper no. 124 (Torino: Centro Studi Luca d'Agliano, 1998).

Frank, A. G., *Capitalism and Underdevelopment in Latin America: Historical Studies of Chile and Brazil* (New York: Monthly Review Press, 1969).

Furtado, C., *Development and Underdevelopment* (Berkeley: University of California Press, 1967).

Grindle, M. S., 'The New Political Economy: Its Explanatory Power for LDCs', in Meier, G. M. (ed.), *Politics and Policy-Making in Developing Countries* (San Francisco: International Center for Economic Growth, 1991).

Haq, K. and U. Kirdar, *Human Development: The Neglected Dimension* (Islamabad: North South Roundtable, 1986).

Haq, M., I. Kaul and I. Grunberg, *The Tobin Tax: Coping with Financial Volatility* (Oxford University Press, 1996).

Helpman, E. and P. Krugman, *Market Structure and Foreign Trade: Increasing Returns, Imperfect Competition and the International Economy* (Cambridge, MA: MIT Press, 1986).

International Labour Organization (ILO), *Towards Full Employment: A Programme for Colombia* (Geneva, 1970).

ILO, *Employment, Incomes and Equality, A Strategy for Increasing Productive Employment in Kenya* (Geneva, 1972).

ILO, *Employment, Growth and Basic Needs: A One-World Problem* (Geneva, 1976).

Kakwani, N., 'Structural Adjustment and Performance in Living Standards in Developing Countries', *Development and Change* 26/3 (1995) 469–502.

Kay, J., *The Role of Business in Society*, Inaugural Lecture no. 3, Said Business School (University of Oxford, February 1998).

Khan, M., 'The Macro-Economic Effects of Fund-Supported Adjustment Programs', IMF Staff Papers no. 37 (Washington, DC: IMF, 1990).

Khan, M. and M. Knight, 'Fund-Supported Adjustment Programs and Economic Growth', IMF Occasional Paper no. 41 (Washington, DC: IMF, 1985).

Killick, T., 'The Possibilities of Development Planning', *Oxford Economic Papers* 28/2 (1976) 161–84.

Killick, T. *et al.*, 'What Can we Know About the Effects of the IMF Programmes?', ODI Working Paper no. 47 (London: ODI, 1991).

Knoke, I. and P. Morazan, 'PRSP: Beyond the Theory. Practical Experiences and Positions of Involved Civil Society Organizations', draft for discussion for the International GTZ Conference 'Beyond the Review: Sustainable Poverty Alleviation & PRSP', 13–16 May 2002 (Washington, DC: Bread for the World, 2002).

Krueger, A., 'The Political Economy of the Rent-Seeking Society', *American Economic Review* 64/3 (1974) 291–303.

Krugman, Paul R., *Strategic Trade Policy and the New International Economics* (Cambridge, MA: MIT Press, 1986).

Lal, D., *The Poverty of 'Development Economics'* (London: Institute of Economic Affairs, 1983).

Lal, D., 'The Political Economy of the Predatory State', Development Research Dept Discussion Paper no. DRD 105 (Washington, DC: World Bank, 1984).

Lall, S., 'The East Asia Miracle Study: Does the Bell Toll for Industrial Strategy?', *World Development* 22/4 (1994) 645–54.

Lewis, A., 'Economic Development with Unlimited Supplies of Labour', *The Manchester School of Economic and Social Studies* 22/2 (1954) 139–91.

Leys, C., *Underdevelopment in Kenya: The Political Economy of Neo-Colonialism* (London: Heinemann, 1975).

Lipton, M., *Why Poor People Stay Poor: Urban Bias in World Development* (London: Temple Smith, 1977).

Little, I. M. D., *Economic Development: Theory, Policy and International Relations* (New York: Basic, 1982).

Little, I. M. D., M. F. Scott and T. Scitovsky, *Industry and Trade in Some Developing Countries: A Comparative Study* (Oxford University Press, 1970).

Lucas, R. E., 'On the mechanics of economic development', *Journal of Monetary Economics* 22/1 (1988) 3–42.

Mahalanobis, P. C., 'Some Observations on the Process of Growth in National Income', *Sankhya* 12/4 (1953) 307–12.

Morley, S., *Poverty and Inequality in Latin America: The Impact of Adjustment and Recovery in the 1980s* (Baltimore: Johns Hopkins University Press, 1995).

Mosley, P., J. Harrigan and J. Toye, *Aid and Power* (London: Routledge, 1991).

Myrdal, G., *Economic Theory and Underdeveloped Regions* (London: Duckworth, 1957).

Nurkse, R., *Problems of Capital Formation in Developing Countries* (Oxford: Blackwell, 1955).

Oman, C. and G. Wignaraja, *The Postwar Evolution of Development Thinking* (Paris: OECD, 1991).

Pack, H. and L. Westphal, 'Industrial Strategy and Technological Change', *Journal of Development Economics* 22 (1986) 87–128.

Palma, G., 'Dependency: A Formal Theory of Underdevelopment or a Methodology for the Analysis of Concrete Situations of Underdevelopment', *World Development* 6/7–8 (1978) 881–924.

Prebisch, R., *The Economic Development of Latin America and its Principal Problems* (New York: United Nations, 1950).

Ranis, G., and F. Stewart, 'Crecimiento Económico y Desarrollo Humano en América Latina', *Revista de la CEPAL* 78 (2002) 7–24.

Ranis, G., F. Stewart and A. Ramirez, 'Economic Growth and Human Development', *World Development* 28/2 (2000) 197–220.

Roemer, P. M.,'Increasing Returns and Long Run Growth', *Journal of Political Economy* 94/5 (1986) 1002–37.

Rosenstein-Rodan, P., 'Problems of industrialisation of Eastern and South-Eastern Europe', *Economic Journal* 53/210–11 (1943) 202–11.

Rostow, W. W., *The Stages of Economic Growth: A Non-Communist Manifesto* (Cambridge University Press, 1960).

Sahn, D. E., P. A. Dorosh and S. D. Younger, *Structural Adjustment Reconsidered: Economic Policy and Poverty in Africa* (Cambridge University Press, 1997).

Sen, A. K., 'Rational Fools: A critique of the Behavioural Foundations of Economic Theory', *Philosophy and Public Affairs* 6 (1977) 317–44.

Sen, A. K., *Commodities and Capabilities* (Amsterdam: Elsevier, 1985).

Sen, A. K., *Inequality Reexamined* (Cambridge, MA: Harvard University Press, 1992).

Sen, A. K., 'Capability and Well-Being', in Martha C. Nussbaum and Amartya K. Sen (eds), *The Quality of Life* (Oxford: Clarendon Press, 1993) 30–53.

Singer, H. W., 'The Distribution of Gains Between Investing and Borrowing Countries', *American Economic Review* 40/2 (1950) 473–85.

Srinivasan, T. N., 'Foreign Trade Regimes' in Meier, G. M. (ed.), *Politics and Policy-Making in Developing Countries* (San Francisco: International Center for Economic Growth, 1991).

Stern, N., 'The Economics of Development: A Survey', *Economic Journal* 99/397 (1989) 597–685.

Stewart, F. and P. Streeten, 'Conflicts Between Output and Employment Objectives in Developing Countries', *Oxford Economic Papers* 23/2 (1971) 145–68.

Stewart, F. and M. Wang, *Do PRSPs Empower Poor Countries and Disempower the World Bank, or Is It the Other Way Round?* (Oxford: Queen Elizabeth House, 2003).

Stiglitz, J. E, *Whither Socialism? Wicksell Lectures, 1990* (Cambridge, MA: MIT Press, 1994).

Stiglitz, J. E. and A. Weiss, 'Credit Rationing in Markets with Imperfect Information', *American Economic Review* 71/3 (1981) 393–410.

Streeten, P. *et al.*, *First Things First: Meeting Basic Needs in Developing Countries* (New York: Oxford University Press, 1981).

Sunkel, O., 'National Development Policy and External Dependence in Latin America', *Journal of Development Studies* 6/1 (1969) 23–48.

The Independent Commission on International Development Issues, *North-South: A Programme for Survival* (London: Pan, 1980).

UNDP, *The Human Development Report 1990* (New York: Oxford University Press, 1990).

UNDP, *Human Development Report 1999* (New York: Oxford University Press, 1999).

Wade, R., *Governing the Market: Economic Theory and the Role of Government in East Asia Industrialization* (Princeton University Press, 1990).

Warren, B., *Imperialism: Pioneer of Capitalism* (London: New Left Books, 1980).

Williamson, J., 'What Washington Means by Policy Reform', in J. Williamson (ed.), *Latin American Adjustment: How Much Has Happened?* (Washington, DC: Institute for International Economics, 1990).

Williamson, J., 'The Washington Consensus Revisited', in L. Emmerij (ed.), *Economic and Social Development into the XXI Century* (Washington, DC: Inter-American Development Bank, 1997).

World Bank, *Report on Adjustment Lending II: Policies for the Recovery of Growth* (Washington, DC, 1990).

World Bank and UNDP, *Africa's Adjustment and Growth in the 1980s* (Washington, DC, 1989).

4
The Hegemony of US Economic Doctrines in Latin America

Paul W. Drake

Introduction

The implantation of US neo-liberalism in Latin America in the closing decades of the twentieth century resembled the installation of US *laissez-faire* doctrines in the opening decades of that same century. Both experiences took place when US hegemony was expanding in the hemisphere. Many of the ideas and even some of the transmitters were similar. However, the second period of penetration was more complex, pervasive, and profound. It involved a far greater paradigm shift in Latin America. Whereas the first transfer of economic technology had built upon the previous British promotion of free-market ideas, the second infusion had to roll back decades of Latin American advocacy of government intervention. The celerity with which most of the Latin American republics capitulated to that US offensive in the 1980s and 1990s was stunning. However, from the perspective of history and hegemony theory, it looks like the most logical move they could have made.[1]

Hegemony theory

From the point of view of hegemony theory, the United States, as the dominant economic and military power, has rationally and repeatedly injected its economic doctrines into the Latin American countries. The hegemon has waged this war of ideas to establish, regulate, and maintain a stable and open international economic order commensurate with its policies and interests. Given the paucity of easily enforced international economic laws and regulations, the United States has sought to put in place broad rules of the game that will be accepted, internalized, and obeyed by all the key players. The participants do not always have to adhere to the letter of the law but only to confine their actions within acceptable boundaries. Such conformity has reduced risks for US capitalists venturing abroad and for their counterparts in the recipient countries.

For the Latin American rulers, consumption of the US economic model has eased their entry into an international system wherein the United States appears to guarantee some stability and a chance at prosperity. Although sometimes resentful of US arrogance and disproportionate gains, most of them have preferred subordination to anarchy or isolation. Therefore, they have agreed repeatedly to adopt US institutions and laws, clamp down on inflation, stabilize exchange rates, restrain government spending, open their economies, and respect foreign property and obligations. In return for such good behaviour, the United States has provided the collective goods of safeguarding the international flow of capital and commodities.

When the Latin Americans have strayed from the path of virtue, they have been reminded to get back on the straight and narrow by the United States, its agents, and its allies. Once admonished, they have repeatedly vowed to behave better in the future, sometimes by adopting the regimens of foreign advisers, such as the IMF. These accommodations between the hegemon and its underlings have required extensively reiterated bargaining and negotiating over such issues as exchange rates, tariffs, and the rights of foreign investors. Whether independently or through international institutions like the WTO, both sides have tried to minimize their costs and maximize their benefits. Even when the hegemon has gained more from this economic version of collective security than have its junior partners, the minions have stayed in the game so long as their long-range benefits seemed to exceed their costs. The only other option for the smaller powers has been to defect to an alternative economic regime, which no longer existed after the end of the cold war, or to go their own way, which became impractical in light of the globalization of capital, production, trade and neo-liberal precepts.

Within the subordinate states, these decisions to collaborate rather than clash with the hegemon have depended on the perceptions of local ruling groups and governing coalitions. Therefore, the United States has sought to shape not only the international arena but also decision-making within the weaker countries. Although willing to use force – including the Marines and the Central Intelligence Agency – to extract concessions at times, the United States has found it far cheaper to obtain consent through pressure, persuasion, and consensus. The salespersons and intermediaries for US economic doctrines have convinced the Latin Americans to play along and have persuaded the hegemon that its clients are behaving properly, within reasonable limits.[2]

The history of US economic doctrines in Latin America

Partial hegemony, 1890s–1920s

At the end of the nineteenth century, the United States began establishing its political and economic pre-eminence in Mexico, Central America and the Caribbean. Following the opening of the Panama Canal and the conclusion of World War I, the Colossus of the North displaced Great Britain in South America as well, bringing the west coast into its orbit in the 1920s and the east coast in the 1940s. After a spate of direct colonization and imperialism in the Caribbean Basin at the turn of the century, the United States opted for the less expensive, controversial, and risky policy of promoting the 'open door'. Because of its enormous comparative advantages, the United States believed that it could prevail over European and Latin American competitors so long as all the countries in the hemisphere gave it equal access to trade and investment opportunities. The more the Latin Americans adopted US economic institutions and practices, the easier that access became. The US demand for openness was generally well received in Latin America in the prosperous 1920s, as it would be again in the 1980s and 1990s (Williams 1962; Tulchin 1971; Rosenberg 1982).

From the Spanish–American War until the Great Depression, US trade as well as direct and indirect investment mushroomed in Latin America. US entrepreneurs, bankers, investors, advisers and government agents prodded Latin America to adopt US economic ideas and organizations to facilitate that commercial interchange. In the Caribbean and Central America, the United States dispatched economists along with troops to install US economic as well as political institutions. In South America, the United States delivered similar economic advice through private agents hired by host countries, the most famous being the 'Money Doctor', Edwin W. Kemmerer. From the 1890s through the 1920s, every Latin American country except Argentina and Brazil contracted US financial consultants.

Throughout the hemisphere, these US economists recommended the gold standard, independent central banks, regulated commercial banking, balanced and monitored government budgets, transparent management and accounting of government finances, national comptrollers, effective taxation, prudent and productive public works, the streamlined judicial review of business disputes, efficient customs administration, free trade, cautious borrowing and reliable debt servicing, and equal treatment for foreign capitalists. They helped these countries attract foreign loans by combating deficit spending, inflation, and exchange instability. Unlike their counterparts in the 1980s, these fiscal physicians did not have to push deregulation and privatization because the Latin American states were not yet deeply involved in their economies. In response to these missionaries, the Latin Americans imbibed their advice mainly in order to improve their access to foreign loans on reasonable terms (Rosenberg and Rosenberg 1987; Eichengreen 1989).

Hegemony challenged, 1930s–1970s

The Latin Americans turned against the US open model first in pragmatic response to the international market havoc caused by the Great Depression and World War II, and second in intellectual response to their unequal share of world growth after the war. During and following the 1931–3 crash, most

Latin American governments scuttled the doctrine that the United States had promoted in the 1920s of the gold standard, autonomous central banks, minimal governments, balanced budgets, punctual debt payments and free trade. They junked the gold standard, captured central banks, enlarged currency emissions, expanded government intervention, ballooned deficit spending, suspended foreign debt payments, installed exchange controls, imposed import restrictions and protected national industry. These measures reflected the diminution of US power, the rise of Keynesian statism and protectionism in the United States itself as well as western Europe, and the arrival of challengers to US domination, especially Germany (Thorp 1984).

The economic catastrophe of the 1930s undermined constitutional republics, which were usually replaced by military dictatorships. By contrast, the debt crisis of the 1980s would usher in democracies as well as neo-liberal economic policies. In other words, classic liberalism took a beating both economically and politically in the 1930s, while it experienced a resurrection on both fronts in the 1980s. This pattern comports with the broader historical experience of severe external economic shocks, which usually inspire countries to experiment with the opposite of whatever political economy combination they had before (Gourevitch 1986).

This inadvertent Keynesianism in the 1930s was rationalized, legitimized, theorized, and institutionalized by ECLA in the 1940s and 1950s. The doctrine came to be known as 'import substitution industrialization' (ISI) or 'structuralism'. More radical versions evolved into 'dependency theories'. What the United States had seen as emergency measures in reaction to the collapse of international trade and finance in the 1930s became, to its dismay, standard Latin American policy from the 1940s to the 1970s (Hirschman 1961; FitzGerald 1994; Love 1994, 1996).

There was no great mystery as to why the Latin Americans turned away from traditional US economic advice in the 1930s. With the disruption of international trade, they needed to protect domestic industries to produce what they used to import and to conserve foreign exchange. With the interruption of international finance, they naturally suspended debt payments and engaged in deficit spending. There was little incentive to follow free-market doctrine in order to attract foreign investment, since there was virtually no investment in the offing. Indeed, no massive influx of private indirect foreign capital arrived again until the 1970s, when some Latin Americans began adopting more classical liberal economic policies, reminiscent of the 1920s, in order to obtain and service foreign loans.

If there was a mystery in this period, it was why Latin America hung onto interventionist doctrines so long in the 1950s and 1960s, when US hegemony might have pushed them 'back into line'. Most US economists and policy-makers roundly criticized ISI strategy and widespread interference with markets. Economists from the US private sector and government, as well as from international agencies like the IMF, urged greater reliance on the private sector. Even though it could extend credits as well as certify credit-worthiness to private investors, the IMF and its austerity policies aroused great resistance in Latin America, especially from labour, the left and nationalists. Despite US strategic and economic domination of the region from the end of World War II through the cold war, the United States was unable to roll back decisively ECLA or dependency schools of thought until the 1980s, although a few inroads were made earlier in Chile, Argentina, Uruguay, Peru and elsewhere (Krueger 1978; Currie 1981; Ramos 1986).

There were six main reasons for the tenacity of the ISI school of thought. First, the United States itself had succumbed to Keynesianism and moderate government intervention in the economy from the 1930s through the 1970s, when even President Richard Nixon declared, 'We're all Keynesians now.' Moreover, during the cold war, the United States exhibited more concern with Latin American geopolitical and ideological loyalty than with its economic conformity. Second, there were viable alternative models available in the world – whether the European welfare state or socialist options – that lent comfort to the Latin American strategy. Third, foreign capital reached Latin America in the form of public aid and direct investments even without total submission to preferred US policies, and private financial largesse did not re-emerge until the 1970s. Fourth, the ECLA formula did produce considerable growth and structural modernization. Fifth, the protectionist policies adopted in the aftermath of the Great Depression had created a coalition of vested interests – industrialists, government bureaucrats, the middle sectors, intellectuals and organized labour, as well as the institutions committed to these policies – that defended that approach until their dominance was shattered by the stagnation of the model and the destruction of the 1980s debt crisis. Sixth, there was a natural inertia and lag once policies were in place and embedded in institutions, so that no major change was likely in the absence of another disastrous external shock.

In the broad sense of general economic regimes, however, Latin America had not completely broken with US hegemony from the 1940s to the 1970s. Just as it had bowed to the essential tenets of the prevalent free-trade doctrine emanating from Great Britain and thereafter the United States from the 1840s to the 1920s, so it had accompanied the United States and Great Britain in their subsequent conversion to Keynesianism. From the 1930s to the 1970s, Latin America had crafted its own regional version of government macroeconomic intervention, however much at odds with the more restrained US variety. When Keynesianism lost favour in the United States after the oil crisis and stagflation of the 1970s, to be replaced by monetarist and neo-liberal concepts, Latin America tagged along once again. In all three eras, Latin America followed the general lead, albeit with its own variations and deviations, especially from the 1930s to the 1970s, of the primary economic power (Hirschman 1989; Ikenberry 1993).

Hegemony unchallenged, 1980s–2000s

From the waning years of the cold war through the dawn of the new millennium, US hegemony in Latin America reached unparalleled heights. In the 1980s, Ronald Reagan reasserted US supremacy after the 1970s malaise associated with Vietnam, Watergate, the oil crisis, and the Iranian and Nicaraguan revolutions. In particular, the White House struck back in Central America. President Reagan also reacted to stagflation under President Jimmy Carter by endorsing monetarism, the shrinking of the welfare state, and 'the magic of the market'. The Latin Americans echoed that change of heart mainly because the international debt crisis left those governments desperate to expand exports and slash expenditures in order to service their external obligations.

Thus in many ways, the conversion to neo-liberalism was like the previous embrace of structuralism. It was a reaction to an externally generated crisis, this time calling for (1) freer trade to expand exports; (2) privatization to reduce government expenditures, to raise revenues and to attract foreign investment; and (3) further restrictions on government interventions (independent central banks, weakened labour unions, deregulation, and so on) in order to block inflation, maintain exchange stability, and woo foreign capital. Then a series of emergency measures once again hardened into a doctrinal orthodoxy, this time emanating from the North rather than the South. Neo-liberalism solidified partly because the United States remained powerful and prosperous enough in the 1980s, unlike in the 1930s, to offer Latin America rewards – that is, investments and trade – in return for obedience to its economic dicta. This cure-all was prescribed not only by the US government but also by most US economists and business leaders, the main multilateral institutions, and many Latin American elites themselves.

The causes of the contemporary hegemony of US neo-liberalism

Basically, there are five explanations for the adoption of US economic ideas as policies in Latin America: (1) the economic and political domination of the United States; (2) the economic conditions at the time; (3) the perceived correctness and cogency of the ideas themselves; (4) the power and effectiveness of their transmitters; and (5) their attractiveness to the recipients, especially the state and a winning political coalition. It was a confluence of these factors that made neo-liberalism so hard to resist. To over-generalize, that formula pervaded the hemisphere – and much of the planet – because of the overwhelming dominance of the United States, the debt crisis and subsequent globalization, the perceived superiority of that model to discredited alternatives, the leverage of carriers like the World Bank, and the receptivity of host governments and transnational socio-economic coalitions (Odell 1982; Hall 1989; Sikkink 1991; Biersteker 1995).[3]

US hegemony

From the 1940s through the 1990s, the United States exerted extraordinary political and economic hegemony over Latin America. As the unequivocal power, it set and enforced the basic rules of the political and economic systems, regardless of defiance and defections in various countries and categories. Although its supremacy suffered some setbacks from the 1960s to the 1980s, analysts who interpreted these partial slippages as evidence of a long-term US decline in Latin America were mistaken. Instead, from the 1980s into the 2000s, the only remaining superpower vigorously reclaimed its hegemony in the western Hemisphere as never before. In Panama in 1989 and Haiti in 1994, the United States showed that it was still willing to invade small countries in the Caribbean Basin in the aftermath of the cold war. Because of such a resurgence of uninhibited and unquestioned political, economic, and strategic superiority in the region, even more so than in the 1920s, most of the Latin American countries fell over themselves to establish better relations with the United States, whether it was Argentina dispatching a ship to the Gulf War or Ecuador adopting the US dollar as its currency (Keohane 1984; Lowenthal 1987; Schoultz 1998; Smith 2000).

US economic doctrine became more hegemonic in Latin America when the US economy became more hegemonic. After decreasing from the 1960s to the 1980s, the US share of foreign trade and investments in Latin America climbed from the 1980s to the 1990s, especially in the Caribbean Basin and above all in Mexico. While the Soviet alternative vanished, the other two possible external sources of a model or leader for Latin America fell short of expectations. As an economic partner for Latin Americans, the United States overshadowed Asian and European countries in the 1990s, even though they scored significant gains in South America. The more statist East Asian strategy lost its lustre with the Japanese recession and the East Asian crisis of the 1990s. At the same time, the main western European powers, even when they made sizeable economic inroads in Latin America, did not offer an approach starkly different from that of the United States, and they were more concerned with Eastern Europe than with the western Hemisphere. Because of US economic pre-eminence, exaggerated after the fall of the Soviet Union and fortified by spectacular growth under the two Clinton administrations, ideas and their purveyors from the United States automatically had more clout than those from less powerful nations. The options for the Latin American republics shrivelled, as most of them toed the line of neo-liberalism (Smith 2000).

Economic conditions

Three economic conditions facilitated the penetration of US neo-liberal doctrines: the recession and debt crisis of the early 1980s, the concomitant rise of globalization, and the subsequent renewal of growth, however slow and selective, in the 1990s.

Economic earthquakes have long opened the way to fresh ideas because they capsize existing orders and beliefs, setting off a frantic search for solutions. What made the concept of free markets so saleable in recent years was their ability to respond to the quadruple crises of the foreign debt, inflation, ISI and the welfare state. Their other major attraction was their ability to lure foreign capital. The Latin American reproduction of policies copied from US blueprints reduced uncertainties for US investors and traders.

Partly caused by anti-inflationary policies and rising interest rates in the United States, the worldwide recession, and the debt crisis devastated Latin America in 1982. Since those debts were owed mainly to US banks, most Latin Americans adopted US formulas to weather the crisis. US economics departments, US economists and their former students, US economic elites, the US government, the western world establishment, and the international financial institutions espoused a ready-made recipe for a situation well suited to its premises, one requiring the husbanding and redirecting of state resources to meet foreign obligations. That stabilizing response promised to simultaneously curb inflation and honour debts.

Countries desperate for debt relief, fresh foreign capital and foreign exchange proved unusually receptive to the neo-liberal marching orders. Development through export promotion became exceptionally attractive to nations that needed to service their staggering debts by expanding sales abroad. Strapped governments frequently heeded the advice of multilateral institutions because the Latin Americans knew that the approval of these institutions sent positive signals to private investors and to first-world public agencies supplying aid (Kahler 1986; Thorp and Whitehead 1987; Sachs 1989; Nelson 1990; Stallings 1992; Goldstein and Keohane 1993; Iglesias 1994; Biersteker 1995; Dominguez 1997; van Dijck 1998).

After initial belt-tightening and liberalizing failed to stem the debt crisis and reignite growth, the 1985 plan by US Treasury Secretary James Baker called for new loans from the banks and the international agencies. He expected that assistance to be contingent on deeper structural reforms from the Latin Americans to further prune the state and unshackle markets. Then, the plan by Treasury Secretary Nicholas Brady in 1989 became the enduring standard for handling the debt crisis. His plan went beyond Baker's in calling for voluntary debt reduction by the banks as well as expanded lending by the multilaterals to countries pursuing structural reforms. The White House linked debt reduction to the further freeing of domestic markets and foreign trade. Foreign capital began returning to Latin America. These escalating incentives propelled more and more compliance with the principles of neo-liberalism. Because these foreign debts malingered and even grew beneath the superficial prosperity in the 1990s, countries remained apprehensive about abandoning neo-liberal commandments (Roett 1992; Varas 1995).

The second economic trend favouring neo-liberalism was so-called 'globalisation'. By the 1990s, the world economy had become more interconnected and interdependent than at any time since the 1920s. Countries saw foreign trade and investment soar as a proportion of GNP. Capitalists reorganized production on a global scale. The increasing flow of international goods, services, and capital undercut the effectiveness of market interventions by either governments or labour unions, especially in smaller, poorer countries. As autonomous monetary and fiscal policies became increasingly futile, governments lost power to internationally mobile capital.

To compete or at least survive in the internationalized economy, many countries threw themselves open to global market forces, and rode up or down with the world economy. Increasingly susceptible to external currents, most nations had little choice but to heed the demands of international economic elites by curtailing independent policy-making, restraining fiscal and monetary practices, deregulating domestic markets, and liberalizing foreign trade and investment rules. As neo-liberal reforms accelerated, they became cumulative. The more ground that governments ceded to the market-place, the less able they were to resist making further concessions to the increasingly powerful domestic and international market forces. Once countries began down the slippery slope of liberalization, deregulation, and privatization, it became very difficult to stop, let alone reverse course. More and more, they were prone to synchronize their economic institutions and practices with the world standard set largely by the United States (Milner and Keohane 1996; Rodrik 1997).

Given the 1980s–1990s sequence of debt crisis followed by globalization, it is easy to see why Latin America generally caved in to US demands for neo-liberal policy packages. That compliance was fortified by a third major trend, as renewed growth lent credence to the neo-liberal doctrine. After the 'lost decade' of the 1980s, the annual average growth-rate for Latin America rose over 3 per cent in the 1990s. Although that growth was modest and very unevenly distributed, it was enough to fan the flames of hope for neo-liberalism, especially when reformed countries like Chile led the way. Equally important, foreign capital returned to the region, partly encouraged by neo-liberal transformations. Moreover, extraordinary US economic success in the 1990s made its model increasingly attractive and hegemonic (Weeks 1995; Smith 2000).

The validity of the ideas

In the 1980s and 1990s, theories supporting market approaches to economic development swept aside emphases on government intervention. This reliance on the private sector became the foundation of what was dubbed 'monetarism', 'neo-liberalism', or the 'Washington consensus'. In that last term, 'Washington' referred to the US government, economic think tanks, the IMF, the World Bank, the Export–Import Bank and the IADB. 'Consensus' signified agreement about the desirability of macroeconomic discipline, monetary and exchange stability, independent central banks, lean governments, tight budgets, effective taxation, privatization, deregulation, foreign investments, export promotion and free trade (Ocampo 1990; Williamson 1990a; Williamson 1990b; Williamson 1990c; Edwards 1995).[4]

It is too soon to know whether neo-liberalism became all the rage because, as its proponents would have it, economic science had finally discovered the truth with a capital 'T'. Although intellectual advances made the model more attractive, the evidence for its success was mixed. Therefore, it seems unlikely that the sudden popularity of US economic ideas in the 1980s and 1990s was mainly a result of their surprisingly self-evident veracity. It seems more plausible that changing conditions rendered longstanding premises more palatable. For over a century, the United States had emphasized the primary role of the private sector in growth and development, both domestically and internationally, albeit with significant intellectual and policy changes within that framework over the decades. The basic litany of monetary and exchange prudence, central bank autonomy, small government, fiscal discipline, broad and efficient taxation, deregulation, private property rights, free markets, free trade and foreign investment had been the US prescription for other countries for a long time (Williamson 1994).

The current economic wisdom formed part of a larger ideological bundle swathed in liberalism. As they sometimes had been in the past, liberal economics and liberal politics were closely linked in this formulation. This ideology formed part of a resurgent crusade against the Soviet Union and its allies in the 1980s, wherein the western protagonists called for both economic and political liberalization. Soon, alternative regimes found it increasingly daunting to challenge the liberal canon in light of the recent failures of communism, socialism, social democracy and populism (Lowenthal 1987; Carothers 1991; Hall 1993; Biersteker 1995).

Although neither neo-liberal economics nor foreign investors required political democracy for their operation, freer markets and politics increasingly coincided in US rhetoric and in the Latin American reality in the 1990s. Many analysts came to believe that authoritarianism really offered more uncertainty than did democracy. A dictatorship might make it clearer who was and was not going to rule, but it put few limits on what that ruler could do, including abrupt and arbitrary changes in the rules of the economic game. By contrast, so long as all major contenders agreed on the fundamental economic paradigm, which had not been true in the 1960s and 1970s but was largely true by the 1990s, democracy provided more checks and balances on policy changes. It also supplied improved feedback and flexibility on policy implementation and outcomes, enhanced transparency of decision-making, greater reliability and less corruption from the bureaucracy and the judicial system, more openness for foreign economic agents, and insulation from charges of consorting with dictators and torturers. Although democracy and all its tumult presented more instability on the surface than did a dictatorship, underneath all the pulling and hauling, it was more sturdy and predictable. Consensus trumped coercion as a guarantor of policy continuity.

Aware of these mutually reinforcing economic and political linkages, more and more US and international opinion leaders – politicians, policy-makers, bureaucrats, academics, and so on – promoted the tandem liberalization of markets and politics. According to proponents of neo-liberalism, the reduction of the state, invigoration of the private sector, expansion of property ownership, and reliance on market mechanisms established the classic economic prerequisites for an individualistic liberal political system. In short order, the US economic and political models encircled the globe together, with the greatest impact in Europe and Latin America (Huntington 1991; Fukuyama 1992; Dominguez 1997; Drake 1998).

The transmitters of the doctrines

The transmitters provided information, legitimacy and leverage for the diffusion of these economic ideas. These authorities helped the Latin American governments choose among competing alternatives, forge a transnational coalition to support the policies, explain and justify the new directions, and receive external funding to facilitate their implementation. In some cases, these messengers also supplied a foreign scapegoat for attacks on the policies. The main broadcasters were government institutions, multilateral agencies, the private sector and economists (Hirschman 1965; Kahler 1994).

One of the most graphic examples of the influence of these transmitters occurred when Peru's Alberto Fujimori, between his 1990 first election and inauguration as president, switched from an opponent to an advocate of rapid and drastic structural adjustment. That conversion took place partly through the lobbying of Peruvian economists and businessmen, but mainly through Fujimori's visit to the IMF and the governments of the United States and Japan. Overnight, they convinced him to jump from heterodox to orthodox programs (Conaghan 1997).

Government institutions

From the US government, emissaries promoting neo-liberalism fanned out from the Federal Reserve, Commerce Department State Department, Treasury, Agency for International Development and even the presidency. Under President Reagan, the White House mounted an aggressive campaign to enlist all the agencies of the US government, multilateral institutions, and its allies overseas in a crusade to replace statist with market strategies. The dominant spokespersons were Ronald Reagan in the United States and Margaret Thatcher in Great Britain, seconded by many others such as Helmut Kohl in Germany. On a much smaller scale, another US promulgator of the Chilean and East Asian export promotion models was the National Bureau of Economic Research. In the 1970s and 1980s, its economists hailed these cases as the triumph of market mechanisms over ISI (Biersteker 1995).

A key US offensive involved the conclusion of NAFTA in 1993 and the continuing promotion of a hemisphere-wide counterpart. NAFTA assured Mexico's commitment to freer markets, and those wishing to compete in the hemisphere felt they had to follow that huge example. The United States made it indelibly clear to the Latin Americans that they had to open their markets – and usually their politics – in order to participate. Thereafter international trade and investment agreements increasingly bound countries to market-friendly policies. Under both the Bush and Clinton administrations (1988–2000), the United States promoted framework agreements to encourage more market-oriented economies in Latin America in exchange for greater access to the US market. At the first Summit of the Americas in 1994 in Miami, the United States and the Latin Americans pledged to negotiate a hemispheric free trade area, the Free Trade Area of the Americas (FTAA), by 2005. Summitry continued to promote free trade – at least verbally – at the second conclave in Santiago in 1998. Despite US procrastination on free trade agreements, these accomplishments and the hopes of more kept most Latin American governments on the approved path of neo-liberalism (Varas 1995; Feinberg 1997; Smith 2000).

Other foreign governments and models reinforced the message from the United States. Along with US examples and preaching, privatization policies in England and Japan provided exemplars for governments drained by fiscal crises. From the mid-1980s onwards, Chile became Latin America's paragon of the success of neo-liberalism, while Peru under President Alan Garcia became the showcase for the failure of statism and populism. The dismal record of heterodox solutions in Brazil and Argentina, accompanied by the scourge of hyperinflation, rendered the Washington consensus even more alluring. Latin American governments learned from each other how to adopt neo-liberalism as well as democracy. Amidst the uncertainty of simultaneous liberalization of the economy and polity, it was tempting to imitate nearby success stories (Ikenberry 1990; Biersteker 1995).

International institutions

Key international advocates of the new economic orthodoxy included, with variations, the World Bank, IMF and IADB, all but especially the first two heavily influenced by the United States. Nevertheless, as multilateral organizations, their advice was seen as somewhat less tainted by national motives than were similar directives from the US government. After the onset of the debt crisis and the increase in the funds of these prestigious and powerful institutions, their ability to sell neo-liberalism to Latin America expanded dramatically, as did their demands for policy reforms.

The World Bank peddled these ideas by promoting the new paradigm, by helping design and implement these policies through 'structural adjustment programs', by training local officials, and by conditioning financial assistance on the carrying out of these programs. The IMF diffused the same doctrine through its research, publications, courses, missions, and conditional loans. Although the IMF, under pressure from the United States, had been promoting a similar monetarist formula for austerity since the late 1950s, mainly to squelch inflation and stabilize the balance of payments, it found states to be more receptive to its entreaties in the wake of the debt crisis. Further enhancing their impact, these multinational institutions could coordinate the participation of foreign lenders and donors in assistance packages. Although neither the IMF nor the World Bank insisted officially on democracy as a condition for loans, their emphasis on 'good governance' (transparency, accountability, and so on) from the late 1980s onward tilted in favour of democratic regimes. In the 1990s, the propensity for these institutions and official Washington to favour capitalist democracies became more blatant (Williamson 1983; Killick 1984; Pastor 1987; Biersteker 1990; Mosley, Harrigan and Toye (eds) 1991; Leftwich 1994:363–86; Nelson 1994; Nelson *et al.* 1994; Williams and Young 1994:84–100; Finnemore 1996; Montecinos 1998:2–3).

According to the IMF and World Bank, the vast majority of their economic compliance conditions were fully implemented by recipient countries in the 1980s. From the early 1980s to the early 1990s, every Latin American country except Cuba enacted IMF and World Bank adjustment programs. The IADB also adopted policy-based lending practices hinged to the ingestion of neo-liberal axioms. Another proponent of deregulating and denationalizing economies was the General Agreement on Tariffs and Trade (GATT), which most Latin American countries did not join until the 1980s. Its promotion of free trade and investment forbade members from favouring domestic over foreign producers (Iglesias 1992; Nelson and Englinton 1992; Weeks 1995).

Private institutions

US and Latin American business leaders and their associations also spread the gospel of neo-liberalism. Foreign investors and financiers joined the chorus in favour of liberalization. Enormous banking consortia pressured the Latin American debtors to go along, using threats as well as credits to extract compliance. It was much harder for the Latin Americans to reject this advice in the 1980s than it had been to spurn thousands of atomized bondholders in the 1930s (Haggard and Maxfield 1996; Conaghan 1997).

Economists

An international 'epistemic community' of economists emerged in these decades. Increasingly trained in the United States from the 1960s onward, they shared a common learning experience, a specialized discourse, a fund of knowledge, a storehouse of expertise, a commitment to certain cause-and-effect concepts, and a set of theoretical and normative beliefs. From the 1970s to the 1990s, that training increasingly reflected the trend among US economists, particularly those specializing in international trade and public choice, to prefer untrammelled markets over government activism. Turning against Keynesianism, that universal doctrine left virtually no room for regional, national, or local idiosyncrasies, let alone what used to be called 'development economics'. As US economics departments stopped producing area specialists, so they turned the rising numbers of economics students from those foreign areas into generalists who believed that 'one size fits all'. Standard training by US universities was supplemented by US government exchange programmes, by visits from US economists, by foreign support for local think tanks, and by socialization in multilateral agencies and multinational corporations.

The commitment of these economists to these universal truths overshadowed nationalistic values. They dazzled politicians and the public with their claims to scientific objectivity and certainty. According to these high-priests of modernity, there were hardly any rational alternatives to neo-liberal policies. After economists themselves converged on these approaches, they presented a united front to governments. By excluding some fundamental economic issues from the public agenda – such as government ownership of industries or massive redistribution of income and wealth – they made unruly democracies safe for domestic and foreign capital (Haas 1992; Goldstein and Keohane 1993; Markoff and Montecinos 1993; Feinberg 1994; Biersteker 1995:183–4; Galjart and Silva 1995; Haggard and Webb 1996:30–1; Camp 1997; Conaghan 1997; Dominguez 1997; Huneeus 1997; Loureiro 1997; Montecinos 1997:135–54; Centeno and Silva 1998).[5]

The recipients of the doctrines

Policy change reflected the influence of not only ideas but also interests and institutions. Whatever the transmission mechanism, neo-liberalism was not simply imposed on the Latin Americans, although many leaders realized that they had very limited choices in the economic climate of the 1980s and 1990s. To a significant extent, neo-liberalism coincided with what some rulers and their supporters wanted to do anyway. The three decisive recipients were the government, technocrats and a winning socio-political coalition (Nelson *et al.* 1989; Goldstein and Keohane 1993; Conaghan and Malloy 1994).

Governments

Assuming that the opposition could be cowed, crushed, or coopted, some governments found neo-liberal ideas attractive because they were simple and cheap. When one of Pinochet's economists asked one of his generals why they had taken their advice, he replied, 'because you agreed with each other and gave us simple answers to our questions' (Pinera 1994). These pro-market policies were also relatively easy and inexpensive to administer. They required little government action or expertise except to get out of the way of market mechanisms. Neo-liberal remedies called for the government to do less, not more, at a time when it had few resources to do anything anyway.

Moreover, they promised that their medicine would bring rapid relief, in terms of both staunching inflation and attracting external credit (Pion-Berlin 1989).

The reliability and stability provided by turning over economic policy-making to neo-liberal technocrats were especially attractive to politicians during democratization, when uncertainty abounded. Civilian leaders were eager to prove that they were at least as skilful as dictators WERE at managing the economy. Appealing to advice from exalted experts helped justify belt-tightening to their own citizens. Their audience was not only foreign investors but also domestic capitalists, whom they wanted to coax away from coup coalitions. Many Latin American leaders, even from the left, were using neo-liberal policies to placate those groups most prone to authoritarianism, while taking for granted those sectors more inclined towards democracy. By winning over or neutralizing the traditional opponents of democracy and by undercutting the traditional proponents of populism and redistribution, neo-liberal reforms were intended to stabilize not only the economy but also the polity. They made democracy safe for and from capitalists (Schneider 1997).

In some cases, the Latin American governments accepted these US rules and regulations with alacrity because they really had little intention of fully implementing or obeying them, for example signing one 'letter of intent' after another with the IMF to slash domestic deficits. After rubber-stamping recommendations to please foreign investors, host governments sometimes circumvented those promises in order to satisfy domestic political and economic pressures. Despite impressive compliance statistics from the IMF and World Bank, some of their programs were implemented partially or not at all (Remmer 1994; van Dijck 1998).

This evasion was scarcely unprecedented, since Latin America has walked a tightrope between external demands and internal expectations for centuries. For example, officials in colonial Spanish America told the Crown in Spain, 'I obey but do not execute,' to avoid implementing royal decrees unacceptable to local elites. In similar fashion, Brazilians in the nineteenth century labelled behaviour mimicking the British in order to propitiate powerful foreigners 'for the English to see'. In the 1920s, Bolivians called economic legislation concocted more to curry foreign favour than to apply to local citizens 'laws for export'. By the same token, some of today's Latin American infatuation with neo-liberalism may have been more strategic than sincere.

Above all, Latin American governments heeded the advice of US economists and their local *protégés* because they mollified capitalists. The appointments and pronouncements of these economists sent reassuring market signals to jittery foreign and domestic investors. Restoring investor confidence was particularly essential after the debt crisis of the 1980s. Given the extreme dependence on foreign funders, governments needed technocrats with contacts and influence with their counterparts in Washington and Wall Street more than ever. Technocrats helped politicians establish credible commitments to discipline budgets and meet foreign obligations, thus enhancing their governments' reputations for creditworthiness with fluid foreign and domestic capital (Schneider 1997).

Technocrats

With the rise of technocrats in Latin American politics in the 1980s and 1990s, a convergence took place between them and their US counterparts. A transnational coalition congealed to install and defend free-market economics. This 'import substitution' of relying on local economists trained abroad instead of foreigners probably shielded some of these programs from nationalistic attacks. The panegyric in favour of neo-liberal economic approaches by multilateral institutions strengthened the hand of these local technocrats steeped in the same tradition (Pion-Berlin 1989; Harberger 1993; Centeno 1994; Dominguez 1997).

Many of those international ties were woven in US graduate schools, particularly in economics. Such training had been denounced in the 1960s by Chilean economists Anibal Pinto and Oswaldo Sunkel. They complained that such foreign education indoctrinated Latin American economists with universalistic theories with no adjustment to conditions in their home countries. Nevertheless, the numbers of Latin Americans undergoing graduate training in the United States and western Europe increased, partly owing to the exile of many Latin American intellectuals during the dictatorships of the 1970s. Other Latin American thinkers and politicians also became enamoured of the private sector, including Hernando de Soto and Mario Vargas Llosa in Peru (de Soto 1989; Puryear 1994; Dominguez 1997; Aslanbeigui and Montecinos 1998).[6]

After returning home, the foreign-trained economists spread their neo-liberal ideas through universities, think tanks, interest associations, consulting firms, the media, political parties, and government agencies. National teams of these professional economists proved most successful at carrying out neo-liberal reforms. The most famous example was the 'Chicago Boys' in Chile (O'Brien and Roddick 1983; Nylen 1993; Valdés 1995; Conaghan 1997; Dominguez 1997; Montecinos 1997). For another example, trade liberalization only caught on in Colombia at the start of the 1990s when a majority of its economists converted to neo-classical doctrines; the economist who was president, César Gaviria, shared their faith; the IMF, World Bank and US trade negotiators pushed the same concept; and so did domestic exporters (Urrutia 1994).

Socio-political coalitions

US economic theories caught on in Latin America also because powerful local interests profited from these concepts. For ideas to become policies, they had to appeal to a winning coalition of international and domestic political actors. As a result of crises and reforms, domestic groups who benefited from internationalization and openness gained in wealth and power, thereby imposing and consolidating their policy preferences, despite the rearguard resistance of domestic losing sectors (Handelman and Baer (eds) 1989; Stallings and Kaufman 1989; Ikenberry 1993; Frieden and Rogowski 1996; Silva 1996; Heller *et al.* 1998).

For the steamroller of neo-liberalism, the supportive coalition included rising interest groups such as new middle-class entrepreneurs, internationalist businesses, exporters, financiers, and entrepreneurial elements of the informal sector. Some capitalists previously dependent on government protection shifted to more competitive strategies. Privatization multiplied the numbers of supporters. Consumers above the poverty line also benefited from neo-liberalism and the importation of foreign goods without high tariff barriers. Foreign capitalists also favoured the new policies. Monetarism and neo-liberalism provided a rationale for anti-statist policies that many conservatives and economic elites had advocated for many years anyway. To a significant extent, the two Latin American groups long most heavily influenced by the United States – the business executives and the military – were won over to neo-liberalism. It fitted with the business magnates' devotion to capitalism and markets, and it comported with the military's faith in technocracy, order, antisocialism and antipolitics.

The neo-liberal coalition opposed declining interest groups, such as protected and inefficient industrialists and agriculturalists (both mainly producing for domestic markets), government bureaucrats and some other white-collar middle sectors, organized labour and segments of the unorganized poor. In short, the old ISI coalition lost out. The sudden drainage of resources caused by the debt crisis diminished the possibility of populist or leftist leaders pumping up state redistribution programs. Even those politicians who promised such outmoded solutions on the hustings, for example Carlos Menem in Argentina, usually surrendered to market realities and neo-liberalism once in office.

Wherever the neo-liberal programme unfolded, its central elements undercut the principal proponent of the previous statist model, organized labour. Unionized workers were also reeling because of the globalization of trade, production, investment and competition. Especially in the early stages of implementation, neo-liberalism's austere fiscal and monetary policies, suppression of inflation, reduction of social services, privatization of public enterprises, unharnessing of markets, restriction of unions, constriction of wages and flexibilization of the workforce further eroded the ability of the traditional labour movement to resist this juggernaut. In some cases, growing income inequality and unemployment exacerbated these trends. For example in Chile, Pinochet adopted neo-liberal policies that rewarded the groups he wanted to favour (for example, internationalist capitalists) and punished those he wanted to disfavour (for example, organized workers and state employees), so that his economic and political agendas dovetailed (Handelman and Baer 1989; Chalmers, *et al.* 1992; Hall 1993:275–96; Conaghan and Malloy 1994; Smith *et al.* 1994a, 1994b; Vilas 1995; Bulmer-Thomas 1996; Drake 1996; Haggard and Webb 1996:18–22; Silva 1996:30, 97, 98, 112, 138, 206, 207).

Conclusion

It was not surprising that US doctrine prevailed in the hemisphere in the 1980s and 1990s. Multiple factors coincided to favour that outcome: (1) a long history of US hegemony over most of the region most of the time; (2) a resurgence of US hegemony to unprecedented heights; (3) a set of economic conditions that rendered Latin America exceptionally receptive to ideas from its premier creditor, investor and trader; (4) a coherent policy package well attuned to the economic and political exigencies of the time; (5) a group of potent and luminous transmitters eager and able to sell that package; and (6) a cluster of Latin American governments, technocrats, and social actors inclined to adopt that remedy. By contrast, the forces outside and inside Latin America that might have resisted the neo-liberal leviathan were in an unusually weak position.

Indeed, neo-liberalism engulfed not only most of Latin America but also vast sections of the entire globe. Consequently, it would have been surprising if Latin America, the region of the world most dependent on the United States, had bucked the tide. Although patterns and choices varied among the countries in the hemisphere, the most striking phenomenon was the uniformity of the general trend.

Of the causal factors, which were the most important? The ideas had been around and gaining strength since the early 1960s, as seen in the standard potion prescribed by the IMF and in stabilization plans adopted by various authoritarian regimes in the 1960s and 1970s. Like the ideas, the hegemon, transmitters, and recipients were not completely new in the 1980s, although their leverage, status, and coherence had increased significantly. Therefore, it seems that the key variables were the crucial international changes in the 1980s and 1990s. The debt crisis delivered a tremendous shock that made many of the other factors fall into place. That crisis propelled the general turn to neo-liberalism, which was accelerated and locked in by the increasingly omnipresent and aggressive hegemony of the United States and its agents, the tidal wave of democratization, the end of the cold war, the contagion of globalization, and the spurt of renewed growth, all rationalized and legitimized by the evangelists of the new economic orthodoxy.

By the turn of the century, some doubters criticized the Washington consensus, and observers expressed more concern about social inequalities and poverty, as well as environmental degradation. However, the essential neo-liberal framework remained in place. If the past was any guide, this policy syndrome seemed likely to persist until a comparable conjuncture of powerful international and domestic forces blew it off course.

Notes

1. For suggestions, I want to thank Richard Feinberg, Peter Gourevitch, Eric Hershberg, David Lake and Peter Smith. I hope that I will be forgiven for over-generalizing in this chapter in order to sketch the major trends. It would require far more time and space to test my variables and arguments across a variety of cases, to explain why some factors had more impact in some countries than in others and to establish why some countries liberalized more rapidly and deeply than others.

2. Much of the above paragraphs as well as significant passages below are adapted from Drake (1989, 1994b), and especially from the introduction to the latter (Drake 1994a). On hegemony theory, see Keohane (1984), who, like many scholars, over-estimated the decline of US hegemony by the 1980s, prior to the end of the cold war and the emergence of the United States as the sole superpower, more hege-monic than ever, particularly in Latin America. He also noted the utility of Antonio Gramsci's concept of ideological hegemony, which does not constantly need to be imposed by force (pp. 44–6). Another key writer on hegemony is Kindleberger (1973, 1981). Also important are Lipson (1985) and Snidal (1985).

3. For the story of how this doctrine took hold in Bolivia, see Conaghan (1994).

4. Later, the need to help the poor and the environment was added to the menu, but this chapter is concerned mainly with the spread of the original thesis.

5. I am grateful to E. V. K. FitzGerald for some of these points about the training of economists.

6. The proportion of US economics doctorates awarded to foreign students rose from 21 per cent in 1972 to 43 per cent in 1988 to about 50 per cent in 1996. Of those enrolled in 1996, 20 per cent came from Latin America and the Caribbean. When these enrolled foreign students were asked why a US economics PhD had value in their countries, the most common responses were that it would improve the qual-ity of economic research, increase rationality in public policy-making, create inter-national networks and help in the implementation of market-oriented reforms and integration of the country into the global economy.

References

Aslanbeigui, N. and V. Montecinos, 'Foreign Students in US Doctoral Programs', *Journal of Economic Perspectives*, 12/3 (Summer 1998) 171–82.

Ayres, R. L., *Banking on the Poor: The World Bank and World Poverty* (Cambridge, MA: MIT Press, 1983).

Biersteker, T. J., 'Reducing the Role of the State in the Economy: A Conceptual Exploration of IMF and World Bank Prescriptions', *International Studies Quarterly*, 34/4 (December 1990) 477–92.

Biersteker, T. J., 'The "Triumph" of Liberal Economic Ideas in the Developing World', in B. Stallings (ed.), *Global Change, Regional Response: The New International Context of Development* (Cambridge University Press, 1995).

Bulmer-Thomas, V. (ed.), *The New Economic Model in Latin America and Its Impact on Income Distribution and Poverty* (New York: St Martin's, 1996).

Camp, R. A., 'Tecnocracía a la Mexicana, '¿Antecedente a la Democracia?', *Pensamiento Iberoamericano*, 30 (1997) 155–76.
Carothers, T., *In the Name of Democracy: US Policy toward Latin America in the Reagan Years* (Berkeley: University of California Press, 1991).
Centeno, M. A., *Democracy Within Reason: Technocratic Revolution in Mexico* (University Park: Pennsylvania State University Press, 1994).
Centeno, M. A. and P. Silva, 'The Politics of Expertise in Latin America: Introduction', in M. A. Centeno and P. Silva (eds), *The Politics of Expertise in Latin America* (New York: St Martin's, 1998).
Chalmer, D. A., M. do. C. Campello de Souza and A. A. Boron (eds), *The Right and Democracy in Latin America* (New York: Praeger, 1992).
Cline, W., *International Debt Reexamined* (Washington, DC: International Institute for Economics, 1995).
Conaghan, C. M., 'Reconsidering Jeffrey Sachs and the Bolivian Economic Experiment', in P. W. Drake (ed.), *Money Doctors, Foreign Debts, and Economic Reforms in Latin America from the 1890s to the Present* (Wilmington, DE: Scholarly Resources, 1994).
Conaghan, C. M., 'Las Estrellas de la Crisis: El Ascenso de los Economistas en la Vida Publica Peruana', *Pensamiento Iberoamericano*, 30 (1997) 177–206.
Conaghan C. M. and J. M. Malloy, *Unsettling Statecraft: Democracy and Neo-liberalism in the Central Andes* (University of Pittsburgh Press, 1994).
Currie, L., *The Role of Economic Advisers in Developing Countries* (Westport, CT: Greenwood, 1981).
De Soto, H., *The Other Path: The Invisible Revolution in the Third World* (New York: Harper & Row, 1989).
Devlin, R., *Debt and Crisis in Latin America: The Supply Side of the Story* (Princeton University Press, 1989).
Di Palma, Giuseppe, *To Craft Democracies: An Essay on Democratic Transitions* (Berkeley: University of California Press, 1990).
Dominguez, J. I., 'Technopols: Ideas and Leaders in Freeing Politics and Markets in Latin America in the 1990s', in J. I. Dominguez (ed.), *Technopols: Freeing Politics and Markets in Latin America in the 1990s* (University Park: Pennsylvania State University Press, 1997).
Drake, P. W., *The Money Doctor in the Andes: The Kemmerer Missions, 1923–1933* (Durham, NC: Duke University Press, 1989).
Drake, P. W., 'From Good Men to Good Neighbors: 1912–1932', in A. F. Lowenthal (ed.), *Exporting Democracy: The United States and Latin America* (Baltimore, MD: Johns Hopkins University Press, 1991).
Drake, P. W. (ed.), *Money Doctors, Foreign Debts, and Economic Reforms in Latin America from the 1890s to the Present* (Wilmington, DE: Scholarly Resources, 1994a).
Drake, P. W., 'Introduction: The Political Economy of Foreign Advisers and Lenders in Latin America', in P. W. Drake (ed.), *Money Doctors, Foreign Debts, and Economic Reforms in Latin America from the 1890s to the Present* (Wilmington, DE: Scholarly Resources, 1994b).
Drake, P. W., *Labor Movements and Dictatorships: The Southern Cone in Comparative Perspective* (Baltimore, MD: The Johns Hopkins University Press, 1996).
Drake, P. W., 'The International Causes of Democratization, 1974–1990', in P. W. Drake and M. D. McCubbins (eds), *The Origins of Liberty: Political and Economic Liberalization in the Modern World* (Princeton University Press, 1998).
Edwards, S., *Crisis and Reform in Latin America: From Despair to Hope* (New York: Oxford University Press, 1995).

Eichengreen, B., 'House Calls of the Money Doctor: The Kemmerer Missions to Latin America, 1917–1931', in G. Calvo, R. Findlay, P. Kouri and J. Braga de Macedo (eds), *Debt, Stabilization and Development: Essays in Memory of Carlos Diaz-Alejandro* (Oxford: Blackwell, 1989).

Feinberg, R. E., 'Comment', in J. Williamson (ed.), *The Political Economy of Policy Reform* (Washington, DC: Institute for International Economics, 1994).

Feinberg, R. E., *Summitry in the Americas: A Progress Report* (Washington, DC: Institute for International Economics, 1997).

Finnemore, M., *National Interests in International Society* (Ithaca, NY: Cornell University Press, 1996).

FitzGerald, E. V. K., 'ECLA and Formation of Latin American Economic Doctrine', in D. Rock (ed.), *Latin America in the 1940s: War and Postwar Transitions* (Berkeley: University of California Press, 1994).

Frieden, J. A., *Debt, Development and Democracy* (Princeton University Press, 1991).

Frieden, J. A. and R. Rogowski, 'The Impact of the International Economy on National Policies: An Analytical Overview', in R. O. Keohane and H. V. Milner, (eds), *Internationalization and Domestic Politics* (Cambridge University Press, 1996).

Fukayama, F., *The End of History and the Last Man* (New York: Maxwell Macmillan, 1992).

Galjart, B. and P. Silva (eds), *Designers of Development: Intellectuals and Technocrats in the Third World* (Leiden University, 1995).

Goldstein, J. and R. O. Keohane, 'Ideas and Foreign Policy: An Analytical Framework', in J. Goldstein and R. O. Keohane (eds), *Ideas and Foreign Policy: Beliefs, Institutions and Political Change* (Ithaca, NY: Cornell University Press, 1993).

Gourevitch, P. A., *Politics in Hard Times: Comparative Responses to International Economic Crises* (Ithaca, NY: Cornell University Press, 1986).

Haas, P. M., 'Introduction: Epistemic Communities and International Policy Coordination', *International Organization*, 46/1 (Winter 1992) 1–35.

Haggard, S. and S. Maxfield, 'The Political Economy of Financial Internationalization in the Developing World', in R. O. Keohane and H. V. Milner (eds), *Internationalization and Domestic Politics* (Cambridge University Press, 1996).

Haggard, S. and S. B. Webb, *Voting for Reform: Democracy, Political Liberalization, and Structural Adjustment – An Overview* (San Francisco: ICS Press, 1996).

Hall, P. A. (ed.), *The Political Power of Economic Ideas: Keynesianism Across Nations* (Princeton University Press, 1989).

Hall, P. A., 'Policy Paradigms, Social Learning and the State: The Case of Economic Policymaking in Britain', *Comparative Politics,* 25/3 (1993) 275–98.

Handelman, H. and W. Baer (eds), *Paying the Costs of Austerity in Latin America* (Boulder, CO: Westview, 1989).

Harberger, A., 'Secrets of Success: A Handful of Heroes', *American Economic Review,* 83/2 (May, 1993) 343–50.

Healy, D., *Drive to Hegemony: The United States in the Caribbean, 1898–1917* (Madison: University of Wisconsin Press, 1988).

Heller, W. B., P. Keefer and M. D. McCubbins, 'Political Structure and Economic Liberalization: Conditions and Cases from the Developing World,' in P. W. Drake and M. D. McCubbins (eds), *The Origins of Liberty: Political and Economic Liberalization in the Modern World* (Princeton University Press, 1998).

Hirschman, A. O. (ed.), *Latin American Issues: Essays and Comments* (New York: Twentieth Century Fund, 1961).

Hirschman, A. O., *Journeys Toward Progress: Studies of Economic Policy-Making in Latin America* (Westport, CT: Greenwood, 1965).

Hirschman, A. O., 'The Rise and Decline of Development Economics', in A. O. Hirschman (ed.), *Essays in Trespassing: Economics to Politics and Beyond* (Cambridge University Press, 1981).

Hirschman, A. O., 'How the Keynesian Revolution Was Exported from the United States, and Other Comments', in P. A. Hall (ed.), *The Political Power of Economic Ideas: Keynesianism across Nations* (Princeton University Press, 1989).

Huneeus, C., 'Tecnócratas y Políticos en la Política Democrática en la Argentina (1983–1995)', *Pensamiento Iberoamericano*, 30 (1997) 207–28.

Huntington, S. P., *The Third Wave: Democratization in the Late Twentieth Century* (Norman: University of Oklahoma Press, 1991).

Iglesias, E. V., *Reflections on Economic Development: Toward a New Latin American Consensus* (Washington, DC: Inter-American Development Bank, 1992).

Iglesias, E. V., 'Economic Reform: A View from Latin America', in J. Williamson (ed.), *The Political Economy of Policy Reform* (Washington, DC: Institute for International Economics, 1994).

Ikenberry, G. J., 'The International Spread of Privatization Policies: Inducements, Learning, and "Policy Bankwagoning" ', in E. N. Suleiman and J. Waterbury (eds), *The Political Economy of Public Sector Reform and Privatization* (Boulder, CO: Westview, 1990).

Ikenberry, G. J., 'Creating Yesterday's New World Order: Keynesian "New Thinking" and the Anglo-American Post-war Settlement', in J. Goldstein and R. O. Keohane (eds), *Ideas and Foreign Policy: Beliefs, Institutions and Political Change* (Ithaca, NY: Cornell University Press, 1993).

Kahler, M. (ed.), *The Politics of International Debt* (Ithaca, NY: Cornell University Press, 1986).

Kahler, M., 'External Actors and Adjustment: The Role of the IMF', in P. W. Drake (ed.), *Money Doctors, Foreign Debts, and Economic Reforms in Latin America from the 1890s to the Present* (Wilmington, DE: Scholarly Resources, 1994).

Kemmerer, E. W., 'Economic Advisory Work for Governments', *American Economic Review*, 17/1 (March 1927) 1–12.

Keohane, R. O., *After Hegemony: Cooperation and Discord in the World Political Economy* (Princeton University Press, 1984).

Killick, Tony *et al.*, *The Quest for Economic Stabilization: The IMF and The Third World* (London: Heinemann, 1984).

Kindleberger, C. P., *The World in Depression, 1929–1939* (Berkeley: University of California Press, 1973).

Kindleberger, C. P., 'Dominance and Leadership in the International Economy', *International Studies Quarterly*, 25/3 (1981) 242–54.

Krueger, A. O., *Foreign Trade Regimes and Economic Development: Liberalization Attempts and Consequences* (Cambridge, MA: Ballinger, 1978).

Kuczynski, P. P., *Latin American Debt* (Baltimore, MD: Johns Hopkins University Press, 1988).

Leftwich, A., 'Governance, the State and the Politics of Development', *Development and Change*, 25 (1994) 363–386.

Lipson, C., *Standing Guard: Protecting Foreign Capital in the Nineteenth and Twentieth Centuries* (Berkeley: University of California Press, 1985).

Loureiro, M. R., 'Los Economistas Como Elites Gobernantes. La Dirección del Plan Real', *Pensamiento Iberoamericano*, 30 (1997) 245–68.

Love, J. L., 'Economic Ideas and Ideologies in Latin America since 1930', in L. Bethell (ed.), *Cambridge History of Latin America*, vol. VI (Cambridge University Press, 1994).

Love, J. L., *Crafting the Third World: Theorizing Underdevelopment in Rumania and Brazil* (Stanford University Press, 1996).

Love, J. L. and Jacobsen, N., *Guiding the Invisible Hand: Economic Liberalism and the State in Latin American History* (New York: Praeger, 1988).

Lowenthal, A. F., *Partners in Conflict: The United States and Latin America* (Baltimore, MD: Johns Hopkins University Press, 1987).

Marichal, C., *A Century of Debt Crises in Latin America: From Independence to the Great Depression, 1820–1930* (Princeton University Press, 1989).

Markoff, J. and Montecinos, V., 'The Ubiquitous Rise of Economists', *Journal of Public Policy*, 13/1 (1993) 37–68.

Milner, H. V. and R. O. Keohane, 'Internationalization and Domestic Politics: An Introduction', in R. O. Keohane and H. V. Milner (eds), *Internationalization and Domestic Politics* (Cambridge University Press, 1996).

Montecinos, V., 'Los Economistas en la Política de Partido. La Democracía Chilena en la Era de los Mercados', *Pensamiento Iberoamericano*, 30 (1997) 135–54.

Montecinos, V., *Economists, Politics, and the State: Chile 1958–1994* (Amsterdam: CEDLA, 1998).

Mosley, P., J. Harrigan and J. Toye (eds), *Aid and Power: The World Bank and Policy-Based Lending*, 2 vols (London: Routledge, 1991).

Nelson, J. M. (ed.), *Economic Crisis and Policy Choice: The Politics of Adjustment in Developing Countries* (Princeton University Press, 1990).

Nelson, J. M., *Intricate Links: Democratization and Market Reforms in Latin America and Eastern Europe* (New Brunswick, NJ: Transaction Books, 1994).

Nelson, J. M. (ed.), *A Precarious Balance: Democracy and Economic Reforms in Latin America* (Washington, DC: Overseas Development Council, 1994).

Nelson, J. M. and S. J. Englinton, *Encouraging Democracy: What Role for Conditioned Aid?* (Washington, DC: Overseas Development Council, 1992).

Nelson, J. M. *et al.*, *Fragile Coalitions: The Politics of Economic Adjustment* (Washington, DC: Overseas Development Council, 1989).

Nylen, W. R., 'Selling Neo-liberalism: Brazil's Instituto Liberal', *Journal of Latin American Studies*, 25/2 (1993) 301–11.

O'Brien, P. and J. Roddick, *Chile: The Pinochet Decade. The Rise and Fall of the Chicago Boys* (London: Latin American Bureau, 1983).

O'Brien, T. F., *The Revolutionary Mission: American Enterprise in Latin America, 1900–1945* (Cambridge University Press, 1996).

Ocampo, J. A., 'New Economic Thinking in Latin America', *Journal of Latin American Studies*, 22/1 (February 1990) 169–81.

Odell, J., *US International Monetary Policy: Markets, Power, and Ideas as Sources of Change* (Princeton University Press, 1982).

O'Donnell, G., P. C. Schmitter and L. Whitehead (eds), *Transitions from Authoritarian Rule*, 4 vols (Baltimore, MD: Johns Hopkins University Press, 1986).

Pastor, M., *The International Monetary Fund and Latin America: Economic Stabilization and Class Conflict* (Boulder, CO: Westview, 1987).

Pinera, Jose, 'Chile', in John Williamson (ed.), *The Political Economy of Policy Reform* (Washington, DC: Institute for International Economics, 1994).

Pion-Berlin, D., *The Ideology of State Terror: Economic Doctrine and Political Repression in Argentina and Peru* (Boulder, CO: Rienner, 1989).

Przeworski, A., *Democracy and the Market: Political and Economic Reforms in Eastern Europe and Latin America* (New York: Cambridge University Press, 1991).

Puryear, J., *Thinking Politics: Intellectuals and Politics in Chile, 1973–1988* (Baltimore, MD: Johns Hopkins University Press, 1994).

Ramos, J., *Neoconservative Economics in the Southern Cone of Latin America 1973–1986* (Baltimore, MD: Johns Hopkins University Press, 1986).

Remmer, K. L., 'The Politics of Economic Stabilization: IMF Standby Programs in Latin America, 1954–84', in P. W. Drake (ed.), *Money Doctors, Foreign Debts, and Economic Reforms in Latin America from the 1890s to the Present* (Wilmington, DE: Scholarly Resources, 1994).

Rodrik, D., *Has Globalization Gone Too Far?* (Washington, DC: Institute of International Economics, 1997).

Roett, R., 'The Debt Crisis and Economic Development in Latin America', in J. Hartlyn, L. Schoultz and A. Varas (eds), *The United States and Latin America in the 1990s: Beyond the Cold War* (Chapel Hill: University of North Carolina Press, 1992).

Rosenberg, E. S., *Spreading the American Dream: American Economic and Cultural Expansion, 1890–1945* (New York: Hill & Wang, 1982).

Rosenberg, E. S. and N. L. Rosenberg, 'From Colonialism to Professionalism: The Public-Private Dynamic in United States Financial Advising, 1898–1929', *Journal of American History*, 74/1 (June 1987) 59–82.

Sachs, J. (ed.), *Developing Country Debt and the World Economy* (University of Chicago Press, 1989).

Schneider, B. R., 'Las bases materiales de la tecnocracia: La confianza de los inversores y el neo-liberalismo en América Latina', *Pensamiento Iberoamericano*, 30 (1997) 109–32.

Schoultz, L., *Beneath the United States: A History of US Policy toward Latin America* (Cambridge, MA: Harvard University Press, 1998).

Sheahan, J., *Patterns of Development in Latin America: Poverty, Repression and Economic Strategy* (Princeton University Press, 1987).

Sikkink, K., *Ideas and Institutions: Developmentalism in Brazil and Argentina* (Ithaca, NY: Cornell University Press, 1991).

Silva, E., *The State and Capital in Chile: Business Elites, Technocrats, and Market Economics* (Boulder, CO: Westview, 1996).

Smith, P. H., *Talons of the Eagle: Dynamics of US–Latin American Relations* (New York: Oxford University Press, 2000).

Smith, W. C., C. H. Acuña and E. A. Gamarra (eds), *Democracy, Markets, and Structural Reform in Contemporary Latin America: Argentina, Bolivia, Brazil, Chile, and Mexico* (New Brunswick, NJ: Transaction Books, 1994a).

Smith, W. C., C. H. Acuña and E. A. Gamarra (eds), *Latin American Political Economy in the Age of Neo-liberal Reform: Theoretical and Comparative Perspectives for the 1990s* (New Brunswick, NJ: Transaction Books, 1994b).

Snidal, D., 'The Limits of Hegemonic Stability', *International Organization*, 39/4 (Autumn 1985) 579–614.

Stallings, B., *Banker to the Third World: US Portfolio Investment in Latin America, 1900–1986* (Berkeley: University of California Press, 1987).

Stallings, B., 'International Influence on Economic Policy: Debt, Stabilization and Structural Reform', in S. Haggard and R. Kaufman (eds), *The Politics of Economic Adjustment: International Constraints, Distributive Conflicts and the State* (Princeton University Press, 1992).

Stallings, B. and R. Kaufman (eds), *Debt and Democracy in Latin America* (Boulder, CO: Westview Press, 1989).

Thorp, R. (ed.), *Latin America in the 1930s: The Role of the Periphery in World Crisis* (London: Macmillan, 1984).

Thorp, R. and L. Whitehead (eds), *Latin American Debt and the Adjustment Crisis* (Pittsburgh University Press, 1987).

Tulchin, J., *The Aftermath of War: World War I and US Policy toward Latin America* (New York University Press, 1971).

Urrutia, M., 'Colombia', in J. Williamson, *The Political Economy of Policy Reform* (Washington, DC: Institute for International Economics, 1994).

Valdés, J. G., *Pinochet's Economists: The Chicago School in Chile* (New York: Cambridge University Press, 1995).

Van Dijck, P., 'The World Bank and the Transformation of Latin American Society', in M. A. Centeno and P. Silva (eds), *The Politics of Expertise in Latin America* (New York: St Martin's, 1998).

Varas, A., 'Latin America: Toward a New Reliance on the Market', in B. Stallings (ed.), *Global Change, Regional Response: The New International Context of Development* (Cambridge University Press, 1995).

Vilas, C. M., 'Economic Restructuring, Neo-liberal Reforms, and the Working Class in Latin America', in S. Halebsky and R. L. Harris (eds), *Capital, Power, and Inequality in Latin America* (Boulder, CO: Westview, 1995).

Weeks, J., 'The Contemporary Latin American Economies: Neoliberal Reconstruction', in S. Halebsky and R. L. Harris (eds), *Capital, Power, and Inequality in Latin America* (Boulder, CO: Westview, 1995).

Williams, W. A., *The Tragedy of American Diplomacy* (New York: Delta, 1962).

Williams, D. and T. Young, 'Governance, the World Bank and Liberal Theory', *Political Studies*, 42/1 (March 1994) 84–100.

Williamson, J., *IMF Conditionality* (Washington, DC: Institute for International Economics, 1983).

Williamson, J., 'Introduction', in J. Williamson (ed.), *Latin American Adjustment: How Much Has Happened?* (Washington, DC: Institute for International Economics, 1990a).

Williamson, J., 'What Washington Means by Policy Reform', in J. Williamson (ed.), *Latin American Adjustment: How Much Has Happened?* (Washington, DC: Institute for International Economics, 1990b).

Williamson, J., 'The Progress of Policy Reform in Latin America', in J. Williamson (ed.), *Latin American Adjustment: How Much Has Happened?* (Washington, DC: Institute for International Economics, 1990c).

Williamson, J. (ed.), *The Political Economy of Policy Reform* (Washington, DC: Institute for International Economics, 1994).

5
The Conflict of Economic Doctrines in Latin America

Valpy FitzGerald

> Today, in spite of the sophisticated analytical techniques, and often highly esoteric specialisms characterizing late twentieth-century economic science, the primary object of the exercise [economics] remains the same as it was in the seventeenth century: to provide national administrators and their responsible agents with the objective knowledge needed to design and implement efficient economic policies. (Deane 1989:v)

> If they were consistent enough to constitute a system, that system might be called the popular political economy. What I first propose to show is that we have to deal with ideas centuries old, on which the thought of professional economists has never made any permanent impression, except, perhaps, in Great Britain, and that in the every-day applications of purely economic theory our public thought, our legislation, and even our popular economic nomenclature are what they would have been if Smith, Ricardo, and Mill had never lived, and if such a term of political economy had never been known. (Newcomb 1893:377)

Introduction

The nature of the relationship between national development and international markets on the one hand, and between economic growth and social welfare on the other, has traditionally been – and continues to be – central to political discourse in Latin America in the twentieth century.[1] Systems of ideas on these topics can be understood as economic *doctrines* to the extent that they constitute 'a body or system of principles ... which is laid down as true concerning a particular department of knowledge' in both the positive sense of Burke's doctrine of the equality of all men, and the normative sense of the Monroe doctrine.[2] These two senses are combined in economic doctrines, because the desire to influence state management of the national economy has always driven economic thought.

Economic doctrine has a central role to play in societies undergoing indus-trialization. As Adam Smith argued, this is the proper role of political econ-omy because the strength and survival of the state itself depends on economic success.[3] By extension, the same can be said of critics of state policies who rely upon an alternative economic doctrine in order to legit-imize their critique and – at least in principle – inform their alternative strat-egy, were they to gain power. In developing countries, the state has a high degree of relative autonomy from civil society owing to both the underde-velopment of the latter and the need to negotiate insertion to the world economy, so economic doctrine has a substantive role in guiding the actions of both state managers and international agencies. In consequence, it is nec-essary to attempt to distinguish, as Gerschenkron does, between the con-struction of 'doctrine as knowledge' from its subsequent use by political actors as ideological discourse – while remembering that this discourse 'reveals the impact of a doctrine but also disguises its perversion, if not aban-donment' (Gerschenkron 1969:2).

The most notable 'conflict of economic doctrines' of the postwar years in Latin America is widely recognized to be the rise of 'developmentalism' (*desarollismo*) as the basis for state-led national industrialization; and its sub-sequent demise in the face of neo-liberalism based on a reduced role of the state and further integration into world markets. This resolution has even been presented as an instance of paradigm shift in economic science, where the former has been superseded by the latter on the basis of both theoretical superiority and empirical evidence, but above all on its proven efficacy in practice as the basis for government policy.[4] However, I argue that the con-flict did not result in a complete victory to either side at the beginning or the end of the period. Central banks (and the IMF) never accepted structuralism in the postwar decades, while 'line' ministries of agriculture and industry (and the UN agencies) have not abandoned structuralism. Moreover, these two doctrines are essentially those of state managers (and their international allies) and not those of Latin American civil society. Domestic business groups and popular opposition movements, meanwhile, have held more radical views of their own with a distinct anti-state bias – again, with specific international dimensions.

In this chapter, I attempt to address this persistently contested nature of economic doctrine in Latin America.[5] In the second section, I examine the changing relationship between 'orthodox economics' and state strategy, where the doctrine of 'neo-liberalism' has clearly regained its traditional dominance as official discourse in the form of market opening, fiscal retrench-ment and monetary orthodoxy. These 'sound economic fundamentals' are associated with the hegemony of central banks, treasury ministries and international institutions over state policy. Nonetheless, the 'old' doctrine of 'developmentalism' is still widely held within sectoral agencies and local administrations. In the third section, I turn to what can be called 'popular economics', which while not always forming a formally consistent body of ideas, does clearly influence non-state actors ranging from trades unions and NGOs to business associations. The content of this latter doctrine is extremely diverse, ranging from mercantilism to socialism, but shares a common commitment to public action in order to overcome market failures.

In each of these sections, the role of universities and international agencies as institutions that transmit economic doctrine is identified. In the fourth section, I use these findings to locate the Latin American experience within a wider debate on the way in which economic doctrines such as Keynesianism are accepted (and later rejected), on the one hand; and the persistence of a systematic gap between the ideas of professional economists (which inform official doctrine) and those of the general public, on the other. The former is used to explain the current primacy of neo-liberal thought, and the latter the persistence of more heterodox ideas. The fifth section concludes by suggesting that the persistent dichotomy of economic doctrine can be explained only by the changing relative influence of the respective representative institutions, transmission mechanisms and external linkages.

Orthodox economics and state strategy

The main channel for the transmission and adoption of economic doctrine in Latin America is the state itself, and in particular 'state managers'. Economic policy is made by key 'technocratic' politicians, supported by teams of advisers, ministers, directors-general and so on who have little or no political base of their own in a presidential system. In the past, economic policy-makers were lawyers or engineers by profession, but increasingly they have received a neo-classical economics education at US universities. It is their technical training that forms part of their political legitimacy as *técnicos*.

The supports for these economic policy-makers are more or less the same now as previously – the political party (and more specifically the president) in power, major domestic economic groups, and international financial institutions. These formed the basis of support for the industrialization strategy in the three postwar decades, which supported government expenditure, import-substitution and state enterprise; and subsequently for the present globalization strategy based on privatization, trade liberalization and deregulation. The change in economic doctrine, therefore, must to a great extent reflect changes in the influence of these three actors.

Modern Latin American political parties do not appear to be the main channels for economic doctrine, let alone originators. This was not the case in the past, when parties represented specific economic interests – such as landowners or trades unions – or when radical parties proposed major changes such as land reform or even communism. Clearly economic failure is a major source of electoral defeat, although major devaluations and hyperinflation seem to be more fatal than low growth or high unemployment. By extension, elections are frequently won by candidates with a reputation (or an image) of skills in economic management. However, the details of economic policy, let alone a doctrine, do not usually form part of the electoral platform – rather the promise to 'depoliticize' the economy, rely on the *técnicos*, banish corruption and enforce the rule of law.[6]

The domestic business lobby in Latin America has traditionally been relatively weak in the sense that the *ilustrados* in power can impose reform measures based on economic doctrines of efficiency (whether forced industrialization or trade liberalization) with a far greater degree of freedom than in Europe, let alone the United States. This is true despite the ability of business groups to lobby successfully for specific government support in the form of tariff protection, tax exemption or changes in labour or environmental legislation. It continues even though major national corporate groups in the region are becoming multinational – particularly in sectors such as banking, energy, and telecommunications – and developing a strong view on economic policy as a whole as well as their own sectoral needs.

The major change in doctrines in the last half-century has thus been associated with a shift in the strategy of state managers' long-term goal of economic modernization and international competitiveness. This has involved a changing balance *within* central government, and changing international institutional alliances as well. Radical economic reforms are not supported by much empirical evidence, nor are they the outcome of complex political negotiation with domestic lobbies. Rather, they are the result of shifts of doctrine – often in response to external shocks – but always appealing to universal ideas of economic modernity.

In the immediate postwar period (and in some cases since the Depression[7]), line ministries such as industry and agriculture, foreign trade ministries and even ministries of planning (often attached to the presidency) had a predominant role in economic reform.[8] They led an attempt to transform the structure of the national economy in order to support rapid industrialization in what were regarded as hostile world markets. Under these circumstances, structuralist economic doctrine naturally appealed strongly to state managers.

This doctrine originated in Central Europe from the classical political economy tradition, but was developed by ECLA and rapidly spread by the *cepalinos* through Latin America.[9] It was a state doctrine *par excellence* and provided the rationale for tariff protection, public investment, regional integration and agrarian reform (Rodriguez 1980). There was a considerable degree of international support for this approach, and not only from UN agencies themselves. Multinational enterprises were keen to invest behind tariff barriers, although not so enthusiastic about technology transfer requirements. Most OECD governments shared similar approaches to industrialization in the postwar period, while the World Bank supported import-substitution as the basis for development until 1980. Washington even made the establishment of a planning agency a condition for economic assistance under the *Punta de Este* agreement in 1961.

However, it is important not to overestimate the duration or depth of the hegemony of developmentalist doctrine. Key institutions such as the central banks (and IMF) remained unconvinced. At most, import-substitution as a strategy was dominant in the region until the mid 1960s, when policy shifted towards export promotion. Nevertheless, state promotion of heavy industry persisted through the 1970s – although they were serious proposi-tions only in the larger economies such as Brazil and Mexico. These last attempts to build national capitalism were based on the example of East Asia rather than anything related to socialism. It was, of course, the debt crisis that brought an end to structuralist doctrine.

In marked contrast, ministries of finance appear to have been subordi-nated in the immediate postwar decades. Indeed, these were the very agen-cies that ran the large fiscal deficits and contracted the enormous external debts. They appear to have had little doctrine of their own – certainly not Keynesianism in any meaningful form. However, after the debt crisis, finance ministries emerged as the command centres of economic reform. In alliance with the IMF, they pushed through stabilization policies based on government expenditure cuts and large nominal devaluations, followed by privatization of state-owned enterprises. Trade liberalization was pushed through by ministries of finance or by ministries of foreign trade under their control. Finally, the development of a domestic capital market as a source of government borrowing (to replace external debt) and the subsequent capital account liberalization (to encourage foreign purchase of government paper) were almost always treasury initiatives.

Ministries of finance were increasingly led by charismatic *técnicos* with domestic and international standing as a 'strong pair of hands'.[10] In the 1980s an ability to negotiate with foreign creditors was crucial, and in the 1990s an ability to convince foreign portfolio investors was equally important. The traditional virtues of the free market and fiscal retrenchment were reinforced by a commitment to high real interest rates, stable nominal exchange rates, and privatization flotations in order to reduce the state's net liability posi-tion. Membership of the GATT/WTO locked in the free-trade policies that had been a central theme in doctrinal conflict since Independence. The intellectual underpinning for this new doctrine was supplied by the IMF and World Bank, making good use of recent advances in the economic theories of institutions, trade and expectations – but above all of open-economy macroeconomics. This 'technical' discourse was particularly important because it permitted the presentation of new policies as both an expression of the findings of 'modern economics' and a manifestation of the 'logic of the world market'.[11]

Of course, for the Latin American elite, study in the United States itself has become essential. Originally confined to postgraduate training, the metropolitan education of the Latin American elite has progressed through undergraduate to secondary schooling. In this way, the US economics profession has extended its influence on Latin American economic doctrine. This indirect influence in promoting a set of values through textbooks and teaching methods was also an explicit professional mission in western Europe and Japan after the war, and more recently in Eastern Europe (Bernstein 1999).

In contrast to the changing fortunes of Latin American economic ministries, the central banks have maintained a relatively steady course. The role of Latin American central banks in developing, transmitting and reconciling ideas on monetary policy in particular and economic analysis in general is often underestimated. There exists a dense web of relationships between these banks, reinforced by the Centro de Estudios Monetarios Latínamericos (CEMLA), which was founded in 1952. Central bank staff members share a similar outlook, and most have been trained by the IMF at some point in their career.[12] Their economic research departments are in many cases the best in the country – and in the small countries, often the only one. They are often the main source of economic statistics and macroeconomic analysis. The explicit links between Latin American central banks and the IMF are well known, and in some cases there have been permanent IMF offices within the institution. There is also some evidence of close relationships with the US Federal Reserve, albeit only in terms of consultations.[13]

Last, but not least, central banks have maintained a strong tradition of commitment to 'sound money' – monetary prudence, commitment to a strong reserve position, and a low external debt – even when they have been subject to expansionary ministers of finance.[14] In contrast to monetary stabilization, central banks have not initiated structural adjustment and state reform – which have been designed and implemented by ministries of finance. In consequence, they do not appear to have evolved new doctrines in this respect. The modern tendency to grant autonomy to central banks is thus the apotheosis of their doctrine of sound money, rather than a new doctrine as such.

Popular economics and non-state actors

Nonetheless, the developmentalist doctrine is still alive within the Latin American state, albeit far from dominant. It can be found in ministries of industry (particularly in attempts to construct a national technology system), and above all in regional governments, where moves towards administrative decentralization have revived interest in regional planning. Social services ministries maintain doctrine based on 'human development', at least among the technicians if not at the ministerial level. This is partly because of the claims of their constituencies, but also because of the need of these *funcionarios*[15] to justify their own role in opposition to that of treasury officials and others determined to reduce the activities (and the budget) of their ministries and agencies. Developmentalist doctrine is still supported by UN agencies such as the UNDP, UNIDO, FAO and UNICEF, by many bilateral aid agencies influential in the poorer Latin American economies, and increasingly by international NGOs.

In marked contrast, the persistence of 'popular'[16] economic doctrine in Latin America is little discussed and even less researched. Two skeins should be distinguished, which I shall term 'left' and 'right' popular economics. The former is broadly identified with NGOs, trades unions and both urban and rural social movements. The latter skein is made up of business groups (especially small business) and many professional associations. In both cases, their economic doctrine has two characteristics: first, it is broadly opposed to state management 'from above'; and second, it tends to be dismissed by professional economists as 'not serious'.

'Left popular' economic doctrine, as might be expected, is mainly concerned with income distribution, employment and poverty reduction, although it also contains a strong element of critique of capitalist society and international dependency theory. To some extent, this *economía popular* derives its doctrine from a prewar tradition of socialist Marxism (stretching back to Mariátegui) (Kay 1989). It also derives elements of its analysis (particularly of trade and technology issues) from the Latin American structuralist version of development economics pioneered by ECLA. The decline of trades unions and of left-wing political parties has not led to the disappearance of this tradition: it has been taken up by the new 'social movements' and NGOs. It is also expressed in practice through cooperatives, microcredit schemes and educational projects at the grassroots level.

Liberation theology has made a significant input to this popular economics, to some extent substituting for traditional socialist views derived from Marxism in the earlier part of the century. It contains a strong critique of capitalism (and dependency in particular) from the point of view of both redistributive justice and social marginalization derived from biblical notions of 'life' (Ellacuría and Sobrino 1990) – rather than economic analysis as such (FitzGerald 1999a). It is used in advocacy against structural adjustment and privatization as a burden on the poor, and in support of international objectives such as debt cancellation. The international connection to progressive church groups abroad is clear enough, although the opposition of both the Catholic hierarchy and Protestant sects limits the domestic impact.

Further inputs have been provided by environmental and feminist critiques of capitalism on the one hand, and the focus on basic needs provision and human development in the international aid discourse on the other. The growth of NGOs within Latin America, which have largely filled the space abandoned by labour unions and socialist parties, has steadily expanded the channel for this doctrine. These NGOs have strong international linkages, depending in many cases for financial and intellectual resources on partner NGOs in developed countries, and particularly the United States and northern Europe.

'Right popular' economic doctrine is even more diffuse and inchoate, but none the less influential for that. Small businessmen throughout Latin America seem libertarian to a degree, claiming that the state is sunk in a sea of bureaucratic corruption and that free markets are the only solution. Strong opposition to taxation is derived not just from direct self-interest, but also from opposition to government expenditure *per se*. Their Smithian opposition to monopoly often extends to a critique of multinational corporations as well as of state enterprise. Another dimension of this 'right populism' is an almost mystical belief in the virtues of small enterprises and micro-credit as a means of organizing the Latin American economy so as to provide employment, apply 'appropriate technology' and reduce reliance on imports. This does not prevent them, of course, from demanding tariff protection and fiscal subsidies for their own sector at every available opportunity.

However, scholastic concepts of 'unfair competition' and 'just price' are also widespread, as is a strong belief in paternalistic labour relations along Christian Democrat (*Rerum Novarum*) lines. Thus, right populism often enjoys the support of the Catholic hierarchy. Arguments for the protection of particular sectors are often combined with exhortations about 'national competitiveness' to be based on skills and enterprise.[17] Chambers of commerce express these views vociferously, particularly in the Latin American newspapers. The external linkages of these channels for doctrine include both foreign chambers of commerce and international associations such as the Rotarians. It would appear that the much of the work of US foundations – which are generally pro-business – has been effectively geared to the same end (Balakrishnan and Grown 1999).

These small-business groups have been swelled by the process of informalization of the Latin American economy consequent upon structural adjustment. Their views cannot be subsumed under the neo-liberal doctrine of the dominant group of state managers – owing to their deep distrust of state action and growing opposition to globalization. An important expression of this distrust is the process of dollarization of the Latin American economies, which has been promoted autonomously by the private sector as a response to hyperinflation and exchange rate instability.[18] The businessman's tendency to hold assets in dollars, to lend only in dollars, and to mark prices to the exchange rate is widespread and independent of government policy. In an extreme case such as that of Ecuador, dollarization has been forced on the state as a means of severely constraining government power in the economy.

The persistence of this heterodox tradition is explained not only by the interests of different social groups, but also by the heterogeneous nature of economics education in Latin America. Traditionally, economics was taught in Latin American law schools, and thus took account of the institutional context of the country in question, along with courses in politics and philosophy. However, in the postwar period, independent faculties of economics were established and a division emerged between neo-classical and 'heterodox' schools of thought.[19] Broadly speaking, economics in the Universidad Nacional tended to range from Marxism to structuralism, and in many countries this tradition is still strong. The international linkages of these faculties appear to have included both France and Russia. Although they have become somewhat isolated over time, their influence on generations of junior civil servants cannot be underestimated. In contrast, private universities have naturally tended to teach neo-classical economics, although Catholic universities have given safe haven to heterodox economists. It is the economics faculties of these private universities that have taught the new generation of state managers; their strong links to US universities provide an effective mechanism for the transmission of economic doctrine.

Moreover, a considerable amount of economic theory is taught outside the faculties of economics. Business schools are probably as, if not more, important than economics faculties as transmitters of economic doctrine. Their teaching is not precisely neo-classical economics[20] and it is oriented to those who will work in large rather than small companies. Nonetheless, an increasing proportion of state managers is trained in this way, which probably contributes to the spread of managerialism in the public sector. The links between Latin American and US business schools are strong; many of the former are subsidiaries of (or franchised by) the latter. Textbooks and teaching methods of US schools are explicitly copied in Latin America; indeed, this is their strongest selling point.

Business schools apart, economic doctrine is also transmitted through other social science faculties.[21] Departments of geography and politics in particular provide a critical analysis of capitalism in general and international economic relations in particular. Radical economic geography is particularly attractive to regional administrations (and the universities they support), where there is logically a considerable resentment of the neo-liberal policies of the national government. Moreover, this is also true of geography faculties in the United States and Europe, which continue to teach 'radical' economics.[22] Interest in radical economic ideas on labour and gender is naturally strong in faculties of sociology, where post-modern ideas are also antithetical to the Newtonian pretensions of neo-classical theory. Faculties of history, ecology and even theology also have a role to play in transmitting heterodox economic doctrine.

Finally, it should be remembered that though the heterodox economic doctrines discussed above have their origins in the United States and Europe, they have also made their way back to the metropolis considerably modified if not mutated. Perhaps the most celebrated is the effect of the structuralist ideas of ECLA on the development economics debate, and of the idea of dependency on international relations theory (Cardoso 1977). The *cepalino* logic of import-substitution, supply-side inflation theories and technological progress were all adsorbed by mainstream development economists in the 1960s, and were taken up by most international organizations. Development sociologists, world system theorists and international political economists – particularly in the United States – took up the notion of dependency. Indeed, it could be argued that these ideas now have as much, if not more, currency outside Latin America than within the region.

Latin American popular economics of the left has enjoyed a considerable international influence, particularly in developing countries, or to be more precise, among NGOs and international NGOs working 'in the field'. Liberation theology influences not only church groups but also international movements as diverse as debt reduction (the Jubilee Campaign) and fair trade movements. More broadly, the influence of 'new social movements' in Latin America on grassroots organization worldwide has been accelerated by the internet, reaching out to threaten the WTO in Seattle and the World Bank in Prague. In contrast, the populism of the right as developed in Latin America has had less international impact.

The adoption and persistence of economic doctrine

My argument so far might appear to suggest that the changing influence of these doctrines in general, and the relative success of neo-liberalism in particular, may have as much to do with the shifting importance of the channels themselves (or rather, the groups they reflect), as with the economics content of the doctrines as such. However, the relative efficacy of the doctrines themselves in explaining the relationship with the changing world economy, and in justifying a realistic policy, is also relevant to their degree of political acceptance. The aim of the dominant doctrine at any one time, of course, is to convince society as a whole that this is the objective, scientific truth – or at least that 'there is no alternative'. This was the claim of structuralism in the immediate postwar decades, as well as the neo-classical economics that displaced it.

Hall suggests that a new system of economic ideas will only take hold in a society when there is a clear need for them, and when there is a clear and congruent political dimension (Hall 1989). He identifies four specific factors that influenced the adoption of Keynesian policy by most industrial countries in the postwar decades: the orientation of the governing party, the structure of the state and state–society relations, the pattern of political discourse, and the exogenous shock of the war itself. Progressive parties tended to commit to full employment and the welfare state, while obliging subsequent conservative governments to continue them. The public administration was capable of implementing reflationary policies, and was supported in its social expenditure by bodies such as trades unions. The pattern of political discourse ranged from avoidance of depression to fear of communism. And finally, the experience of war itself had legitimized economic planning and welfare provision.

The decline of Keynesian economic ideas as the dominant form of economic doctrine in industrialized countries can be attributed to shifts on these four points. Political parties moved to the right, partly because of the failure of progressive governments to cope with the inflationary consequences of full employment – in other words, with the consequences of the success of Keynesian economic ideas. The nature of state–society relations changed as the corporate sector grew in size and strength, while trades unions were weakened by the technological decline of basic industries. Political discourse shifted towards a critique of bureaucracy and the promotion of the virtues of private property as the basis of liberty. Finally, the challenge of war was replaced by the challenge of globalization, and the need for industrial competitiveness and flexible production.

The parallels with the rise of structuralism in Latin America are not difficult to identify. The orientation of the governing parties did not generally shift to the left in the postwar period, but did become more nationalist, supporting state-led industrialization. The structure of state–society relations was affected by the strength of trades unions in some cases, but as I have argued above, it was the relative autonomy of state managers, rather than their competence, which determined economic policy. Political discourse in Latin America was dominated by the need to overcome backwardness rather than full employment as such, but to some extent the need to create jobs (even by land distribution) in order to forestall communism was also present. Although Latin America had not participated directly in the war, the experience of relative isolation from the world economy had stimulated government intervention in the economy too.

The decline of structuralism mirrors the fall from grace of Keynesianism, but not exactly. Political parties of both left and right moved towards market-based policies, led by authoritarian Chile and followed by a succession of governments engaged in the transition to democracy. In a sense, economic policy became ostensibly 'depoliticized' as the *técnicos* encouraged the shift towards autonomous central banks, privatized public utilities, free-trade treaties, and legislative fiscal and currency rules. However, external debt and currency collapse[23] did become central to political discourse, displacing concerns over industrial progress and poverty. The nature of state–society relations changed, as the corporate sector became transnationalized, while trades unions were weakened by the informalization of labour markets and successive stabilization programmes. The capacity of the state to promote industrialization was in doubt, while the new doctrine was predicated precisely on the incapacity of governments to manage the economy. Finally, the principles of structural adjustment replaced those of development planning as a means of coping with globalization.

An additional factor in the Latin American case, of course, is the fact that the United States as the dominant power in region has always exercised a major influence on the economic doctrines adopted by Latin American governments – both by example and through the conditions for financial support. Before World War II, the US economic model and its interests in the region both underpinned a pre-Keynesian economic doctrine based on the classical principles of the gold standard, independent central banks, balanced and reduced government budgets, efficient courts and customs, free trade, open investment and sustainable debt.[24] However, as pointed out above, there was considerable US support for Latin American developmentalism in the postwar period. This was derived in part from Keynesian policy in the United States itself,[25] but also from the transfer of lessons learned from counter-insurgency wars in Asia that seemed to imply that poverty reduction, and the creation of employment and a domestic middle class would act as bulwarks against communism. The geopolitical strategy of successive US administrations has thus always contained a strong element of economic reform, a key aspect of which has been the propagation of the corresponding economic doctrine.

However, the sort of economic reform espoused by Washington changed radically in the early 1980s, as the cold war drew to a close. The emphasis shifted towards trade openness, financial liberalization and utilities privatization. Institutional leadership shifted from the State Department and USAID towards the Department of Commerce and the US Treasury. The Treasury strengthened its links with its Latin American counterparts and began to intervene more actively through the Bretton Woods institutions, which also strengthened the hand of reforming ministers of finance. Moreover, debt renegotiations, particularly for the larger Latin American economies, involved the solvency of US banks and were thus of domestic policy concern to Washington. Successive treasury secretaries became directly concerned with the debt problem in the 1980s,[26] and were subsequently to steer the rescue operations after financial liberalization in the 1990s.

These factors are more than sufficient to explain the shift in the official doctrine of the Latin American state. What they do not explain is the persistence of heterodox ideas that I have stressed above. This is not just a question of 'backwardness' because divergence between the views of professional economists and those of the general public is also a characteristic of advanced industrial countries such as the United States itself. Reports on survey data for the United States indicate that

> for example, economists are vastly more likely [than the general public] to see foreign trade and downsizing as economically beneficial, accept supply-and-demand rather than monopolistic explanations of price changes, and believe living standards have and will continue to increase. (Caplan 2002:433)[27]

This divergence cannot be explained by level of education, class or political affiliation of the respondents – it is a general characteristic of the 'lay' public. Nor does this gap between economic beliefs and economic theory correspond to the usual model of information diffusion, where more knowledge reduces the dispersion of opinion but not the mean (Walstad 1996). It is no surprise, perhaps, that popular economic doctrine tends to be disregarded by social scientists.[28]

However, in cases of key economic policy decisions – such as the NAFTA debate in the early 1990s – political discourse and decision-making pass rapidly from the hands of technical economists to popular concerns even in the United States. This is partly because technical economics does not produce a clear answer and economists as professionals are inevitably reduced to rhetoric, while politicians can no longer refer to market logic and are reduced to calls to the national interest (Klamer and Meehan 1999). Such popular views are widely present throughout Latin America among similar civil-society groups. Popular economics does seem to reflect people's life experiences and should be considered as a valid discourse in its own right – if only as a means of making sense of economic life as actually experienced (Amariglio and Ruccio 1999).

A further factor may be the nature of the situation faced by Latin American governments attempting to manage semi-industrialized economies on the periphery of world markets. As a consequence, most political leaders in the region (whether of the left or the right) are still fundamentally *mercantilist* in their approach to such varied topics such as exchange parities, trade negotiations, labour skills, population size and national money. In the doctrine that preceded what we now call classical political economy, the state was both the subject and object of mercantilist economic policy, and in its historical setting, was an agent of unification. How to create a strong and wealthy state was the issue, rather than the wealth and freedom of individuals as in Smith, through domestic market protection, monetary and reserves policy, business and industry regulation, and defence and foreign market access (Heckscher 1934).[29] This problematic remains in Latin America today.

Further, the study of the origins of modern political economy indicates that there is a moral or ethical dimension to politics that may explain the persistence of non-orthodox economic ideas. Initially the debate between mercantilists and free-traders in seventeenth-century Britain had been won by the 'modernizers'. However, in the context of European war and chronic unemployment, protection was successfully presented as a *moral* policy, whereas the free-traders had no equivalent political vision.[30] Adam Smith's successful reversal of the policy debate was thus based mainly not on his new economic principles, but rather on his restatement of free trade as a logical derivative of commutative justice (Fitzgibbon 1995). In this context, the attempts by the many neo-liberal governments (supported by the

World Bank and IADB) to include popular concepts of poverty reduction and small-enterprise promotion in their market-based economic strategies might well be regarded as an attempt to capture the moral high ground of social equity currently still held by popular economics in Latin America.

Conclusion

The notion – widely shared by supporters and critics of neo-liberalism – that 'modern economics' has triumphed over 'old developmentalism' is thus far too simplistic. Within the Latin American state itself, distinct economic doctrines are held: the orthodox views of central banks and ministries of finance supported by the Bretton Woods institutions on the one hand; and the heterodox views of the line ministries and United Nations agencies, the latter still espousing state-led industrialization, on the other. In civil society proper, large business groups and much of the media form a channel for economic orthodoxy, while trades unions and NGOs form a channel for heterodox views. Both enjoy their own international support.

Two competing popular economic doctrines are current in Latin American civil society. They are distinct from the two state doctrines and are less formally articulated, but are nonetheless influential. The first is 'popular economics of the left' the doctrine of associated with radical theologians and NGOs concerned with poverty elimination and national independence. The second is the more ambiguous but nonetheless pervasive doctrine of 'popular economics of the right', concerned with reducing bureaucratic control of the economy and ultimately the rejection of national money.

The role of Latin American and international universities in the teaching of these rival economic doctrines is very different in economics faculties as such, and related faculties such as business, law and sociology. However, the acceptance of any one economic doctrine, and the presence of 'superseded' doctrines, depends not only on the educational system. Nor does the experience of industrial democracies indicate that the orientation of the governing party is sufficient explanation. Rather, the nature of the state and state–society relations, the structure of political discourse and major external shocks are key explicators of changes in economic beliefs. Indeed, popular economics seems to be as persistent in the United States as in Latin America.

In sum, my main argument in this chapter is that economic doctrine in Latin America is more diverse than is usually recognized, and that its constituent elements are remarkably resistant. This is particularly true of doctrines that are *not* the dominant orthodoxy at any one point in time. Possible explanations of the changing fortunes of these doctrines go well beyond their relative efficacy in practice. This coexistence is partly a question of the complex nature of economic reality itself, but it is also the case that these doctrines reflect the interest of different social groups, their corresponding institutions, and their international 'partners'.

However, it may well be that the process of globalization has transformed the terms of reference for national or even regional economic doctrine. Policy debate in Latin America in the latter half of the twentieth century focused on the best way to accommodate the national economy and society to the exogenous dynamic of the world market. It has also had to accommodate to successive economic crises and the need for assistance from Washington to resolve them. The contrast with Asia, where developmentalism and industrialization are still the economic doctrines of the state and much of civil society, only serves to underline this point. It is now becoming clear that the central issue of economic doctrine in Latin America is the institutional basis of the world economy itself.

Notes

1. This chapter focuses on recent decades, but clearly much the same debate has been going on since Independence, if not before.
2. Both these are cited as illustrations of this definition in the *Oxford English Dictionary*.
3. 'Smith was very much concerned with the survival of political states; and although he is supposed to have replaced moral and political speculations with economic theory, his economic theories were really intended to advance this fundamentally political objective' (FitzGibbon 1995:v).
4. See, for instance Edwards (1995). This book reflects the 'high tide' of optimism about the virtues of economic liberalization in Latin America.
5. I am well aware of the dangers of generalizing about the whole region, but there does seem to be sufficient similarity of economic doctrines between them to do so – even though the balance of forces and timing of the debate clearly differ widely. This chapter does not refer to anti-capitalist regimes such as Cuba since 1959, or the radical interludes in Chile and Nicaragua; but even in these very different contexts of geopolitical and social conflict, the debate revolves around similar themes.
6. There is a strong contrast here with platforms in the United States or Europe, where tax proposals, for instance, are key commitments.
7. See the case studies in Thorp (1984) for the inter-war origins of industrialization policy.
8. The case of Mexico is instructive: as late as 1978, the Secretaría de Hacienda was split to provide a Secretaría de Hacienda y Crédito Publico dealing with taxation and debt, and a separate Secretaría de Programación y Presupuesto to handle national planning and the government expenditure.
9. See FitzGerald (1994) for the origins of the doctrine, FitzGerald (1998) for a discussion of its evolution and FitzGerald (2000) for the technical details of *cepalino* industrialization.
10. Although figures such as Simonsen in Brazil and Ortíz Mena in Mexico had enjoyed great standing in earlier decades, they were not autonomous political actors.
11. In other words, the 'TINA (there is no alternative) Factor'.
12. Central banks in Latin America have traditionally been a career 'open to all talents', recruiting bright young staff from all social classes, promoting by

technical ability, offering lifetime employment and being largely immune to political appointments. In this (and in their strong *esprit de corps*), there are interesting parallels with the church and the army.

13. Although in the case of Mexico, this was of little avail in the 1994–95 crisis when there was a fatal lack of coordination between the Banco de Mexico and the Federal Reserve.

14. In passing, it is worth remembering that Prebisch himself retained a conservative position on monetary affairs, remaining unconvinced by structuralist explanations of inflation in terms of supply bottlenecks and mark-up pricing behaviour (FitzGerald 1994).

15. From the French *fonctionnaire*: the contrast with the English 'civil servant' and the American 'federal employee' raises an interesting semiotic question.

16. I deliberately use the term 'popular' rather than 'populist'; the latter has pejorative overtones and is used in this way by Dornbusch and Edwards (1994).

17. Which Krugman (1994) has appositely titled 'airport economics'.

18. I develop this argument further in FitzGerald (1999b).

19. For some reason, these faculties are known as *ciencias económicas*, a claim that even US faculties do not make, although faculties of political science do exist.

20. It contains too much realism about markets, for a start.

21. Microeconomics is also taught in engineering schools, but this is generally limited to project appraisal.

22. I am indebted for this point to Andy Hurrell.

23. The result of fiscal problems rather than import-substitution (FitzGerald 2000).

24. As is shown by the Kemmerer missions between 1923 and 1933, on which see Drake (1989).

25. On which see Hall (1989).

26. Which is why the Latin American secondary debt market is based on Brady Bonds and not 'Camdessus Bonds', of course.

27. See also Blendon *et al.* (1997), who report similar findings, with most members of the US public believing that inflation is caused by the speculative activities of large firms, and that free trade causes job losses, for example.

28. Even the leading post-modern analyst of economic discourse compares it to astrology (McCloskey 1994).

29. In a reference to contemporary inter-war Europe, he observes, 'even to-day – or perhaps one should say once again today – popular ideas in *this* respect are in the main mercantilist. To study this special aspect of mercantilism is thus to deal with the rise of an outlook which is still prevalent, at least among layman' (p. 26).

30. 'The English ruling class swiftly closed ranks behind a program to create employment, protect English industry, capture lost European markets in North and South America, and coerce the lower class through the work provisions of the Poor Laws' (Appleby 1978:277).

References

Appleby, J. O., *Economic Thought and Ideology in Seventeenth Century England* (Princeton University Press, 1978).

Amariglio J. and D. F. Ruccio, 'The Transgressive Knowledge of "Ersatz" Economics', in R. F. Garnett (ed.), *What Do Economists Know?* (London: Routledge, 1999).

Balakrishnan, R. and C. Grown, 'Foundations and Economic Knowledge', in R. F. Garnett (ed.), *What Do Economists Know?* (London: Routledge, 1999).

Bernstein, M. L., 'Economic Knowledge, Professional Authority and the State: The Case of American Economics During and After World War II', in R. F. Garnett (ed.), *What Do Economists Know?* (London: Routledge, 1999).

Blendon, R. J., J. Benson, M. Brodie, R. Morin *et al.*, 'Bridging the Gap Between the Public's and the Economists' Views of the Economy', *Journal of Economic Perspectives*, 11/3 (Summer 1997) 105–18.

Caplan, B., 'Systematically Biased Beliefs about Economics: Robust Evidence of Judgemental Anomalies from the Survey of Americans and Economists on the Economy', *Economic Journal* 112/479 (2002) 433–58.

Cardoso, F. H., 'The Originality of the Copy: CEPAL and the Idea of Development', *CEPAL Review* 4 (1977) 7–40.

Deane, P., *The State and the Economic System: An Introduction to the History of Political Economy* (Oxford University Press, 1989).

Dornbusch, R. and S. Edwards, *The Macroeconomics of Populism in Latin America* (Chicago University Press, 1991).

Drake, P. W., *The Money Doctor in the Andes: The Kemmerer Missions 1923–33* (Durham, NC: Duke University Press, 1989).

Edwards, S., *Crisis and Reform in Latin America: From Despair to Hope* (New York: Oxford University Press, 1995).

Ellacuría, I. and J. Sobrino (eds), *Mysterium Liberationis: Conceptos Fundamentales de la Teología de Liberación* (Madrid: Trotta, 1990).

FitzGerald, E. V. K., 'ECLA and the Formation of Economic Doctrine', in D. Rock (ed.), *Latin America in the 1940s: War and Post-War Transitions* (Berkeley: University of California Press, 1994).

FitzGerald, E. V. K., 'ECLA and the Theory of Industrialisation', *CEPAL Review, Special Fiftieth Anniversary Issue* (1998) 47–62.

FitzGerald, E. V. K., 'The Economics of Liberation Theology' in C. Rowland (ed.), *The Cambridge Companion to Liberation Theology* (Cambridge University Press, 1999a).

FitzGerald, E. V. K., 'Trade, Investment and NAFTA: the Economics of Neighbourhood', in V. Bulmer-Thomas and J. Dunkerley (eds), *The United States and Latin America: The New Agenda* (Cambridge, MA: Harvard University Press for David Rockefeller Centre, 1999b).

FitzGerald, E. V. K., 'ECLA and the Theory of Import-Substituting Industrialisation in Latin America', in E. Cardenas, J. A. Ocampo and R. Thorp (eds), *Industrialisation and the State in Latin America: The Post-War Years* (London: Macmillan, 2000).

Fitzgibbon, A., *Adam Smith's System of Liberty, Wealth and Virtue: The Moral and Political Foundations of the Wealth of Nations* (Oxford: Clarendon, 1995).

Gerschenkron, A., 'History of Economic Doctrines and Economic History', *American Economic Review* 59/2 (1969) 1–17.

Hall, P. A. (ed.), *The Political Power of Economic Ideas: Keynesianism across Nations* (Princeton University Press, 1989).

Heckscher, E. F., *Mercantilism* (London: Allen & Unwin, 1934).

Kay, C., *Latin American Theories of Development and Underdevelopment* (London: Routledge, 1989).

Klamer, A. and J. Meehan, 'The Crowding Out of Academic Economics: The Case of NAFTA', in R. F. Garnett (ed.), *What Do Economists Know?* (London: Routledge, 1999).

Krugman, P., *Peddling Prosperity* (New York: Norton, 1994).

Love, J., 'Economic Ideas and Ideologies in Latin America since 1930', in L. Bethell (ed.), *The Cambridge History of Latin America Volume VI* (Cambridge University Press, 1994).

McCloskey, D. N., *Knowledge and Persuasion in Economics* (Cambridge University Press, 1994).

Newcomb, S., 'The Problem of Economic Education', *Quarterly Journal of Economics* 7 (1893) 375–99.

Rodriguez, O., *La Teoría del Subdesarrollo de la CEPAL* (Mexico City: Siglo XXI, 1980).

Thorp, R. (ed.), *Latin America in the 1930s: The Role of the Periphery in World Crisis* (Basingstoke: Macmillan, 1984).

Walstad, W., 'Economic Knowledge and the Formation of Economic Beliefs', in P. Lunt and A. Furnham (eds), *Economic Socialisation: The Economic Beliefs and Behaviours of Young People* (Cheltenham: Elgar, 1996).

6

'*Liberalismo Tropical*': The Career of a European Economic Doctrine in Nineteenth-Century Latin America

Nils Jacobsen

Introduction

In this chapter, I argue that the power of economic liberalism over the minds of intellectuals and policy-makers in nineteenth century Latin America has tended to be exaggerated, both in its duration and in its reach. While specific aspects of liberalism were discussed and gained influence among certain groups from the late-colonial era on, it held sway as the dominant paradigm over much of the region – in the sense of being viewed as undoubtable truth questioned only by those considered reactionary, subversive or irrelevant – between *circa* 1850 and 1890. Even then, the various liberalisms dominant in different regions and nations of Latin America often were combined elements that either originated in non-liberal thought and traditions, or in practice countermanded the presumed economic effect of paradigmatic liberal policy.

It is hardly surprising that liberalism has been viewed as so powerful in Latin America. After all, the doctrine's proponents made extraordinarily confident claims about its economic efficacy. Moreover, those North Atlantic nation-states, whence the doctrine originated and which had become paragons of its policy prescriptions to a greater or smaller degree, were the most modern and economically successful countries to be found anywhere during the mid nineteenth century. These North Atlantic nations – most notably, of course, Britain – also happened to be the ones with which Latin America then sustained its most intense commercial, political and cultural ties. Thus, it is not particularly surprising that in subsequent eras – especially between the 1920s and 1980s – intellectuals and policy-makers were wont to place primary blame on the doctrine of economic liberalism for Latin America's post-independence economic woes. Against this long history of overestimating economic liberalism's power and efficacy, I attempt to show that in Latin America during the century in which the doctrine became ascendant – roughly between 1790 and 1890 – it was neither as strong as economic nationalists feared nor as weak as doctrinaire liberals fretted (Jones 1992:222).

This chapter outlines the ascent of economic liberalism towards becoming the dominant paradigm through four periods: (1) enlightened reform-mongering and proto-liberalism (1760s–1795); (2) crisis management and internationalisation of the Latin American economies (1796–1825); (3) an inconclusive struggle between liberalism and other economic doctrines and ingrained practices (1825–48); and (4) liberalism triumphant (1849–1880/90). My task is twofold. On the one hand, I discuss the cultural, political, and institutional processes and mechanisms, as well as the economic contexts through which liberal economic ideas were transmitted and gained influence until achieving dominance. On the other hand, I sketch the reception of such ideas and their assimilation to local conditions and climates of thought and debate.

Useful models of the spread of economic ideas, at a minimum, need to account for the following variables: the 'code' in which they are written (technical jargon, methodology, and underlying cultural and political conceptions); the quantity and quality of the channels of communication (the intensity, density, and speed of transportation networks for people and texts, circulation of print material); the audience(s) (their education, interests, pre-existing ideologies, and values); the power structure of the region or nation where the ideas are disseminated; the openness of institutions, both public and private, in the host region or country to the dissemination of novel ideas; and the economic conjuncture and structure of the host region or nation. When economic doctrines are identified with national interests, power constellations between nations also need to be considered.

For economic liberalism in nineteenth century Latin America, I would argue that domestic power structures, the education, interests, and ideologies of potential audiences, and government and civil society institutions were the direct variables upon which the chances for the doctrine's spread and influence hinged. These variables, in turn, were powerfully affected by the quantity and quality of communication channels between Europe and Latin American ports, capitals, and major regional centres; by economic conjuncture and structure; and by the interests and economic policy notions of major foreign groups of businessmen and governments.

Conclusions about the transmission, evolution and rise to dominance of a pristine economic doctrine require defining the doctrine. Economic liberalism was on the rise for a minimum of one hundred years, and underwent important changes during this long era. The following rough definition only touches the essentials of economic liberalism during the dominance of classical economics before the 1870s. Economic liberalism declares the propensity of the individual for self-improvement and of the macroeconomy for growth and productivity increases to coincide through the workings of an invisible hand – a kind of benevolent Newtonian equilibrating mechanics – as long as individual and economy are free of distorting interferences. At least in its north-west European cradle, this was the economic component of a broader liberalism embraced by emerging new social groups – manufacturers, independent farmers, merchants working without privilege – who pushed for their emancipation from *ancien régime* regulations and authorities. Based on the notion of many small producers and consumers in the market-place, economic liberalism's policy prescriptions included free trade, the notion of comparative advantage in international trade, a rejection of monopolies, and 'a strong presumption against government activity'.[1] Willingness to brook government intervention in the economy generally diminished among theorists from the 1770s to the 1820s, remained low through the 1850s and then slowly increased again, although not decisively so before the late nineteenth century. David Ricardo (1772–1823) and Richard Cobden's (1804–1865) Manchester Club of Political Economy advocated a more stridently *laissez-faire* position than Adam Smith had done.

Enlightened reform-mongering and proto-liberalism (1760s–1795)

The Bourbon and Pombaline reform era was crucial in setting the stage for the later transmission of full-blown liberal economic ideas, for it introduced Latin American elites to ideological debates about political economy. Although economic conflicts began to become ideologized, the transmission of proto-liberal ideas to the small reading public was relatively smooth, largely because such ideas were often at least tolerated by the crowns. The transmission of economic ideas found fewer obstacles from Iberian colonial governments than enlightened texts on political philosophy and religion.

More than 50 years ago, a slim volume edited by Arthur Whitaker provided solid evidence for surprisingly dense communication networks between Latin America's late-colonial intellectuals and major currents of west European enlightenment (Whitaker 1942). The quantity and quality of communication channels between Europe and Latin America underwent significant growth between the 1760s and early 1790s as a direct expression of the growth and shifting pattern of the Atlantic economy. With the multiplication of the volume of trade came more frequent and faster voyages. *Comercio libre* put more American ports into direct contact with a greater number of peninsular ports, especially those (as Barcelona, La Coruña and Santander) more closely attuned to the economic changes sweeping the world of western European commerce and industry.

Increased communication also heightened the flow of people between the peninsula and Latin America. Between the 1700s and 1780s, immigration to Spanish America and Brazil was larger than at any time since the late sixteenth century. In cities from Mexico and Guatemala to Villa Rica and Santiago, Basques, Catalans and northern Portuguese set themselves up as merchants or joined an established business of an uncle or cousin. Especially after José de Gálvez became Minister of the Indies in 1776, many of Spanish America's upper-echelon bureaucrats were hand-picked to vigorously push the economic reform ideas of Charles III and his enlightened ministers. Scientific expeditions, several sponsored by the crown, brought Spaniards, Portuguese, Italians, French and Germans fully versed in the ideas of their time.

Americans also travelled to Spain and Portugal, and from there visited other European countries. Many came to study, not only in Coimbra or Salamanca, but also in Montpellier and other foreign universities. When they found the curriculum in the Spanish and Portuguese universities too stifling and anachronistic, some, as the young Manuel Belgrano in the late 1780s, joined the *academias* and *sociedades de amigos del país*, where much of the latest enlightened literature was discussed. Conservative efforts to stop the spread of the new ideas, such as the spectacular 1778 inquisition trial against the prominent Peruvian-born reformer Pablo de Olavide, for many years a correspondent of Voltaire and Rousseau, were rearguard actions. Even if they expressed prevailing religious orthodoxy, they failed to stop the dissemination of enlightened ideas among the small reading public, in either the peninsula or the American colonies (Herr 1958:209–10).

By the late 1780s and early 1790s, in most larger Latin American towns, at least one or two private libraries, owned by men from the professions, the clergy or upper-class families, contained important contemporary works on political economy, including texts by Quesnay, Condillac, Turgot, Necker, Filangieri, Genovesi and, in a few cases, French editions of Smith. French and Italian authors were more numerous in these libraries than English authors were. By 1789, Claudio Manoel da Costa, leading Brazilian poet of the day and co-conspirator in the Inconfidência Mineira, was already at work translating Adam Smith's *The Wealth of Nations* (Marchant 1942:107). But before the Napoleonic wars, more Latin Americans learned of physiocratic and early liberal ideas indirectly through the texts of Spanish writers, especially Jovellanos, Campomanes and Bernardo Ward, whose works appeared on no Inquisition index and circulated more freely, at least until 'Floridablanca's great fear' after 1790.[2]

The institutions allowing discussion and dissemination of new ideas were becoming more numerous by the late 1780s. *Tertulias*, literary salons in the homes of well-to-do *ilustrados*, had constituted a rather exclusive public sphere for decades. Since the 1760s and 1770s, coffee houses made a belated appearance in the largest Latin American cities. Between the early 1770s and early 1790s, academies and learned societies were founded with official encouragement, in cities like Mexico, Havana, Guatemala, Rio de Janeiro, Quito and Lima, dedicated to the promotion and diffusion of scientific and practical knowledge useful for the development of their own colony.[3] Political economy was not conceived as a clearly defined field of study. Rather it was part of a broader field of empirical and practical knowledge, which stood in sharp juxtaposition to the deductive scholastic approach to learning dominant until mid-century. Until the end of the colonial regime, political economy would not become a separate field of knowledge taught at any institution of learning in Latin America.[4]

Some of the newspapers and journals that began to be published were little more than gazettes announcing the latest official events in the vice regal capital, decrees and ordinances, *te deums* and festivities held at the occasion of the arrival of a new viceroy, the birth of an *infante*, or the inauguration of a new school. But others, especially the ones edited by the learned societies themselves, such as the *Mercurio Peruano*, edited by Hipólito Unánue for Lima's Sociedad Económica de Amantes del País from 1791 to 1796, published studies about socio-economic issues. They had a powerful effect on the formation of a reading public, which read with a mindset different from those of previous centuries exposed primarily to scholastic works and tomes on virtuous Christian living (Chiaramonte 1979:xxvii). Moreover, this reading public, however small in absolute numbers, was more diverse socially. Pharmacists, engineers, medical doctors, military officers, merchants, and even perhaps well-to-do master artisans joined the enlightened elite of high-level crown officials, clergymen and scions of the landed aristocracy. This intelligentsia liked to view itself as egalitarian, without deference to rank and social prestige. Yet, as Chowning (1999:60–6) pointed out for the case of Valladolid, Mexico, these *ilustrados* 'thought of themselves as part of a social world whose boundaries were generous but not ambiguous or confusing'. The intelligentsia was largely urban and excluded manually labouring social strata and the indigenous and African-American ethnic groups.[5]

However, what did Latin America's *ilustrados* actually make of the new economic ideas? How did they assimilate them to their own world and to their goal of advancing the well-being of their particular region? Furthermore, what effect did Spanish and Portuguese reform policies and domestic, colonial, and international conflicts of interests have on their economic thinking? While enlightened economic thought in Latin America showed some commonalities, at the same time there began a process of differentiation according to regional and social priorities, perceptions, and interests. In the decades preceding the Napoleonic Wars, most writers on economic affairs in Latin America called for the promotion of new sectors of economic enterprise and for better regulations for pre-existing ones. They believed this would redound to the benefit of the entire 'nation', by which nearly all writers meant both the colonies and the metropolis. Depending on the economic structure of their specific colony, the writers' emphasis could fall more heavily on liberalization or protection, but the two strategies were not seen as contradictory as long as they fostered production and trade.

Most writers accepted the physiocratic creed that the true wealth of a society rested on agriculture (see for example, Belgrano 1796). Many accepted the physiocratic notion of a 'natural order'. José Joaquim da Cunha de Azeredo Coutinho (1742–1821), scion of sugar planters and Bishop of Olinda, went so far as to suggest that trade outside the empire for colonial agricultural goods would be beneficial for both Brazil and the metropolis de Lima (Sobrinho 1978:61–84; Burns 1975:238). However, most authors merely called for the removal of trade barriers within the colony, between colonies of the same empire, and between colony and metropolis. Many, as Arango y Parreño for Cuba and Lavardén for the River Plate, still justified the liberalization of trade with neo-mercantilist balance of trade arguments: it would facilitate the flow of commodities between colony and metropolis, and thus diminish the loss of specie through purchases from foreign powers (Chiaramonte 1979:xxv; Chiaramonte 1982:71). In 1781, Ramón de Posada, fiscal de la Real Hacienda in New Spain, extolled the virtues of a free grain trade for stabilizing prices and increasing production; but for him freedom of trade seemed to mean nothing more than government stimulation of exports.[6] Even those who had read Adam Smith by the mid-1790s praised the Scottish author profusely and then ignored his ideas. As late as 1796, Manuel Belgrano was still unwilling to embrace the notion that trade could be an autonomous source of wealth, insisting that 'everything depends on and results from the cultivation of land'.[7] In a telling example of selective neglect of European economic ideas, no Latin American writer, as far as I am aware, picked up the key physiocratic notion of the single tax to be paid by the proprietors of land, so intimately linked to the notion of net rent and to the centrality of landed property, a centrality which the Latin Americans frequently underscored. Nor do we find Latin American writers taking up the notion that the state's role in the economy should follow the motto of *laissez-faire*, even though they enthusiastically embraced the physiocrats' 'natural order', on which it is based.

José Carlos Chiaramonte (1982) adduced three reasons for the eclecticism of the economic thought of *ilustrados* in Spanish and Portuguese America. First, especially before 1796, they relied heavily on Spanish and Italian writers in their reception and understanding of French and English economic thought. Where the physiocrats and Smith were formulating abstract ideas – the supposedly universal 'natural laws' of economics – Italian authors as Galiani and Genovesi outlined a partial critique and commentary based on the notion that economic analysis should take into account each nation's climate, geography, production, and culture. This was music to the Latin American *ilustrados*' fears, as it perfectly matched their own programme of discovery and development of their country's natural bounty.[8] Second, most *ilustrados* still viewed it as their task to advance their own colony as an integral part of the Spanish or Portuguese empire. Thus, they formulated projects in such a way as to indicate the advantage they would bring to the metropolis.

This imposed limits on the type of policies they could embrace, a powerful motive pushing their thought towards eclecticism. Third, quite a few writers represented specific economic interests and wrote more from the perspective of policy advocate than from than of detached scholar. Men like Arango y Parreño, Azeredo Coutinho, Belgrano, and Lavardén were closely associated with specific social groups and economic interests, such as sugar-growers, *estancieros* or local merchant groups. Their selective appropriation of economic thought in good measure reflected the interests of those groups.

The impact of reforms of trade, production, and taxation introduced by enlightened despots in Madrid and Lisbon varied from colony to colony, and thus created rather distinct policy debates among and between crown officials, miners, merchants, agricultural and livestock producers, and the circles of *ilustrados* in Havana, Mexico City, Santa Fé, Rio de Janeiro and Buenos Aires. In some cases, the reforms added insult to the injury suffered by certain regions and economic sectors because of the accelerating economic changes of the Atlantic world.[9] John Fisher's characterization of the 1778 Ordinance of Free Trade summarizes the goals and philosophy behind the entire reform effort. They were

> to provide the combination of freedom and protection which would promote the settlement of empty territory, eliminate contraband trade, generate increased customs revenues ... and above all develop the empire as a market for Spanish products and a source of raw materials for Spanish industry. (Fisher 1985:14)

Not surprisingly, the strongest resistance against the reforms came from the old centres of the Habsburg monopoly trade, the viceroyalties of New Spain and Peru, and specifically from the merchant guilds of their capitals. Those colonies whose business elites were already sensing their enhanced opportunities in the rapidly evolving Atlantic economy – from Cuba to coastal Venezuela, Buenos Aires and the Norte Chico and central valley of Chile – could most easily agree with the free-trade plank of the reforms. However, strong differences appeared also between superficially similar economic regions, as, for example, the very different political effect of the Bourbon tax increases in Mexico and Peru (O'Phelan Godoy 1986:340–56; Deans-Smith 1992; Vizcarra 2001). Most importantly, the reforms engendered contradictory reactions in one and the same colony. In Nueva Granada, for example, coastal dye-wood and cacao producers opined that trade liberalization was not going far enough, while the Spanish merchants in Cartagena and merchants, grain, and textile producers in Santa Fé and the surrounding Andean countryside complained about the loss of markets for their trade goods. This conflict was immediately reflected in the economic debates of the *ilustrados*. Antonio Nariño made the call for more encompassing free trade one of his rallying cries against the colonial regime, while Pedro Fermin de Vargas became convinced of the futility of free trade for Nueva Granada and the need for a development strategy based on securing the home markets for Andean agricultural and industrial goods (McFarlane 1993:128–63).

As the activist economic policies inevitably shifted costs and benefits for distinct groups of traders and producers in the various colonies, they contributed to the fragmentation of Latin American societies (Halperin 1985:73). These increasingly atomistic clashes of interest – fostered both by the broad trends of the Atlantic economy and by metropolitan policies – now found a more vigorous public expression in the *ensayos, memorias, discursos, representaciones*, and *reflexiones* published by the *ilustrados*. In short, by the 1790s they rapidly became ideologized.

For the case of late-colonial Brazil, Bradford Burns nicely described the feedback mechanism between new ideas and institutional infrastructures for their dissemination:

> The flow of new ideas into Brazil increased as the intellectual infrastructure expanded. The input of new ideas and the construction of the infrastructure buttressed each other. The more ideas that entered, the stronger the infrastructure became; and as the infrastructure strengthened, it became easier for ideas to migrate. (Burns 1975:224)

While capturing the intensifying circulation of new ideas in the final decades of the colonial era, Burns is silent on the tremendously varied appropriation of those new ideas within each colony and between them. The debates among *ilustrados* set the stage for more vigorous or acrimonious debates about economic liberalism over the next half-century.

Crisis management and internationalization of the Latin American economies (1796–1825)

Napoleonic Wars and Latin American revolutions of independence completely transformed the atmosphere in which economic ideas were discussed. By 1825 (earlier in specific regions), economic liberal thought among Latin American elites had become the most probable and legitimate body of thought for organizing post-colonial economies to contend with the body of corporate or state-interventionist thought that in part survived the enlightened reforms and in part had found new fodder in those reforms.

I have chosen to place the break at 1796 because the acceleration of external shocks began during the years of Spain's renewed warfare with England. These shocks – both economic and political – would open up the climate of opinion in the American colonies. The crises that befell the Spanish Empire since the defeat of the joint Franco-Spanish fleet at Cabo San Vicente in 1796 necessitated a series of *ad hoc* commercial and fiscal measures, and created sustained disruptions of transatlantic trade that slowly but steadily pushed the colonial business elites as well as the *ilustrados* into the widening gyre of economic and political change beyond the bounds of empire. The authorization of direct trade with foreign colonies (1795), *Comercio neutral* (1797–9, although special *permisos* continued thereafter), the *consolidación de vales reales* (applied in America since 1803), the interruption of mercury shipments from Almadén, and, more broadly, periodic interruptions of commerce, flows of specie and imperial communications, forced the debate upon the colonials as to whether even the reformed regulatory framework tinkered with in Madrid was still adequate for their American economies. The increasing weakness of the imperial nexus thus emboldened the debate about economic models (Halperin 1985:75–93). In Brazil, this development set in more abruptly (and yet less disruptively) with the destruction of Portuguese neutrality through the French invasion of 1807 and the subsequent transfer of the court and centre of the empire to Rio de Janeiro.

The political events of 1810–25 would, of course, entirely explode the regulatory framework of mainland Latin American economies by exploding the colonial nexus itself. The earliest significant codifications of this shift came with the decree allowing ships of friendly and neutral nations – this time most importantly those of Great Britain – into Buenos Aires harbour in 1809 and the Treaty of Navigation and Commerce between Portugal and Great Britain of February 1810 that gave Great Britain preferential access to the Brazilian market.[10] But the line from these early measures to the internationalization of trade throughout mainland Latin America as a consequence of the revolutions for independence was anything but straight. This is not the place to rehearse the shifts of economic policies during the prolonged period of transition from colony to nation-state. Nevertheless, it is important to recall that their timing, form and rationale varied significantly from region to region. Often they were not unequivocal expressions of a suddenly expanded conviction in new economic doctrines, but merely dire economic necessity (to give vent to accumulating stockpiles of hides, for example), fiscal emergency, or even, as in the case of the Portuguese–British treaty, coercion.

During this period, new channels for transmission of economic ideas opened up. More coffeehouses were established, the first public libraries were founded, and Freemasons mingled discussions of politics with debates about new books and doctrines. A new generation of newspapers, including exile patriot papers in London, more freely discussed political and economic issues (Bethell 1985:178). Just as importantly, during these years printing presses spread in Latin America. The first printing press arrived in the capital of the Inca Empire, Cuzco, together with the last viceroy, in 1821 (Walker 1999:173). Brazil, astonishingly, received its first two presses only in 1808 and 1811, after the arrival of the royal court. Almost immediately, they became active in the publication of studies on political economy, including translations of French-, English- and German-language works. In 1811 and

1812, the first two Portuguese editions of Adam Smith's *The Wealth of Nations* were published (the first Spanish edition was published in Madrid in 1794). Smith now was widely read and cited among all major Brazilian writers on economics (Burns 1975:229). The two decades before 1825 saw the rapid rise in the availability and influence of English authors on political economy, at least in cities like Rio de Janeiro and Buenos Aires.

With the opening of the ports to direct trade with western Europe and the United States, the book trade became more lively as well. By the 1820s, most new general treatises on political economy published in France and England were available practically without delay in Rio de Janeiro, and, we may assume, in other large cities. This is evident from the literature cited by José da Silva Lisboa in his *Estudos do Bem Comum e Economía Política*, published in Rio in 1819, probably the most important work on economics published in Latin America during the first quarter of the nineteenth century. The modern historian of economic theory may be hard put to name authors that are missing from Lisboa's discussion. The author had already read David Ricardo's main work, *The Principles of Political Economy*, which had appeared in 1817. He cites other works that had just appeared in Europe in 1819, in other words, a few months before the publication of his own book.[11]

However, the most important new channel for the transmission of economic ideas during the first quarter of the nineteenth century consisted in the swift establishment of sizeable foreign communities in all the major port and capital cities of Latin America. By the early 1820s, many cities counted hundreds of foreign longer-term residents as well as a constant trickle of shorter-term visitors. These were British, North American, French and – in smaller numbers – other continental European merchants, diplomats, engineers, whalers, ex-combatants in the wars of independence and naturalists. As trade with their nations replaced that with Spain or Portugal, the foreign merchants almost immediately became an interest group seeking to influence government decisions about tariffs, port fees, and regulations, and, more broadly, the rights of foreigners to participate in all aspects of wholesale and retail trade. Although their full integration into local elite circles could take years or even decades, from the first moment the foreign merchants opened their offices and shops they became strategic conduits for information about North Atlantic economic debates.

Charles A. Jones has called attention to the formation of a 'cosmopolitan bourgeoisie', a transnational group of merchants – frequently intermarrying – who functioned as nodes for the international flow of goods, capital, and information in the centres of trade throughout the world. This cosmopolitan bourgeoisie came into being between the 1760s and 1860s through the destruction of the mercantilist trading world coupled with the development of machine-based manufacturing techniques. 'Merchants trading internationally were inclined to see themselves, and to be seen by others, as agents of an individualistic and progressive liberal revolution' (Jones 1987:1).

Clearly, this was how, by the early 1820s, they were perceived, for better or for worse, among Latin Americans. As William Glade puts it, trade flows were 'the chief "growth industry" of that day'. 'Had anyone in emancipated colonies doubted the importance of trade amongst nations and the policies shaping it, he would have been swimming against the prevailing current of international opinion' (Glade 1989:381). In this new cosmopolitan trading world '*laissez aller, laissez faire* [has become] the aphorism which is proclaimed so much today', as da Silva Lisboa commented in 1831.[12] In short, the international merchant communities now settled in port and capital cities throughout Latin America were the vital links of a rapidly modernizing global economic network of cities and their hinterlands for whom economic liberalism constituted the necessary framework for their operation and growth.

Nevertheless, this was hardly a network of nations by the early nineteenth century, as David Ringrose recently underscored (Ringrose 1996). Since the second half of the seventeenth century, the economic developments that began to fashion economies of sustained productivity growth are better understood as being driven by an expansion of a network of regions based on one or more core cities; national boundaries were as yet of secondary importance for these regions. This network, originating in the regions around London, Amsterdam and Paris, between the late eighteenth and mid nineteenth century expanded more explosively to include cities and their hinterlands in the Americas and parts of Asia. Such regions could be relatively numerous or extensive within certain national spaces, while in others there might exist only one such region (or indeed none), with the overwhelming part of the national space unaffected by the developing international economy of sustained productivity growth. Given that productivity growth through market integration was one, but of course, not the only source of productivity growth, the 'cosmopolitan merchants' were crucial nodes in this expanding network, both contributing to its expansion and reflecting growing productivity outside of trade.

Before the mid nineteenth century it makes little sense to talk of national economies and thus of a *national* political economy, common to and integrating all regions and sectors, for most Latin American states.[13] Capital, labour and commodity markets were not integrated on a national scale, while productivity levels must have varied considerably between a few modernizing nodes and other regional and sectoral economies. Insufficient infrastructure and human resource development, and 'burdensome' and 'inefficient' public regulatory frames, from taxation to property rights, did nothing to advance such integration (Coatsworth 1998:33–4). It is thus essential to locate the analysis of economic change on the level of the regions and their urban centres. The Latin American nodes of the modernizing international network of regions and the other regions within a national space faced off politically on the level of other networks, both social and political. It is these political struggles through which 'the dominant discourses about economics and politics change their vocabulary' (Ringrose 1996:36).

The relation between the modernizing international network of regions and economic liberalism that interests us here was anything but straightforward. While the firms and individuals operating within this largely commercial network clearly flourished within a liberal framework – which does not *ipso facto* prove its adequacy for *national* economies – we cannot presume that they automatically *caused* the ascendancy of economic liberal institutions. The tremendous expansion of the modernizing network between the late eighteenth and mid-nineteenth centuries itself had been in good measure the consequence of political events. Over fairly long periods, merchants and producers of the modernizing nodes could survive in niche economies (their limited region and specific trades) within larger polities and societies not adopting the economic liberal framework. Under such conditions, the modernizing nodes could give little impulse for extending a sustained productivity economy to other regional economies of the national space. On the other hand, situations were also thinkable in which economic liberalism became politically dominant before the majority of economic regions within the national space had become part of the modernizing network (Ringrose 1996). This would powerfully affect the nature of the liberal institutions being forged, and might even result in a national economic framework in which the putative liberalism was so statist or clientelist as to render the very notion of a liberal economy a contradiction in terms. In short, while the characteristics of the various regional economies within a national space clearly influenced economic policies and institutional frameworks, they did not determine them, at least not in the short run.

By 1820, the basic doctrines of economic liberalism had become commonplace knowledge among politicians, intellectuals, and businessmen in Latin America (although probably less so in the Andes than on the east coast of South America). What was at stake now was to which degree and in which form they could become politically dominant. Before turning to this drama, I would briefly like to present some ideas of one Latin American economist writing at this moment of intellectual breakthrough for liberalism.

José da Silva Lisboa (1756–1835), a native of Salvador and graduate of Coimbra with a distinguished career in royal administration, had written studies and reports on economic issues since the 1790s. In 1804, his *Principios de Economía Política* appeared, which already demonstrated a strong influence of Adam Smith. However, his key work was the *Estudos do bem comum e economía política*, published in three instalments in 1819 and 1820. The work was planned on a much vaster scale consisting of 12 parts, with extensive sections not only on underlying principles of political economy, and 'theories' of 'general industry', value, capital, rent, and interest, but also on the various sectors of the economy; on labour and the importance of machines;

on money, credit and banking; on industrial promotion and more generally economic policy-making and administration to stimulate national wealth and increase of population; on the relation between the wealth of nations and their power, and other subjects. Unfortunately, da Silva Lisboa never wrote the last nine sections. Still, in this plan one can glimpse the tremendous change compared with Latin American writing on economic issues until the 1790s. While the writers of the 1780s and 90s stressed the particular, in the *Estudos* da Silva Lisboa outlines the natural law by which wealth is created everywhere; it only allows 'accidental, but not substantive' modifications according to place and time (da Silva Lisboa 1975:169). Although guided primarily by Smith, Malthus and Ricardo, whom he considers the major contributors to the study of the economy as the common good, he rejects certain parts of their doctrines, adds original ideas, and stresses elements peripheral to classical economics. The laws governing the wealth of nations are given by the Supreme Being; da Silva Lisboa frequently cited the bible in support of his maxims, and viewed political economy as 'auxiliary' to morals.[14]

Da Silva Lisboa explicitly rejected the Malthusian trap. Rightly, he saw no evidence in Brazil for the notion that increasing population would result in subsistence crises, given the unlimited supply of land. He was much influenced by Lord Lauderdale (1759–1839), today viewed as one of the precursors of welfare economics because he saw a conflict between national wealth and private riches (Spiegel 1991:299–302). Da Silva Lisboa followed Lauderdale (and the French economist Canard) in recognizing land, labour and capital as the sources of national wealth. For the Brazilian, the 'progress of civilization' was derived from human intelligence, the capacity to develop machines, devices, means of communication, ways of exploiting land and so on that increased productivity. Thus, the increase (or decrease) of the wealth of a nation depended directly on the proportion between intelligence and manual labour in the production of goods (da Silva Lisboa 1975:187–8, 236–8, 241–3).

While fervently calling for free trade, and leaving as much autonomy to the individual as possible, da Silva Lisboa was primarily concerned with the welfare of the entire nation and saw it as not automatically congruent with that of the individual. Given that the employment of all hands in the nation was one of the goals of political economy for him, he sought a careful balance between producing as much domestically as possible and not 'absurdly' disrupting the principle of 'natural advantage'. He considered slavery anti-economical, and called for a broad distribution of land. Thus, as he wrote in 1832,

in everything there ought to be a fair mean between the extremes of governing a lot and not governing at all ... In the old governments, it was censured – and rightly so – that in nearly everything the hand of authority could be seen. But neither is it convenient, without modifications, to adopt the aphorism proclaimed so much these days: *laissez aller – laissez faire*.[15]

In short, José da Silva Lisboa, growing old in the service of the Braganças, professed a flexible economic liberalism. It was shaped as much by his tremendous erudition as by his understanding of the specific Brazilian situation, and his Catholicism. Moreover, his innovative discussion of intelligence as the ultimate font of human progress and increasing wealth demonstrates that even by 1820 the development of modern economic thought should not be construed as a one-way diffusion from European knowledge producers to Latin American knowledge consumers.

Inconclusives struggle between liberalism and other economic doctrines and ingrained practices (*c.* 1825–48)

The first 25 or 30 years after the conclusion of the revolutions for independence are one of the two eras for which scholars disagree about the dominance of economic liberalism.[16] This divergence of opinion in part stems from distinct national perspectives – liberal influences were decidedly weaker in Bolivia, Peru or Mexico than in Argentina – but they also reflect different conceptual and ideological positions. Scepticism about the influence of economic liberalism in many parts of Latin America before 1850 has grown over the past 15 years, and I believe that scepticism is – for many regions – justified. While most sectors of Latin American elites realized by the 1820s that the growth of foreign trade and especially exports would be crucial for national economic development, and while they expressed general knowledge of the new science of political economy, this did not automatically make them economic liberals. As Chilean Minister of Finance José A. Rodríguez put it in 1822, 'we are liberals in all that does not tend to ruin us' (Will 1964:6–7). And before mid-century, policy-makers in most countries frequently perceived free trade, not to mention free labour and property markets, as ruinous.

In the theoretical enthusiasm of political and intellectual elites for the new science of political economy, efforts were made during the immediate post-independence years to disseminate the doctrine through courses in schools and universities. In 1823, the Mexican Congress debated at great length the proposal by several deputies to establish 'a chair for political economy in each provincial capital, under the direct inspection of the *diputaciones provinciales*'. All those training in law were to be required to take a course in political economy for at least six months, and all those applying for a career position in the foreign and finance ministries were to undergo an examination in political economy administered by three *catedráticos* in the field.

After arduous debate, the project was returned to committee, because it was unclear how it could be implemented (Reyes Heroles 1957:I, 123–7). The liberal educational reforms of 1833 created a *Colegio de Humanidades y Ciencias Ideológicas*, apparently directed by José María Luis Mora himself, which was to teach courses in political economy (Hale 1968:173). In Chile, the famous *Instituto Nacional* taught a course in political economy – based on Say's *Traité d'économie politique* – beginning in 1819. Over the next 30 years the number of students enrolled declined, instruction was based on rote learning, and instructors had the reputation of being boring and rather uninformed. However, nobody seemed to care before the late 1840s (Will 1964:4, 17–18; Villalobos and Sagredo 1987:17–21). During the days of Unitario rule in Buenos Aires in the 1820s, a utilitarian approach to political economy was taught at the university and perhaps in other schools. However, it seems to have disappeared from the university curriculum during the decades of the university's 'evisceration' by Rosas (Adelman 1999:167–8). And in Lima the first 'cursantes de economía política' appeared on the scene only during the late 1840s (Gootenberg 1989:88–9). In short, before mid-century efforts to train a generation of elites in political economy remained feeble or were defeated during the 1830s and 1840s.

The fledgling press of the independent nations now became a vital channel for the discussion of economic ideas. But most of the papers were tied to specific circles of politicians, and frequently adopted a shrill and combative tone in the day-to-day political struggles. Governments supported the papers that supported them through multiple subscriptions, direct financial subventions, preferred access to newsprint and other favours. Opposition papers were harassed, fined, had to pay higher licensing fees, or were unceremoniously shut down. In ideologically doctrinaire liberal or conservative regimes, this meant that publicized opinion tended to be supportive of the regime. Hence, while disseminating interested interpretations of political economy, the press mostly served to buttress reigning economic policies rather than to bring about their change.

Foreign influence on economic policy directions in Latin America between the 1820s and late 1840s has long been debated in the context of studies on informal imperialism and dependency.[17] I shall limit myself largely to the issue of direct and active foreign influences on economic policy debates and outcomes. Yet, the structural changes in regional economies in which communities of Jones's cosmopolitan bourgeoisie played such a prominent role in themselves constituted a major cause for changing economic policies. On that structural level, however, the differentiation between 'foreign' and 'domestic' influences tends to be blurred, because the 'modernizing networks' included both foreign and national traders and producers.[18]

For the narrower consideration of their direct influence on economic policy formulation, we must differentiate between private foreign interferences and those of foreign governments. For most nations, the influence of foreign merchants, miners and financiers was stronger during the first post-independence decade, then diminished during the 1830s and 1840s. The internationalization of the Latin American economies went hand in hand with a brief investment boom and loan cycle between 1821 and 1825. The speculative opening of the London money market and stock exchange for Latin American loans and mining company stocks was accomplished through groups of British merchants and bankers in close association with Latin American politicians and diplomatic representatives. These groups mutually reinforced their convictions in the importance of opening markets, and creating legal prerequisites for foreign investments (Marichal 1989:ch. 1). Thus, in this first ebullient moment, foreign merchants, miners, and financiers primarily gained influence on economic policy not through bribery and hard-ball pressure politics – although these were never absent – but rather through an imagined community of interest between them and specific groups of Latin American politicians.[19]

After the crash of the London stock exchange, the general financial–commercial crisis across Europe from late 1825 to mid 1826, and the bust of most mining ventures, as well as the default of nearly all Latin American loans during those same months, the climate for foreign merchants in Latin America changed and it became more difficult for them to influence government economic policies. Most nations (with the prominent exception of Brazil) did not have access to foreign loans for at least 25 years, and direct foreign investment diminished sharply. Hence, the leverage exercised by the foreign merchants declined considerably. This does not mean they did not keep trying. However, the risks for merchants in trying to influence Latin American politics directly were greater now, increasing proportionally with the weakness of the regime and the threat of breakdown and civil war (and these were, paradoxically, the regimes where foreign money or pressure presumably could have achieved results most easily). As Paul Gootenberg has suggested for the foreign merchant community in Peru during the 1830s and 1840s, the larger and more established merchants tended to be risk-averters, intent on keeping good relations with each of the revolving-door regimes before 1845 (Gootenberg 1989:21–2).

Foreign governments were another matter. They clearly influenced economic policies of Latin American governments throughout the period – mostly in the direction of economic liberalism, although not always.[20] Their tools included everyday representations of ministers, chargés d'affaires or consuls concerning bills or decrees thought averse to the economic interests of their business community, protests and demands of compensation for losses incurred by their nationals (from unpaid loans to confiscations and wartime destruction of property), negotiation over commercial treaties, support for one political party against another, and gunboat diplomacy or war. There were numerous instances in which such negotiation, pressure and threat or use of force did result in changes of government policy in the general direction of economic liberalism, from Chatfield's direct participation in the design of Guatemala's fiscal policies, to the numerous treaties of trade and navigation that promised lower tariffs, to the survival of the economically liberal Colorado government in Uruguay through British military intervention in 1843 (Miller 1993:48–59). However, there were many other cases in which such meddling proved counter-productive, if anything strengthening the cohesion of anti-liberal coalitions. Paul Gootenberg has made this case for Peru between the late 1820s and late 1840s, and it applies equally for British military intervention in Argentina during much of the 1840s. Even in Brazil, where Great Britain had gotten pretty much everything it wanted between 1808 and the late 1820s, by the 1840s, both conservative and liberal governments were less willing to give in to British pressures (Bethell and de Carvalho 1985:724–6).

An overall assessment of foreign private and governmental influence on the acceptance of economic liberalism in early post-independence Latin America thus needs to draw some careful distinctions. On a structural level, the European and North American businessmen and their diplomatic protectors were critical elements of the modernizing international economy for which economic liberalism was imagined as doctrinal justification and the only legitimate operative paradigm. Their very presence and their constant hectoring brought the presumed identity between the new international economy and its liberal rules before the mind's eye of their business partners and government officials in Latin America. Yet this does not mean that specific targeted interventions of foreigners had much success in shoving economic liberalism down the throats of hapless Latin Americans. Such intervention had indifferent success after the late 1820s, because many Latin Americans were not convinced any more that the liberal formula for achieving a nation's wealth applied to their particular nation. After a brief moment of classicist universalism around the time of independence, by the late 1830s, romanticism gave legitimacy once again to viewing each nation as singular in its endowments. While in Argentina's generation of 1837, such introspection was combined with liberalism, in other intellectual circles of the continent this was much less the case.

How economic liberalism fared in this new atmosphere of disillusionment depended on a host of variables: the benefits and costs of an open economy accruing to various regional and sectoral economies within the national space; the need for revenue (such as import duties) after the collapse or abolition of several colonial taxes; and more intangible factors about power structures (articulation of regional, sectoral, social, and ideological dimensions) as well as ingrained practices of how to deal with diverse groups (ranging between the extremes of conciliation and imposition by force). In Rosista Buenos Aires the solution was the forcible imposition of a rigid politics of export promotion for the *estancieros* of the province against the interests of all other regions, both those also hoping to benefit from open trade and those where costs of economic liberalism were for a long time greater than its benefits. In the 1830s the drift of Buenos Aires away from the liberal trade regime of the 1820s had more to do with revenue shortfalls and with strategies to stabilize the Rosista regime than with deep-seated socio-ideological challenges to economic liberalism. As Tulio Halperin has put it, initially in Buenos Aires and after 1852 or 1862 in Argentina, liberalism wanted to be – and with good reason – 'the political expression of this society itself' (Halperin 1987:150).[21]

More surprising perhaps is the case of New Granada, where, according to Frank Safford, a credible alternative to economic liberalism was formulated for only a few short years during the early 1830s, although the chances for developing new export sectors only emerged after the mid 1840s (Safford 1988:35–62). Rather than economic interests, I think this surprising strength of economic liberalism in post-independence New Granada probably owed a lot to the power constellation between various regions, especially mining Antioquia, the region between Cundinamarca and Santander with its grain producers and strong crafts sectors, the badly integrated Caribbean coast, and the sugar and livestock slave-based complex of the Cauca valley. Perhaps here economic liberalism must be understood as expression of a kind of balance of power arrangement with a weak central state incapable of imposing a more centralist, corporatist vision of economic development. The Chilean case of successful export promotion combined with a cautious, moderate protectionism – with surprisingly little variation of trade regimes between the 1811 Free Trade law of the first republic, those of the liberal era and those of the Portalian era, even through the 1850s – in some ways appears as the polar opposite of that of New Granada. For a long time it proved possible to hold together the interests of central valley *fundo* owners, miners of the Norte Chico and the merchants of Santiago-Valparaíso – both national and foreign – under such a programme, perhaps in part because of the close social integration of all these sectors, and also because the Chilean elite was imbued with an ongoing mission of economic emancipation from the colonial mercantile and bureaucratic overlords in Lima.[22]

The cases of Mexico and Peru, although distinct in some regards, not surprisingly represent some of the most significant defeats of economic liberalism during the two decades after the early 1820s enthusiasm. As Salvucci *et al.* have argued for Mexico, and Gootenberg for Peru, the social groups that could sustain a free-trade policy were either absent (the Salvuccis' interpretation for the Mexican case), or weak and easily defeated (Gootenberg on Peru). In both cases, protectionism by the 1830s became wedded to an overconfident nationalism (Salvucci *et al.* 1994:95–114; Gootenberg 1989:esp. chs. 2, 3).

An encompassing analysis of the limits of economic liberalism's influence over Latin American elites needs to go beyond an analysis of trade policies, and consider notions about property and labour regimes. And here very little change is visible in most parts of Latin America, except for those regions whose economies were already growing strongly before 1850 *and* slavery or some form of peonage were not used to fill the growing labour requirements. According to Hilda Sabato, Buenos Aires sheep ranches already counted with a virtually free labour market by the 1850s, and there do not seem to have been strong sentiments among *estancieros* to push for legislation that could have constrained that market. Buenos Aires is the only case of a fairly free market for rural labour anywhere in Latin America up to 1850. Even in Chile, with its growing export economy, *inquilinaje*, the labour tenancy on most central valley estates, was becoming more rigid, demanding, and manorial between the 1830s and 1870s, not unlike contemporary trends in Prussian estates (Bauer 1975:ch. 2). No liberal state administration interfered to loosen this tightening seigniorial grip.

Liberalism triumphant (1849–1880/90)

What accounts for economic liberalism becoming dominant in most parts of Latin America sometime between the late 1840s and early 1870s? First, it clearly could not have happened without the preceding 70 to 80 years of intellectual ferment and structural changes sketched above. Second, changing international political constellations, as the abolition of the corn laws in Great Britain in 1846, the revolutions of 1848, and the subsequent general tendency to lower tariffs in many parts of Europe, helped to make economic liberalism more credible. Finally, the real issue is whether the improved outlook for many regional economies in Latin America was a major *cause* for the rise to dominance of economic liberalism, or whether this improvement is the *consequence* of economic liberal reforms themselves. Put differently (and more like questions about the rise of neo-liberalism between the 1970s and early 1980s): was economic liberalism adopted because Latin American elites saw no alternative, as their national economies and/or the fiscal health of the nation had failed to respond to the experiments of the preceding decades, or did they adopt economic liberalism precisely because improved economies made them more optimistic about the nation's place in the international market-place and order?

Tulio Halperin has suggested that in both Argentina and Mexico, key intellectuals advocated opening up the economy not because they truly wanted it, but because they felt there was no alternative.[23] John Coatsworth offers the following linkage between liberal reforms and changing economic performance:

In the second half of the nineteenth century, virtually every Latin American country carried out a series of similar (occasionally identical) reforms that eliminated or substantially reduced the most important of the institutional constraints inherited from the colonial era. In most cases the process began with the elimination of state monopolies, church and military *fueros*, and other privileges, a wide array of domestic taxes and fees, and archaic property rights (entail, ecclesiastical and indigenous mortmain, and slavery), and continued with the privatisation of public lands, the enactment of new civil and commercial codes, and efforts to attract foreign capital and labour to the development of railroads and other public works as well as a wide range of productive activities. The timing and the sequence of the reforms varied with the political fortunes of contending parties and factions in each country. In those that took longer, economic growth was delayed until later than elsewhere. (Coatsworth 1998:39)

This succinct summary of the substance of the liberal economic reforms seems to suggest two things: a tremendous uniformity of the reforms across most Latin American nations, only differentiated by time-lags, and, second, a causal link making the reforms – the removal of institutional obstacles – the precondition for growth. That seems to coincide with Tulio Halperin's judgement: the elites had to do it in order to grow the economy, whether they wanted to or not. And the growth is a consequence of the reforms, not its cause.

Perhaps I am pursuing a rather irrelevant 'chicken and egg' question here. But in at least some cases, economic growth had set in well before the reforms. For example, in Peru, guano revenue was swelling by the late 1840s, years before the central liberal reforms were undertaken. In Bolivia, the recovery of silver production and exports preceded most of the major liberal reforms freeing the circulation and export of unminted silver. Admittedly in the Bolivian case, more spectacular growth-rates of silver production occurred in the 1870s, after the crucial liberalizing reforms (and improvement of transport conditions) had been accomplished. Still, economic growth often created the space (fiscal and thus political) to undertake economic liberal reforms, which previously were viewed as divisive and impolitic.

The crucial missing link which helps to overcome the circular *cause/consequence* conundrum in the rise of economic liberalism thus concerns politics. In every case of a breakthrough for liberalism, it went hand in hand with some type of political reaccomodation. The nature and depth of that reaccomodation varied. But coalitions needed to be realigned, and the pre-existing proponents of liberalism needed to gain a broader set of allies in order to be able to carry out their desired reforms. In some greatly varying fashion, different regions – badly articulated in most cases until mid-century – needed to be brought into the national fray. This could happen through formulas that heeded the interests of regions previously neglected, or through imposition by force, or a combination of both. Such a combination seems to have been at play in the foundation of the modern Argentine state between 1859 and 1862, which Carlos Marichal has described as an articulation of local issues, national politics, and fiscal reforms aimed at the conciliation of diverse regional elites (Marichal 1996:90–110). In Brazil, by contrast, the liberal reforms during the moderate conservative and moderate liberal governments of the Saquaremas and *conciliacão* in the early 1850s were rather meagre, limited mostly to the abolition of the slave trade and the land law abolishing *sesmarias* and *posses*, largely because all the provincial elites clung to the primacy of saving slavery and the institution of the emperor as its guarantor. In fact, the land law can easily be interpreted as an anti-liberal measure, based on Wakefield's scheme to maintain an abundant supply of labour for plantation agriculture by keeping land scarce.[24]

Because nearly everywhere the nations continued far from integrated, regionally, socially, ethnically and in terms of transportation and governmental infrastructure, the liberal reforms represented nation-building programs, that is the attempt to develop the nation through a feedback mechanism between building modern institutions and economic growth through exports. The interests of the nation and of those elites forming part of the liberal political accommodation were seen as identical. This could require repression of wayward regional elites and of broad popular sectors. There was a broad range in the role assigned to the state for achieving this nation-building: minimal in Granada, where until 1864 the liberals believed that even road and school construction should not be in the purview of the state, and quite large in the Peruvian guano state.

We also need to query John Coatsworth's contention of the uniformity of the liberal reforms. It is at least exaggerated. After Bolivar's and La Mar's feeble attempts of 1825 and 1828, Peru never had a decree privatising indigenous communal lands as Mexico's Ley Lerdo of 1856 or Bolivia's laws of 1866 and 1874, or El Salvador's privatisation of communal and municipal lands of 1882. While El Salvador was trying to foster a free rural labour market and did not use state force to recruit labour for the coffee haciendas, this is precisely what the 'liberals' in neighbouring Guatemala were doing with the mandamiento laws of the 1870s and thereafter. And even when two countries carried out formally equivalent reforms, these could have drastically different meanings and consequences. Take the establishment of liberal property laws. In Argentina, as Jeremy Adelman has shown recently, this was one of the important successes of the accommodation of the 1860s; henceforth property owners enjoyed secure titles and the legal apparatus to ward off challenges. In Andean Peru, however, the highly modern Civil Code of 1852, with its complex, formalistic instruments to establish guarantees for private property, over the next six or seven decades became a favourite tool for gamonal land grabbers to take control surreptitiously of properties from indigenous peasants and weaker *hacendados* with minimal outlays of cash. There were export complexes, then, which flourished between the 1850s and

1920, that felt only minor effects from liberal reforms enacted on the national level.

In short, while the doctrinal domination of economic liberalism in most Latin American countries for part or most of the years between the late 1840s and 1890 is beyond doubt, the nature and consequences of this domination varied tremendously. In addition, putatively liberal regimes passed laws and continued practices, which either by intent or in their consequence flatly contradicted economic liberalism, as for example Brazil's land law of 1850, Guatemalan *mandamiento laws*, and Peru's *Código Civil*.

After 1890, I believe, economic liberalism came to be doubted in some elite circles and was slowly undermined regarding certain policy aspects (indigenous property, social legislation and in some cases even tariff policies).[25] The era between the 1890s and 1920s is thus better understood as a transition period, a slow and gradual expansion of notions of state intervention, rather than as a full-blown continuation of the liberal era. This view does not draw into doubt the continued primacy of the export economy through 1930, but I see no inevitable identity between export-economies and liberalism.[26]

Conclusions

The rise of economic liberalism to dominance in Latin America was the consequence of a drawn-out (although at times explosive) concatenation of mutual influences between structural economic transformations in the Atlantic world, dissemination of intellectual currents, and political accommodations between sectors of the elites within national spaces. While foreign interests (private and governmental) at crucial moments played an important role in disseminating or reinforcing economic liberalism as a doctrine and as policy prescription, in the long run their impact could come to fruition only when an elite coalition of sufficient political strength considered adoption of economic liberalism to be in their own interests. Methodologically it is important not to locate the influence of economic liberalism on the national level from the onset of independence or before, given that we are dealing with badly integrated economic regions with strong, weak, or non-existent ties to the modernizing regions in Europe and North America. Such regional integration into modernizing networks clearly influenced the chances for the acceptance of economic liberalism.

This chapter cautions about a model of diffusion of pristine ideas from one or a few source(s). Economic liberalism was adapted or transformed in Latin America according to distinct interest and intellectual/cultural traditions, and such transformations needed not always to remain one-way streets. The form, content and effect of economic liberalism on various regions and nations in Latin America were far from uniform. There was a long lag time between its broad dissemination and its rise to dominance. Since export economies do not require to be accompanied by a full-blown policy program of liberalism, I believe the doctrine to have been less influential in Latin America than has often been assumed.

Notes

1. Viner (1928: 140), cited in Skinner (1989:31).
2. Chiaramonte 1979: xvii, xxiv–xxv; Herr 1958:ch. 8; Sarrailh 1957:pt iii, ch. 5.
3. On the earlier dissemination of rationalist and empiricist ideas in Salvador, see Burns 1975:217–18 and Marchant 1942:102–4. On 1780s literary salons in provincial New Spain, see Chowning 1999:60–1.
4. It appeared in the curriculum of Chile's Instituto Nacional in 1813, but was not actually taught before 1819 (Will 1964:4).
5. Chowning 1999:60–6. However, on 'popular enlightenment' in the Andes, see Estenssoro Fuchs (1996) and Serulnikov. For rising literacy rates in late-colonial New Spain, see Guerra 1993:276–82.
6. Arcila Farías (1974:vol. i, 19) considers Posadas's views on foreign trade closer to Smith than to the physiocrats.
7. As cited by Adelman 1999:59. For Belgrano's pragmatic yet doctrinally confused call for the liberalization of export trade, and simultaneous protection of local industries, see Chiaramonte 1982:125–6.
8. Chiaramonte 1982:122. On the Peruvian José Baquijano y Carrillo's express rejection of the physiocrats' emphasis on agriculture as inimical to the centrality of mining for the Andes, see his 'Disertación histórica y política sobre el comercio del Perú [1791],' in Chiaramonte 1979.
9. On the at times limited impact of these reform measures on structural changes, see Halperin 1985:85.
10. On forerunners to Portugal's 1810 preferential treaty with Great Britain, see Halperin (1985:105) and Bethell (1985:171).
11. Da Silva Lisboa (1975:part I, chs. 3–10).
12. Da Silva Lisboa 1832, cited in da Silva Lisboa (1975:20).
13. Possible exceptions were a few of the small states, especially Costa Rica, Paraguay and Uruguay.
14. Da Silva Lisboa (1975:62). For da Silva's comparison of the economist with the catechist, see p. 73.
15. Cited in Almeida (1975:20).
16. The other one concerns the years between the 1890s and 1920s, which I merely mention in the conclusion.
17. For an overview of the debates, see Kay (1989). For a less Eurocentric and more interactive treatment of imperialism, see Smith (1981), and also Cains and Hopkins (1993). For a balanced treatment of British actions in Latin America, see Miller (1993).
18. This is one of the points stressed by Gootenberg (1989:esp. 15). There also existed transnational networks of the 'nationalists', conservatives or groups with more corporate views, including ties with power groups in neighboring republics and with the representatives of the major powers. One may think of the alignments of conservatives and liberals in Guatemala and neighboring Central American republics during the 1840s and 1850s with the United Kingdom and the United States respectively.

19. Cf. Bernecker 1993:177–212, esp. 191.
20. The French–Haitian agreement of 1824, through which France would recognize the independence of Haiti against indemnity payments for planters, included a clause that would increase import tariffs on British manufactured goods; that is France was seeking preferential trading privileges, not liberalization of trade; see Marichal (1989:35).
21. See also Adelman (1999:121–7).
22. Maurice Zeitlin's (1984) analysis of the failed Chilean 'bourgeois revolutions' of the 1850s, while suggestive for the gradual differentiation of elite social groups, overemphasizes the class base of the differentiation of Chile's political party system. For a distinct interpretation, see Collier and Sater (1996:ch. 5).
23. Halperin (1987: 146). For a similar view on the adoption of free-trade policies in Colombia, see Ocampo (1984: 46).
24. See da Costa 1985:ch. 4, but compare the more subtle interpretation by Dean 1971:606–25.
25. On tariff policies in the belle époque, now see Coatsworth and Williamson (2004:205–32).
26. I present details of this argument for the Peruvian case in Jacobsen (2002); for evidence of post-1890s protectionism as explicit industrial policy, see also Coatsworth and Williamson (2004).

References

Adelman, J., Republic of Capital: Buenos Aires and the Legal Transformation of the Atlantic World (Stanford: Stanford University Press, 1999).

Almeida, J., 'Atualidade das idéias econômicas do Visconde de Cairu', in da Silva Lisboa, J., Estudos do Bem Comum e Economía Política; ou Ciência das Leis Naturais e Civis de Animar e Dirigir a Geral Indústria e Promover a Riqueza Nacional e Prosperidade do Estado (Rio de Janeiro: IPEA/INPES, 1975 (orig. 1819)).

Arcila Farías, E., Reformas económicas del siglo XVIII en Nueva España, 2 vols (Mexico: SepSetentas, 1974).

Bauer, A., Chilean Rural Society from the Spanish Conquest to 1930 (Cambridge University Press, 1975).

Belgrano, M. (1796), 'Medios Generales de Fomentar la Agricultura, Animar la Industria y Proteger el Comercio en un país Agricultor', in J. C. Chiaramonte (1979) (ed.), Pensamiento de la Ilustración: Economía y Sociedad Iberoamericanas en el Siglo XVIII, vol. 51 (Caracas: Biblioteca Ayacucho).

Bernecker, W., 'Las Relaciones entre Europa y Latinoamérica durante el siglo XIX: Ofensivas Comerciales e Intereses Económicos', Hispania, 53/1 (1993) 177–212.

Bethell, L., 'The Independence of Brazil', in L. Bethell (ed.), Cambridge History of Latin America, vol. III (Cambridge University Press, 1985).

Bethell, L. and J. M., de Carvalho, 'Brazil From Independence to the Middle of the Nineteenth Century', in L. Bethell (ed.), Cambridge History of Latin America vol. III (Cambridge University Press, 1985).

Burns, E. B., 'The Intellectuals as Agents of Change and the Independence of Brazil, 1724–1822', in A. J. R. Russell-Wood (ed.), From Colony to Nation: Essays on the Independence of Brazil (Baltimore: Johns Hopkins University Press, 1975).

Cains, P. J. and A. G. Hopkins, British Imperialism: Innovation and Expansion, 1688–1914 (London: Longmans, 1993).

Chiaramonte, J. C. (1979), 'Prólogo', in J. C. Chiaramonte (ed.), *Pensamiento de la Ilustración: Economía y Sociedad Iberoamericanas en el Siglo XVIII*, vol. 51 (Caracas: Ayacucho, 1979).

Chiaramonte, J. C., *La Crítica Ilustrada de la Realidad: Economía y Sociedad en el Pensamiento Argentino e Iberoamericano del Siglo XVIII* (Buenos Aires: Centro Editor de América Latina, 1982).

Chowning, M., *Wealth and Power in Provincial Mexico: Michoacan from the Late Colony to the Revolution* (Stanford University Press, 1999).

Coats, A. W. and D. C. Colander, 'An Introduction to the Spread of Economic Ideas', in A. W. Coats and D. Colander (eds), *The Spread of Economic Ideas* (Cambridge University Press, 1989).

Coatsworth, J. H., 'Economic and Institutional Trajectories in Nineteenth Century Latin America', in J. H. Coatsworth and A. Taylor (eds), *Latin America and the World Economy since 1800* (Cambridge, MA: Harvard University Press, 1998).

Coatsworth, J. H. and J. G. Williamson, 'Always Protectionist? Latin American Tariffs from Independence to the Great Depression', *Journal of Latin American Studies* 36:2 (May 2004) 205–32.

Collier, S. and W. F., Sater, *A History of Chile, 1808–1994* (Cambridge University Press, 1996).

Da Costa, E. V., *The Brazilian Empire: Myths and Histories* (University of Chicago Press, 1985).

Da Silva Lisboa, J., *Estudos do Bem Comum e Economía Política; ou Ciência das Leis Naturais e Civis de Animar e Dirigir a Geral Indústria e Promover a Riqueza Nacional e Prosperidade do Estado*, Rio de Janeiro: IPEA/INPES, 1975 (orig. 1819)).

Da Silva Lisboa, J., *Manual de Política Ortodoxa* (Rio de Janeiro: Tipografía Nacional, 1832).

De Lima Sobrinho, A. E., *Etapas das Idéias Econômicas no Brasil* (Brasilia: Editorial Universidade de Brasilia, 1978).

Dean, W., 'Latifundia and Land Policy in 19th Century Brazil', *Hispanic American Historial Review*, 51/4 (1971) 606–25.

Deans-Smith, S., *Bureaucrats, Planters, and Workers: The Making of the Tobacco Monopoly in Bourbon Mexico* (Austin: University of Texas Press, 1992).

Estenssoro Fuchs, J. C., 'La Plebe Ilustrada: El Pueblo en las Fronteras de la Razón', in C. Walker (ed.), *Entre la Retórica y la Insurgencia: Las Ideas y Los Movimientos Sociales en los Andes*, siglo XVIII (Cusco: CBC, 1996).

Etzioni, A., *The Moral Dimension: Towards a New Economics* (New York: Free Press, 1988).

Fisher, J., *Commercial Relations Between Spain and Spanish America in the Era of Free Trade, 1778–1796* (University of Liverpool Centre for Latin American Studies, 1985).

Glade, W. P., 'Commercial Policy in Early Republican Latin America', in R. Liehr (ed.), *América Latina en la Época de Simón Bolívar: La Formación de las Economías Nacionales y los Intereses Económicos Europeos 1800–1850* (Berlin: Colloquium, 1989).

Gootenberg, P., *Between Silver and Guano: Commercial Policy and the State in Post-Independence Peru* (Princeton: Princeton University Press, 1989).

Guerra, F. X., *Modernidad e Independencia: Ensayos sobre las Revoluciones Hispánicas*, (México: Fondo de Cultura Económica, 1993).

Hale, C., *Mexican Liberalism in the Age of Mora, 1821–1853* (New Haven: Yale University Press, 1968).

Halperín Donghi, T., *Reforma y Disolución de los Imperios Ibéricos, 1750–1850* (Madrid: Alianza, 1985).

Halperín Donghi, T., *El Espejo de la Historia: Problemas Argentinos y Perspectivas Hispanoamericanas* (Buenos Aires: Sudamericano, 1987).

Herr, R., *The Eighteenth Century Revolution in Spain* (Princeton University Press, 1958).

Jacobsen, N., 'Pensamiento Económico y Políticas Económicas en el Perú, 1885–1899: Los Limites a la Ortodoxia Liberal', in C. Contreras and M. Glave (eds), *Estado y Mercado en la Formación de la Economía Peruana* (Lima: Editorial de la Pontificia Universidad Católica del Perú, 2002).

Jones, C. A., *International Business in the Nineteenth Century: The Rise and Fall of a Cosmopolitan Bourgeoisie* (New York University Press, 1987).

Jones, C., *El Reino Unido y América: Inversiones e Influencia Económica* (Madrid: MAPFRE, 1992).

Kay, C., *Latin American Theories of Development and Underdevelopment* (London: Routledge, 1989).

Marchant, A., 'Aspects of Enlightenment in Brazil', in A. Whitaker (ed.), *Latin America and the Enlightenment* (Ithaca, NY: Cornell University Press, 1942).

Marichal, C., *A Century of Debt Crises in Latin America: From Independence to the Great Depression, 1820–1930* (Princeton University Press, 1989).

Marichal, C., 'Liberalism and Fiscal Policy: The Argentine Paradox, 1820–1862', in V. C. Peloso and B. Tenenbaum (eds), *Liberals, Politics and Power: State Formation in Nineteenth Century Latin America* (Athens: University of Georgia Press, 1996).

McFarlane, A., *Colombia before Independence: Economy, Society and Politics During the Bourbon Era* (Cambridge University Press, 1993).

Miller, R., *Britain and Latin America in the 19th and 20th Centuries* (London: Longmans, 1993).

O'Phelan Godoy, Scarlett, 'Las Reformas Fiscales Borbónicas y su Impacto en la Sociedad Colonial del Bajo y Alto Peru', in N. Jacobsen and Hans-Jürgen Puhle (eds), *The Economies of Mexico and Peru During the Late Colonial Period, 1760–1810* (Berlin: Colloquium, 1986).

Ocampo, J. A., *Colombia y la Economía Mundial, 1830–1910* (México: Siglo Veintiuno Editores, 1984).

Reyes Heroles, J. (1957), *El Liberalismo Mexicano*, part 1 of 3 vols (Universidad Nacional de México, 1957).

Ringrose, D., *Spain, Europe and the 'Spanish Miracle', 1700–1900* (Cambridge University Press, 1996).

Safford, F., 'The Emergence of Economic Liberalism in Colombia', in J. Love and N. Jacobsen (eds), *Guiding the Invisible Hand: Economic Liberalism: Economic Liberalism and the State in Latin American History* (New York: Praeger, 1988).

Salvucci, R. J., L. K. Salvucci, and A. Cohen, 'The Politics of Protection: Interpreting Commercial Policy in Late Bourbon and Early and Early National Mexico', in K. J. Andrien and L. L. Johnson (eds), *The Political Economy of Spanish America in the Age of Revolution, 1750–1850* (Albuquerque: University of New Mexico Press, 1994).

Sarrailh, J., *La España Ilustrada de la Segunda Mitad del Siglo XVIII* (México: Fondo de Cultura Económica, 1957).

Serulnikov, S., 'The Parish, the Universe and the Space in Between: Andean Political Imagination During the Late Eighteenth Century', in N. Jacobsen and C. Aljovín (eds), *Political Cultures in the Andes, 1750–1950* (Durham: Duke University Press, 2005).

Skinner, A. S., 'Adam Smith', in J. Eatwell, M. Milgate and P. Newman (eds), *The New Palgrave: The Invisible Hand* (New York: Palgrave, 1989).

Smith, T., *The Pattern of Imperialism: The United States, Great Britain and the Late-Industrializing World Since 1815* (Cambridge University Press, 1981).

Solow, R. M., 'How Economic Ideas Turn To Mush', in A. W. Coats and D. Colander (eds), *The Spread of Economic Ideas* (Cambridge University Press, 1989).

Spiegel, H. W., *The Growth of Economic Thought*, 3rd edn (Durham, NC: Duke University Press, 1991).

Villalobos R. S. and B. R. Sagredo, *El Proteccionismo Económico en Chile, Siglo XIX* (Santiago: Blas Cañas, 1987).

Viner, J., 'Adam Smith and Laissez Faire', in J.M. Clark et al., *Adam Smith 1776–1926: Lectures to Commemorate the Sesquicentennial of the Publication of 'The Wealth of Nations'* (Chicago: University of Chicago Press, 1928).

Vizcarra, C., 'Markets and Hierarchies in Late Colonial Spanish America: The Royal Tobacco Monopoly in the Viceroyalty of Peru, 1752–1813', PhD dissertation, (University of Illinois at Urbana-Champaign, 2001).

Walker, C., *Smouldering Ashes: Cuzco and the Creation of Republican Peru, 1780–1840* (Durham, NC: Duke University Press, 1999).

Whitaker, A. (ed.), *Latin America and the Enlightenment* (Ithaca, NY: Cornell University Press, 1942; 2nd edn 1961).

Will, R. M., 'The Introduction of Classical Economics into Chile', *Hispanic American Historical Review* 44/1 (February 1964) 1–21.

Zeitlin, M., *The Civil Wars in Chile (or the Bourgeois Revolutions That Never Were)* (Princeton University Press, 1984).

7
Institutional Foundations of Economic Ideas in Latin America, 1914–50

Joseph L. Love

Introduction

This chapter reviews the international economic theories, broad ideas, biases and outlooks that tended to prevail in Latin America from World War I to the early 1950s, and shows how institutional responses were central to the success of some schools over others. The quality of understanding and depth of penetration of imported doctrines depended critically on the nature of the academic and research settings, as would the later 'indigenous' (if eclectic) structuralist school. 'Institution' here includes formal institutions, plus relevant practices and networks that constitute informal ones, and rules by which formal and informal institutions operate internally and relate to others in society.[1]

The state

The Latin American state was obviously the most important institution in each national setting. Not only did it fund the universities, but the state also included agencies which directly affected the economy, and often had economic research and training functions as well. In Whitehead's opinion, 'stateness' in terms of government income, outlay and efficiency rose markedly between the late 1920s and the late 1950s, so that 'modernizing' states had replaced 'oligarchic' states by the end of the period (Whitehead 1994:90). Gains were especially notable in direct taxation, as Argentina, Brazil, Chile and Venezuela, among others, introduced taxes on income. On the outlay side, governments had acquired new obligations in social spending; Brazil, Chile and Uruguay put social security systems in place before the war, and Argentina and Mexico followed in the 1940s (Whitehead 1994:76).

Of particular relevance for the spread of economic knowledge was the creation of central banks – with the power to control the money supply and interest rates, and serve as a lender of last resort – which in fact constituted a major advance in 'stateness' in the period in question. On the west coast of

South America, where US interests were dominant by the 1920s, Professor Edwin Kemmerer of Princeton University shaped such institutions in a series of missions from Colombia to Chile. On the east coast, where British capital, though in decline, was still dominant, British advisers, and especially Sir Otto Niemeyer of the Bank of England, were influential. However, the governments of Argentina and Brazil extensively revised Niemeyer's recommendations in creating the Banco Central (1935) and the Superintendency of Currency and Credit (SUMOC, 1945), respectively.[2]

Central banks aided in the professionalization of economics in Latin America, both in terms of their research functions and in training economists on the job. For the Cuban central banker Felipe Pazos, the Argentine Bank under the direction of Raúl Prebisch set a standard for the whole region, not only in its building of financial and trade indices, and conducting counter-cyclical policy, but also in its accurate economic analysis as well (Pazos 1953:565). As early as 1928, the Argentine Central Bank's predecessor, the Banco de la Nación, had established a research division under Prebisch, and launched the publication of the *Revista Económica* (Banco de la Nación Argentina 1928:2). The Banco de México established a research unit in 1934,[3] and ten years later Prebisch helped reorganize it into a central bank, led by Daniel Cosío Villegas and others.[4] The Banco de México seminars quickly became a research venue of international importance. In Brazil, SUMOC, along with the Federal Council of Foreign Trade (CFCE), became important 'practical schools for training in economics' (Loureiro 1997:23, 25).

In the postwar period, development banks, tending to focus on industrialization, would also be training grounds for economists. In the larger countries, they had been established in the 1930s and 1940s. In Mexico, Nacional Financiera, SA (NAFINSA), a partly government-owned development bank, had been established in 1934, though it became seriously committed to manufacturing only after its reorganization at the end of 1940. During World War II, the pace quickened.[5] Meanwhile in 1938, Chile had created its Corporación de Fomento de la Producción, but in 1940, the sum budgeted for the development of manufacturing was less than each of those allocated to agriculture, mining, energy and public housing (Presidente de la República 1940:21–2, 95). In Brazil, a division for industrial development in the Bank of Brazil began to make significant loans in 1941, but from then until the war's end it only disbursed an annual average of 17.5 per cent of its private sector loans to manufacturing concerns (Vargas 1940:91, 1941:179; Villela and Suzigan 1973:352). Meanwhile, other Latin American governments were also establishing development banks: Bolivia, Colombia and Venezuela all did so between 1940 and 1946 (Santos 1945; Whitehead 1994:74), even if everywhere the role of such banks remained modest at the war's end.

Whether one emphasizes gains in the boom years of the 1920s or the depression years that followed, it is evident that industrial growth made major strides in the inter-war years in the larger countries. Traditional exports tended to be undynamic, as shown by deteriorating terms of trade for all primary products between 1913 and 1929, even though the impressive import-substitution industrialization of the 1930s, excepting Argentina, depended significantly on the recovery of exports (Bulmer-Thomas 1994:224; Thorp 1998:104). During the 1930s, industrial growth in seven Latin American countries – including the six largest ones – exceeded that of the GDP (Thorp 1998:113).[6] Growth was qualitatively different also, from earlier years, establishing the foundations for a transition to the 'pure import-substitution model' of the postwar period (Bulmer-Thomas 1994:224, 232).

Concomitant with the industrialization trend came a rising emphasis on state intervention in the economy, notably in the form of planning – however much or little that meant in practice. By the end of World War II, planning was nearing the zenith of its prestige. In Europe, the imperial German government's experience with *Kriegswirtschaft* in 1916–18 was followed by the first Soviet five-year plan (from 1928), and in the following two decades western governments initially attempted to stimulate economic growth through fiscal policies and public works programs, and then introduced extensive controls during the war effort that followed. Keynes had provided a theoretical basis for economic management in capitalist economies, Wassily Leontief had shown that planning could be 'scientific' through his input–output model of the American economy in 1941, and the Soviet five-year plans, emphasizing industrialization, were widely credited for the Soviet Union's successful resistance to the German onslaught in the same year. Toward the end of the war, the earliest 'economic development theses', those of Rosenstein-Rodan and Mandlebaum, had emphasized planning and industrialization as a central element in stimulating growth in 'backward' countries. In Britain, the Political and Economic Planning group brought together leading economists, many of them continental exiles, who would open the new field of development economics in the first postwar decade.

How could Latin Americans not be influenced by these trends towards state intervention and planning? Already, intervention in the economy had an established history in the region, but until the eve of World War II, not for the purpose of developing industry. Brazil intervened in the international coffee market in the years 1906–30, and Chile did so, though much less effectively, in the world nitrate market in 1931–3.

By the time of World War II, governments supported industrialization not only in the form of industrial credit banks, but also in the creation of basic industries, of which Brazil's Volta Redonda Steel Mill was the most important. Getúlio Vargas, the president-turned-dictator of Brazil, exacted a national steel mill from the United States as part of the country's price for sending troops to Italy during the war. Although the Cárdenas government in Mexico had officially introduced multi-year planning for the *sexenio* beginning in 1934, industrialization at the time had taken a back seat to agrarian reform.[7] A decade later, the economist Víctor Urquidi called for 'an organic plan of development and industrialization' for Latin America. However, Urquidi had doubts that the new World Bank, just created at Bretton Woods, would adequately support planning. Two years later, he repeated the case for planning in his native country, stating that Mexico needed an 'organic national plan of investment' to support industrialization, although he cautioned against seeing industrialization as a panacea (Urquidi 1944:614–15; Urquidi 1946:2, 25). In *Trimestre Económico* (*TE*), Urquidi's colleague Gustavo Polit praised the intentions of the Perón regime's first five-year plan of 1946. Polit approved Perón's attempts to industrialize Argentina in order to overcome the problem of disguised unemployment (in the new postwar sense), and he cited Kurt Mandelbaum's *Industrialization of Backward Areas* (1945) for theoretical support.[8] Thus the state, by the end of the period, had gained unprecedented power, prestige and legitimacy as an economic actor, and as we shall see, stimulated economic research through new institutions.

Journals and research institutes

Let us turn to the specific means of the diffusion of economic knowledge in the inter-war period. No institutions, perhaps, were more basic to the spread of ideas than professional journals and the organizations which produced them.[9] In this area, Argentina led the way with the *Revista de Ciencias Económicas* (*RCE*), the review of the Facultad de Ciencias Económicas, created at the University of Buenos Aires in 1913. The RCE was published continuously from 1913 until 1947, when Perón purged the Argentine universities and took over the journal. From the beginning, however, its editors did not see the *RCE* as a theoretical vehicle, but as a more general review on problems related to the Argentine economy, with an occasional excursion into theory relevant to Argentine issues. Political economy was the rule, with frequent references to law.

Two more important journals followed the *RCE* in Argentina before the Great Depression. Both were primarily concerned with 'real-world' issues, but had a professed interest in research. Alejandro Bunge – among other attributes, a professor at the Facultad de Ciencias Económicas – launched the *Revista de Economía Argentina* in mid 1918. In an editorial statement appearing in every issue, Bunge's journal called for 'the use of a rigorously scientific method' in economic research, and 'the publication and diffusion of the ideas that can in any way help solve our [economic] problems'. In an article titled 'Positive Economics and Argentine Political Economy' (1918), Bunge condemned 'the lack of the habit of research, the absence of university discipline in the direct examination of the [economic] facts'.[10]

Yet in many ways the most important journal of the inter-war period in Argentina was the *Revista Económica* of the Banco de la Nación Argentina, also published in English as the *Economic Review*, first appearing in 1928. Focused on banking, business cycles and foreign trade, the journal was the product of a new Bureau of Economic Research created the same year. The *Economic Review* proposed to provide accurate data series (on prices, the volume of sales and so on), based on techniques used by the US Department of Commerce and the Federal Reserve System; such data could serve as the basis for research on Argentine business cycles (de Estrada 1928:2). The director of the journal was Raúl Prebisch, Bunge's former student and himself now a professor at the University of Buenos Aires. The Bureau was Latin America's first real research institute. The unit and its review passed to the new Banco Central when the latter was created in 1935, with Prebisch as the Bank's first director; its *Memorias* (annual reports) became an important source of economic information and analysis even beyond Argentina (see Pazos, above).

In the Depression era, however, leadership in journal publication and institutional innovation was passing to Mexico, where there was an increasingly dense network of research-related institutions. A number of economists (*lato sensu*) led by Manuel Gómez Morín, director of the Escuela Nacional de Jurisprudencia, and including Narciso Bassols, Jesús Silva Herzog, and Daniel Cosío Villegas, had begun to formalize the study of economics as early as 1925. In 1928, an Instituto Mexicano de Investigaciones Económicas appeared, though it was to have a brief existence and was less committed to research than Prebisch's Bureau in Argentina. Meanwhile, the study of economics remained in the Law School until 1934, when Enrique González Aparicio returned from study in England to establish the Escuela de Economía as an independent entity in the Universidad Nacional Autónoma de México (UNAM) (Becerra Maldonado 1989:vol. 1, 22). It was Silva Herzog, however, the long-time director of the Escuela, who was 'the most important founder of economics at UNAM' (Babb 2002:31).

In the same year, Cosío Villegas and Eduardo Villaseñor established *El Trimestre Económico*, which was arguably the most important economics journal published in Latin America during the twentieth century.[11] Not only did the *Trimestre* deal with issues in agrarian and agricultural economics in Mexico and elsewhere in Latin America, but it also published translations of articles by distinguished scholars coming from such diverse perspectives as Friedrich von Hayek, Joseph Schumpeter, Maurice Dobb and Oskar Lange.

In 1934, Cosío and Villaseñor also established the Fondo de Cultura Económica, which soon became Latin America's most important economics publishing house. Before mid century, the Fondo had published not only many translations of European and North American works in neo-classical, Marxist and Keynesian traditions, but also a survey of contemporary Latin American economic thought (Gondra *et al.* 1945), and Prebisch's widely used *Introducción a Keynes* (1947). Cosío, who had studied agricultural economics and other subjects at Harvard, Cornell and Wisconsin, had a talent for raising funds, and the Fondo was supported by the Asociación de Banqueros de

México, of which he was director. More important was the financial support of the Banco de México and the Finance Ministry (Babb 2002:58). In 1937, *Trimestre Económico* became an organ of the Fondo (Villaseñor 1953:550–1; Cosío Villegas 1986: 102–18; Lida and Matesanz 1990:64). Another Mexican journal appeared in that year, the *Revista de Economía*, edited by Jesús Silva Herzog. This was something closer to an economic bulletin, appearing biweekly, and less given to theory and 'big issues' than the *Trimestre*. In the war years, the *Revista*, now directed by Gustavo Martínez Cabañas – later to be the first executive secretary of ECLA – focused on problems of industrialization (Bagú 1944:37; 'Industrialización' 1945:5–6).

Still another Mexican journal began in 1941, this one the organ of the Escuela Nacional de Economía of UNAM. Its articles were true to its title, *Investigación Económica*, but the subjects studied were again largely problems of sectoral production, especially in the early years.

Daniel Cosío Villegas was not only a founder of the *Trimestre* and the Fondo de Cultura, but from its creation until 1963 was the chief administrator and later president of a third institution that perhaps was even more influential in shaping Mexico's social sciences – the Colegio de México, whose mission was the creation of a Mexican intellectual elite (Cosío Villegas 1986:177–8). The Colegio had been preceded in 1939 by the Casa de España, the academic fruit of President Lázaro Cárdenas's policy of welcoming Spanish exiles fleeing Franco Spain. The Spanish sociologist José Medina Echavarría, who would later head the Instituto Latinoamericano de Planificación Económica y Social (ILPES), a dependency of ECLA, collaborated with Cosío to found the Centro de Estudios Sociales at the Colegio in 1943 (Lida and Matesanz 1990:205). There, Josué Sáenz and Víctor Urquidi, an employee of the Banco de México, and the Spanish exile Javier Márquez taught economics, while Medina introduced Weberian sociology.[12] Economic offerings included a theoretical course on international economics, statistics and an interdisciplinary seminar on 'the consequences of the industrial revolution in Mexico' (Lida and Matesanz 1990:209, 222–3). Of the 18 students at the Centro, Cosío Villegas had recruited 8 from the Escuela Nacional de Economía, where he was a professor. One was the future ECLA economist and leading contributor to the structural inflation thesis, Juan Noyola Vázquez. Foreign students at the Centro included three future economic historians, each to become well known in his own country – Eduardo Arcila Farías of Venezuela, and Julio LeReverend and Manuel Moreno Fraginals, both of Cuba (Lida and Matesanz 1990:149, 210).

The Centro was closed in 1946, perhaps because of a dispute between Cosío and Medina, who left the Colegio that year. In 1948, Cosío turned to historical studies, for which he obtained grants from the Rockefeller Foundation and the Carnegie Endowment for the creation of a Centro de Estudios Históricos.[13] During the lifetime of the Centro, the Colegio also published short monographs, based on seminars by professors and other authorities in the social sciences and humanities. In this series, called 'Jornadas', Márquez published a study on integration in Latin America, Gonzalo Robles wrote one on industrialization in the region, and Raúl Prebisch published a third on the gold standard and economic vulnerability in Latin America (Prebisch 1944).

Brazil trailed Argentina and Mexico in the development of professional journals and research institutes, but it began to catch up at the end of the war. The central institution was the Fundação Getúlio Vargas (FGV) in Rio de Janeiro, established as a training and research institute for high-level bureaucrats in 1944, with close government ties. The FGV sought to generate price indexes and did basic work on establishing Brazil's national accounts. It would soon have formal teaching functions too, but was initially linked with the Faculdade de Ciencias Econômicas of the University of Brazil.

Through the 1930s in Brazil as elsewhere, 'economics' generally meant monetary issues, rather than issues of economic development, GDP measurement or employment – all of which appeared on the agenda in the 1940s (Gudin 1972:86). The man most responsible for changing this situation in Brazil was Eugênio Gudin, an engineer by training who had taught himself economics. He had been a frequent adviser to the Vargas government during the Estado Novo dictatorship (1937–45), was named to the chair of money and banking at the University of Brazil when the Faculdade de Ciencias Econômicas opened in Rio in 1945, and would become Minister of Finance in the mid 1950s.

It was Gudin who set up the Brazilian statutes on economics training in 1945, basing the curriculum on his contacts with professors at Harvard, which he visited after the Bretton Woods Conference (Loureiro 1997:35, 37). In 1946, he established an economics research institute at the FGV, which was soon renamed the Instituto Brasileiro de Economia. In 1947, the Instituto launched the publication of its research journal, the *Revista Brasileira de Economia*, as well as a bulletin of current economic data and analysis, the *Conjuntura Econômica*.

The *RBE*, which was to be the most important Portuguese-language economics journal of the twentieth century, did not appear until 1947, but aspired to a high standard. In its first editorial, the editors announced their intention to be guided by the orientation of the FGV, namely, to pursue 'the systematic treatment of the diverse issues related to the national economy – notably those concerning ... the theory and application of economic science' (*RBE* 1947:7).

Gudin put the Instituto de Economia on the map in part by inviting internationally renowned economists to Rio de Janeiro to deliver lectures on development issues, broadly defined. Each series of lectures was then translated and published in the *RBE*. The scholars chosen covered a broad ideological spectrum. Beginning in 1947 with Gottfried Habeler, they also included Hans W. Singer, Jacob Viner, Ragnar Nurkse, Kenneth Boulding,

Lionel Robbins, Nicholas Kaldor and Edward Bernstein (director of research at the IMF) in the first decade of the *RBE*'s existence.[14] Of equal interest perhaps, was the fact that the lectures generated Brazilian responses, notably Celso Furtado's reply to Nurkse (Furtado 1954a:124–44).

The training of economists

Everywhere in Latin America, the teaching of economics in the inter-war period provided less than full-time employment – usually considerably less. In Mexico, Sarah Babb has convincingly argued that government was overwhelmingly the most important employer of economists in the 1930s and 1940s,[15] and this situation was probably true elsewhere. Only in this period or later, depending on the country, was economics 'liberated' as a separate discipline, no longer to be the hobby of autodidacts employed at engineering and law schools. The Facultad de Ciencias Económicas in Buenos Aires, founded in 1913, led the way as a stand-alone department, and Professor Luis Roque Gondra offered South America's first course in mathematical economics there in 1918 (Gondra 1945:32).

Yet, the legitimate existence of economics as a distinct field came slowly elsewhere. Foreign professors, such as France's François Perroux, who taught at the University of São Paulo (USP) in the mid 1930s, was himself the product of the Faculté de Droit at Lyon, and taught in the Faculdade de Direito at the USP. At the USP, even after Gudin's reforms 'liberating' economics from other disciplines in 1945, most of the professors had come from the law school (Loureiro 1997:34, 37).

Forward-looking but conservative statesmen like Vargas's Minister of Education Gustavo Campanema wanted to create an 'elite' with technical expertise – not least in formal economic analysis. However, there was a related issue of prestige: if economics was not an adjunct field to engineering or law, then it was sometimes seen as a complementary field to commercial sciences, in an era in which accounting also lacked prestige, compared to the traditional professions of law, engineering, and medicine.[16] For youth who could aspire to being doctors and lawyers, who wanted to be a bookkeeper? Economics probably meant little more than bookkeeping to students at elite secondary schools, who had to choose a professional curriculum on entering the university.

Before World War II, as indicated, there had been almost no tradition in Latin America of seeking foreign research (PhD) degrees – in contrast to that of Eastern Europe, where the pattern began in the third quarter of the nineteenth century. In Charles Hale's survey of Latin American social and political thought over the half-century ending in 1930, only one intellectual of some 90 treated, the Mexican anthropologist Manuel Gamio, held a PhD.[17] Such a fact might serve as a proxy for the weakness of a research tradition. In the field of economics, we might take as representative Jesús Silva Herzog's survey, *El Pensamiento Económico en México* (Economic Thought in

Mexico), which covers Mexico's national history through the mid 1920s. Revealingly, all of his 'economists' are autodidacts (Silva Herzog 1947).

Patently, the professionalization of economics, defined rather strictly here in university teaching and in advanced research venues as requiring a PhD, was not achieved in the first half of the twentieth century. Latin American students of economics began to appear in modest numbers in North American and European universities in the 1930s and 1940s, but it seems that only a couple of dozen at most obtained foreign PhDs before 1960, and the next 20 years was decisive in bringing the profession up to international standards, at least in the most developed countries.[18]

Among the earliest Brazilian students taking course work abroad were Otávio Bulhões and Roberto Oliveira Campos, both in the diplomatic service, who began their graduate studies at American and George Washington Universities in the US capital in the early 1940s. After the war, Campos took further work at Columbia University, when he was stationed in New York. Sikkink (1988:113–15) mentions other Brazilian diplomats who followed this pattern, and suggests that high bureaucrats associated with developmentalism ('*desenvolvimentismo*') during the 1950s and 1960s in Brazil were more likely to have studied abroad than their counterparts in Argentina.[19] However, during his years as director general of the Argentine Central Bank (1935–43), Prebisch did send Argentinian students to Harvard (Pollock *et al.* 2002).

For a number of students, the foreign experience was decisive in their education as economists. Dênio Nogueira, a member of Brazil's National Economic Council in the 1950s, had studied economics with Gudin before the economic reform, graduating in 1944. In 1949, he spent a year at the University of Michigan studying with Kenneth Boulding. In retrospect, Nogueira declared his Brazilian-acquired knowledge of economics as '*fraquíssimo*' (extremely weak), and attributed his knowledge of theory to his year at Michigan.[20] Among the earliest Brazilians to take a PhD was Celso Furtado, at the University of Paris in 1949, who wrote a thesis for Maurice Byé at the Faculté de Droit.[21] Like Campos and Bulhões, he was a Brazilian civil servant.

Mexicans who studied economics abroad in the 1940s likewise usually had positions in the government (Cosío Villegas 1986:198; see also Babb 2002:83), and this situation was almost certainly typical throughout the region. Mexico probably set the pace in foreign study, though a student's residence abroad was generally not for more than a year at a time at any single institution. Already in the 1930s, several Mexicans, some of them in the diplomatic service, had studied abroad – Antonio Espinoza de los Monteros had studied at Harvard; Manuel Gómez Morín at Columbia; Miguel Palacios Macedo at the University of Paris; Eduardo Villaseñor, Josué Sáenz and Víctor Urquidi at the University of London (Becerra Maldonado 1989:21; Camp 1995). As noted above, Cosío Villegas studied economics at three American universities.

In 1940, when Villaseñor became head of the Banco de México, Cosío Villegas assumed control of its Department of Economic Studies, and sent a sizeable number of government officials – and not only those in the Bank – to study abroad (Cosío Villegas 1986:198). In 1948, Edmundo Flores completed a doctorate in economics at Wisconsin (Flores 1983),[22] and in 1949, the same year Furtado took his doctorate in Paris, Alfredo Navarrete completed an economics dissertation at Harvard on the Mexican balance of payments (Navarrete 1950).

Foreign study, however, had its critics. In 1966, Anibal Pinto and Osvaldo Sunkel sharply criticized the training economists received abroad, especially in the United States. They argued that the macro models to which Latin Americans were exposed were focused on the short run, and were closed (that is, had no foreign sector). They further alleged that many of the sophisticated mathematical tools taught in the United States were unfit for the poor quality of data available in Latin America, and that many development problems were not quantifiable. They called for training in a world area in which the economists had previous work experience – presumably at ESCOLATINA of the University of Chile and ILPES,[23] both internationally-focused programs in Santiago connected with ECLA, the organization where Pinto and Sunkel were employed (Pinto and Sunkel 1966:79–90). However, the two critics can now be said to have lost the battle, as evidenced by the symbolic fact that the man named to direct ECLA in 1997, José Antonio Ocampo, was trained at Yale University.[24]

Of course, the creation of an economics profession was not simply a matter of setting up a modern curriculum at home and sending promising students abroad. Broader cultural and institutional problems had impeded the development of social science in Latin America. The intellectual traditions of the region through the inter-war years largely revolved around the *pensador* (lit., thinker), a man who prided himself on his broad culture and who eschewed specialization; he often wrote as readily about contemporary sociology and politics as he did about literature, and his studies frequently crossed disciplinary lines. The *pensador's* vehicle was the essay, a literary form which in Latin America retains the prestige which it has all but lost in the English-speaking world. The style perhaps was appropriate to highly stratified, pre-industrial societies; in any case, the writer on social matters usually wrote without reference to monographic studies. The essayist's judgments tended to be definitive, his treatment historical. Formal, rule-based social research was scarce, poorly funded and unappreciated.

The *pensador* tradition was dying, but slowly. In 1960, Professor Howard Ellis of Berkeley and two Latin American colleagues wrote a report on the teaching of economics in Latin America for ECLA, the OAS and UNESCO. Although noting that several universities had plans underway to offer the equivalent of a US or European doctorate, hurdles remained, and not only in preparation in mathematics. One problem was language: '[F]ew Latin American university students have a sufficient mastery of English to be able to read the literature of economics' (Ellis *et al.* 1961:53, 59). Foreign missions were still important, such as that of University of Chicago professors at the Universidad Católica in Santiago in the late 1950s and Vanderbilt professors at USP, beginning in 1965 (Ellis *et al.* 1961:80; Teixeira Vieira 1981:368; Harberger 1996:301–3).

In brief, the achievements of the postwar era, and the maturation of several domestic doctoral programs in the larger Latin American countries in the mid 1970s, had an indispensable foundation in the inter-war years. During that time, the first economics programs were liberated from allied disciplines, and governments began to pay for the economics training of civil servants and subsequently to employ them. The interaction of universities, central banks and research institutions all began in those years. However, one must also acknowledge the role of individual actors in providing the continuity in policy in governmental, educational and research institutions (Sikkink 1988:24–5). It was, after all, men like Daniel Cosío Villegas, Raúl Prebisch and Eugenio Gudin who established a network of institutions and facilitated their interaction. Is it extending the notion of institutions too far to suggest that such men and their teams and networks, like rules and practices, were themselves institutions? Mortal, to be sure, but so were many institutions.

Conclusion

This chapter has explored the institutional framework underlying the development of economic ideas and ideologies in Latin America from the end of World War I, through a largely pre-theoretical phase in the 1930s to the early 1950s, when the formal study of economics became a legitimate field in its own right.

I have shown how certain institutions, beginning with the state and its component agencies – especially the central bank (or closest approximation) – crucially affected the reception and diffusion of European and North American economic ideas in the inter-war years. States supplied new development banks, offered opportunities for on-the-job training, began to send their best employees to study abroad, subsidized journals in central banks and public universities, and provided a critical public sector demand for trained economists. In the academy, economics was liberated from engineering and law schools, and the field began to acquire a new level of prestige as an academic subject and as a profession, though its triumph was not yet consolidated by 1950.

The institutions at issue, however, were not only state agencies, universities, journals, publishing houses and research institutes, but also individuals and groups who supplied the necessary 'connectivity' among the formal institutions and practices that were associated with the teaching and research processes that moved Latin America away from *ensayismo* and toward professional economics. In a part of the world where formal institutions frequently led short lives because of economic shocks, radical shifts in government priorities, or political upheaval, the role of individuals, groups and networks was critical.

In the years 1914–1950, economics as a profession in Latin America began the fundamental shift toward a formal, independent academic discipline that linked theory to research, and the field broadened from monetary problems to issues of cyclical behaviour, development, national accounting and employment. In the process – inevitably perhaps, given the nature of the problems at hand and the power of the constituents who wanted them solved – neo-classical economics triumphed easily over other schools of thought, though a rising enthusiasm for Keynesian economics emerged at the end of the period. This enthusiasm would pave the way for the rise of structuralism, propagated by ECLA and Raúl Prebisch, in the decade to come.

Notes

1. This definition follows that in Sikkink 1991:23. It is more useful for my purposes than Douglass North's definition (1981:201–2) consisting of rules, compliance procedures, and ethical norms related to maximizing wealth or utility – without explicitly including formal institutions.
2. Niemeyer was probably not surprised by the Brazilian revisions. In a confidential letter following a mission to Brazil in 1931, he wrote: '[I]n Brazil the law of cause and effect evidently does not apply to the sphere of economics and ... since nothing here seems to be certain but the unexpected, [I] suppose things are really not as bad as they [seem]' (cited in de Paiva Abreu 1977:47).
3. See Cosío Villegas 1986:198.
4. Meanwhile, Chile's Banco Nacional appointed Hermann Max as Director of Economic Research in 1933 (Keller 1945:215).
5. For sources, see Love (1994:401, n. 22).
6. The countries were Argentina, Brazil, Chile, Colombia, Costa Rica, Peru and Venezuela.
7. On the almost wholly symbolic nature of the first Mexican plan, see Solís 1975:190–1.
8. Polit (1948: 194–201, citing Mandelbaum 1945).
9. On the importance of journals in the diffusion of economic ideas in the United States, see Day (1989:61–72).
10. Editorial, *Revista de Economía Argentina*, 1/1:1 (1918: July–Dec.); Alejandro Bunge, 'La economia positiva y la política económica argentina', in ibid., 212.
11. Aníbal Pinto testified to the *TE's* continental significance in Pinto (1953:571–3). Among other things, he said, it had served to diffuse theory and proper practice throughout Latin America.
12. In 1944, Medina published his translation of Max Weber's magnum opus, *Economy and Society*, which appeared in Spanish (at the Fondo de Cultura Económica) two decades before its English-language counterpart.
13. Lida and Matesanz (1990:227–8) (on the Cosío–Echavarría dispute) and Cosío Villegas (1986:198–9) (on foundations).

14. *RBE*, table of contents, various issues, 1947–56.
15. She mentions Chile in the 1930s as a comparable case (Babb 2002:40, 45, 67).
16. Campanema, quoted in Loureiro (1997:34); Loureiro (1997:37 (prestige)).
17. Gamio studied at Columbia University with Franz Boas (Hale 1986:434, n. 138).
18. In Brazil, dozens of economics graduate students were sent to study in the United States with support from USAID and the Brazilian Ministry of Education from the late 1960s (Prado 2001:14).
19. See also Gouvea de Bulhões (1990:19).
20. Dênio Nogueira (depoimento, 1989). Transcript of interview at Centro de Pesquisa e Documentação, FGV, Rio, 1990.
21. In fact, Furtado's dissertation was an exercise in economic history, with a minimum of formal economic analysis (see Furtado 1948). However, his *A Economia Brasileira* (1954b) offers a structuralist analysis of Brazil's economic history.
22. It is possible that Flores and Cosío Villegas, both of whom studied at the University of Wisconsin, were affected by the American Institutionalist School, because Wisconsin was its focal point; Flores (1983:263) mentions using a text by Richard Ely, a Wisconsin professor and a leading Institutionalist. However, the influence of the school on Mexican economics seems slight at best, and in their memoirs, neither Flores nor Cosío mention studying directly with any Institutionalist.
23. ESCOLATINA is the Programa de Estudios Económicos Latinoamericanos para Graduados.
24. Moreover, he was the first head of ECLA to have obtained a doctorate in its half-century of existence.

References

Babb, S., *Managing Mexico: Economists from Nationalism to Neoliberalism* (Princeton University Press, 2002).

Bagú, S. 'Industrialización', *Revista de Economía* (Mexico) 8:10 (15 October 1915) 5–6.

Bagú, S., '¿Y Mañana, Qué?', *Revista de Economía* (Mexico) 7: 5–6 (30 June 1944) 37.

Bagú, S., 'Industrialización', *Revista de Economía* (Mexico) 8:10 (October 1945) 5–6.

Banco de la Nación Argentina, *Economic Review* 1/1 (August 1928).

Becerra Maldonado, F., 'Prólogo', in F. Becerra Maldonado (ed.), *Antología del Pensamiento Económico de la Facultad de Economía, 1929–1989* (México City: Facultad de Economía de la UNAM, 1989).

Bulmer-Thomas, V., *The Economic History of Latin America since Independence* (Cambridge University Press, 1994).

Bunge, A. 'La Economía Positiva y la Política Económica Argentina,' *Revista de Economía* 1:1 (July–December 1918) 212.

Camp, Roderic Ai, *Mexican Political Biographies 1935–1993* (Austin: University of Texas Press, 1995).

Coats, A. W. and D. C. Colander, 'An Introduction to the Spread of Economic Ideas', in A. W. Coats and D. C. Colander (eds), *The Spread of Economic Ideas* (Cambridge University Press, 1989).

Cosío Villegas, D., *Memorias* [orig. 1976] (Mexico City: Joaquín Mortiz, 1986).

Day, C., 'Journals, University Presses and the Spread of Ideas', in A. W. Coats and D. C. Colander (eds), *The Spread of Economic Ideas* (Cambridge University Press, 1989).

De Estrada, T. E. (1928), 'Purpose of This Publication', in Banco de la Nación Argentina, *Economic Review*, 1/1: 2 (August, 1928).

De Paiva Abreu, M., 'Brazil and the World Economy, 1930–1945: Aspects of Foreign Economic Policies and International Economic Relations under Vargas', PhD dissertation (University of Cambridge, 1977).

Flores, E., *Historias de Edmundo Flores: Autobiografía, 1919–1950* (Mexico City: Martín Casillas, 1983).

Furtado, C., *L'Économie coloniale brésilienne (XVIe et XVIIe siècles): éléments d'histoire economique appliqués*, PhD dissertation Université de Paris, Faculté de Droit, 1948.

Furtado, C., 'Capital Formation and Economic Development', *International Economic Papers* 4 (1954a) 124–44.

Furtado, C., *A Economia Brasileira* (Rio de Janeiro: Noite, 1954b).

Ellis, H. S., B. Cornejo and L. Escobar Cerda, *The Teaching of Economics in Latin America* (Washington, DC: Pan American Union, 1961).

Gondra, L., 'Argentina', in L. Gondra *et al.* (eds), *El Pensamiento Económico Latinoamericano: Argentina, Bolivia, Brasil, Cuba, Chile, Haiti, Paraguay, Perú* (México City: Fondo de Cultura Económica, 1945).

Gudin, E., 'Notas Sobre a Economia Brasileira', *Revista Brasileira de Economia*, 26/3 (July–September 1972).

Hale, C. A., 'Political and Social Ideas in Latin America, 1870–1930', in L. Bethell (ed.), *Cambridge History of Latin America*, vol. IV (Cambridge University Press, 1986).

Harberger, A. C., 'Good Economics Comes to Latin America, 1955–95', in A. W. Coats (ed.), *The Post-1945 Internationalization of Economics* (Durham, NC: Duke University Press, 1996).

Keller R. C., 'Chile', in L. Gondra *et al.* (eds), *El Pensamiento Económico Latinoamericano: Argentina, Bolivia, Brasil, Cuba, Chile, Haiti, Paraguay, Perú* (Mexico City: Fondo de Cultura Económica, 1945).

Lida, C. and J. A. Matesanz, *El Colegio de México: Una Hazaña Cultural 1940–1962* (México: El Colegio, 1990).

Loureiro, M. R., *Os Economistas no Governo* (Rio de Janeiro: Fundação Getúlio Vargas, 1997).

Love, J. L., 'Economic Ideas and Ideologies in Latin America since 1930', in L. Bethell (ed.), *Cambridge History of Latin America*, vol. VI, 1 (Cambridge University Press, 1994).

Mandelbaum, K., *The Industrialization of Backward Areas* (Oxford: Blackwell & Mott, 1945).

Navarrete, R. A., 'Exchange Stability, Business Cycles, and Economic Development: An Inquiry into Mexico's Balance of Payments Problems, 1929–1946', PhD dissertation (Harvard University, 1950).

North, D., *Structure and Change in Economic History* (New York: Norton, 1981).

Pazos, F., 'Veinte Años de Pensamiento Económico en América Latina', *Trimestre Económico*, 20:4 (October–December 1953).

Pinto, A., 'El Trimestre en el Sur', *Trimestre Económico*, 20/4 (October–December 1953) 571–73.

Pinto, A. and O. Sunkel, 'Latin American Economists in the United States', *Economic Development and Cultural Change* 15:1 (October 1966) 79–86.

Polit, G., 'La Argentina se Decide por la Planificación Económica', *Trimestre Económico*, 15/2 (July–September 1948) 194–201.

Pollock, D., D. Kerner and J. L. Love, 'Aquellos Viejos Tiempos: La Formación Teórica y Práctica de Raúl Prebisch en Argentina. Una Entrevista con David Pollock', *Desarrollo Económico: Revista de Ciencias Sociales* 164: 41 (January–March 2002), 531–54.

Prado, Eleutério F. S., 'A Ortodoxia Neoclássica', in *USP: Estudos Avançados* 41 (2001) 4.

Prebisch, R. 1944, *El Patrón Oro y la Vulnerabilidad Económica de Nuestros Países*, Jornadas no. 11 (Mexico City: El Colegio).

Presidente de la República [de Chile, Pedro Aguirre Cerda], *Mensaje ... en la apertura ... del Congreso Nacional 21 de Mayo de 1940* (Santiago, 1940).

Revista Brasileira de Economia (various, 1947–56).

Revista Brasileira de Economia 1, 1 (September 1947), p. 7.

Revista de Economía Argentina 1:1 (July–December 1918) 1.

Santos, G., *La Industria Colombiana y su Base Económica y Social* (Buenos Aires: Unión Industrial Argentina, 1945).

Sikkink, K. A., 'Developmentalism and Democracy: Ideas, Institutions, and Economic Policy Making in Brazil and Argentina (1954–1962)', PhD dissertation (Columbia University, New York, 1988).

Sikkink, K., *Ideas and Institutions: Developmentalism in Brazil and Argentina* (Ithaca, NY: Cornell University Press, 1991).

Silva Herzog, J., *El Pensamiento Económico en México* (México: FCE, 1947).

Solís, L., *Planes de Desarrollo Económico y Social en México* (Mexico City: SepSententas, 1975).

Teixeira Vieira, D., 'História da Ciência Econômica no Brasil', in M. Guimarães Ferri and S. Motoyama (eds), *Historia das Ciencias no Brasil*, vol. 3 (São Paulo: EDUSP, 1981).

Thorp, R., *Progress, Poverty and Exclusion: An Economic History of Latin America in the xx[th] Century* (Washington, DC: Inter-American Development Bank, 1998).

Urquidi, V. (1944), 'Elasticidad y Rigidez de Bretton Woods', *Trimestre Económico*, 9/44 (January–March 1944) 614–615.

Urquidi, V., 'El Progreso Económico de México: Problemas y Soluciones,' *Trimestre Económico*, 13/1 (1946).

Vargas, G. *A Nova Política*, VI , VIII (Rio de Janeiro: J. Olympio, 1940, 1941).

Villaseñor, E., 'XX aniversario de *"El Trimestre Económico"* ', *Trimestre Económico* 20/4 (October–December 1953) 550–1.

Villela, A. and W. Suzigan, *Política do Governo e Crescimento da Economia Brasileira, 1889–1945* (Rio de Janeiro: IPEA/INPES, 1973).

Whitehead, L., 'State Organization in Latin America since 1930', in L. Bethell (ed.), *Cambridge History of Latin America*, vol. vi, part 2 (Cambridge University Press, 1994).

8

The Rise and Fall of Structuralism*

Joseph L. Love

Introduction

This chapter focuses on the evolution of structuralist doctrine in Latin America in the 1950s and 1960s, and the role played by Raúl Prebisch and the UN Economic Commission for Latin America (ECLA) in its propagation. It examines the antecedents to and academic origins of structuralism, before turning to the main theoretical innovations of the ECLA school – notably regarding terms of trade, comparative advantage, structural causes of inflation and the need for industrial promotion – all of which represented a sharp challenge to traditional neo-classical theory. The chapter explores how the promotion of the doctrine was made possible by the institutional developments outlined in the previous chapter – above all, the growing influence of ECLA as a source both of policy advice and of training. Its theoreticians became increasingly critical with time of the theory's implementation; however, those criticisms were not effectively translated into policy modification by ECLA's member governments.

Antecedents

Of the several schools of economics circulating in the inter-war years, one that had already reached Latin America in the nineteenth century was the German Historical School. The first writer of the Historical School, Friedrich List, whose name is associated with the infant industry argument, was known in Argentina, Brazil and Chile among other places, and his writings played a role in the Argentine tariff debates of the 1870s (Concha 1889:327–8, 1909:25–7).[1] Malaquias Concha, List's leading champion in Chile, also cited

* This chapter uses material originally printed in *The Cambridge History of Latin America* (Cambridge University Press, 1994), vol. 6, part 1, pp. 393–460. Permission from Cambridge University Press to draw on this material is gratefully acknowledged.

Gustav Schmoller, but in a French translation. Members of later generations of the Historical School were little noted except for the late maverick, if not chameleon, Werner Sombart, the last part of whose *Der moderne Kapitalismus* (1928) appeared in French in 1933 and Spanish in 1946. This book was the first work to distinguish between an industrial centre and an agricultural periphery in the world economic system, a notion later employed by Prebisch in his Latin American version of structuralism. However, Sombart did not provide any theory of relations between centre and periphery; in particular, he offered no analysis of the relation between business cycles and the international distribution of income, the focus of Prebisch's postwar analysis.[2]

Another work using a centre–periphery scheme was that of the Chilean–German theorist, Ernst Wagemann, whose *Struktur und Rhythmus der Weltwirtschaft* (1931) had been translated into Spanish in 1933. Wagemann, a specialist in business cycles, used 'central cycle' (*zentrische Konjunktur*) to designate money income movements *within* a given country, and 'peripheral cycle' (*periphere Konjunktur*) to designate capital movements at the international level.[3] Thus, Wagemann employed a centre–periphery scheme in connection with a cyclical movement, but not in the sense which Prebisch shared with Sombart. Wagemann directed the Institut für Konjunkturforschung in Berlin in the inter-war years, and had his greatest influence in Chile, the land of his birth, after returning there in 1948 to direct the economics department at the Universidad de Chile.[4]

Corporatism was a rising doctrine in the inter-war years, and some corporatist writers anticipated the concerns and approaches of the Latin American structuralist school associated with ECLA in the postwar era. This was especially true of the Romanian writer Mihail Manoilescu, who argued that agrarian countries should industrialize to capture the benefits of spillover and growth effects which manufacturing offered and agriculture did not. Another corporatist who took an explicit structuralist approach to the organization of national economies was the French professor François Perroux, who taught and published in Brazil and Portugal in the 1930s.[5]

Marxism was poorly diffused and understood in Latin America during the inter-war period. An underlying reason for the school's slow penetration was the lack of a sturdy Hegelian foundation in the Latin American intellectual milieu. Hegel's philosophy had opened the road for Marx in Russia, but was largely absent in Latin America, except in the limited circles of academic philosophers. Moreover, before World War II, Latin Americans' greater familiarity with French, British, and Spanish than German thought probably tended to limit their knowledge of Marxism, if one accepts Perry Anderson's judgement that there were no significant contributions to Marxist theory in Britain, France, or Spain before the 1930s.[6] Rudolf Hilferding's *Finance Capital* (1981 [German ed. 1910]), which was influential in Eastern Europe during the 1920s and 1930s,[7] was not available in English, French or Spanish until the 1970s. Even fewer Marxist works were available in Portuguese than Spanish, partly because Spanish texts were easily understood by Portuguese speakers. The first full text of Marx's *Capital* translated directly from German into Portuguese only appeared in 1968 (do Amaral Lapa 1980:23).

Marxism was even less well understood before Lenin founded the Third International in 1919, setting up national communist parties around the globe, though prewar Marxism probably enjoyed greater currency and comprehension in Argentina than elsewhere.[8] Radicalism in most of Latin America, like its Iberian counterparts, tended to revolve around anarchism more than socialism at least until the 1920s, and in many nations, perhaps until the early 1930s.[9] In addition, most socialist parties were not exclusively or predominantly Marxist-oriented until the Third International forced the issue in the early 1920s.

As for the peasant economics (neo-populism) of Alexander Chayanov, his works appear to be altogether unknown in inter-war Latin America, in sharp contrast to his popularity in the 'succession states' of Eastern Europe at the time. Part of the reason may have been the perceived irrelevance of peasant economics in Argentina and Uruguay, where the man–land ratio was low. Yet the Mexicans certainly would have wanted to consider Chayanov, had they known of his work, since agricultural and agrarian economics was at the top of their concerns in the inter-war years.[10] In any event, Latin Americans did not have access to the nineteenth-century Russian debate about capitalism between Marxists and populists, as did Eastern Europeans. In the 1920s, Chayanov's works revitalized and transformed populism, providing a theoretical basis for 'peasantist' parties' agendas in Eastern Europe, where universal male suffrage brought the rural masses new power after 1918. By contrast, Latin America – Mexico and Costa Rica excepted – lacked a land-holding peasantry as a political base for the diffusion of Chayanov's ideas. Further, here is an instance where language may have played a considerable role in impeding the diffusion of the economic ideas. Whereas the medium of Chayanov's influence in Eastern Europe had been his German and Russian publications in the 1920s, his impact in Latin America was based on the rediscovery of his theories through an English-language compendium of his work edited by Daniel Thorner and others in 1966.[11]

Clearly, most people who called themselves economists in the inter-war period would have thought Chayanov's peasant economics and Marxism were exotic theories, without much practical application, at least for the problems that concerned them. Taking the perspective of government or established economic interests, they were trying to solve concrete and often pressing economic problems. If such writings had any theoretical basis – and they almost invariably did – the bulk of the economic literature generated in, or imported into, Latin America in the years 1914–45 was reasoned in the neo-classical framework of 'standard economics'.

Through the 1930s Latin American writers rarely aspired to publish on theoretical issues, and to the extent that they wrote on 'non-practical' matters, they tended to be concerned with large policy issues. A good example is Otávio Paranaguá's *Tariff Policy* (1935). Informed by neo-classical trade theory but looking at the real world at the moment of beggar-thy-neighbour protectionism, Paranaguá tried to relativize the notion of 'natural' economic activities and denied that the assumptions of Ricardian trade theory were valid for the world he lived in.[12]

The vast majority of economic studies by Latin Americans had to meet a criterion of practicality, as Felipe Pazos noted in his survey, 'Fifty Years of Economic Thought in Latin America' (1983), revisiting the theme he had treated 30 years earlier in *Trimestre Económico*. Pazos wrote: '[T]he function of our economists is not to describe [*sic*] new general principles, but to apply the existing ones to the analysis of our concrete reality and to the formulation of the necessary means of improving it.' However, he did add the qualification that 'only when foreign science [didn't] supply the adequate intellectual instruments' did Latin Americans attempt to 'speculate about general problems', referring to structuralist theories of ECLA of the postwar era (Pazos 1983:1916).

Earlier, the editors of *Trimestre Económico* had agreed on the prevalence of the practical criterion – and lamented it. Writing in 1953, Víctor Urquidi and Javier Márquez complained about the practical nature of economic research in Latin America. There was a 'lack of originals' in Latin American economic writing, they asserted. There were few opportunities for theoretical research in the region's universities in the early 1950s. Furthermore, many economists had little time for examining new literature, and frequently their employment in administrative posts did not really require training in economics (Urquidi and Márquez 1953:576).

The practical issues of which Pazos, Urquidi and Márquez wrote concerned money and banking, exchange rates, the balance of payments and specific sectors of production – transport, energy, and agriculture. To the extent that 'practical' men, including leaders of central banks and heads of producers' organizations, paid attention to economic theory, it usually had to do with the utility of theory for their own purposes. Prebisch's career offers a good example. In 1927, he published a study sponsored by the Argentina's Sociedad Rural (Stockbreeders' Association) that became the basis for government action on behalf of cattlemen in the British meat market. Prebisch's study offered statistical proof that the meat pool's interference in the market had been beneficial for the British packinghouses, but not for the Argentine stockbreeders.[13] The impact of this study on the Sociedad Rural and its interlocking directorate with the Banco de la Nación can only have helped him make a successful case for opening a research division at the bank a year later.

As Prebisch's case illustrates, the economic theory that commended itself to businessmen and government was frequently self-serving, but in any case, it was written in neo-classical language, which prevailed everywhere in the journals. A survey of the articles in *Trimestre Económico* during the 1930s and 1940s establishes the overwhelming preponderance of studies written in a neo-classical tradition. In addition to Mexican and other Latin American writers, such neo-classical economists as Gustav Cassel, Irving Fisher, D. H. Robertson, Piero Sraffa and Jan Tinbergen were published in the journal.[14] Moreover, leading Latin American economists of both early and later generations had been trained in the neo-classical school – Gondra, Prebisch, Cosío Villegas, Urquidi, Gudin, and Bulhões among them. Moreover, they read the English-language literature: Urquidi and Prebisch, for example, were corresponding in 1944 about the merits of Charles Kindleberger's argument that agricultural and raw-material producers should industrialize, because of the (alleged) long-term deterioration of the terms of trade.[15]

Toward the end of the period, an interest arose in the Keynesian variant of neo-classical economics. During the decade 1934–43, *Trimestre Económico* published three articles by Keynes and four others about Keynes's theories (one of them by J. R. Hicks). Keynes's prestige was further heightened by his leadership of the British delegation at Bretton Woods, where he presented the Keynes Plan for postwar monetary stability. Even more attention was focused on his *General Theory* after Prebisch published his *Introducción a Keynes* (1947), a Latin American predecessor and counterpart to Alvin Hansen's *Guide to Keynes* in the Anglo-Saxon world (Hansen 1953). By the late 1950s, Keynes was the most widely cited author in Mexican academic theses (Babb 2002:95, 103).

The rise of a Latin American school: ECLA structuralism

As noted in the previous chapter, Prebisch was a leading teacher at the University of Buenos Aires from the 1920s, the organizer of Latin America's first economic research unit in Argentina's Banco de la Nación in 1928, and the first director general of the country's Banco Central from 1935 until 1943, when he was fired following the coup that quickly brought Perón to power. As director general of the Central Bank, Prebisch had been much concerned with his nation's passive reaction to business cycles emanating from the economies of the North Atlantic basin. In particular, he was concerned with the dramatic decline in Argentina's terms of trade during the depression years, and he increasingly associated that fact with the country's great dependence on agricultural exports.[16]

Freed from his duties at the Central Bank, Prebisch was twice in Mexico during the mid 1940s at the invitation of Mexico's central bank (Banco de México). On both occasions, he participated in international meetings: in 1944, at a gathering of intellectuals from Latin America at the Colegio de México on problems the region would face in the postwar era,[17] and in 1946 in Mexico City at an inter-American meeting of central bankers.

Prebisch's interest in industrialization as a solution to Latin America's economic problems arose originally from the desire, shared by many Argentine contemporaries, to make Argentina less economically 'vulnerable', a vulnerability painfully evident for the whole period 1930–45. The Argentine Central Bank, under Prebisch's leadership, had begun to advocate industrialization in its 1942 report. By implication, Prebisch was recommending similar policies to other Latin American governments in his Colegio de México lecture of 1944.[18] In his 'Conversations' at the Banco de México that same year, Prebisch again noted that the periods of greatest industrial development in Argentina had been the Great Depression and times of war, periods in which the nation had to produce for itself what it could not import.[19] Later, ECLA theorists would explore the implications of this observation, as they elaborated the concept of 'inward-directed development'.

In a 1944 article in Mexico's *Trimestre Económico*, Prebisch noted that the United States, unlike Argentina, had a low propensity to import (defined as the change in the value of imports generated by a given change in the national product). Since other countries, he implied, had high propensities to import, and the United States had replaced Britain as the chief industrial trading partner of the Latin American states, Prebisch expanded on the League experts' argument in 1933, warning that the postwar international trading system faced the danger of permanent disequilibrium (Prebisch 1944:188, 192–3).

Prebisch first used the terms centre–periphery in print in 1946, at the second meeting mentioned above, of the hemisphere's central bankers at the Banco de México. Prebisch now identified the United States as the 'cyclical centre' and Latin America as the 'periphery of the economic system'. The emphasis, as indicated, was on the trade cycle, whose rhythms the US economy set for the whole international system. Fiscal and monetary authorities in the United States could pursue a policy of full employment without producing monetary instability, Prebisch argued. Furthermore, such authorities did not need to be especially concerned about the impact of full employment policies on the exchange rate of the dollar in other currencies. By contrast, Prebisch asserted, the nations of the periphery could not apply the same monetary tools as the centre did. Extrapolating from his 1944 argument with reference to Argentina, Prebisch contended that the money supply in peripheral countries could not be expanded in pursuit of full employment, because, with a high propensity to import, any expansion of income would quickly exhaust foreign exchange, assuming no devaluation.

This 1946 statement and previous writings of Prebisch implied that peripheral countries faced three options, all with undesirable consequences. They could have strong currencies and maintain high levels of imports at the cost of high unemployment. They could fight unemployment with an expansionary monetary policy, but would thereby create inflation and put pressure on the exchange rate – thereby raising the cost of repaying foreign debts. Finally, if they used monetary policy to maintain high levels of employment but failed to devalue, their reserves would disappear. When prices of the periphery's products fell during the downswing of the cycle, furthermore, governments of peripheral countries – at least in isolation – could not affect world prices for their goods as could the centre. Thus, equilibrium theories in international trade were not acceptable (Prebisch 1944:199, 1946:25–8). This was an assault on the policy prescriptions of neo-classical economics. Prebisch's message in Mexico City was in tune with the pessimism then prevailing in Latin America regarding international trade as a long-term engine of growth. Even the improving terms of trade of the early postwar years were widely viewed as transient.

In the classroom in Buenos Aires in 1948, Prebisch specifically attacked the theory of comparative advantage. He noted that its precepts were repeatedly violated by the industrialized nations, whose economists nonetheless used neo-classical trade theory as an ideological weapon. He also implied that industrial countries acted as monopolists against agricultural countries in the trading process. Historically, in both the United States and Britain, he asserted, technological progress did not result in a decrease in prices, but in an increase in wages. 'The fruit of technical progress tended to remain in Great Britain' in the nineteenth century; yet because Britain had sacrificed its agriculture, part of the benefits of technological progress had been transferred to the 'new countries' in the form of higher land values. Britain's nineteenth-century import coefficient (defined as the value of imports divided by real income) was estimated by Prebisch as 30–35 per cent, whereas that of the United States in the 1930s was only about 5 per cent. All of this implied a blockage to growth for the agricultural-exporting periphery under the new largely self-sufficient centre.[20]

Despite the fact that some of the key ideas of Prebisch's later analysis were set forth in international meetings in 1944 and 1946, there were no discussions on these occasions of an ECLA, the agency that was subsequently to be Prebisch's principal theoretical and ideological vehicle. Rather, it resulted from a Chilean initiative in 1947 at UN headquarters in Lake Success, New York. The agency was approved by the UN Economic and Social Council in February 1948, and ECLA held its first meeting in Santiago, Chile, in June of that year, with Alberto Baltra Cortés, the Chilean minister of the economy, presiding. For the future of ECLA, or at least its most famous thesis, the chief outcome of the meeting was a resolution calling for a study of Latin America's terms of trade.[21]

Without Prebisch's leadership, ECLA was not yet ECLA. His personality, theses, and programs so dominated the agency in its formative phase that it stood in sharp relief to the Economic Commission for Asia and the Far East (established in 1947) and the Economic Commission for Africa (1958), agencies with more purely technical orientations. The year of ECLA's founding, 1948, seemed propitious for obtaining Prebisch's services: in Juan Perón's

Argentina he was excluded from official posts, perhaps because of his long and close association with the nation's traditional economic elite. Meanwhile, his reputation as an economist in Latin America had been enhanced by the publication in Mexico of his *Introducción a Keynes* (1947).

In any event, Prebisch was again invited to go to Santiago to work on special assignment as editor and author of the introduction to an economic report on Latin America, authorized at the initial ECLA meeting. In Santiago, he elaborated his thesis on the deterioration of the terms of trade in *El Desarrollo Económico de América Latina y sus Principales Problemas*, published in May 1949.[22] Prebisch had already formed his opinions about the direction of Latin America's long-range terms of trade. Now, a new study, *Relative Prices of Exports and Imports of Underdeveloped Countries*, by Hans W. Singer of the UN Department of Economic Affairs, provided an empirical foundation for Prebisch's thesis. This work examined long-term trends in relative prices in the goods traded by industrialized and raw material-producing countries, and concluded that the terms of trade from the late nineteenth century till the eve of World War II had been moving against the exporters of agricultural goods and in favour of the exporters of industrial products. Singer wrote:

> On the average, a given quantity of primary exports would pay, at the end of this period, for only 60 per cent of the quantity of manufactured goods which it could buy at the beginning of the period. (United Nations 1949:7)

ECLA explained this finding in part by arguing that gains in productivity over the period in question were greater in industrial than in primary products, thus challenging basic assumptions of the theory of comparative advantage. If prices of industrial goods had fallen, this development would have spread the effects of technical progress over the entire centre–periphery system, and the terms of trade of agricultural goods would have been expected to have improved. They did not do so, and the significance of this fact had to be understood in terms of trade cycles. During the upswing, the prices of primary goods rise more sharply than those of industrial goods, but they fall more steeply during the downswing. In the upswing, the working class of the centre absorbs real economic gains, but wages do not fall proportionately during the downswing. Because workers are not well organized in the periphery (least of all in agriculture), the periphery absorbs more of the system's income contraction than does the centre (CEPAL 1950:8–14). Thus in current jargon, Prebisch focused on the 'double factorial terms of trade' – domestic labour's compensation versus that of its foreign counterpart.

In the *Economic Survey of Latin America, 1949* (CEPAL, 1951 [Spanish edn, 1950]), Prebisch expanded on these arguments. He held that there were two distinct sources of the potential deterioration of the terms of trade: technological productivity gains in the centre and those in the periphery. He assumed the centre's gains would be greater, and if the system worked normally, these would, to some extent, spread to the periphery. In that case, over the long run, the centre's terms of trade would deteriorate, and the periphery's would improve. If the periphery's terms deteriorated, this would indicate that it was not only failing to share in the centre's presumably larger gains, but was transferring some of its *own* productivity gains to the centre (CEPAL 1951:47). Since Singer's *Relative Prices* had established deterioration in the periphery's terms, protection for industry was a *sine qua non* to arrest the concentration of the fruits of technological progress in the centre.

The basic cause of the deterioration was the surplus labour supply and the underlying population pressure in the pre-capitalist, largely agricultural, sector of the periphery's economy. As modern agricultural technique penetrates and reduces the size of the pre-capitalist sector, the *Survey* stated, a labour surplus develops. It then adduced historical data to show that the export sector in Latin America could not absorb this surplus. Industrialization, in part to absorb the labour surplus, was the centrepiece of a policy of economic development. Even when protection was needed, industries were 'economical in so far as they represent a net addition to real income'. National income could be increased by selectively lowering components of the import coefficient.[23]

Another initial ECLA argument grew out of Prebisch's observations on Argentina's import problems in the 1930s. The United States, the principal cyclical centre, had a much lower import coefficient than export coefficient, and the former was also much lower than those of the Latin American countries. The United States tended to sell more to Latin America than it bought from the region, exhausting Latin American reserves and creating a tendency toward permanent disequilibrium. The US economy even grew by closing. ECLA produced statistics showing that the United States's import coefficient had fallen from the 1920s to the late 1940s. The explanation was that technological progress in some industries was much greater than on average; this allowed such industries to pay much higher wages, driving up wages in general – and in some other industries, above productivity gains. Therefore, rising costs led to greater average protectionism and a 'closing' of the centre (CEPAL 1951:35, 75).

However, Prebisch and the ECLA team he organized were also interested in another dimension of the problem – monopolistic pricing at the centre. The original analysis in 1949–50 laid much more emphasis on the rigidity of wages in the downward phase of the cycle than on monopolistic pricing as such, but the latter argument was there (CEPAL 1951:59).[24] In any event, both wage rigidities and monopoly were assumed to be nonexistent in neoclassical trade theory. Peripheral countries did not have monopolies on the goods they offered in the world market, with rare and temporary exceptions, just as they lacked well-organized rural labour forces that would resist the fall in wages during the downswing of the cycle.

The preceding analysis, taken as a whole, pointed to negative features in the periphery's economy: structural unemployment, external disequilibrium and deteriorating terms of trade – all of which a properly implemented policy of industrialization could help eliminate.

In 1950, the year after the appearance of the original Spanish version of the 'ECLA manifesto', another UN economist independently made a case related to the ECLA theses. Hans W. Singer alleged that technological progress in manufacturing was shown in a rise in incomes in developed countries, while such progress in the production of food and raw materials in 'underdeveloped' countries was expressed in a fall in prices. He explained the differential effects of technological progress in terms of different income elasticities of demand for primary and industrial goods – an extrapolation of Engel's law that the proportion of income spent on foods falls as income rises – and in terms of the 'absence of pressure of producers for higher incomes' in poor countries. Since consumers of manufactured goods in world trade tended to live in poor countries, and the contrary was true for consumers of raw materials, Singer continued, the latter group had the best of both worlds while the former had the worst.[25] This idea was linked to Prebisch's, and quickly termed the Prebisch–Singer thesis, though both economists later stated that there was no direct exchange of views at the time the related sets of propositions, based on the same UN data, were developed.[26] (Prebisch was then in Santiago, and Singer in New York.)

By 1951, the year that ECLA became a permanent organ of the United Nations, the agency was referring less to import coefficients than to disparities in income elasticities of demand at the centre for primary products, and those at the periphery for industrial goods.[27] This adoption of Singer's terms was significant, because it dealt with the centre countries as a group and not just the United States, which had unusually low import requirements because of its tremendous agricultural output. Though ECLA first emphasized differential productivities, by the late 1950s it was tending to emphasize differential income elasticities of demand, possibly because of perceived export stagnation in Argentina and Chile.[28]

Prebisch's ideas were probably influenced by an array of economic theorists who published in the 1930s and 1940s, among them Keynes, Mihail Manoilescu, Ernst Wagemann, François Perroux, Charles Kindleberger, Werner Sombart, Gustav Cassell, and the Argentinian Alejandro Bunge. Having examined their possible impact on Prebisch's ideas elsewhere,[29] I believe it suffices here to remark here that Prebisch put together the various terms, themes, propositions and emphases in their writings in a unique synthesis, though indeed his argument bore close similarities to the roughly contemporaneous thesis of H. W. Singer.[30]

In any case, ECLA's theses, from their initial appearance in 1949, were hotly contested by neo-classical trade theorists such as Jacob Viner. The economics profession in 1948–49 had just been treated to a formal demonstration by

Paul Samuelson that, under certain conventional (but unrealistic) assumptions, trade could serve as a complete substitute for the movement of factors of production from one country to another, indicating that international trade could potentially equalize incomes among nations. Thus the less rigorous, but much more realistic, arguments of Prebisch and Singer burst upon the scene just after Samuelson had raised neo-classical trade theory to new heights of elegance, and the new ideas would have to struggle against this theory.[31] In particular, the terms of trade thesis came under severe attack, as the validity of the data was challenged on a variety of grounds.[32]

ECLA: apogee and crisis

Despite the disputations that ensued, the terms of trade argument was a point of departure for a structuralist school which would seek to restrict the applicability of neo-classical economics in Latin America, and by extension in all 'underdeveloped' countries. In this endeavour, Prebisch was able to attract to or retain in his agency a pleiad of talented economists, in the early years including Jorge Ahumada, Aníbal Pinto and Pedro Vuscovic, all of Chile; Aldo Ferrer of Argentina; Víctor Urquidi and Juan Noyola Vázquez of Mexico; and Celso Furtado of Brazil.[33] These men were entering economics just as the field was becoming a profession in a number of Latin American countries.

Furtado, who joined the ECLA staff shortly before Prebisch officially took over, quickly drew further conclusions from Prebisch's analysis of the business cycle and high import coefficients. Arguing that income tended to concentrate in Brazil during the upswing of the cycle, owing to a highly elastic labour supply, he then hypothesized that much of the effect of the Keynesian multiplier 'leaked' abroad, owing to the high propensity to import. Furtado anticipated, by four years, W. Arthur Lewis's famous analysis of an infinitely elastic labour supply as the source of wage 'stickiness' in poor countries. Such analysis, of course, pointed again to the importance of an industrialization policy.[34]

According to a study of ECLA's theoretical innovations by Octavio Rodríguez, a former staff economist, its major theoretical contributions, beyond its analysis of the terms of trade, have fallen in the areas of problems of industrialization; the analysis of structural obstacles to development; and the related problem of the causes of inflation. Rodríguez further argues, in a work that is far from uncritical, that ECLA's period of greatest originality was from 1949 through the late 1960s, after which few new theses were presented.[35] Other contributions cited in ECLA publications were the promotion of Latin American economic integration, implicit in the agenda of the 1949 'manifesto'; 'programming' or planning economic development; and helping to create the Inter-American Development Bank (IADB) and UNCTAD (CEPAL 1973:34; CEPAL 1978). Although some governments in the 1950s, notably Brazil's, openly acknowledged ECLA as a source of their developmentalist policies, Argentina's *desarrollistas* were quick to distance themselves from ECLA, possibly because of Prebisch's previous activity in national policy formation.[36] In any event, such activities of ECLA were in applied fields, not theory, and many policy prescriptions had little success, as noted below, when implemented by Latin American governments. Yet regional integration, part of ECLA's strategy from 1958, began to produce complementary industrial structures by the late 1960s. Intra-regional trade, and that in manufactures particularly, grew faster than extra-regional trade overall and that in manufactures between 1965 and 1979 (Baer 1972:104; IADB 1985:98).

Prebisch and his collaborators at ECLA were interested not only in theorizing, but also in convincing Latin American government officials and university professors of the validity of structuralist doctrines, and the urgency of applying them. To this end, the fact of career civil servants moving in and out of their national governments (such as Furtado in Brazil, Ahumada in Chile and Urquidi in Mexico) was critical. However ECLA as an institution was even more important in the middle and longer terms – it organized courses in modern economic techniques and structuralist-infused theory at ECLA headquarters from 1952, and ESCOLATINA (at the University of Chile) from 1954. These two institutions, often in collaboration with others outside Chile, trained and indoctrinated middle-ranking Latin American bureaucrats in central banks, development and finance ministries, and university faculties. Over a hundred such men and women studied at ECLA itself in courses varying from several months' duration to a year before the creation of ILPES in 1962. After that, ILPES continued to train aspiring economists in Santiago, but also offered short courses in a majority of Latin American countries. Multiple sites were available in several countries, including eight in Brazil alone between 1963 and 1969.[37] If one takes into account the briefer seminars, between 1962 and 1992, ILPES offered over 300 hundred courses and seminars, registering over 12,000 participants (Montecinos 1996:296). ECLA personnel also found employment in the ILO, in development institutes and planning agencies such as ODEPLAN in Chile and CENDES in Venezuela, and in the IADB.[38] The peak years of ECLA's influence were the late 1950s and early 1960s, especially in the Brazilian governments of Juscelino Kubitschek and João Goulart, and the Chilean government of Eduardo Frei.

Of the theoretical endeavours, the 'structuralist' explanation of inflation as a challenge to 'monetarism' is sometimes viewed as only second in importance to the terms of trade thesis.[39] Despite the fact that a number of ECLA economists helped develop it, ECLA never accorded it recognition as part of its official doctrine, though at times Prebisch himself endorsed it in the agency's publications.[40]

Inflation was more rampant in Latin America during most of the postwar decades than in any other area of the world. The basic structuralist proposition was that *underlying* inflationary pressures derive from bottlenecks produced by retarded sectors, especially agriculture, whose backward state yields an inelastic supply, in the face of rapidly rising demand by the burgeoning urban masses. In Chile, where the analysis was first applied, the stagnation of the export sector was also recognized as a structural cause. Repeated devaluations to raise export earnings automatically boosted the price of imports. A related cause in this view was deteriorating terms of trade, fuelled by a demand for imports that rose faster than the demand for exports (see below on ISI). Also associated with the foreign trade problem was a shift in the fiscal system: as exports stagnated, the relative weight of revenues provided by regressive domestic taxes tended to rise, allowing more income for the already import-oriented upper classes. To a lesser degree, the ECLA economists noted as a cause of inflation national industrial monopolies and oligopolies, shielded by high tariffs, which could raise prices quickly.[41]

The several 'structural' features of inflation were distinguished from 'exogenous' or adventitious causes (for example, natural disasters, changes in the international market), and 'cumulative' causes (action by government and private groups to raise wages and prices in a climate of inflationary expectations). It is important to recognize that the thesis did not deny that orthodox 'monetarist' explanations of inflation had some validity – for example, that some supply inelasticities were caused by distortions in exchange rates and prices, following an inflationary spiral.[42]

A number of ECLA economists, especially those concerned with Chile, developed the structuralist interpretation of inflation in the mid and late 1950s. The contributors were so numerous and the contributions so nearly simultaneous that attribution is difficult – but the Mexican Juan Noyola may have been the first in print to emphasize the role of the backward agrarian sector. He and the Chilean Aníbal Pinto in 1956 were the first to distinguish between 'structural' causes and 'propagating mechanisms' – fiscal policies, credit and the wage–price spiral (Noyola 1956; Pinto 1956).[43]

The inherent weakness of the structuralist thesis on inflation as a policy guide is that any increase in economic efficiency – even if agriculture is the most notorious offender – will diminish 'basic' inflationary processes; 'it is therefore always possible to claim that inflation is due to the failure to carry out one particular improvement', and it can be associated with a variety of social problems (Hirschman 1963:216). Therefore, the emphasis on 'underlying' or 'structural' causes could be interpreted in different ways: it could be used as a rationale either for government-sponsored reform, or, in the absence of reform, to explain government powerlessness to stem an inflationary tide. Structuralism became the dominant interpretation of inflation – and a stimulus for reform – in two Latin American administrations in the 1960s, those of João Goulart in Brazil (1961–4) and of Eduardo Frei in Chile (in his first 18 months of office, 1964–6). Structuralists lost their influence on the inflation issue because of their relative neglect of monetarist measures necessary in times of hyperinflation.[44] However, beyond that, the hyperinflations in the Southern Cone of the 1970s and 1980s were attributed by some critics to ECLA's influence, and such attribution contributed to the eclipse of the structuralist school.

The reformist views implicit in structuralism were part of an increasing concern with social issues by the ECLA staff after the Cuban Revolution began in 1959. More dramatic than ECLA's contribution to the Alliance for Progress (for which it helped win acceptance for the goals of agrarian reform, commodity price stabilization, and economic integration) was Prebisch's call for social reform in his 1963 essay, *Towards a Dynamic Development Policy for Latin America*. Here he appealed for specific reforms in agrarian structure, income distribution and education (Prebisch 1967). Beyond this, he wrote that Latin American industrialization was based on the technology appropriate to the labour-saving needs of the developed countries, and that the consumption patterns of Latin America's upper strata exacerbated the problem through their preferences for capital-intensive consumer goods. It was 'absolutely necessary [*ineludible*] for the state to deliberately compress the consumption of the upper strata.' Given the sharply skewed pattern of income distribution and the upper classes' high propensity to consume, deteriorating domestic terms of trade between agriculture and industry had their explanation:

> in the insufficient dynamism of development, which does not facilitate the absorption of the labor force [because such absorption is] not required by the slow growth of demand [for agricultural products] and the increase of productivity in primary activities. This insufficient dynamism prevents a rise of wages in agriculture parallel to the increase in productivity, and ... [thus] primary production loses in part or in whole the gains from its technological progress. (Prebisch 1967)

Prebisch further denounced the actual pattern of industrialization in Latin America, pointing out that the exaggerated pattern of protection had allowed grossly inefficient industries to arise. Latin America had, on average, the highest tariffs in the world, depriving it of economies of scale and opportunities to specialize for export (Prebisch 1967:21, 41, 90, 99). In retrospect, this 1963 statement anticipates the sombre Prebisch of *Capitalismo Periférico* (1981).

In the same period, Prebisch acknowledged that 'social' as well as economic forces had to be 'influenced' if reforms were to be achieved (Prebisch 1961:24). To this end, ECLA had established ILPES in 1962. Meanwhile, ECLA's long-standing proposals for restructuring the international trading system were largely shifted in 1963 to the new UNCTAD, which, under Prebisch's leadership as its first executive secretary, was clearly the international body most appropriate for such efforts. The original UNCTAD programme, adopted at its first world conference in 1964, was that of ECLA, *mutatis mutandis*, at the global level. Prebisch's reports to the organization in 1964 and 1968, if not fully *cepalismo*, were definitely international adaptations of the regional agency's programme as it had evolved by the early 1960s (Prebisch 1964:14–17, 20–6; Prebisch 1968:27–8).

However, at the moment when ECLA's message had reached the global stage, its authority and prestige, and even its self-confidence, began to wane. This process was partly owing to the United States's reversion to a traditional policy of anti-communism and protection of American investment under Lyndon Johnson, with a simultaneous de-emphasis on the reforms envisioned in the Alliance for Progress.[45] But ECLA's own reformist agenda of the 1960s was conditioned and increasingly made irrelevant by a long evolution of ECLA's views on its initial key policy recommendation, import-substitution industrialization (ISI). An ISI policy had seemed a brilliant success, especially in Brazil and Mexico, during the 1950s, but this success was owed in part to unusually high commodity prices during the Korean War. In the latter 1950s, ECLA began to consider the complexities of ISI. By 1957, the organization had distinguished between two types, which in the 1960s would be seen as phases of import-substitution. The first involved the relatively easy substitution of simple domestically produced consumer goods for previously imported items. The second, more difficult type involved the production of intermediate goods and consumer durables, a shift from 'horizontal' to 'vertical' ISI – so denominated because of the substitution of simple goods on a broad front in the first phase, to an integrated line of production of fewer final goods and their inputs in the second. A third phase, the production of capital goods, would ensue at a later date (CEPAL 1957:116; CEPAL 1966:19–20; Rodríguez 1980:202–3).

In 1956, ECLA had still assumed the existence of a threshold in structural changes in the economy, beyond which 'dependence on external contingencies' would diminish. Yet, the following year the agency first suggested that dependence on 'events overseas' might even increase as ISI advanced; all the same, it still held that 'import-substitution' consisted of lowering 'the import content of supplies for the home market'.[46]

Argentina was Latin America's most industrialized country, and despite its unique political phenomenon of *perónismo*, ECLA tended to view it in 1957 as a trendsetter for other Latin American nations. Argentina, ECLA noted, had reduced its imports of finished goods to one-third the total dollar amount. Yet its declining capacity to import had meant that reducing the importation of consumer goods was not sufficient to contain balance-of-payment difficulties. Capital goods and fuels also had to be reduced, and this fact was reducing the rate of growth. Chile was seen as facing similar though less dire problems. ECLA seemed to wonder aloud whether the Argentine experience was the future of Latin America. Two conclusions followed: that primary exports and food production for domestic consumption had to be increased (the latter to relieve pressure on imports), and that a region-wide common market must be developed to assure the future development of efficient manufacturing industries (CEPAL 1957:128, 150, 151).

Why should industrialization bring rising import requirements in its train? Using a simple two-sector model, Furtado in 1958 explained the problem as one in which, by assumption, the advanced sector, A, had a larger import coefficient than the backward sector, B. As the economy developed, A's coefficient grew ever larger as a share of the whole economy's coefficient, and *pari passu*, the average import coefficient tended to rise (Furtado 1958:406). If the terms of trade were deteriorating, the pressures on the balance of payments became even more acute.

Thus, for ECLA economists in the mid and late 1950s, the import requirements in the later stages of ISI, unless offset by capital inflows or rising exports, could cause 'strangulation' – a favourite ECLA metaphor for stagnation caused by insufficient imports of capital goods and other industrial inputs. As a partial solution to stuttering ISI, ECLA in 1957–8 formally appealed to its sponsoring states for a Latin American common market, which, ECLA held, would provide incentives (through economies of scale) for the production of capital and intermediate goods.[47]

Yet in its early years, the Latin American Free Trade Area, established in 1960, was only an expression of hope for alleviating the ills associated with ISI, and it had to struggle against the protectionism that had originally been encouraged by ECLA. Already in 1959, Prebisch had observed that the more economically advanced Latin American countries were becoming increasingly the hostages of external events, because they had compressed their imports to the absolute essentials for the maintenance of growth. Two years later he wrote: 'It remains a paradox that industrialization, instead of helping greatly to soften the internal impact of external fluctuations, is bringing us a new and unknown type of external vulnerability.'

The agonizing reappraisal of ISI came in 1964. In that year an ECLA study, though blaming Latin America's declining rates of growth on deteriorating terms of trade in the 1950s, also noted that 80 per cent of regional imports now consisted of fuels, intermediate goods and capital equipment. Consequently, there was little left to 'squeeze' in the region's import profile to favour manufacturing (CEPAL 1964:14, 21). Meanwhile, two monographs highly critical of ISI appeared in the agency's *Economic Bulletin* – one on the Brazilian experience in particular, and the other on Latin America in general (Tavares 1964; Macario 1964). These articles pointed to problems that, by the 1960s, were beginning to affect other parts of the developing world as well.

Examining the Brazilian case in the 1950s and early 1960s, Tavares argued that ISI had failed because of the lack of dynamism of the export sector, coupled with the fact that ISI had not diminished capital and fuel import requirements. Other problems were apparent ceilings on the domestic market, owing in part to highly skewed income distribution, which also determined the structure of demand, as well as to the constellation of productive resources – for example, the lack of skilled labour and the capital-intensive nature of industrialization in more advanced phases of ISI, which implied little labour absorption. In the advanced stages of ISI, Tavares contended, the low labour absorption of manufacturing tended to exaggerate rather than to terminate the dualism of Brazil's economy. Among other things, she argued that bottlenecks in the food supply, partly owing to the antiquated agrarian structure, put unsustainable pressures on the import bill. Tavares recommended agrarian reform as a partial solution (Tavares 1964:7–8, 11, 12, 55).

In the same number of the *Bulletin*, Santiago Macario wrote a blistering critique of the way in which ISI had been practised in Latin America, following up Prebisch's observation the previous year, 1963, that the region had the highest tariffs in the world. Macario observed that the governments of the four most industrialized countries – Argentina, Brazil, Chile and Mexico – had used ISI as a deliberate strategy to counteract a persistent lack of foreign exchange, and to create employment for expanding populations. However, in those four countries, and in most of the others of the region, protectionism, primarily in the form of tariff and exchange policies, had been irrational, in that there was no consistent policy to develop the most viable and efficient manufacturing industries. On the contrary, the most inefficient industries had received the greatest protection; there had been over-diversification of manufacturing in small markets in the 'horizontal' phase; and these factors had contributed, in some instances, to real dissavings (Macario 1964:65–7, 77, 81).

Nor did Latin American manufactures hold their own in international markets, continued Macario, at a time when exchange earnings had become critical for the future of industrialization. On the positive side, there were tendencies in the early 1960s to abolish exchange controls, quantitative restrictions and multiple exchange rates, and a related tendency to begin tariff reduction; yet Macario asserted that Latin American tariffs were still being built on a makeshift basis, resulting in a gross misallocation of scarce resources (Macario 1964:67, 78, 81).

Rational criteria were needed to develop industries – such as the use of factors in greatest abundance (for example, labour), or the promotion of industries that could earn foreign exchange. Equally important, thought Macario, was the establishment for each country of a 'uniform level of net protection'. Overall, his thesis was less that ECLA's policy prescriptions had initially been wrong – which Tavares's analysis in some ways implied – than that the region's governments had flagrantly ignored ECLA's technical advice, pursuing, in Macario's words, 'import-substitution at any cost'.[48] Though Albert Hirschman suggested four years later that Tavares and Macario had issued the death certificate of ISI somewhat prematurely, other scholars soon added new charges, such as ISI's having increased the concentration of income with regard both to social class and to region (within countries).[49]

Conclusion

In the 1950s, the turn to Keynes was a sign of the times, resulting from several factors. Among them were the increasing legitimacy of state intervention in the economy, authorized by Keynes; the tolerance of protectionism in developing nations by the newly created IMF and World Bank;[50] the generalized 'export pessimism' deriving from the Depression era; and the rise of an 'unanticipated' and un-theorized industrial economy in several countries. These developments all contributed to a new climate in which Prebisch found a favourable reception for his structuralist approach. By capturing a UN agency, ECLA, Prebisch and his group obtained a firm institutional platform from which to propagate their unorthodox ideas. ECLA was in a position to influence governments through diagnostic and prognostic missions to its member states, through the passage of its personnel to government ministries and university chairs, and through its training programs at ILPES and on site in more than a score of cities across Latin America. When Prebisch became head of UNCTAD in 1963, he used the new international organization to bring ECLA doctrines to a Third World audience. Structuralists also extended their influence through other UN agencies (notably the ILO), and national planning agencies and development institutes.

On the theoretical plane, there were two phases in the period under review, corresponding to perceived failures in economic performance, which both implied inadequacy in analysis. The first was the failure of export-led growth, giving rise to the Prebisch–Singer thesis. The second was the decline, in the most advanced countries, of ISI as a viable strategy, and this is where our story ends. Beyond it lies the rise of a dependency school within and beyond the ECLA camp, and a Marxist riposte to dependency in the form of a modes-of-production literature.

A broader attack on the perceived failures of structuralism by neo-classical theorists, contemporaneous with that of dependency, resulted in the wave of liberalization and privatization that coincided with and was reinforced by the decline and collapse of socialism in the Soviet Union and Eastern Europe.[51] Structuralism's influence began to wane as import-substitution was not succeeded by dynamic export-substitution, as in East Asia. In the neo-liberal attack on rent-seeking, waste, and inefficiencies associated with the Latin American state during the 1970s and 1980s, ECLA was frequently charged with providing the ideological justification for rampant protectionism and other excesses. However, we have seen that in fact, Prebisch and other ECLA economists were already highly critical of such policies by the early 1960s.[52]

To summarize, in the 1940s, Prebisch formulated his thesis of unequal exchange between centre and periphery, resulting in part from his two decades of involvement in economic and financial policy. He came to reject the thesis of comparative advantage via his partial rejection, in the context of peripheral economies, of the monetary and banking policies of Keynes. Prebisch was an eclectic, however, and also drew on the writings of Kindleberger and others. He had formulated the elements of his thesis before the appearance, in 1949, of the empirical base on which the thesis would rest in its first published form – Singer's UN study, *Relative Prices* (United Nations, 1949). 'Structuralism' had been present in embryonic form in Prebisch's institutional arguments as to why neo-classical economics did not apply to the periphery without modification. The analysis contained some historical elements from the outset (for example, the decisive shift, in Prebisch's view, of the principal centre after World War I), and a younger group of ECLA economists subsequently employed structural analysis in formal historical studies.[53]

Structuralism gave the state a key role in the development process, in contrast with the dependency school, whose members viewed the state as less autonomous of social forces and more bound to particular class interests. In any event, structuralism distinguished itself from neo-classical analysis in its emphasis on macroeconomics, institutions, and interdisciplinary approaches to economic issues, as well as in treating long-term (trans-cyclical) changes.

Notes

1. List was also championed by Luis Vieira Souto in turn-of-the-century Brazil.
2. Sombart (1928:vol. 1, xiv–xv (quotation), 64; vol. 2, 1019).
3. See Wagemann (1931 [Span.trans., 1933]:70–1).
4. In addition, Joseph Schumpeter, who used both neo-classical and historical approaches, was known through his publications in English and Spanish.
5. See Manoilescu (1929, 1934). Both these books were published in Spanish and Portuguese translations. On Perroux, see his *Lições de Economia Política* (1936: ch. 2, 138–225), and his numerous articles published in Brazil, cited in Love (1996:273). On the influence of the two economists on Prebisch and structuralism, see Love (1996:111–12, 134–7).
6. Anderson (1976:25–37). Anderson notes a new generation of French intellectuals entering the Parti Communiste de France in 1928, but perceives no 'generalization of Marxism as a theoretical currency in France' until the German occupation (p. 37).
7. E.g., on Romania, see Love (1996:173, 282).
8. On the relatively early appearance of Marxism in Argentina, see Ratzer (1969). The Argentine socialist leader, Juan B. Justo, was the first translator of *Capital* into Spanish in 1895, though he only translated the first volume.
9. On Brazil, see Dulles 1973:514.
10. Recall also that Cosío Villegas, Edmundo Flores and other Mexicans had studied agricultural economics abroad (Chapter 6).
11. See Chayanov (1966) and Heynig (1982:124) on the importance of the English-language anthology of Chayanov's works. Spanish translations of Chayanov appeared in the 1970s.

12. In the mid 1950s, Paranaguá, a professor at the University of São Paulo, served as the Brazilian representative to the IMF. See Paranaguá (1935:22–3) and *passim*; Campos (1994:309).
13. See Prebisch (1927:1302–21).
14. See the annual indexes to *Trimestre Económico* (1934–51).
15. Urquidi to Prebisch, Mexico City, 2 June 1944, in Prebisch Archive (private collection, Santiago, Chile), referring to Kindleberger (1943*a*:supplement, 347–54, 1943*b*:375–95).
16. For details on his views and actions as bank director in the 1930s, see Love (1994:404–08).
17. At the same time Prebisch gave a series of lectures at the Banco de México on 'the Argentine monetary experience (1935–1943)', that is, covering the period in which he was the director general of the central bank. See Banco Central de la República Argentina (1972:1, 249–588; 2,599–623).
18. Prebisch (1944:234); Banco Central (1942:30).
19. Banco Central (1972: 1, 407). See the similar judgments on ISI by Dorfman (1942:74), on World War I and the Great Depression, and Ferreira Lima (1945: 17), on São Paulo, World War II.
20. Prebisch 1948:88–97 (quotation on 97).
21. UN ECOSOC E/CN.12/17 (7 June 1948), 2; E/CN.12/28 (11 June 1948), 6; E/CN.12/71 (24 June 1948).
22. Published in English as *The Economic Development of Latin America and its Principal Problems* in 1950 (CEPAL, 1950).
23. CEPAL (1951: 78 (quotation), 79). At that time, Prebisch believed that by changing the composition of imports from consumer to capital goods, Latin American countries could reduce their import coefficients (CEPAL 1964:44–5).
24. More ambiguously, *Economic Development* stated, 'the income of entrepreneurs and of productive factors' in the Centre increased faster than did productivity in the Centre from the 1870s to the 1930s; but in another passage, the document placed exclusive emphasis on the role of wages in the Centre (pp. 10, 14).
25. Singer (1950:473–85, quotation on 479). Income elasticity of demand for a good refers to the relative response of demand to a small percentage change in income, $(\Delta q/q)/(\Delta y/y)$, where q is the quantity demanded, and y is disposable income).
26. Prebisch to author, 29 June 1977; Singer to author, Brighton, England, 21 August 1979.
27. E/CN.12/221 (18 May 1951), p. 30. In fact, Prebisch had made *two* arguments, of which one was better stated by Singer. (Singer in turn had touched on Prebisch's theme of contrasting degrees of labour organization in centre and periphery.) Prebisch's central argument related to differential productivities in centre and periphery. His other argument, dealing with disparities in import coefficients, was roughly analogous to Singer's more elegant argument on differential income elasticities.
28. E.g., see Prebisch (1959:251–73).
29. See Love (1994:418–22).
30. Singer's own debt to structuralist tradition, in the form of the German Historical School, can be inferred from the fact that he was the student of Arthur Spiethoff, the long-time editor of *Schmollers Jahrbuch* (see Meier and Seers 1984:273).
31. Hirschman (1977:supplement, p. 68). Samuelson's articles were 'International Trade and the Equalisation of Factor Prices' (1948) and 'International Factor-Price Equalisation Once Again' (1949).

32. The principal arguments and sources in this long debate have been summarized and evaluated by John Spraos, who concludes that Prebisch was right about long-term deterioration of net barter terms of trade for 1870–1939, but that the trend was weaker than Prebisch thought. Furthermore, for 1900–75, Spraos concludes that the data were trendless. Yet Prebisch would still argue, one assumes, that anything less than a *favourable* trend for primary products would show that the centre was benefiting more than the periphery in the trading process (assuming greater technological productivity gains in the centre); see Spraos (1980:107–28, esp. 126). More recent studies of long-term data have tended to support Prebisch and Singer. For an extensive review of the literature, generally supporting Spraos's findings, see Diakosavvas and Scandizzo 1991 (on Spraos, p. 237). For recent developments, see Love, 'The Rise and Decline of Latin American Structuralism: New Dimensions,' to appear in *Latin American Research Review*, 40: 3 (Fall, 2005).
33. On the early institutional development of ECLA, see Burger (1998:ch. 3).
34. Furtado (1950:11); Lewis (1954:132–91). ECLA was also referring to highly elastic labour supplies in 1950, and it is not clear whether Furtado introduced this concept.
35. Rodríguez 1977:196; Rodríguez 1980:297. More strictly, Rodríguez believes ECLA's best years for theory ended with the 1950s (Rodríguez 1980:15).
36. For an instructive comparison of Argentine *desarrollismo* and Brazilian *desenvolvimentismo* in the 1950s and 1960s, analysing the latter's greater success, see Sikkink 1988.
37. Compiled from ILPES Archive, CEPAL, Santiago.
38. CEPAL 'played a significant role in spreading modern economic analysis and statistical techniques and in developing ... schools of public administration and planning ministries' (Cárdenas *et al.* 2000:12).
39. E.g., (Sachs 1976:137).
40. Prebisch (1961:1–25, esp. 3), where agriculture is cited as a structural cause of inflation (because of antiquated land-tenure systems). Rodríguez (1980:4, 190) stresses personal, rather than official, contributions of *cepalistas*. CEPAL's *XXV Años* (1973) and *Aporte* (1978) do not mention any contribution by CEPAL as such on inflation.
41. See Noyola Vázquez (1956:603–18); Sunkel (1960:107–31); Rodríguez (1980:ch. 6). In Chile, as Sunkel pointed out, prices for agricultural goods were favourable. In Perón's Argentina, one would have expected an inelastic supply in agriculture, because of government price and foreign exchange controls.
42. On the origins of the 'structural' inflation thesis and its antecedents, see Love (1994:424–27).
43. On their priority, see Rodríguez (1980:190). In his memoir, Furtado (1985:185) puts Noyola first. Other contributors include Sunkel, Jorge Ahumada, Jaime Barros and Luis Escobar, all from Chile. Hirschman independently developed an analogous approach (see Hirschman 1963:213, n. 1).
44. See Hirschman (1981:183).
45. E.g., see Burger (1998:137).
46. CEPAL (1956:30); CEPAL (1957:115).
47. CEPAL (1958:4) The seventh session of CEPAL in 1957 adopted a resolution calling for steps toward the creation of a region-wide common market.
48. Macario (1964:67) (quotation), 84 (formula for 'uniform level of net protection', 87).
49. *Inter alia*, Hirschman (1971:85–123, esp. p. 103) argued that the failure of ISI was not inevitable, but depended on the interaction of social and political factors with

economic elements. On ISI failures and other economic and social problems of the mid 1960s, see the literature surveyed in Baer (1972:95–122, esp. 107).

50. Cárdenas *et al.* (2000:5–8) note that through the 1960s, economic orthodoxy, as defined by the positions of the World Bank and IMF, accepted the necessity of industrialization and a moderate protectionism in the process of economic development.

51. On these matters, see Love (1994:432–57).

52. For a theoretical reconsideration of structuralism and ECLA's theorization of import-substitution, showing that the agency anticipated most of its critics, see FitzGerald (1998:47–61).

53. Furtado (1959); Pinto Santa Cruz (1959); Ferrer (1963); Sunkel and Paz (1970). Later a more specialized structuralist work appeared on Mexico: Villareal (1976). Villareal argues, however, that structuralism accounts more adequately for Mexico's external disequilibrium in the period 1939–58 than in 1959–70.

References

Anderson, P., *Considerations on western Marxism* (London: Verso, 1976).

Babb, S., *Managing Mexico: Economists from Nationalism to Neoliberalism* (Princeton University Press, 2002).

Baer, W. 'Import Substitution and Industrialization in Latin America: Experiences and Interpretations', *Latin American Research Review*, 7/1 (Spring 1972) 95–111.

Banco Central de la República Argentina, *Memoria, 1942* (Buenos Aires: Banco Central, 1943).

Banco Central de la República Argentina, *La Creación del Banco Central y la Experiencia Monetaria Argentina Entre los años 1935–1943* (Buenos Aires: Banco Central, 1972) 1: 249–588; 2: 599–623.

Burger, H., 'An Intellectual History of the ECLA Culture, 1948–1964', PhD dissertation, Harvard University, 1998.

Campos, R. [de Oliveira], *A Lanterna na Popa* (Rio de Janeiro: Topbooks, 1994).

Cárdenas, E., J. A. Ocampo, and R. Thorp, 'Introduction', in E. Cárdenas, J. A. Ocampo, and R. Thorp (eds), *An Economic History of Twentieth-Century Latin America, vol. 3: Industrialization and the State in Latin America: The Postwar Years* (New York: Palgrave, 2000).

CEPAL, *Economic Survey of Latin America: 1949* (New York: United Nations, 1951).

CEPAL, *The Economic Development of Latin America and its Principal Problems* (New York: United Nations, 1950 [Sp. orig., 1949]).

CEPAL, 'The situation in Argentina and the New Economic Policy', *Economic Bulletin* 1:1 (January 1956) 30.

CEPAL, *Economic Survey of Latin America: 1956* (New York: United Nations, 1957).

CEPAL, 'Bases for the Formation of the Latin American Regional Market, *Economic Bulletin*, 3(1)(1958).

CEPAL, *The Economic Development of Latin America in the Post-war Period* (New York: United Nations, 1964).

CEPAL, *The Process of Industrial Development in Latin America* (New York: United Nations, 1966).

CEPAL, *XXV Años de la CEPAL* (Santiago: CEPAL, 1973).

CEPAL, *El Aporte de las Ideas-Fuerza* (Santiago: CEPAL, 1978).

Chayanov, A. *On the Theory of Peasant Economy*, Daniel Thorner, Basile Kerblay and R. E. F. Smith (eds) (Homewood, IL: Irwin, 1966).

Concha, M., 'Balanza de Comercio', *Revista Económica* II: 23 (March 1889) 327–8.

Concha, M., *La Lucha Económica: Estudio de Economía Social Presentado al IV Congreso Científico Americano Reunido en Santiago de Chile en 1908* (Santiago: Imp. Nacional, 1909).

Diakosavvas, D. and P. L. Scandizzo, 'Trends in the Terms of Trade of Primary Commodities, 1900–1982: The Controversy and Its Origins', *Economic Development and Cultural Change*, 39/2 (January 1991) 231–64.

Dorfman, A., *Evolución Industrial Argentina* (Buenos Aires: Losada, 1942).

Dulles, J. W. F., *Anarchists and Communists in Brazil: 1900–1935* (Austin: University of Texas Press, 1973).

Ferreira Lima, H., 'Evolução Industrial de São Paulo', *Revista Industrial de S. Paulo* 1/7 (June 1945).

Ferrer, A., *La Economía Argentina: Las Etapas de su Desarrollo y Problemas Actuales* (Mexico City.: Fondo de Cultura Económica, 1963).

FitzGerald, E. V. K., 'La CEPAL y la Teoría de la Industrialización', *Revista de la CEPAL*, número extraordinario [CEPAL: Cincuenta Años] (October 1998) 47–61.

Furtado, C., 'Características Gerais da Economia Brasileira', *Revista Brasileira de Economia*, 4/1 (March 1950).

Furtado, C., 'The External Disequilibrium in the Underdeveloped Economies', *Indian Journal of Economics* 38/151 (April 1958) 403–10.

Furtado, C., *Formação Econômica do Brasil* (Rio de Janeiro: Fundo de Cultura, 1959).

Furtado, C., *A Fantasia Organisada* (Rio de Janeiro: Paz e Terra, 1985).

Hansen, A., *A Guide to Keynes* (New York: McGraw-Hill, 1953).

Heynig, K., 'The Principal Schools of Thought on the Peasant Economy', *CEPAL Review* 16 (April 1982).

Hilferding, R., *Finance capital: a study of the latest phase of capitalist development* (London: Routledge and Kegan Paul, 1981 [German ed., 1910]).

Hirschman, A. O., 'Inflation in Chile', in A. Hirschman, *Journeys toward Progress: Studies of Economic Policy-Making in Latin America* (New York: Twentieth Century Fund, 1963).

Hirschman, A. O., 'The Political Economy of Import-substituting Industrialization in Latin America', in A. O. Hirschman, *A Bias for Hope* (New Haven: Yale University Press, 1971).

Hirschman, A. O., 'A Generalized Linkage Approach to Development, with Special Reference to Staples', *Economic Development and Cultural Change* 25, Supplement, Essays in Honor of Bert Hoselitz (1977) 67–98.

Hirschman, A. O., 'The Social and Political Matrix of Inflation: Elaboration of the Latin American Experience', in A. O. Hirschman (ed.), *Essays in Trespassing: Economics to Politics and Beyond* (Cambridge University Press, 1981).

Inter-American Development Bank (IADB), *Economic and Social Progress in Latin America: Economic Integration: 1984 Report* (Washington, DC, 1985).

Kindleberger, C., 'Planning for Foreign Investment', *American Economic Review* 33/1, Supplement (March 1943a), 347–54.

Kindleberger, C., 'International Monetary Stabilization', in Seymour E. Harris (ed.), *Postwar Economic Problems* (New York: McGraw-Hill, 1943b).

Lapa, J. R. do Amaral, *Modos de Produção e Realidade Brasileira* (Petrópolis: Vozes 1980).

Lewis, W. A., 'Economic Development with Unlimited Supplies of Labour', *Manchester School*, 22 (May 1954) 132–91.

Love, J. L., 'Economic Ideas and Ideologies in Latin America since 1930', in L. Bethell (ed.), *Cambridge History of Latin America*, vol. VI, pt 1 (Cambridge University Press, 1994).

Love, J., *Crafting the Third World: Theorizing Underdevelopment in Rumania and Brazil* (Stanford University Press, 1996).

Love, J., 'The Rise and Decline of Latin American Structuralism: New Dimensions,' to appear in *Latin American Research Review*, 40:3 (Fall 2005).

Macario, S., 'Protectionism and Industrialization in Latin America', *Economic Bulletin for Latin America*, 9 (1964) 61–101.

Manoilescu, M., *Théorie du protectionnisme et de l'échange international* (Paris: Alcan, 1929).

Manoilescu, M., *Le siècle du corporatisme: Doctrine du corporatisme intégral et pur* (Paris: Alcan, 1934).

Meier, G. M. and D. Seers, *Pioneers in Development* (New York: Oxford University Press for World Bank, 1984).

Montecinos, V., 'Economists in Political and Policy Elites in Latin America', in A. W. Coats (ed.), *The Post-1945 Internationalization of Economics* (Durham, NC: Duke University Press, 1996).

Noyola Vázquez, J., 'El Desarrollo Económico y la Inflación en México y Otros Países Latinoamericanos', *Investigaciones Económicas*, 16/4 (1956) 603–18.

Paranaguá, O. *Tariff Policy* (Oxford: Clarendon, 1935).

Pazos, F., 'Cincuenta Años de Pensamiento Económico en la América Latina', *Trimestre Económico* 50/4 (October 1983) 1916.

Perroux, F., *Lições de Economia Política* (Coimbra: Ed. Coimbra, 1936).

Pinto [Santa Cruz], A. *La Intervención del Estado* (Santiago: Ed. Universitaria, 1956).

Pinto Santa Cruz, A., *Chile, un Caso de Desarrollo Frustrado* (Santiago: Ed. Universitaria 1959).

Prebisch, R., 'El Régimen de Pool en el Comercio de Carnes', *Revista de Ciencias Económicas* 15 (December 1927) 1302–21.

Prebisch, R., 'Observaciones Sobre los Planes Monetarios Internacionales', *Trimestre Económico* 11/2 (July–September 1944).

Prebisch, R., 'Panorama General de los Problemas de Regulación Monetaria y Crediticia en el Continente Americano: A. América Latina', in Banco de México, *Memoria: Primera Reunión de Técnicos Sobre Problemas del Banco Central del Continente Americano* (Mexico City, 1946).

Prebisch, R., *Introducción a Keynes* (Mexico City: Fondo de Cultura Económica, 1947).

Prebisch, R., 'Commercial Policy in the Underdeveloped Countries', *American Economic Review: Papers and Proceedings* 49/2 (May 1959) 251–73.

Prebisch, R., 'Economic Development or Monetary Stability: The False Dilemma', *Economic Bulletin for Latin America*, 6/1 (March 1961) 1–25.

Prebisch, R., *Towards a New Trade Policy for Development* (New York: UNCTAD, 1964).

Prebisch, R., *Hacia una Dinámica del Desarrollo Latinoamericano* (Montevideo: Banda Oriental, 1967 [orig. 1963]).

Prebisch, R., 'Towards a Global Strategy of Development', *UNCTAD Second Conference* (New York: UNCTAD, 1968).

Prebisch, R. *Capitalismo Periférico* (Mexico City: Fondo de Cultura Económica, 1981).

Ratzer, J., *Los Marxistas del 90* (Córdoba: Pasado y Presente, 1969).

Rodríguez, O., 'On the Conception of the Center Periphery System', *CEPAL Review*, 1st half of 1977 (1977).

Rodríguez, O., *La Teoría del Subdesarrollo de la CEPAL* (Mexico City: Siglo xxi, 1980).

Sachs, I., *The Discovery of the Third World* (Cambridge, MA: MIT Press, 1976).

Samuelson, P., 'International Trade and the Equalisation of Factor Prices', *Economic Journal* 58/230 (June 1948), 163–84.

Samuelson, P., 'International Factor-Price Equalisation Once Again', *Economic Journal* 59/234 (June 1949), 181–97.

Sikkink, K. A., *Developmentalism and Democracy: Ideas, Institutions, and Economic Policy Making in Brazil and Argentina (1955–1962)*, PhD dissertation, Columbia University, New York, 1988).

Singer, H. W., 'The Distribution of Gains between Investing and Borrowing Countries', *American Economic Review: Papers and Proceedings*, 40/2 (May 1950) 473–85.

Sombart, W., *Der moderne Kapitalismus* (Munich: Duncker & Humblot, 1928).

Spraos, J., 'The Statistical Debate on the Net Barter Terms of Trade between Primary Commodities and Manufactures', *Economic Journal* 90/357 (March 1980) 107–28.

Sunkel, O., 'Inflation in Chile: An Unorthodox Approach', *International Economic Papers*, 10 (1960), 107–31 [orig. in *Trimestre Economico* (1958)].

Sunkel, O. and P. Paz, *El Subdesarrollo Latinoamericano y la Teoria del Desarrollo* (Mexico City: Siglo XXI, 1970).

Tavares, M. da Conceição, 'The Growth and Decline of Import Substitution in Brazil', *Economic Bulletin for Latin America*, 9 (1964) 1–59.

Trimestre Económico (1934–51).

United Nations, *Relative Prices of Exports and Imports of Under-Developed Countries: A Study of Postwar Terms of Trade between Under-Developed and Industrialised Nations* (New York: United Nations Department of Economic Affairs, 1949).

Urquidi, V. and J. Márquez, 'Nuestro Problema Editorial: La Falta de Originales', *Trimestre Económico* 20/4 (October–December 1953) 576.

Villareal, R., *El Desequilibrio Externo en la Industrialización de México (1929–75): Un Enfoque Estructuralista* (Mexico City: Fondo de Cultura Económica, 1976).

Wagemann, Ernst *Struktur und Rhythmus der Weltwirtschaft* (Berlin: Von Raimar Hobbing, 1931 [Spanish trans., 1933]).

9
Knowledge is Power: The Case of Colombian Economists[1]

Marco Palacios

Knowledge and power

Professional economists appear to society at large to be legitimate bearers of scientific economic knowledge. Accordingly, they are the agents entrusted with professional responsibility for formulating and developing economic policies. With their command of a specialized body of knowledge, members of the profession's elite become indispensable to politicians, to economically powerful groups and to congressional lawmakers. They become public actors when they enter the institutional and political structure. At that moment knowledge and power are linked; that link is the main subject of this chapter.[2]

According to Max Weber's classic definition, the modern state transforms policy into action through human resources and organizations that meet the conditions of procedural and substantive rationality, legality and administrative responsibility. In this process, the intellectual becomes a functionary and critique becomes bureaucratic reasoning. Power is the probability that one actor within a social relationship will be in a position to carry out his or her own will despite resistance. Economic knowledge is transformed into power when its bearers act as state officials and make key decisions on economic policy that seem 'technical', that is, divested of political responsibility. However, the fact that a decision is prepared and presented as technical does not prevent it from affecting or promoting specific interests within society. That is, it does not in any way alter its eminently political nature. However, the technician is often viewed as apolitical and 'neutral'. The problem lies in the confusion of political neutrality, should it be found to exist, with so-called ideological neutrality, ensured by 'the objective science of the economy'.

Given the central political role of economists, it is clearly of the utmost importance to study the different systems of awarding fellowships to do doctoral studies, and of recruiting graduates to occupy important positions in the Colombian state. The chapter will explore this through a study of the Universidad de los Andes 'model', and will suggest that the latter

(UNIANDES) was successful owing to the central role that its Faculty of Economics and its research centre, Centro de Estudios para el Desarrollo Económico (CEDE), played as centres of recruitment into the upper ranks of public service and private sector management. The point is developed by contrast with the National University (UNAL).

Although there are some studies of the role played by politicized professionals in the Colombian state, there are no monographs similar to the studies available for Argentina, Brazil, Chile and Mexico.[3] To place our study of the formation of a policy-making elite in context, this chapter perforce first needs to examine topics which need more thorough research: the access of Colombian economists to positions of power and influence in the context of the pragmatic tradition that has given meaning to the values and ideals of Colombian elites since the end of the eighteenth century; the emergence of economics in the university; the launching of an economic elite and its possible explanation as a social phenomenon; the relationship of this elite to the higher reaches of the state, and their integration into the power elites.

The origins and place of economic discourse

The emission and reception of economic discourse in Colombia follows the historical pattern of other Latin American countries in so far as it is a public and institutional matter. It began with the *hacendistas*, public finance experts of the Bourbon era (lawyers, politicians and businessmen supplemented by engineers a century later). In our days it is in the hands of national and international officials and ex-officials, in the majority graduates of North American universities who hold the title of PhD in economics. According to Paul Streeten, the 'development community' is made up of three groups: (1) academic and research community; (2) the community of officials of multilateral and bilateral development institutions; and (3) the wider community of fieldworkers in development programmes.

The officials who make decisions in developing countries are incorporated in group 2 and the lower-level national officials in group 3.[4] However, two well-known economists maintain that, in contemporary Colombia,

> the evidence suggests the non-existence of an active and consolidated academic community ... the target audiences seem to be located abroad, whether in the context of a virtual community now under development or in the international academically-oriented, financial or development institutions.[5]

We can suppose that high-ranking Colombian economists feel that they are part of an international epistemological community whose main nerve-centres are located in the most prestigious universities of the United States and occasionally Britain. However in these two countries, the epistemological communities act independently of the governments, while in Colombia, as in many Latin American countries, the epistemological authority on matters of economic policy is in the hands of economists who hold high positions in the state. This authority is a form of power.

Doctrine and ideas do not exist in the abstract. They require a subject that formulates them as discourse, and discourse requires language:

> Language is an instrument of control as well as communication ... Language is ideological in another, more political, sense of the word: it involves systematic distortion in the service of class interest ... [And] ideology involves a systematically organized presentation of reality. (Kress and Hodge 1979: 6, 15).

The systematized language of economists is directed at multiple social and institutional audiences and stakeholders. How then is this language developed, and for whom, and from where is it emitted?

The primordial mechanisms for framing discourse or doctrine have historically been the big government projects and plans, foreign missions and the universities, as we will see below. The main disseminators have been as follows:

1. The Finance Ministry (hereafter FM), responsible for guiding and putting into practice macroeconomic policy, formulating the budget, and effectively managing the control of tax collection and central government expenditures. Moreover, it is probable that the pressure of the political class on appointments in the FM serves as an effective counterweight to the domination of the professional economists, except in areas where macroeconomic policy is formulated.
2. The National Planning Department (hereafter NPD), whose functions are limited to the approval of public investment, including projects financed with international loans. Its role could, however, be more significant in that it is the technical coordinator of two government institutions that are key to the formulation of the national budget – CONPES (Consejo Nacional de Política Económica y Social) and CONFIS (Consejo de Política Fiscal).
3. The central bank, in Colombia called the Bank of the Republic (BR), has enjoyed increased legal autonomy since the 1991 constitutional reforms, and its governors can play a stronger hand in relation to the FM. In any case, the BR shows great bureaucratic stability, as seen in the longevity of its leadership and technical staff.
4. The specialized press. Since the 1980s, a number of economic periodicals have appeared and consolidated themselves. These, according to Juan Luis Molina Londoño, form new 'power points for economic opinion'.[6] Two observations are in order here: first, these new means of expression

originate in different groups that have already consolidated power, such as the large economic conglomerates or the World Bank, and have no fundamental disagreements in terms of the economic 'model'. Second, the economic discourse promoted in these magazines, whether propaganda or political pedagogy, is not directed at citizens in order to communicate, in the sense of seeking and effecting an exchange of ideas and arguments about the intricate workings of democratic society. The economist speaks as a teacher or prophet to passive audiences that acknowledge his or her role as the valid interpreter of economic science. The only challenge then comes from another economist, and the exchange that is established among them often calls itself public debate.

The practical republic: less politics, more administration

From the time of the eighteenth-century New Granadian Enlightenment, those interested in reaching the pinnacle of the social system and the centre of the political system needed to demonstrate a discursive capacity to define and defend values and projects, and the talent to create and mobilize public opinion. These were virtues brought to life by the networks built up in the late-colonial era around the *tertulias* (soirées), the press and university colleges. In the process of politicizing these networks, the objective of the discourse was increasingly to attain state power and maintain legitimacy.

The undertaking to adapt universal economic doctrine to the Colombian setting, on the one hand, and the strength of the idea of progress, on the other, form part of a complex cultural learning process. This came harnessed to an elitist dream of Bourbon roots constructed around political stability and material progress. To some extent, this refers to 'alternative values': apolitical in a climate of party fervour and technical in the face of the needs of material development – what Frank Safford has termed 'the ideal of the practical' (Safford 1976:240).

Despite the durability of the ideal of the practical, successive ruptures in the process of nation-building took their toll in the nineteenth century. That century's experiences of nation-building led to a dichotomous view of Colombian reality, according to which the market functions well but the country exists on the edge of ingovernability. Traditional aristocratic values were hybridized in the incubator of representative liberal institutions, and political passions became rooted in the republic's body politic. So, once the last fratricidal war of the nineteenth century ended and the province of Panama separated to form a sovereign republic, the solution to the ongoing deficit of public finance and 'public order' (the two connected by the civil wars) seemed to be found in the divorce of politics and administration.

From the dawning of the twentieth century, sectors of the elites believed that they had found the 'open sesame' of stability and development, in isolating as far as possible economic institutions from the electoral cycle. According to this view of order, the state can modernize itself using a professional technical staff that administers rationally and in a politically neutral fashion. The duty of politicians leading the state is to decide on the options (for example in political economy) that will be carried out by a qualified team of neutral, hierarchically organized administrators. However, twentieth-century Colombian experience seems to suggest that the constant expansion of public bureaucracy does not lend itself to the appearance of a body of officials with a modern ethos capable of transforming the patterns of a legalistic, personalistic, patronage-based and short-sighted political culture. Rather, the expansion of even the most highly technical administrative bureaucracy entails new forms of struggle for power, of which those of the policy-makers of the last quarter of the twentieth century could serve as a good example.

In other words, the plan to separate administration from politics was a failure. One of the reasons perhaps was the firmly established conception that it was possible to modernize the country and its institutions while altering only minimally the structure and orientation of the traditional social hierarchies. The constitution of 1886 established 'political centralization and administrative decentralization', a myth that was functional for conservatives and liberals in the twentieth century in so far as it legitimized their power struggles by masking the true fragility of the state. It also hid the chasm between an impressive and varied body of law and the weakness of the rule of law, as well as the absence of an inclusive social consensus.

Economic discourse finds an echo and relevance in Colombia's relations with the international system and in internal struggles for power and legitimacy. In the internal arena, it is important to keep in mind the following:

1. The lengthy duration of the ideal of modernity with its core values of rationality and scientific approach.
2. The early twentieth-century separation between institutions that formulate economic policy and the representative bodies that are formed through the electoral process.
3. The defining effect that the liberal model (c. 1910–40), erected on the coffee economy, would have on relations between the state and the private sector throughout the twentieth century; the pragmatic orientation outweighed doctrinaire stances on economic policy.
4. The weakness of populist pressure in the modernization process.[7]

From the international point of view, the continuity of an elitist model of legitimization from, for and against the outside can be appreciated. This model, which dates from the nineteenth century, was deployed by the elites in their domestic struggles. In Colombia, the model came into play during the first Kemmerer mission in 1923, which rationalized the increase in the level of technical competence of the state's economic branches.

The foreign missions adapted astonishingly well to the paternalistic environment of the Colombian elites. They provided a breeding ground for groups which replaced the parties and Congress. Using the state, they propagated notions of 'public interest' in the name of 'reason' and of a 'technical rationality' that soon assumed a halo at once mysterious and sacred. They were called upon to centralize decision-making and to legitimate the redistribution of economic and social power. Independent of their relative success, the internal resistance that they faced, and their impact on the formation of Colombia specialists, the foreign technical expert appeared 'above suspicion'; they did not flirt with regional interests and pork-barrel politics (Palacios 1995:78–9).

The pragmatism that characterized economic policy limits the impact of different doctrines and schools of thought, reflecting the changing perceptions of business groups, especially those linked to coffee, industry, and the financial and banking sector. If in the abstract it can be maintained that coffee and importer interests are internationalist, and that the industrial interests are nationalist, then the gentle and even tardy process of import-substitution in Colombia is proof of the pragmatic negotiation that occurred among these groups.[8] This negotiation was facilitated by the absence of a populist era in the country, with the resulting marginalization of trade unions and popular organizations in economic policy-making, and explains the weakness of the intermediaries, the populist politicians.

Although the attempt to isolate government from the personalistic and patronage-based networks failed, the set of strategic alliances between the state and coffee was institutionalized. Thus a set of values derived from the dichotomy 'politics/administration' developed, rooted in the 'ideal of the practical'. These values have guided the action of social and economic elites, although they have not succeeded in embracing the entire spectrum of the political elite.

We can identify four core values and sets of choices which characterized the Colombian policy-making system, as follows:

1. party moderation or an apolitical approach above sectarianism;
2. economic and business pragmatism ahead of doctrinal purity;
3. collaboration and consensus between the private and public sectors over struggle and conflict;
4. priority to agreed-upon and limited state intervention over open competition among economic agents.[9]

These values defined ground rules in a structure framed by the intersection of two axes: state/private sector and nation-state/world-system. This intersection forms the backdrop against which political and business elites act and, with them, the professional economist.

Emergence and development of the professional economist

Economic discourse, originally an appendage of political discourse, is found from the eighteenth century onwards in the classic debates on fiscal policy, protection and free trade, and the financing and endowment of infrastructure. The discourse eventually gained some independence and its own profile as economic and social development advanced. As modern professions established and consolidated themselves, Colombia had to begin institution-building.

The aura of rationality attributed to the economist during the era of the National Front governments (1958–74) has its clearest precedent in the engineer. The social prestige of the engineer was derived from his or her association with the icons of national progress: the railroad, power plants, highways, tunnels, streetcars, aqueducts and sewage systems. The graduates of the National University's Faculty of Civil Engineering or the National School of Mines in Medellín were associated with the early development of this infrastructure. One study relates the active role of the National School of Mines to the formation of a business group, and the development of the public and private sectors of Antioquia and the country.[10]

From the creation of the Colombian Society of Engineers in 1887, the amalgam of scientific prestige and a public role for the professional was evident, inexorably linked to the inner circles of the state in what became a powerful Ministry of Public Works based on the 'dance of the millions' (1926–9). Their rise to prominence accelerated in 1931 with the change of transportation strategy from railroads to highways. There are even references to a 'government of engineers' between 1946 and 1957 since the three presidents during this period – Mariano Ospina Perez, Laureano Gomez and Gustavo Rojas Pinilla – were engineers.[11]

On the road to the professionalization of the economist, the two Kemmerer missions (1923 and 1931) are landmarks.[12] A more technical approach to the presentation and analysis of economic statistics gained relevance in institutions created in 1923 such as the Bank of the Republic and the Comptroller General's Office. The public finance experts who represented Colombia before the foreign missions, such as the Kemmerer missions and later the 1949–53 World Bank mission, Economy and Humanism (1955), and the two CEPAL missions (1954 and 1958) were able to rationalize a practical economic policy that, in some cases had to be theorized *ex post facto*.

During the 1940s, university-level economic studies were established successively in the socially exclusive Gimnasio Moderno in Bogotá, the University of Antioquia in Medellín, and in the National University and UNIANDES. The Gimnasio Moderno's first graduates in economics began to appear in 1946; however, systematic training of professional economists was firmly established only in the mid 1950s. (In 1955, the programme merged with the UNIANDES programme, which had been suspended since 1952.) This was some 10 years after Chile, 20 years after Mexico and almost 40 years after Argentina.

The number of academic programmes in economics and the number of students and professors increased rapidly, beginning in 1960 (see Table 9.1). As the programmes were consolidated, the interest of graduates in doing graduate work abroad became more evident, something that UNIANDES systematically encouraged.[13]

However, a 1961 report on the teaching of economics in Latin America criticized the proliferation of faculties and programmes, high student

Table 9.1 Students and programmes in economics, 1960–97

	1960	1970	1980	1990	1997
Higher education Graduates	1,928	7,532	24,816	9,487	18,771
Degrees in economics	60	394	1449	697	812
Economists (%)	3.1	5.2	5.8	7.4	4.3
Economics faculties / Colombia	9	15	34	35	48
Master's programmes in economics / Colombia			5	3	2
Economics students				5,367	10,071
National University					
Graduates in economics	29	81	18	39	n.a.
Graduates master's programme in economics			0	3	n.a.
UNIANDES					
Graduates in economics	18	18	31	37	94
Graduates master's programme in economics			0	21	12

Source: Data provided by Dr Carlos Becerra, Director of the ICFES Office of Statistics, Bogotá. The fall in absolute terms in numbers of graduates between 1980 and 1990 appears to be the result of a change in classification. In 1980, students in technical streams (averaging three years) were included along with those in professional degree programmes (4 to 5 years on average). Beginning in 1990, only those in the latter category were included.

drop-out rates, the shortage of full-time professors and students, and problems of instructional quality (Ellis *et al.* 1961).

Table 9.1 summarizes the main indicators of professional training. The number of faculties grew from 3 in 1952 to 9 in 1960, increased to 34–35 in 1980–90, and took off in the 1990s, reaching 48. The number of graduates increased from 60 in 1960 to a peak of 1449 in 1980, and later dropped to 812 in 1997. But the student failure rate (those enrolled in year 1 divided by the number who graduate 5 years later) was 79 per cent on average during the last decade. This reveals a great social waste verging on a social fraud on the part of many of the faculties. Based on scattered official statistics, we can estimate that from 1955 to 2000, Colombian universities graduated about 29,000 economists.

Little is known about the specific occupations that attract economists. Many are employed in the public sector, protected by professional laws, while a significant group works in areas more closely related to business administration. Some characteristics of this mass of economists appear in studies conducted by Hugo López Castaño in Antioquia (Lopéz 1996:85–92). He documents the educational attainment of the Colombian labour force. In Colombia's four main cities (Bogotá, Medellín, Cali and Barranquilla), 20 per cent of the labour force begins tertiary education, while just 10 per cent completes it. Of the professionals who have completed their studies 90 per cent are salaried, a figure above the national average in 1989, and only 10 per cent work independently. The unemployment of professionals tended to diminish between 1984 and 1992 and to be less than total unemployment in the same cities. In 1991, in the seven principal cities, 79 per cent of university graduates worked in professional occupations, including directors and upper-level public officials. Graduate economists represented 2.8 per cent of all degrees. Like other professions, the state is the main employer, although its weight is diminishing.

Table 9.2   Unemployment and income in three professions in Medellín

Rate	Economics	Accounting	Law
Unemployment rate A	2.4%	0.0	2.4%
Unemployment rate B	5.0%	0.0	2.0%
Average expected income	638	1,029	1,051
Average income A	719	1,292	1,183
Average income B	638	846	988

Average monthly income in pesos (thousands).
A = 1990/91 graduates.
B = 1993/94 graduates.
Source: Lopéz (1996).

Focused on Medellín, the study produced the first significant results on labour market outcomes for professionals as measured by rates of employment, unemployment and visible underemployment, and expected and actual income (Table 9.2). The economists are in the intermediate group; the accountants, lawyers and systems engineers are above while the agronomists, historians and social scientists fall below.

It is important to emphasize that average incomes in Medellín include those received by graduates of public and private universities. But private-university alumni receive systematically higher incomes than public-university graduates do, despite that fact that one measure of 'academic reputation' shows that the public university faculties are more highly regarded (Lopéz 1996:85–92).

Economics and economists in the modernizing context

While keeping in mind the growth in number of economics faculties, in this chapter the analysis will be restricted for practical reasons to the two most prestigious faculties: the National University and UNIANDES. These from their founding projected the image of paradigmatic schools for the preparation of Colombian economists, and they are faculties that, from their beginnings, were involved in the political and ideological conflicts of Colombian society. Suffice it to mention two of their most important founders: the socialist intellectual Antonio García in the National University and the great liberal capitalist and businessman Hernán Echavarría Olózaga in UNIANDES.

A hypothesis concerning Colombian social structure can be developed on the basis of the contrast between the universities: after the traumatic events that followed the assination of Jorge E. Gaitán on 9 April 1948 (the impetus for the social elite to found UNIANDES), militancy in political parties ceased to be a channel of social mobility, particularly for professionals. These had to find other ways to reach the highest positions in the state. In the decade 1948–58 access to positions of power and influence were severely limited, from the social as well as political and ideological points of view. To the extent to which the National Front (1958–74) was successful, there was more room for the expert, given their bipartisan or apolitical modernization project. To study in a politicized university closed the road to the top.

In the 1960s, economics took the stage as the science of capital, a science that would allow the conflicts of the new society and the new state to be rationalized. With optimism, the leaders of the National Front, in particular the Liberals, applied themselves to laying the foundations for a new political, administrative and institutional rationality. The middle classes would be simultaneously the main source of adepts of this type of modernity and of specialists at the service of the state and the private sector.

The growth and complexity of the economic functions of the state brought onto the scene the economist-administrator or 'young economist', a new prophet who discreetly displaced the public finance expert and the politician-lawyer. To the extent to which Colombian economic policy based itself on statistics, it embodied this myth of ideological neutrality, essential in a regime that had outlawed controversy. In the collective imagination, the young economist emerged as the disciple of modernity.

The country needed their professional knowledge, and the politicians and the press adopted an open attitude to their prognostications and recommendations. In this way, the politician was relegated to the position of representing the traditional. This dichotomy was popularized during the 1960s. In practice, and with the conflicts that accompany all cohabitation, the specialists and politicians learned to work together and to derive mutual advantage from the situation.

Like the lawyers who preceded them, the economists now took on an essential role in the functioning of the machinery of the state. However, while the former had to work within the parameters of the national legal system and within a profession often chided for being legalistic or 'Santanderian', the economists turned themselves into transnationals, rotating among high-level positions in the Colombian government, the private sector and Washington bureaucracies. They were socialized into the norms and values of the latter, which provided the models for their focus, language and technique. More importantly, economists had access to pertinent information, almost always originating abroad. This converted them into the passkey to an invisible power, reinforced by the conditionality of the IMF's balance of payment loans and other more subtle forms of conditionality in World Bank and IADB loans. They were obligatory partners to the loans, and an expeditious method to remove investment and public expenditure policies from the legitimate sphere of the Congress and place them further out of the reach of the equally legitimate pressures of social forces, and trade and professional associations.

This became even more evident in the country's three largest cities, which were converted into the main clients of the multilateral banks. Their (relatively) gigantic electricity, water and telephone companies expanded at 10 per cent per annum over the period 1960 to 1990, and stepped onto a Möbius strip controlled by Colombian bankers and international technocrats, mainly from the World Bank, who made strategic decisions on expansion, equipment, rates and management. Here the marginalization of local authorities is evident although invisible (Palacios 1995:244–6).

In short, the experts' arrival on the scene gave the National Front regime a non-partisan (supra-party) character. The regime's main project was to build a civil service impermeable to traditional party shenanigans. At the beginning of the 1960s, the Alliance for Progress rewarded regimes like the FN that were considered a democratic alternative to Castro's Cuba. Colombia was converted into one of the showplaces of the Alliance and, in conformity with its recommendations, the country created the NPD. The NPD served to bridge the gap to more traditional institutions such as the FM and to the technically more established institutions like the central bank. From its establishment it has served as the headquarters of the different missions and international advisers.

Within the general context of the socio-demographic and economic changes, very visible in the 1960s, the first serious symptoms of the crisis of the model of import-substitution industrialization arose. This sense of crisis put the brakes on the positive moves toward the professionalization and development of the social sciences and generated two long-run negative effects: a surplus in the supply of professionals and a weakened research mandate. First, the surplus in the supply of professionals (in relation to the demand in the formal market not to the social need) produced a consequent relative stagnation in levels of remuneration and possibilities of social betterment. In the case of doctors and engineers, this was resolved through emigration, mainly to the United States, at a high rate compared with other Latin American countries (Pan-American Health Organization 1966).

Second, research activities in social sciences were concentrated in the economic area and in a very few centres. One example is CEDE, created in 1958 at UNIANDES, and well connected with foreign foundations, the upper reaches of government and international expert missions. Without ignoring the undeniable contributions to knowledge derived from project development, this research model sidelined the areas of theory and economic policy and problems that were not of interest to the funders, dedicating itself to case-studies. Some of these studies were very important, such as the CEDE research on urban employment and unemployment. It should be mentioned also that the urgency to respond to international lending institutions such as the Eximbank and USAID further limited the range of topics for economic research.[14]

The marginalization of the Faculty of the National University probably contributed to this result. The school was considered dysfunctional from the beginning of the 1960s up to the mid 1980s. Like the public university as a whole, the Faculty of Economics at the National was perceived by the elites, who identified strongly with cold war ideologies, as a centre for the propagation of subversive doctrines with socialist and Marxist leanings. The student disturbances and the state of permanent academic abnormality that reigned in the National University between about 1970 and 1984 could justify in part this reaction. But there is no doubt that it was exaggerated and that it created a false image. For example, although the study of the classic works of Marx had a prominent place in all the social sciences, the economic programme could be described as 'developmentalist'. Moreover, at least during the tenure of Currie as dean of the faculty and the director of the CID (Centre for Development Research) in 1966–7, the highest academic standards were demanded. The CID tried to emulate UNIANDES' CEDE in the field of urban development policy and agrarian modernization. Also, the social bias in recruitment (relatively high fees in UNIANDES and virtually free tuition at the National) should be remembered when making comparisons. This was a time when the well-off middle classes began to desert the public universities.

More than Marxism, the reason for the overthrow of the Faculty of Economics at the National University as the centre of elite training was administrative bureaucratization and the closed *esprit de corps*, or ghettoization, of its professors. Once Currie resigned, his programme could not advance much, and the Faculty returned to routines and to rigidity. The administrative and academic shake-up did not occur until the appointment of Juan José Echavarría as dean in 1984, who exercised a modernizing effort in meritocracy; he was followed by Clemente Forero and Salomón Kalmanovitz. However, despite these periods of forward-looking and innovative leadership, the faculty seemed subsequently to return to its lethargic days of cronyism. This was despite efforts to revive research, which was undertaken by travelling a road full of pitfalls: the doctorate.[15]

The economist's road to the top

If we agree with Abbott that a professional is one who receives payment from a client who contracts the individual to diagnose and treat a condition (Abbott 1988:40–8), we must conclude that the economist with no more than a degree from a Colombian university has restricted access to these 'two general forms of knowledge' – diagnosis and treatment – that are central to the claim of professional jurisdiction.

To reach the professional level in the field of economics, it is necessary to invest in more education – doing a PhD – preferably in the United States. Tables 9.3, 9.4, 9.5 and 9.7 outline the academic training of the upper levels of the economic leadership in the Colombian state and describe the support of the BR and the Fulbright Commission for doctoral studies in economics abroad. They show that the alternative offered by UNIANDES has been the most successful and suggest how the Colombian social elites reproduce themselves through the accumulation of educational capital in Bourdieu's terms.

Of some 29,000 economists in Colombia, some 164 have done doctoral studies abroad, mainly in the United States, and of these 48 per cent are graduates of UNIANDES (Table 9.3).

Of those who received financial support from the BR for doctoral study abroad, 70 per cent held a degree from UNIANDES (Table 9.4). In the case of the Fulbright Commission awards, 50 per cent held a degree from UNIANDES (Table 9.5).

A tale of two schools: National University (UNAL) and UNIANDES

To do a master's degree in economics in Colombia can represent the first step in the process of rising above the mass. It is a critically important move, not

Table 9.3 Doctorates in economics/doctoral studies in economics (July 2000)

		Number	%
Total		164	100
Gender	Males	133	88.7
	Females	31	18.9
UNIANDES graduates		80	47.6
Country of destination	United States	120	73.2
	United Kingdom	31	18.9
	France	4	2.4
	Spain	4	2.4
	Other	4	2.4
University	University of Illinois	17	10.4
	New York University	10	6.1
	London School of Economics	9	5.5
	Yale University	8	4.9
	Boston University	8	4.9
	Stanford University	7	4.3
	University of Chicago	6	3.7
	University of Pennsylvania	6	3.7
	University of Columbia	6	3.7
	Harvard University	4	2.4
	University of Oxford	4	2.4
	University of Warwick	4	2.4
	Other	75	45.7
Source of financial	BR	80	48.8
support	NPD	12	7.3
	NPD/BR	2	1.2
	FB	16	9.8
	FB/BR	4	2.4
	n.a.	50	30.5

Sources: Meisel (1996). Table updated with data (which includes PhD students as well as doctorates) provided by: BR, Human Resources Department, 2000; NPD, General Secretary, 2000; Fulbright Commission (FB); and UNIANDES, Admissions and Registrar's Office, 2000.

only for the individual but also from the social perspective. In this section we will examine this step, considering questions such as student profiles, intellectual interests and aspirations. Some criteria will now be established that can contribute to a better understanding of the differences in discourse between the faculties at the National University and UNIANDES, discourses that acquire their own inertial force.

The Colander and Klamer (Colander and Klamer 1987) survey was applied to students in the final two semesters of the master's programme in Economics in the two universities. The fact that the overwhelming majority responded

Table 9.4 Fellowship recipients of the BR for doctoral study abroad in economics

		Number
Fellowship recipients	Pre-1982	2
	1982–90	20
	1991–95	23
	1996 to date	41
Average length of award	33 months	

			%
Alma mater of recipients	UNIANDES	Undergraduate programme[a]	58.1
		master's	11.6
	Other universities	Undergraduate and master's programmes	30.2
Destination country		United States	69.0
		United Kingdom	24.1
		France	2.3
		Spain	3.4
Universities		Other	58.1
		Boston University	4.7
		Yale University	5.8
		New York University	7.0
		University of Pennsylvania	7.0
		University of Illinois	8.1
		London School of Economics	9.3
Gender distribution		Males	77.9
		Females	22.1

[a] Some also did a master's degree in UNIANDES.

Sources: BR, Human Resources Department, Bogotá, 2000 and UNIANDES, Admissions Office and Registrar.

to the questionnaire without difficulty and with interest could be a sign of the instrument's international validity, or of the internationalization of the programmes that train economists.

However, in a research project as preliminary as the one reported here, the validity of this questionnaire should be considered limited. Nonetheless, the results suggest some features that could be common to professional economists throughout the world, and, at the same time, point to differences of style and focus between schools within the same country.

Table 9.6 gives the profile of masters students at the two universities. The differences in average age, marital status and birth place between the

Table 9.5 Fulbright Commission awards for doctoral studies in economics in the USA

		Number
Fellowship recipients	Pre-1982	4
	1982–90	12
	1991–95	2
	1996 to date	2
Average length of award	n.a.	

			%
Alma mater of recipients	UNIANDES	Undergraduate [a]	50
		Master's	0
	Other universities	Undergraduate and master's	50
Universities		Other	50
		University of Colombia	15
		University of Notre Dame	15
		Boston University	10
		New School for Social Research	10
Gender distribution		Males	75
		Females	25

[a] Some also did a master's degree in UNIANDES.

Sources: Fulbright Commission, Colombia, 2000; and UNIANDES, Admissions Office and Registrar.

UNIANDES and UNAL masters students, as well as their expectations of continuing their studies and work preferences, could reflect class differences and fit with the well known differences between students of public universities with a good academic reputation and students of private elite universities. Research from the province of Antioquia reveals that deans and programme directors in faculties of economics consider that the two large public universities in Medellín, Antioquia and National, have the best reputations. However, the graduates of these two faculties obtain the lowest paid work. It can then be said that the private university opens more possibilities of entering networks and gaining prestige (educational capital) that, independent of the quality of the professional training, have a decisive impact on students' futures in the workplace.

The responses to the survey in the Colander and Klamer survey (Appendices 1 to 6) offer, on first inspection, differences in each university's typical student profile. These differences, if significant, could reflect patterns of discourse, style and technique transmitted by the professors.

From this material, two themes in particular emerge in the training of economists that have not been satisfactorily debated since Lauchlin Currie

Table 9.6   Masters student profile

		UNIANDES	UNAL	Total
		23.6	27	25.7
Average age		%	%	%
Birthplace	Bogotá	60.9	54.0	56.7
	Medellín	8.7	0.00	3.3
	Cali	8.7	5.4	6.7
	B/quilla	13.0	2.7	6.7
	Other	8.7	37.8	26.7
Undergraduate faculty	Economics	73.9	70.3	71.7
	Engineering	26.1	18.9	21.7
	Other	0.0	10.8	6.7
Marital status	Married	4.4	24.3	16.7
	Single	95.7	70.3	80.0
Planning to do doctoral studies?	Yes	73.9	59.5	65.0
	No	26.1	40.5	35.0
Preferred country	United States	47.1	27.3	35.9
	United Kingdom	17.6	22.7	20.5
	France	0.0	18.2	10.3
	Other	0.0	18.2	10.3
	Don't know	35.3	13.6	23.1
Preferred workplace	Public sector	25.0	50.0	41.7
	Private sector	12.5	12.5	12.5
	Independent	12.5	0.0	4.2
	Teaching and research	25.0	37.5	33.3
	Other	25.0	0.0	8.3

Sources: Data obtained in a survey of students in the master's programmes of UNAL and UNIANDES in August 2000. 23 of 55 students enrolled in UNIANDES and 37 of 162 students enrolled in UNAL responded. The gender distribution in these programmes is: in UNIANDES 35 males and 20 females; in UNAL 113 males and 49 females.

put them on the table more than 30 years ago. The first is the development of a far more radical separation of economics as a social science on the one hand and as a means of earning money or administering businesses on the other (Currie 1965:42). The second concerns the emphasis of study: whether it is theoretical-conceptual, leading to a greater development of the humanistic and social sense; or mathematical-statistical, which often ends up producing a narrow and instrumental vision of the economy and the society.[16] It is probable that the inertial force of the discourse referred to above implies differences of emphasis, such as those Currie identified: the style of UNAL is more theoretical-conceptual (and perhaps more 'developmentalist') and that of UNIANDES more mathematical-statistical (and perhaps more 'neo-classical').

We find, for example, that a UNIANDES graduate supports a stronger mathematical training: 91 per cent consider it 'very important' (as opposed to 62 per cent of the UNAL graduates) (Table 9A.1 in the appendix to this chapter). The UNIANDES graduates are more interested in macroeconomics, international economics, microeconomics and econometrics (Table 9A.2) and hold opinions like 'inflation is a strictly monetary phenomenon' or 'neo-classical economics is important in solving contemporary economic problems' (Table 9A.4) more strongly. They give more importance to the assumption of 'economic rationality'.

In contrast, the UNAL student, without ignoring the importance of mathematics, gives greater weight to economic development (95 per cent), history and political science (Table 9A.3) and to having 'a broad knowledge of the world economy and the country's economy'. They are more emphatic that 'the market discriminates against women' (Table 9A.4) and do not believe so much in the virtues of neo-classical economics or that 'economics is the most scientific of the social sciences' (Table 9A.5). They hold more doubts about the validity of the assumptions of economic rationality (Table 9A.6).

These different responses can also be interpreted in combination with the data in Table 9.6 related to the expectations held by those hoping to continue on to doctoral study (74 per cent of UNIANDES students and 60 per cent of UNAL students). Of the UNIANDES group 47 per cent preferred the United States while only 27 per cent of their UNAL peers chose the US. No UNIANDES student hopes to undertake the doctorate in France, but 18 per cent of his or her peers from UNAL would like to study there.

The only question that reveals a conspicuous contrast between the two groups in consolidated responses, and that with a difference of 30 percentage points, is the one related to the 'capacity to relate to outstanding professors'. The group that in a large majority maintains that these relations are important for professional success is the group less favoured thereby, that is, the students of the National University.[17]

Reaching the inner circles of the state

Mention has to be made of the importance that entering and belonging to certain modernizing groups assumes in the process of striving for high positions in the state. In particular, entry into the National Department of Planning, the BR and the FM, the three most important government economic entities, and certain prestigious academic communities, such as CEDE and FEDESARROLLO, can be important. From the latter, some talented individuals enter into contact with the upper reaches of the political and business world, and the successful ones end up rotating among the IFIs, top-level positions in the state, business associations, and their think tanks, such as ANIF. If this is the case, the economist is moving in openly elite circles that obviously are not neutral concerning economic policy. Their role is to provide a base of scientific neutrality to these policies and in this way they serve an indispensable legitimating function for the national and world-system.

In Table 9.7, we observe that since 1958, 62 individuals have held the positions of finance minister, board members and director of the Bank of the Republic, and director of the National Department of Planning. The over-whelming majority have had training as an economist, although, as is logi-cal, there were also lawyers and engineers, especially in the period prior to 1970. Only two women (without PhDs), María Mercedes Cuellar and Cecilia López, have held high-level decision-making positions (which for the purpose of this study are defined as the positions enumerated above). Of these 62 high-level officials, 32 graduated from UNIANDES. Evidently, this

Table 9.7 Public officials with decision-making roles and the influence of UNIANDES, 1958–2000

Category	1958–82 Number	1982–2000 Number	1958–2000 Number
Public officials[a]	30	32	62
Positions as public officials[b]	34	38	72
Women	0	2	2
Officials with PhDs	3	9	12
Finance ministers	16	11	27
Heads of NPD	13	12	25
Directors of BR[c]	5	3	8
Board members BR	0	12	12
Individuals holding more than one position	4	6	10
	%	%	%
Finance ministers from UNIANDES	19	36	26
NPD heads Uniandes	54	25	40
BR directors Uniandes	0	33	13
BR board members Uniandes	0	50	50
Total officials from Uniandes	33	44	39

[a] Officials included are finance ministers, directors of the NPD and directors and board members of the BR.
[b] The number of positions is greater than the number of officials because some individuals have held more than one position.
[c] At the moment, two of the five co-directors of the Bank of the Republic are graduates of the Economics Faculty of the National University; the director and one of the board members did all their university studies in the United States.

Sources: Annual reports of the FM, BR and the NPD to Congress; UNIANDES, Admissions Office and registrar.

definition of the elite is very restricted. It should include deputy ministers and top public servants in ministries and heads of public and state-owned utilities, companies and institutes. However, if this was done, it is probable that the distribution between UNIANDES graduates and others would not alter very much. The table also shows how the participation of UNIANDES has increased since 1982, with the exception of the National Department of Planning.

The prominence that economists attained in the governments of western Europe, the United States and Japan began about 1940. The 'golden age' was in the 1960s and the 'hard times' started in the 1970s. The process appears to be a little out of step in Latin America (Pechman 1989). The golden age arrived in the 1980s in Latin America, and the difficult years for economists are only starting at the beginning of the twenty-first century.

The positive public image of economists, constructed in the early days of the National Front, has marked the governing styles of presidents up to the present.[18] According to the public perception of the importance that each president gives to his economic cabinet Colombia has 'technocratic' governments (for example Carlos Lleras Restrepo 1966–70, Misael Pastrana Borrero 1970–4, Alfonso López Michelsen 1974–8 and César Gaviria Trujillo 1990–4) or 'clientelistic' governments (among them the terms of Guillermo León Valencia 1962–6, Julio César Turbay Ayala 1978–82, and Ernesto Samper 1994–8, stand out).

In an appraisal of the National Front, this union of specialists and politicians was termed 'technocracy'.[19] But the Colombian state did not become more technical in the sense of creating an autonomous civil service and a good part of the technical segment was politicized in the traditional sense of the term.

Since the days of the National Front, it has been possible to group the economists in two camps. The first group consists of those specialists who bring stability and continuity to institutions such as the BR and the NPD. To the second camp belong those who rotate among the top jobs in the public administration, the international agencies, and the management groups of private enterprise, using political knowledge but without touching the electoral process or partaking of 'clientelistic politics', and without losing the aura of the scientists of the economy. That is, the expression 'modernizers', used to refer to the experts, gains clarity when it is opposed to the 'traditionalists', grouped in the political class.

The economists and political power: three phases

Economic orthodoxy changes. In some Latin American countries, there was a movement from 'nationalist-populist' to 'developmentalist' and, from the beginnings of the 1980s, a swing toward the 'neo-liberal'. Other efforts at classification have not considered the separation of populist and developmentalist to be of such importance.[20] In Colombia, a group of developmentalist doctrines (*c.* 1940–85) yielded to a so-called neo-liberalism in the mid 1980s, rather late for Latin America. The transition was unmistakable by 1990. As in the case of developmentalism, the new doctrine came face to face with the pragmatic environment or the practical republic. The relations of the economists and the state in this period can be divided into three phases.

First, at the beginnings of the 1970s, and perhaps as a result of the increasing technical character and capacity of sectors of the state, the symbiosis of the professional politician and the expert began to be clearer. In this phase, the community of economists seemed to validate different economic doctrines. Miguel Urrutia, the Director of the Bank of the Republic and one of the most influential economists in the country since the 1970s, emphasizes that 'since the 1970s the majority of Finance Ministers and Directors of the NPD have been professional economists with the result that economic policy has a bias toward orthodoxy' (Urrutia 1994:304). The second phase began around the end of the 1980s, on the basis of poorly defined alliances of politicians and experts, and gained impetus in 1990–4. In 1990, the Gaviria government adopted the neo-liberal canon, a set of economic policies known as the Washington consensus. This consisted of a practical form of political discourse elaborated out of the inevitability and convenience of globalization. In this phase, the IFIs privileged the dialogue with neo-liberal PhDs in each country and thus gave advantages to their coalitions of politicians and experts. Symptomatic of this phase was the radical attempt, in the pragmatic Colombian tradition, to establish a type of unitary thought and with this to legitimate the neo-liberal hegemony in the state.[21]

The Washington consensus intensified the dialogue among officials of the international institutions and the upper reaches of the Colombian government. The interlocutors found common ground in a systematic presentation of reality, dressed up as science, that prescribed: the recognition of market forces as the essential dimension of human liberty; the security of property rights; state deregulation; the privatization of public companies; the encouragement of competition; fiscal restraint; and financial and trade liberalization.

The Colombian story may be highlighted by a contrast. In Mexico, we have a paradigmatic example of the application of these doctrines: the government of Salinas de Gortari (1988–94) which closed an experiment in economic internationalization that had begun in 1982 and which was a paradigm for the Gaviria administration (1990–4). In Mexico under Salinas, anyone who questioned in any manner the scientific principles that the international economy and the macroeconomic policy were supposedly based on, 'was ridiculed and marginalized by colleagues in economics both inside the country and abroad' (Babb 1998:331).

In Colombia, however, neo-liberalism had neither the duration nor the intensity of the Mexican experience. Although during the Gaviria administration members of the economic team and a circle close to the president tried to form a *de facto* political group, once the presidential term was over the strength of the traditional political system showed itself anew, in the pragmatism of the business elite and the necessity of calling on a discourse of redistribution to woo voters. Thus, the economist's capacity to organize was diluted.

We can date our third phase by continuing with the paradigmatic Mexican case. In Mexico, we can locate the point at which the experts' lunge for power fell apart in the term of Zedillo (1994–2000). This was caused by the December mistake of 1994, which started an internal fight in the PRI between the technocracy and the politicians, and ended up in a 'historical defeat' in the presidential elections of 2 July 2000.

It was proven that the best formal training and the highest flying PhD did not necessarily mean greater social and political achievement. Pedro Aspe (PhD, MIT), Carlos Salinas's finance secretary, Zedillo's recently appointed minister of finance, Jaime Serra (PhD, Yale), and the director of the Bank of Mexico, Miguel Mancera (MA, Yale) 'were responsible for what was perhaps the worst financial disaster in Latin American history' (Babb 1998:22–3). Known as the tequila effect, its impact was felt throughout Latin America.

Beginning in 1994, neo-liberalism in Colombia lost some of its initial force, at least in its rhetoric. Economic debate was renewed. Some economists who graduated from the National University held high positions in the economic team. Many sectors of the elites, other than the Catholic hierarchy, formulated new critiques of the dominant dogma. The Colombia equivalent of the Mexican 'December mistake' was perhaps the strong economic recession that began to be felt in 1997 and intensified in 1999. It was accompanied by the aggravating factors of unemployment and a fiscal crisis that originated in the expansionary state bureaucracy implied in the constitution of 1991 and that, paradoxically, was well received by the Gaviria government.

The 1997–2000 recession, added to the political crisis, weakened the movement toward the reforms called for in the Washington consensus and halted the rise of the PhDs. For political reasons, Presidents Samper (1994–8) and Pastrana (1998–) have been less 'orthodox' than Gaviria and have been less concerned with continuity in the top jobs. Samper had three finance ministers and three heads of the NPD; in the first two years of the Pastrana government Colombia had two finance ministers and three heads of NPD, and the former did not hold to the image of the 'UNIANDES graduate with an American PhD'.

But it should be clarified that the Colombian case of knowledge and power is distinctive in the Latin American context. Colombia is alone among the large nations in not experiencing a populist phase, with the result that the state is weaker in the confrontation with the private sector, mainly the large economic groups. This means that the pre-eminence of Colombian economists in leading the state has not been as prolonged, exclusive and decisive as that of their Mexican or Chilean peers, beginning in 1982. In Colombia a critical mass of PhDs, like the Chicago Boys in Chile, did not form. In Chile, economists promoted the discourse that, in the stability of a long political dictatorship, could rationalize coherently the step from developmentalism to neo-liberalism on the ideological level and act on the formulation and enactment of economic policy. It is also important to remember that in the transition to democracy Chilean economic policies have not departed in fundamental ways from the prescriptions of the Chicago Boys.

The case of Colombian economists, experts in a practical republic, immersed in a closed world of political-business pragmatism, could provide an interesting case-study to evaluate the hypothesis that globalization has meant a unification of economic discourse, a counter-case to the Chilean 'ideological transfer' that is used to explain the birth, development and ascent of the Chicago Boys in Chile.[22]

Conclusion: further research and pointers for the future

This chapter has documented the development of economic discourse and the gradual growth of the power of the economist as the source of economic knowledge. In the course of this story, I have also sought to document the particular character of Colombian economic thought and practice: its ability to be pragmatic. I have also chronicled the growth of the economics profession and documented two parallel processes. As economists have increased in number, so by various means the accession to power only of an elite has been preserved. We explored this through examining the characteristics of the main economics departments in the country: UNIANDES and UNAL. We explored the social backgrounds of the students, their distinct approaches to economic issues and their access to doctoral education outside the country, and their subsequent representation at the highest levels of economic policy-making. The UNIANDES group evidently had a stronger neo-liberal formation and commanded the majority of external scholarship places. Not surprisingly, they were strongly represented in the economic elite in government in the 1990s.

Yet while the ideological formation is strong, it never dominates the peculiarly Colombian nature of economic policy-making: its pragmatism. We explored the historical roots of this pragmatism and showed how the economic elite that emerges in Colombia performs in a quite distinct way from its neighbours in the management of the economy in the 1990s. The contrast is developed both with Mexico and with Chile.

Before closing, let us look to the future and to issues that need to be confronted, both in policy terms and in research. We can certainly expect changes, given that recently there has been a certain devaluation of the economic expert in public opinion and an enormous influx of new blood (some 80 PhDs in the last six years). These two factors will surely change the correlation of forces among the top officials and the epistemological community of economists, but how this will happen remains unclear.

We may affirm with more confidence that for the success of a democratic project, the established forms of recruiting personnel for top technical positions in the state will *have* to change. What is required is a set of more inclusive principles that, were they enacted, could perhaps lead to a re-evaluation of the political and of politics. For this to occur, it is indispensable to put an end to the current coupling of cronyism and violence. However, in the practical republic, it is possible to start a debate on the feasibility of the so-called economic technocracy yielding to other professional interests and viewpoints, especially from social sciences. It is true that the system has been functional in producing prophets with no political responsibility. For IFIs, they represent the positive values of bureaucratic continuity and stability. But in a state under the rule of law, their weight should be balanced by that of other professional groups that move in a less closed and elitist world, like the politicians and the lawyers who make up the courts or the members of Congress.

Significant changes to the educational system that *de facto* legitimizes exclusion will also have to be considered. Changes are needed to push toward a just and egalitarian society, that is, the uses and customs that socially segregate will have to be overcome, beginning with access to high-quality education at all levels.

Turning to needed research, two of the hypotheses of this study should receive more rigorous examination: the first is the centralism of state decisions and the advantage this gives Bogotá and its universities, principally the two most important: UNIANDES and UNAL. The other hypothesis requiring further research is still more central to an interpretation of the role of professionals in the country's public spaces: whether it is the case that since 9 April 1948, the political parties and the political arena have ceased to be a route of social mobility. This would generate still more questions since social mobility is one of the main attributes of democratic society.

Finally, although the significance of the weight of economists trained in UNIANDES in the state and in economic discourse has been established, further research is needed to establish how this power and influence has translated into welfare, growth and social justice. As has been pointed out throughout, this chapter does not evaluate the merits of orthodox economic policies of the last 30 years, the formulation of which has been the domain of the high-level and well-connected professional economists.

Appendix

Table 9A.1 The importance of studying another discipline

All numbers are percentages.

Discipline	Very important			Important			Little importance			Not important			No opinion		
	UA	UN	Total	UA	UN	Total	UA	UN	Total	UA	UN	Total	UA	UN	Total
Mathematics	91	62	73	9	38	27	0	0	0	0	0	0	0	0	0
History	52	54	53	35	43	40	13	3	7	0	0	0	0	0	0
Political science	9	41	28	39	54	48	48	5	22	4	0	2	0	0	0
Sociology	9	24	18	39	54	48	43	22	30	4	0	2	4	0	2
Philosophy	9	19	15	39	51	47	43	24	32	9	5	7	0	0	0
Psychology	0	11	7	30	35	33	43	49	47	26	5	13	0	0	0
Computer sciences	61	35	45	26	35	32	13	27	20	0	3	3	0	0	0
Physics	17	16	17	30	14	20	30	59	48	22	11	15	0	0	0

Sources: Data in this and the following tables were obtained from a survey carried out in August 2000 among students in the master's programmes of the National University (Bogota campus) (UN) and UNIANDES (UA).

In UNIANDES 23 of the 55 students enrolled responded. In the National 37 of 162 enrolled in the programme responded.

Table 9A.2 Interest by area

All numbers are percentages.

Area	High interest			Moderate interest			No interest			No opinion		
	UA	UN	Total	UA	UN	Total	UA	UN	Total	UA	UN	Total
Macroeconomics	78.3	59.5	66.7	21.7	40.5	33.3	0.0	0.0	0.0	0.0	0.0	0.0
Political economy	21.7	45.9	36.7	60.9	48.6	53.3	17.4	5.4	10.0	0.0	0.0	0.0
Microeconomics	69.6	40.5	51.7	30.4	56.8	46.7	0.0	0.0	0.0	0.0	2.7	1.7
International economics	78.3	56.8	65.0	21.7	37.8	31.7	0.0	5.4	3.3	0.0	0.0	0.0
Industrial organization	47.8	29.7	36.7	34.8	62.2	51.7	17.4	5.4	10.0	0.0	2.7	1.7
Monetary policy and banking	52.2	56.8	55.0	34.8	29.7	31.7	13.0	13.5	13.3	0.0	0.0	0.0
Economic development	65.2	94.6	83.3	30.4	2.7	13.3	4.3	2.7	3.3	0.0	0.0	0.0
Labour economics	30.4	21.6	25.0	47.8	59.5	55.0	21.7	18.9	20.0	0.0	0.0	0.0
Econometrics	65.2	45.9	53.3	30.4	51.4	43.3	4.3	2.7	3.3	0.0	0.0	0.0
Public finance	47.8	48.6	48.3	34.8	43.2	40.0	17.4	8.1	11.7	0.0	0.0	0.0
History of economic thought	30.4	29.7	30.0	56.5	67.6	63.3	13.0	2.7	6.7	0.0	0.0	0.0
Economics of law	17.4	16.2	16.7	39.1	59.5	51.7	43.5	24.3	31.7	0.0	0.0	0.0
Comparative economics	13.0	5.4	8.3	52.2	56.8	55.0	34.8	37.8	36.7	0.0	0.0	0.0
Urban economics	13.0	13.5	13.3	39.1	56.8	50.0	43.5	29.7	35.0	4.3	0.0	1.7

Table 9A.3 Factors contributing to success

All numbers are percentages.

Element	Very important			Somewhat important			Not know			Doesn't		
	UA	UN	Total	UA	UN	Total	UA	UN	Total	UA	UN	Total
To be intelligent in the sense of being good at problem-solving	73.9	70.3	71.7	26.1	24.3	25.0	0.0	2.7	1.7	0.0	0.0	0.0
Excellence in mathematics	34.8	35.1	35.0	56.5	56.8	56.7	8.7	8.1	8.3	0.0	0.0	0.0
Know a particular field very well	73.9	64.9	68.3	21.7	32.4	28.3	4.3	2.7	3.3	0.0	0.0	0.0
Ability to develop good relations with outstanding professors	17.4	24.3	21.7	39.1	62.2	53.3	39.1	10.8	21.7	4.3	2.7	3.3
Interest and ability in empirical research	52.2	62.2	58.3	43.5	37.8	40.0	4.3	0.0	1.7	0.0	0.0	0.0
Wide knowledge of the economic literature	43.5	51.4	48.3	47.8	45.9	46.7	8.7	2.7	5.0	0.0	0.0	0.0
Wide knowledge of the country's economy and the world economy	56.5	67.6	63.3	39.1	32.4	35.0	4.3	0.0	1.7	0.0	0.0	0.0

Table 9A.4 Economic views

All numbers are percentages.

Opinion	Yes			Probably			Not sure			No opinion		
	UA	UN	Total	UA	UN	Total	UA	UN	Total	UA	UN	Total
Fiscal policy can be an effective tool in stabilization policy	52	46	48	39	51	47	9	3	5	0	0	0
The central bank (BR) should maintain a constant rate of growth of the monetary supply	17	8	12	48	59	55	30	30	30	4	3	3
Increases in the minimum wage worsen unemployment among unqualified workers and youth	30	16	22	39	46	43	17	38	30	13	0	5
Customs tariffs and import quotas reduce general economic well-being	30	16	22	35	49	43	26	30	28	9	5	7
Inflation is basically a monetary phenomenon	57	30	40	22	46	37	13	22	18	9	3	5

Continued

Table 9A.4 Continued

All numbers are percentages.

Opinion	Yes			Probably			Not sure			No opinion		
	UA	UN	Total	UA	UN	Total	UA	UN	Total	UA	UN	Total
Wage and price controls should be used to control inflation	13	24	20	57	57	57	17	16	17	13	3	7
Worker democracy increases productivity	22	22	22	22	41	33	48	35	40	9	3	5
The market tends to discriminate against women	17	38	30	39	16	25	35	43	40	9	3	5
The capitalist system has an inherent tendency to crisis	13	27	22	22	30	27	57	41	47	9	3	5
Income distribution in developing countries should be more equal	48	54	52	26	32	30	22	11	15	4	3	3

Table 9A.5 Opinions on economics as a science

All numbers are percentages.

Statement	Strongly agree			Agree			Disagree			No opinion			N/C		
	UA	UN	Total	UA	UN	Total	UA	UN	Total	UA	UN	Total	UA	UN	Total
Neo-classical economics is important to solve contemporary economic problems	43	14	25	43	41	42	4	41	27	9	5	7	0	0	0
Economists are in agreement on the basic issues	13	0	5	17	22	20	65	70	68	4	5	5	0	3	2
There is a clear dividing line between positive economics and normative economics	13	8	10	26	30	28	48	43	45	9	16	13	4	3	3
Economics is the most scientific of the social sciences	35	22	27	17	27	23	26	38	33	22	11	15	0	3	2

Table 9A.6 Importance of economic assumptions

All numbers are percentages.

Assumption	Very important			Impt in some cases			Not important			No opinion			N/A		
	UA	UN	Total	UA	UN	Total	UA	UN	Total	UA	UN	Total	UA	UN	Total
Assumption of rationality	61	41	48	30	49	42	0	8	5	0	0	0	9	3	5
Rational expectations	30	27	28	61	54	57	0	14	8	0	3	2	9	3	5
Price rigidities	22	14	17	65	68	67	0	8	5	4	5	5	9	5	7
Imperfect competition	52	51	52	39	41	40	0	3	2	0	0	0	9	5	7
Cost-plus-markup pricing	30	32	32	43	51	48	0	5	3	9	5	7	17	5	10
Normative behaviour	26	24	25	43	46	45	13	14	13	9	11	10	9	5	7

Notes

1. Translated by Jennifer L. Newton. The text has been enriched by the generous comments of many specialists. I should like first to mention Alicia Puyana, the first Colombian woman to receive a doctorate in economics (Oxford 1979), who has allowed me insight into the world of professional economists. In the Oxford seminar, I received valuable comments and suggestions from Valpy FitzGerald, Malcolm Deas and José Antonio Ocampo. I would like to thank the following for their comments and critiques: Frank Safford, Fernado Uricoechea, Alberto Carrasquilla, Roberto Steiner, Renán Silva, Boris Salazar, Gonzalo Cataño and Fernado Cubides. I also received written critiques from the Mexican economist Jesus Seade, now in the IMF, and from Salomón Kalmanovitz, Miguel Urrutia, Jorge Hernán Cárdenas, Juan Luis Londoño, Gonzalo Sánchez, and Herbert Braun. I am very grateful to Rosemary Thorp for her excellent editing work. Of course, the opinions expressed here are exclusively my responsibility.

   This work was possible thanks to generous assistance provided by the Faculty of Administration of UNIANDES. In particular, I thank José Felipe Bastidas, economist from the university and research assistant in the Faculty of Administration, and the deans and directors of the master's programmes of the National University and UNIANDES. Their support allowed me to undertake the survey of graduate students. Directors of the Bank of the Republic, UNIANDES and the Fulbright Commission provided valuable information on their graduates and fellowship holders.

2. In itself an extension of the paper 'Modernidad, Modernizaciones y Ciencias Sociales' (Palacios 1999).

3. The majority of the Colombian studies, produced by professional economists, refer to economic thought, to the institutional histories of the Faculties of Economics, or to problems of employment and unemployment in the field. Even so, they offer valuable insights into the topic of the economist as bearer of economic ideas. See, among others, the following works, which also offer good bibliographies: Kalmanovitz (1993); and Enciso (2000:83–125). See also Mayor and Tejeiro (1993) and Buendía (1995).

4. Streeten (1995:9–10).

5. Jalil and Salazar (1999:143–4).

6. I appreciate this observation, sent to the author by Juan Luis Molina Londoño, who served as a minister in the Gaviria government and is now the director of an important economic magazine. In addition to the specialized economic newspaper *La República*, the country now has *Portafolio* and the economic supplement of *El Espectador* as well as the magazines *La Nota* and *Dinero*.

7. In Colombia, unlike the cases of Mexico, Brazil, Argentina, Chile, Peru and Venezuela, no populist movement has governed. However there were populist features in the governments of the 'liberal republic' (1930–46), especially in the first term of López Pumarejo, and populism had one of its clearest expressions in Gaitán's movement. But the economic policies were much more along the lines of orthodox liberalism and after the assassination of Gaitán in 1948 populism was for a time discredited, reappearing under the ANAPO banner in the 1960s. However, from the 1970s onward there has not been a populist movement worthy of the name in Colombia, although a populist style is far from absent in many old-style politicians with clientelistic leanings.

8. See Saenz (1992).

9. On this pragmatism in action, see Thorp (1991).
10. Mayor (1985:18–35). The cultural context, penetrated by the ideal of the practical, carried weight in the orientation of the institution's engineers. This could be seen in the curriculum. We know, for example, the importance given to preparation in industrial economics after 1892. This was soon followed by a course on political economy. However, it is also known that these courses were relatively marginal in the overall academic load. If we review the titles of 178 theses approved for a degree in the School of Mines between 1893 and 1939, some 18 treat socio-economic aspects. See Santa María (1994) – for curriculum, see vol. 1:155–64 and for the thesis projects, see vol. 2, appendix 5:464–8.
11. Safford (1976:239). During his presidency, Ospina demanded to be informed daily on water levels in the Magdalena River. See Abel and Palacios (1991:587).
12. The utilitarian proposition was evident: the invitations to the prestigious Princeton economist were couched in the expectation that he would open the doors to the international bank during a time when access was difficult. See Banco de la República (1994) and Drake (1994).
13. On this educational strategy, see Molina (2000b:18–24).
14. We mention in passing that Lauchlin Currie, in his role as consultant to the Colombian Association of Universities, argued in 1964 about the high cost that would be entailed in doing theoretical research 'always more advanced than practice … since it is less limited by occurrences, emotions and even politics', and, on the contrary, underlined the importance of training Colombian economists on topics that were 'significant for the solution of the country's problems'. See Currie (1965:26–30).
15. When I served as chancellor of the National University (August 1984–July 1988), I offered another term as dean to Chucho (Jesus Antonio) Bejarano, who turned me down and offered a list of possible successors. I decided however to offer the job to Jorge Mendez Munevar, who had served as vice-chancellor of the university but he declined. Then I offered it to Juan José Echavarría, one of the economists suggested by Bejarano. In those years, the prestige of the National University was at one of the lowest points in its history. A simplified version of the incident is recounted in Kalmanovitz (1999:195).
16. Currie (1965:37–8). Two recent examinations of this problem of instruction, characterized by their insight and depth, are González (1999) and Sanz de Santamaría (2000).
17. Uricoechea (2000).
18. On the opposition of specialist and politician during the 1960s, see Nelson (1971).
19. Consult Cepeda and Mitchell (1980) on National Front technocratic tendencies. In this text, the authors show themselves to be quite critical of figures like Virgilio Barco, the future president of the country.
20. So, for example, Sikkink (1988) clearly distinguishes a developmentalist phase from the populist phase, while Babb (1998) treats two large phases: developmentalist (1940–82) and neo-liberal (1982–). For a debate among Colombian economists on neo-liberalism, see, for example, de la Torre (ed.) 1982.
21. A significant incident reflecting this attempt is the following: a group of top-level officials acted as the thought-police for the Faculty of Economics at UNIANDES, alleging problems of quality and pertinence (Palacios 1999:68–70).
22. In addition, it is debatable whether the neo-liberal discourse in Chile spoke with a single voice in a Ford Foundation–Catholic University of Chile–University of Chicago–Pinochet government conspiracy (Valdés 1995). See also Montecinos (1998).

References

Abbott, A., *The System of Professions: An Essay on the Division of Expert Labor* (University of Chicago Press, 1988).

Abel, C. and M. Palacios, 'Colombia 1930–1958', in L. Bethell (ed.) *The Cambridge History of Latin America*, vol. VIII (New York: Cambridge University Press, 1991).

Babb, S. L., 'The Evolution of Economic Expertise in a Developing Country: Mexican Economics, 1929–1998', PhD dissertation, 2 vols, Northwestern University, Evanston, Ill., December 1998.

Banco de la República, *Kemmerer y el Banco de la República: Diarios y Documentos* (Bogotá, 1994).

Buendía, H. G. (ed.), *Economía y Opinión. 25 años de Fedesarrollo* (Bogotá 1995).

Cepeda, F. and C. Mitchell, 'The Trend Towards Technocracy: The World Bank and the International Labor Organization in Colombian Politics', in A. R. Berry, R. G. Hellman and M. Solano (eds), *Politics of Compromise: Coalition Government in Colombia* (New Brunswick, NJ: Transaction Books, 1980).

Colander, D. and A. Klamer, 'The Making of an Economist', *Economic Perspectives*, 1/2 (Fall 1987) 95–11.

Currie, L., *La Enseñanza de la Economía en Colombia* (Bogotá: Tercer Mundo, 1965).

Currie, L., *The Role of Economic Advisers in Developing Countries* (Westport, CT: Greenwood, 1981).

De la Torre, Cristina (ed.), *Modelos de Desarrollo Económico. Colombia, 1960–82* (Bogotá, La Oveja Negra, 1982).

Drake, P. W., *Money Doctors, Foreign Debts, and Economic Reforms in Latin America from the 1890s to the Present* (Wilmington, DE: Scholarly Resources, 1994).

Ellis, H., B. Cornejo, and L. Escobar, *La Enseñanza de la Economía en América Latina* (Washington, DC: Unión Panamericana, 1961).

Flórez Enciso and Luis Bernardo, 'Apuntes Sobre el Pensamiento Económico Colombiano en la Segunda Mitad del Siglo XX', in F. L. Buitrago and G. Rey (eds), *Discurso y Razón: Una Historia de las Ciencias Sociales en Colombia* (Bogotá: Tercer Mundo, 2000).

González, J. I., 'La Fetichización del Currículo y la Absolutización del Libro de Texto', in J. A. Bejarano (ed.), *Hacia Dónde va la Ciencia Económica en Colombia. Siete Ensayos Exploratorios* (Bogotá: Tercer Mundo, 1999).

Jalil, M. and B. Salazar, 'El Estado de la Investigación Económica: del Vacío a la Comunidad Virtual', in J. A. Bejarano (ed.) (1999) *Hacia dónde va la ciencia económica en Colombia. Siete ensayos exploratorios* (Bogotá: Tercer Mundo, 1999).

Kalmanovitz, S., 'Notas para una Historia de las Teorías Económicas en Colombia', in *Historia Social de la Ciencia en Colombia*, vol. IX, *Ciencias Sociales* (Bogotá: COLCIENCIAS, 1993).

Kalmanovitz, S., 'El Debate Debe Continuar. Bejarano y la Enseñanza de Economía', *Cuadernos de Economía* 31 (1999) p. 195.

Kress, G. and R. Hodge, *Language as Ideology* (London: Routledge & Kegan Paul, 1979).

López, C., H., *La Educación Superior en Antioquia* (Medellín: SENA, 1996).

Mayor, A., *Ética, Trabajo y Productividad en Antioquia* (Bogotá: Tercer Mundo, 1985).

Mayor, A. and C. Tejeiro, 'La Profesionalización de la Economía en Colombia', in R. Dombois and C. M. López (eds), *Cambio Técnico, Empleo y Trabajo en Colombia. Aporte a los Estudios Laborales en el VIII Congreso de Sociología* (Bogotá: FESCOL, 1993).

Meisel, A. R., 'Why not Hyperinflation in Colombia? On the Determinants of Stable Economic Policies', *Borradores Semanales de Economía* 54 (1996) 31.

Molina Londoño, L. F., *Historia de la Universidad de los Andes*, mimeo (Bogotá: Universidad de los Andes, 2000a).

Molina Londoño, L. F., 'Historia del Estamento Estudiantil en la Universidad. Qué Vivan los Estudiantes!', *Nota Uniandina* 118 (2000b) 18–24.

Montecinos, V., *Economists, Politics and the State: Chile 1958–1994* (Amsterdam: CEDLA, 1998).

Nelson, R. R. 'The Political Determinants of Colombian Foreign Exchange Policy', in R. R. Nelson, T. P. Schultz and R. R. Slighton (eds), *Structural Change in a Developing Country: Colombia's Problems and Prospects* (Princeton University Press, 1971).

Palacios, M., *Entre la Legitimidad y la Violencia: Colombia 1875–1994* (Bogotá: Norma, 1995).

Palacios, M., *Parábola del Liberalismo* (Bogotá: Norma, 1999).

Pan-American Health Organization (PAHO), *Migration of Health Personnel, Scientists and Engineers from Latin America* (Washington, DC: PAHO, 1966).

Pechman, J. A. (ed.), *The Role of the Economist in Government: An International Perspective* (New York: Harvester Wheatsheaf, 1989).

Saenz, E., *La Ofensiva Empresarial: Industriales, políticos y violencia en los años 40 en Colombia* (Bogotá: Tercer Mundo, 1992).

Safford, F., *The Ideal of the Practical: Colombia's Struggle to Form a Technical Elite* (Austin: University of Texas Press, 1976).

Santa María, A. P. (1994), *Origen, Desarrollo y Realización de la Escuela de Minas de Medellín*, 2 vols (Medellín: Diké).

Sanz de Santamaría, A., 'La Enseñanza de la Economía: Aspectos Metodológicos y Pedagógicos', in *Discurso y Razón: Una Historia de las Ciencias Sociales en Colombia* (Bogotá: Tercer Mundo, 2000).

Sikkink, K. A., 'Developmentalism and Democracy: Ideas, Institutions and Economic Policy-Making in Brazil and Argentina (1954–1962)', PhD dissertation, Columbia University, New York: 1988.

Streeten, P., *Thinking About Development* (Cambridge University Press, 1995).

Thorp, R., *Economic Management and Economic Development in Peru and Colombia* (Basingstoke: Macmillan with OECD Development Centre, 1991).

Uricoechea, F. 'Comments on the Paper, "Saber es Poder: el Caso de los Economistas Colombianos"', presented by Marco Palacios in UNIANDES, Centre for Studies of Economic Development (Bogotá: CEDE, 2000).

Urrutia, M., 'Colombia', in J. Williamson (ed.), *The Political Economy of Policy Reform* (Washington, DC: Institute for International Economics, 1994).

Valdés, J. G., *Pinochet's Economists. The Chicago School in Chile* (Cambridge University Press, 1995).

10
The Bretton Woods Institutions and the Transmission of Neo-liberal Ideas in Mexico

Ngaire Woods

Introduction

The IMF and World Bank have been involved for over two decades in advising states in Latin America on economic policy. Their role has been described in a vast literature about the debt crisis (Griffith-Jones 1988; Biersteker 1993); their responsibility (especially the IMF's) for sustaining international economic activity (Gwin and Feinberg 1989; Goodman and Pauly 1993; James 1996); the relationship between adjustment, restructuring and democratization (Haggard and Webb 1994; Haggard and Kaufman 1995); and the influence of the United States in these institutions (Sanford 1988; Ascher 1992; Kahler 1992b; Gwin 1994). Less examined, however, has been the question of how the international financial institutions (IFIs) influenced economic policy ideas within Latin America and through what political processes within countries.[1] This chapter sets out more specifically to ask under what conditions the institutions enjoyed a high degree of influence in Mexican economic policy-making in the 1980s, recognizing that several other cases highlight the limits of IFI influence.[2]

The chapter is based on research undertaken both in Mexico and in Washington, using archives, papers and interviews to trace Mexico's relations with the IFIs. It argues that the institutions have been highly instrumental in Mexico's embrace of a neo-liberal foreign economic policy. The institutions did not 'impose' a set of neo-liberal ideas on an unwilling Mexican political system, even though the policies expressed by Mexican policy-makers by the mid 1990s looked indistinguishable from those of their interlocutors in Washington – and hence became labelled the 'Washington consensus' (Williamson 1990). Equally, the shift in Mexican policy was not the result of a simple rational 'learning'process about technically 'best' economic policies (Haas 1990; Ikenberry 1990; Kahler 1992a). Rather, it is argued that Mexico's

217

policy shift was affected by more subtle mechanisms of influence which operate between domestic and external actors. It is these mechanisms that this chapter seeks to illuminate.

The overall argument links competing sets of ideas and policies to a struggle for influence within the bureaucracy. It highlights the way key policy-makers in Mexico were able to use the IFIs to enhance their own policies and position, and those of their part of the bureaucracy. The IFIs could offer material rewards and incentives in return for policy changes. Furthermore, they could propound or endorse particular policy ideas, bringing to bear the prestige associated with research undertaken within the rubric of the IMF and World Bank.

The general argument of the chapter is that the IMF and World Bank played into a process of political contestation and institutional change in Mexico. In the short term, the IFIs supported government officials who were prepared to pursue neo-liberal policies. In the longer term, the support of the IMF and World Bank led to institutional change and the entrenchment of neo-liberal policy. In this environment, government officials became ever more reluctant to make policy choices from alternative paradigms.

The chapter is organized in the following way. The second section explains why an analysis of international influence is necessary to explain Mexico's foreign economic policy transformation. The third section outlines the analytical approach of the chapter, highlighting what the study adds to existing frameworks for studying international influence. The fourth section presents the empirical study of Mexico's relations with the IMF and World Bank, describing in three stages the evolution of relations with the IFIs and their impact on successive Mexican administrations from 1976 to 1994. A brief fifth section comments on crisis of 1994–5, before the sixth and final section presents conclusions and the wider lessons about international influence drawn from the Mexican case.

Mexico's transformation

Like many other countries, Mexico radically reshaped its economic relations with the world during the 1980s, throwing open borders to trade, finance and investment.[3] Although the IMF and World Bank played an important role in this process, most accounts of the transformation give little hint of this.[4] The 'traditional' view favoured by economists in Washington is that Mexico simply undertook the most rational technically sound policies available. The period of transformation (1982–94) is portrayed as both planned and inevitable from the start. Ignored are the tough debates and vociferous contestation that preceded each step of liberalization. In 1984, the idea of replacing the gradual, negotiated trade liberalization with rapid unilateral liberalization was opposed by President de la Madrid and most major agencies of the Mexican government.[5] Furthermore, both unions and large business associations such as CANACINTRA and CONCAMIN also opposed trade liberalization.[6] The government's view on investment was that foreign investment did not replace existing national enterprises, nor remove more resources from Mexico than it earned in exports.[7]

Despite widespread domestic political opposition to accelerated liberalization, the Mexican government launched a rapid series of trade liberalization measures in 1985, acceded to GATT in 1986, and eventually signed up to NAFTA and undertook investment and financial liberalization. Having once extolled the benefits of independence and controlled relations with world markets, the Mexican presidency now became an evangelist of the benefits of foreign investment and open access to world markets (Salinas 1989). The transformation looks inevitable with hindsight. Yet closer investigation reveals pervasive political contestation.

Political explanations of Mexico's economic turnaround focus on the impact of external shocks on both policy choices and domestic political coalitions, portraying Mexico's stabilization and structural reform as the inevitable consequence of tight international economic constraints. In this explanation, policy change was contested but the victory of neo-liberalism was assured by the impact of international economic shocks – in one version, because they created new powerful interests which supported neo-liberal policies (Frieden 1991), or in other versions, because it meant the government had no alternative (Pastor and Wise 1994). For example, it is argued that Mexico's radical trade liberalization was a response to economic problems (mid 1985), compounded by earthquakes (19–20 September 1985), an IMF announcement that Mexico had failed to meet the conditions set down in its agreement (21 September 1985) and a crash in oil prices (January 1986) (Szymczak 1992). Under these conditions, the Mexican government had no choice but dramatically to speed up liberalization.

Ignored here is the fact that at the end of 1984, the Mexican government was enjoying a modest sense of economic recovery, having completed two years of economic adjustment, reduced inflation to an annual rate of around 60 per cent, and rescheduled the external debt into multi-year arrangements. The successes of 1983–4 were diminished towards the end of 1984 when the government began to loosen up its fiscal policy – some would say in order to achieve a growth spurt so as to help to secure victory in the 1985 mid-term elections. However while inflation picked up, the public financial deficit grew, the trade balance deteriorated and foreign reserves dropped. Nevertheless, the pace of economic activity remained strong well until the second half of 1985.[8]

Paradoxically, it was during the more positive phase described above that the Mexican government decided to accelerate trade liberalization. For this reason, 'crisis' and lack of choice are not accurate determining factors. Furthermore, the evidence shows that within the Mexican cabinet, at least three different alternatives were recognized and debated.[9] Gradualists within the government favoured continuing hard-debt negotiations with the IMF, the commercial banks and the US government, and maintaining the gradual process of liberalization started in 1983. Radicals favoured using a debtors' cartel to negotiate for better terms, limiting debt repayments to an amount set aside from export earnings and negotiating trade issues separately. Neo-liberals argued that the government should undertake a rapid, unilateral dismantling of trade protections, and use structural reform to deal with inflation and debt. Why and how, then, did the neo-liberals win? Why, furthermore, in the late 1980s and 1990s, when neo-liberal policies were not producing hoped for results, did the neo-liberals continue to dominate? The argument made here is that the IFIs were highly instrumental in this process.

The influence of the IFIs

There is a wealth of literature on the influences and processes of economic policy change which has been excellently summarized and reviewed elsewhere.[10] Two arenas of policy-making are focused on by different scholars. First, there is 'society', and the role interest groups have played in promulgating or supporting (or impeding) reform (Frieden 1991; Bates and Krueger 1993; Silva 1996). Second, there is the arena of government, that is, the institutions and bureaucracy of government, the party system, and the role of electoral cycles (Silva 1993; Haggard and Webb 1994; Geddes 1994, 1995; Haggard and Kaufman 1995). In each of these explanations, internal crisis and external economic shocks usually catalyse the process of change. However, other forms of international influence – such as the role played by the IFIs – are seldom traced.

One literature which does attempt to analyse the impact of international negotiations on domestic politics (and vice versa) is the two-level game analogy which highlights the ways in which bargaining between external actors and domestic politicians can lead to each influencing the other (Gourevitch 1978; Putnam 1988; Lehman and McCoy 1992; Evans *et al.* 1993). Policy-makers play a double game. Although international interlocutors impose new constraints on politicians, the foreign officials also provide new possibilities and leverage for use within the domestic sphere.[11] In other words, interactions in one arena can be used to push for change in the other. A finance minister, for example, might use IMF terms and conditions in order to bolster the case for his or her preferred economic policy.

The relationship between international and domestic negotiations depends upon a number of factors, several of which have been usefully detailed by Stallings (1992). First, the influence of international interlocutors depends upon the level of external financing *international markets* are providing or refusing to provide to governments. Second, there is the *linkage* among negotiators through shared interests and beliefs. Third, there is the level of *leverage* which international actors can exercise by offering incentives or imposing sanctions. These factors are in turn influenced by: the time period of the negotiations (we might compare conditions in the 1970s and 1980s); the phase of reform in the borrowing country (it is easier to be 'decision-making' than 'implementing'); the issue area (stabilization brings out different forces than structural reform); and the country's characteristics (for example, regime type, predisposition to integrate into the world economy).

Overall, negotiations with international agencies such as the IMF and World Bank influence domestic policy in a way which is both significant and contingent. This chapter will argue that there is also a further dimension to external influence. While the existing literature tends to focus on particular episodes of bargaining and bargaining power, the case of Mexico suggests that a longer-term process of change occurs. The evidence indicates that as Mexican policy-makers and interlocutors in the IMF and World Bank negotiated from the late 1970s into the 1990s, a 'third arena' of politics came to evolve. This comprised a small group of actors who participated in negotiations (from both the Mexican government and the IFIs). Relations among these actors were characterized by increasingly shared sets of beliefs about economic policy; insulation from other political pressures due to their own position and that of their government agency; and growing levels of trust and cooperation which greatly increased access to information and the potential to use research and ideas as a lever of influence. In these ways, negotiations between Mexico and the IFIs did not result only in a shifting set of bargains. Rather, relations with the IFIs constituted a political process which affected the distribution of power among agencies within Mexico as well as among policy-makers within the Mexican government. These conclusions are further elaborated upon in the final section of this chapter.

The IMF, the World Bank and political change in Mexico, 1976–94

Over two decades and three presidencies (1976–82, 1982–8, 1988–94), Mexico 'converted' to neo-liberalism. As will be seen below, in the first phase, the government bargained with the IMF and World Bank, which used material incentives to nudge officials towards neo-liberal solutions. In the second phase, government officials became more closely linked to their interlocutors in the IFIs as they increasingly used the incentives and advice of the IMF and World Bank to enhance their own power and position, and that of their ministry in relation to other parts of government. Finally, in the third phase, there was a high level of collusion between both institutions' staff and government officials. Neo-liberal officials (whose careers began in the Finance Ministry or Central Bank) headed virtually all important parts of government, and in policy discussions, no alternatives to neo-liberal foreign economic policy were represented.

The changes described were affected in three domains. First, there was change in the configuration of power *among* government agencies.

Government departments typically compete with each other for power and influence, and in Mexico, the key economic ministries rose to the top. They gained control of the determination of policy priorities, the control of resources, and, most crucially, the framing of policy ideas. The IFIs facilitated this both by pushing particular policy priorities which empowered the economics agencies, and through their capacity to direct resources to specific arms of government. In a similar and related fashion, the endorsement of a particular approach led to change *within* the agencies. Neo-liberals, supported by the IFIs, rose to the top of key arms of the government. Finally, an ever closer relationship of trust and shared purposes emerged among IMF, World Bank and Mexican finance officials. This relationship went beyond the notion of 'linkage' described above – where shared *interests* link the elite with international counterparts. In Mexico, linkage led to collusion, and finally to a form of 'super-linkage'. Cooperation and trust between neo-liberal Mexican policy-makers and their interlocutors in the IMF and World Bank became so strong that it dissolved some of each side's concerns about information and standards of evidence in their dealings with the other.

In the sub-sections below, material drawn from interviews with many of the key players in both the Mexican government and the IFIs is used both to depict the evolution of the relationship between key Mexican neo-liberals and the IFIs, and to analyse the impact of these relations on the policy-making process.

Phase one: bargaining, incentives and alternatives, 1976–82

When the administration of President López Portillo came into office in 1976, it was greeted by a debt crisis and negotiations with the IMF for short-term balance-of-payments financing. The crisis brought two competing views of economic policy into sharp contrast. Economic nationalists prioritized development and growth. Neo-liberals and monetarists argued that Mexico needed to adjust, stabilize, and liberalize in order to lessen inflation, capital flight, and foreign debt.

Among the neo-liberals were two of the future presidents of Mexico, the then head of the newly-created Budget Ministry, Miguel de la Madrid, and the under-secretary of that same ministry, Carlos Salinas de Gortari.[12] The neo-liberals' solutions matched those advocated by the IMF, whose programme required devaluation and fiscal tightening, and encouraged Mexico to open up to world trade and investment. This group came to the fore in 1976, when Mexico was forced to seek assistance from the IMF and to negotiate its first bilateral trade agreement with the United States in 35 years. So too, after several years of denying the World Bank access to Mexican economic data, the government agreed to participate in a World Bank review of Mexico's economic performance, and President López Portillo forged a new closer relationship with the World Bank. This was kicked off by a meeting with World Bank President Robert MacNamara on 17 February 1977, which led to a doubling of the World Bank's portfolio in Mexico.

Although the neo-liberals prevailed, there were alternative voices in the Mexican cabinet. The new policies were criticized by structuralists (or economic nationalists) who argued that Mexican development was best served by decreasing dependence on the United States, and by protection or any measures against the vagaries of uncontrolled international markets. Also advocating a strong state and intervention was the new Ministry of National Patrimony and Industrial Development (SEPAFIN), which emphasized the need to balance economic growth with equity and welfare considerations, and to prioritize production for domestic consumption.[13] For a brief period in the late 1970s, the structuralists won. Loans from international banks permitted Mexico to turn its back on the IMF, to turn away from GATT, and to embark on a nationalist set of trade and investment policies (Story 1982; Mares 1985).

The heyday of the economic nationalists was brought to an abrupt halt when Mexico was hit by a series of economic shocks. A damaging drought caused widespread crop failures in 1979–1980, and was followed by a more damaging rise in US interest rates in 1979 which hiked up Mexico's foreign debt repayment obligations. Furthermore, in 1981 and again in 1982, the price of oil, Mexico's thriving export, dropped. Mexico's economy soon unravelled.

The crisis brought out two contradictory responses. The neo-liberals in the government appealed to the international financial community for help. The economic nationalists (including J. A. Oteyza and V. Brailowsky) nationalized the banks (1 September 1982), imposed unwieldy exchange and interest rate policies, and castigated the exploitative international financial community.[14] The contradictions were resolved when the crisis brought the incoming government directly back into the arms of the IFIs – in dire need of their assistance. Indeed, even as the nationalists within the cabinet of 1982 pursued policies which ought to have completely undermined the confidence of the international financial community, the neo-liberals managed to negotiate agreements with both the IMF and Mexico's commercial creditors. Although President-elect Miguel de la Madrid had not yet taken office, the IMF negotiated with the technocrats in his team, as did the Bank Advisory Group set up in the wake of the crisis.[15] These negotiations are often presented as a series of confrontations between Mexico, and the IMF and commercial banks. Yet, in some ways the real differences of view lay among the Mexicans involved.[16]

The incentives offered to Mexico in 1982 to persuade its policy-makers to stay in line with Washington's vision of debt management were substantial. The Mexican government requested a new commercial bank loan of US$5bn with a tenor of 6 years and 3 years' grace, and the IMF backed up their request by requiring banks to confirm their commitment to new lending as a prerequisite of its approval for Mexico to draw some US$3.9bn from the

Extended Fund Facility (Story 1982; Mares 1985). On 8 December 1982, the Finance Minister communicated to the IMF that Mexico would abide by an economic programme supported by the IMF, and to the banks, the restructuring scheme for Mexican public sector external debt as formally agreed with the Bank Advisory Group.

Along with the incentives the IMF could offer, it also had a clear definition and 'solution' to Mexico's difficulties. They could offer a government which was disenchanted with the ideas behind the old foreign economic policy and without the finances to continue it, an instant, ready-made solution. Here the content of the IMF's ideas – the theoretical logic, prescriptive simplicity, and optimistic prognosis (Woods 1995) – contributed to the ascendance of the agencies and personnel that promulgated them.

The political impact of the adjustment Mexico undertook was immediate. The IMF required Mexico to meet macroeconomic criteria that required stabilization and adjustment. The necessary measures, unlike deeper microeconomic reforms, did not require a wide consensus within Mexico but rather could be undertaken by a very small group of senior officials. As a result, the Finance Ministry and Central Bank began to increase their power relative to other agencies. For although both the Finance Ministry and Central Bank had always been powerful in Mexico,[17] previously their power had been counterbalanced both by competing views of economic policy and by other powerful political ministries. *Gobernación*, for example, controlled the security and the patronage apparatus of the state through the appointment of governors, municipal authorities, and the leaderships of corporatist organizations. However, the power of *gobernación* began to erode as soon as the budget cuts required to meet IMF-favoured macroeconomic criteria were introduced. At the same time, the recipients of IMF assistance, the Finance Ministry and Central Bank, began to expand their own networks – as did the Budget Ministry (headed by Miguel de la Madrid from 1979 and then by Salinas from 1982), creating a network of regional offices whose heads had more direct access to the budget (Centeno 1994:ch. 4).

However, in spite of the rise of neo-liberals, throughout the late 1970s and early 1980s, there remained competing views inside the cabinet. The new technocrats in the Finance Ministry and Central Bank were continually forced to rebut alternative policies propounded by radical voices in the cabinet. The neo-liberal prescriptions were continually subject to critical scrutiny. Furthermore, cabinet opposition served as an important source of 'reverse leverage' for Mexican officials negotiating with the IFIs – they could use the threat of more radical alternatives to get better terms.

Phase two: linkage, socialization and the neo-liberal ascendancy, 1982–8

The 1982 debt crisis forced Mexico to seek help from Washington, from both the multilateral institutions and the US government. Yet, Mexican policy-makers had some reverse leverage which they put to good use. Negotiators were able to play upon US fears that the Mexican government would give in to political demands for a radical policy which would further jeopardize banking stability (owing to the heavy exposure of US banks) and exacerbate US concerns about political instability (from fears of immigration to fears of the communist threat[18]). In the early 1980s, Mexican government officials could point to radical alternatives, such as a moratorium on debt repayments, being advocated within the cabinet.

The Mexican cabinet, however, was in the process of changing. The 1982 elections had sealed the outgoing president's choice of his successor – Miguel de la Madrid – whose new cabinet alarmed radicals. The loser in the race for the presidential nomination attributed the change to the domination of the party by the 'technocrats of SPP' (the Budget Ministry) (Centeno 1994:158). The criticism was to some degree an accurate one. A study of de la Madrid's 1983 cabinet reveals that some 59 per cent of positions were taken by officials who had started their careers in the banking or planning sectors of the bureaucracy, and just over 44 per cent were trained in economics, many in US universities (Centeno 1994:139). Young technocrats like de la Madrid and Salinas had, during the López Portillo administration, already set out their own neo-liberal view of Mexico's foreign economic policy.[19]

The neo-liberals in the incoming cabinet were an important *linkage* for both the IMF and World Bank. Indeed, some would say that neo-liberals had been appointed so as to send out a signal of confidence to Mexico's creditors and private sector, which were haemorrhaging capital abroad. In his memoirs, the outgoing president recalls that he appointed Miguel de la Madrid because as he saw it, de la Madrid was better equipped to deal with Mexico's 'financial' problems than was his rival, Javier García Paniagua (López Portillo 1988). From the World Bank's point of view, Miguel de la Madrid was already perceived back in 1979 as 'very willing' to collaborate with the World Bank, as were several members of his team.[20]

The power and status of the young technocrats were immediately enhanced by their role in dealing with the debt crisis. As of 1982, debt posed the most determinative constraint and incentive on Mexico's economic policy. The position of a small group of technocrats was enhanced by the fact that the IMF negotiated – confidentially – with as small and as specialized a group as possible. Access to the relevant documents, and the deliberations and outcomes of negotiations was tightly restricted. The negotiations concentrated power in the hands of key agencies (the Finance Ministry and Central Bank), and neo-liberals within them. Furthermore, the *type* of policy being advocated by the IMF further enhanced their power since 'top-down' macroeconomic policies did not require 'deep' political implementation – a small group of technocrats *could* take these kinds of decisions (Nelson, Kachanowicz, Mizsei and Muñoz, 1994; Naím 1995). The result was that other agencies of government became marginalized. The Ministry of Foreign

Affairs, for instance, lost any role in foreign economic policy (in 1986, losing even the post of under-secretary for economic relations in the ministry), and was relegated, in the words of one official, to 'dealing with the Third World'.[21]

Yet, in the mid 1980s, there was still strong concern about international infringement of Mexican sovereignty. A debate about this was engendered when the World Bank proposed in 1983 to deepen its dialogue with Mexico. Having been denied access for many years, the Bank proposed a new, high-quality macroeconomic dialogue, focusing on three areas: fiscal policy, trade, and public enterprises. It argued that such an intensive dialogue could potentially lead to several structural or sectoral adjustment loans. The proposal created a storm within the Mexican cabinet. The only Mexican agency then borrowing from the World Bank was NAFINSA, and its head, Gustavo Petricioli, argued strongly that such an arrangement would impinge upon Mexico's sovereignty and independence.

Petricioli lost this argument. Signalling the growing power of the Ministry of Finance, the Minister (and key debt negotiator) Jesús Silva Herzog, over-ruled Petricioli's objections and the government ended up accepting the proposal.[22] Hence, the World Bank gained deeper access to information across many sectors of the Mexican economy (with notable exceptions of oil and agriculture), permitting ever more specific analyses and advice to be presented to the government.

As of late 1983, the World Bank's advisory role became a regular, institutionalized feature in Mexico with six-monthly country strategy implementation meetings occurring throughout the 1980s, alternately in Washington and in Mexico City. In preparation for each meeting, the Bank would prepare a ten-page memorandum aimed at senior officials, giving the Bank's analysis of the country's macroeconomic situation. Initially these consultations involved junior officials from the Finance Ministry, but they quickly became fora for higher-level officials in which the Minister of Finance would take the lead.

The World Bank's agenda was radical liberalization. Trade liberalization was seen as a crucial lever to more fundamental reforms of public enterprises and fiscal reforms.[23] Throughout consultations in the 1980s, the World Bank gradually concentrated more and more on advising Mexico of the links between its fiscal problem and the need for trade liberalization. The Bank's influence on trade reform offers a useful example of influence.

Incentives were the most obvious source of influence. The Bank could offer fast-disbursing loans such as their first Export Development Loan to Mexico in 1983, and the subsequent Trade Policy Loans of 1986 and 1987 which were worth US$500m. each, in return for trade policy reform. Significantly, these loans were considered by the World Bank as 'rewards' for past and for future performance in trade liberalization – that is, not only incentives for policy-makers to pursue particular policies, but also articles of faith in these policy-makers.

A second type of support the World Bank could offer, as mentioned above, was intellectual. In 1985 when the Mexican cabinet was wrestling over crucial decisions on trade liberalization, the Bank very discreetly, without using the World Bank's name, sponsored a conference on trade liberalization using the private university ITAM and the Mexican Agency BANCOMEXT.[24] Conference speakers included the likes of Anne Krueger and many other World Bank staff or consultants who presented the benefits of trade liberalization. One particularly persuasive argument was that liberalization could assist in controlling inflation. Here the World Bank lent important intellectual support to neo-liberals pushing for trade liberalization within the Mexican cabinet.

The example of trade liberalization also highlights the way in which competition among different departments in the Mexican government opened up a conduit for the World Bank view. Unsurprisingly, the Ministry of Trade did not want to relinquish the control and patronage it had gained from administering Mexico's deep range of protectionist instruments. The Central Bank, however, was in a different position. Once the World Bank persuaded key Central Bank officials that trade liberalization was a way of controlling inflation, it created an enthusiastic liberalizer – a Central Bank keen to control inflation without having to limit its own control over interest and exchange rates. The task of persuasion was made easier by the fact that the governor of the Bank, Miguel Mancera, shared the Bank's conviction on this issue. Here, the 'knowledge' and research of the World Bank influenced a bureaucratic turf battle, thereby creating a hefty partner with whom the World Bank could pursue trade liberalization.

The linkage between the World Bank and Mexico's Central Bank became a collusive one in the subsequent 1985 negotiations. Mexico was represented by senior officials from the Finance Ministry, the Central Bank, and the Trade Ministry. The Mexican officials were in clear disagreement with one another over the right approach to trade policy. The Central Bank favoured rapid liberalization, afraid that any gradualist approach would create resistance that would stall the process. The Trade Ministry favoured a gradualist approach, concerned that many small and medium-sized enterprises would otherwise be destroyed overnight. During the negotiations, according to a senior trade official involved in the negotiations, the Central Bank went behind the backs of the Trade Ministry, and gave the World Bank a set of figures (calculated on the basis of production weights as opposed to import weights) which seriously undermined the Trade Ministry's claims about liberalization undertaken to that date.[25] Such manoeuvres illustrate how domestic actors can use the IFIs in order to carry out interdepartmental struggles. We must recall, however, that the debate which created the struggle was one fostered by the World Bank and its proposition that trade liberalization could assist in controlling inflation.

Although the Central Bank won the battle over trade liberalization in 1985, the stakes were altered by renewed economic crisis in Mexico and a crash in oil prices in January 1986. Radicals, greatly weakened but still present in the cabinet, strengthened their demands for an alternative strategy and gained some support from others in the cabinet. The radical strategy included calling a meeting of the debtors' group established at Cartagena in 1984 and reactivating a more assertive, less cooperative approach to debt. Washington's response was rapid. After the Mexican government called for an emergency meeting of the Latin American debtors' group in Punte del Este in January 1986, the United States and the IFIs sped up a revision of arrangements with the Mexican government and came up with important concessions. The terms of the World Bank's trade liberalization deal were immediately lightened, as were the conditions in the IMF agreement signed soon after.

Two points emerge as particularly important from the 1986 episode. First, it underlines that at this point in time, Mexico still retained some bargaining power based on US (and IMF and World Bank) fears of more radical policy. Second (and paradoxically), it also emerges from the 1986 agreements that the IMF and World Bank were becoming increasingly confident of the commitment of the neo-liberals in the cabinet to their style of reform. As one senior official who lightened Mexico's conditions explained in private: there was no longer any *need* to push Mexico to sign up to such vigorous written terms, since the new breed of Mexican policy-makers were committed to liberalizing as far and as fast as they could anyway.[26]

In summary, as the 1980s progressed, the economic policy-making agencies (the Budget Ministry, Finance Ministry, Central Bank and Office of the Presidency) acquired more extensive control of overall policy within the Mexican political system. These agencies were able to use the resources and conditionality of the IMF and World Bank as leverage within the cabinet. Both the IMF and World Bank lent them support and influenced their policy choices through incentives, as well as extensive technical expertise and analysis. The *quid pro quo* from the Mexican government was that it granted the institutions ever greater access to information and policy debates within Mexico.

Phase three: super-linkage and the neo-liberal victory, 1988–94

The result of Mexico's 1988 presidential election was hailed from the outset as one which would cement close ties with (and the confidence of) the international financial community. Like his predecessor, Carlos Salinas de Gortari had been head of the Budget Ministry after a career in the Finance Ministry. Foreign financial press all stressed that the new president-elect had a degree in economics from Harvard and feted him through to the end of his presidency, with *The Economist* citing him in their 1993 Special Survey of Mexico as quite possibly one of the greatest men of the twentieth century.[27] Critics deprecated the choice of Salinas as the new presidential candidate. He was described as a man controlled by international financial interests;[28] and his nomination was described as 'the result of private sector forces associated with the multinationals which desire the development of a privatising, monetarist, and free-trade PRI'.[29] Both those who celebrated and those who criticized the president-elect were right about his close links to the international financial community.

In October 1988, in a 'dramatic confidence-building gesture' for the Mexican government and its new president-elect (and amidst allegations of massive electoral fraud), the United States stepped in to assist Mexico's severe economic and political crisis with a US$3.5bn bridging loan from the Treasury Exchange Stabilization Fund. The US loan was soon rolled over into arrangements with the IMF and the World Bank (under the auspices of the Brady Plan announced in March 1989) totalling some US$4.135bn of IMF financing over a period of three years, and credits from the World Bank of US$1960m. for 1989. There was also financial support for debt reduction and new loans of US$2000m. per year on average over 1990–2. Importantly, the Brady Plan permitted the IMF and the World Bank to support debt rescheduling in Mexico, even in the absence of Mexico completing a deal with its commercial bank creditors.[30]

In this case, although both the IMF and World Bank had been working discreetly on the technicalities of debt reduction, neither had been able to move forwards with debt reduction schemes until the US government gave the nod. Once the 'fax arrived saying that we had to help Mexico', the IFIs went into overdrive to implement debt reduction in deep consultation with Treasury officials.[31] Deviating from all its norms of practice, the World Bank put together a major series of loans to Mexico in just over three weeks: writing reports in the field, agreeing the loans by special committee without the Bank's chief economist (who disagreed with the new US policy of debt reduction), and skipping some of the review mechanisms and appraisals.

What few people know is that even before Mexico's 1988 elections, the World Bank had become involved in preparing a series of short briefs on major policy issues for Salinas (the PRI candidate) and the PRI. The substance of many of these proposals appeared subsequently in the PRI's manifesto.[32] Furthermore, immediately after the elections and before Salinas actually took power, the World Bank organized a workshop for Salinas and his prospective cabinet in the mountains a couple of hours' drive outside of Mexico City. Here, in seminar-style discussions, World Bank officials claim in private that they cemented relations of mutual trust and confidence with the new team which subsequently played a major part in expediting loans and agreements with the World Bank. 'It became clear', recalls one World Bank official, 'that these people wanted the World Bank's involvement in virtually everything. They said things in the same way as the Bank.' In the words of another Bank official, describing the evolution of relations with the new team: '[I]t no longer mattered what was written down, more important was that these policy-makers could be trusted.'[33]

The participants in the seminar soon became key members in the cabinet appointed by Carlos Salinas de Gortari. Marking a departure from the Mexican tradition of appointing heterodox cabinets which ensured that the heads of the various Ministries had different views and were supported by different factions within the party, Salinas made appointments to key agencies from an overwhelmingly small group of officials who had come up through the Finance Ministry, the Budget Ministry or the Central Bank (Centeno and Maxfield 1992; Centeno 1994:140). The four key economic policy-makers in the new cabinet were all neo-liberals: José Córdoba, head of the office of economic advisers set up within the Presidency; Pedro Aspe, an MIT-trained Budget and Finance Ministry official; Jaime Serra Puche, a Yale-trained Finance Ministry official; and Ernesto Zedillo, a Yale-trained Central Bank and Budget Ministry official. Even the new head of the PRI was University-of-Pennsylvania-trained and Budget-Ministry-experienced Luis Donaldo Colosio.

The stake which the IFIs (and the wider international financial community) had in these men was clear from the outset. Furthermore, if a member of the cabinet did not 'play ball', the IMF and World Bank were now in a position to make it clear to the government that they would find it easier to work with someone else.[34] Overall, the relations between the IMF and World Bank, and the Salinas administration became ever more marked by trust, evidenced by high levels of access, and by a high degree of acceptance on all sides of each other's figures, prescriptions, and promises.[35]

Increasing trust, access and acceptance was, of course, always handled (as was the workshop in the mountains discussed above) with the utmost discretion. For example, immediately prior to the unveiling of the 1989 Mexican budget, it was vital that the IMF was not seen in Mexico City (where it might be construed as 'dictating' a budget to the Mexican government). Indeed, the IMF did not officially send a mission to Mexico until after the Budget had been announced. Nevertheless, before the announcement, two IMF officials flew yet more secretly (even than was normally the case for the IMF) into Mexico City to meet with and advise the Mexican team.[36] The secrecy of the meeting was crucial to subsequent events. In the cabinet negotiations on the budget, Finance Minister Pedro Aspe (along with the head of the Central Bank) invoked the need to comply with IMF terms and conditions to bolster their argument for continuing restrictive anti-inflationary policies. Yet, this was in fact a ploy to outmanoeuvre cabinet colleagues. Crucially, the restrictiveness and secrecy of both monetary policy and IMF negotiations meant that many in the cabinet were unaware that Mexico no longer needed the IMF resources for which compliance with the criteria of the Extended Arrangement was necessary.[37]

The closeness of relations between key Mexican policy-makers and the IFIs was cemented during 1989 by negotiations on the details of Mexico's Brady Plan debt reductions. Here, the special relations between the Mexican neo-liberal elite and the IFI staff seemed at times even to supersede the desires of IMF and World Bank Board members. Fund officials were flying in and out of Mexico at least every two months. World Bank officials were there almost permanently. In addition, even though many governments wanted their banks to negotiate directly with Mexico, the IMF and World Bank continued to assist Mexico throughout. A senior World Bank economist involved at the time recalls spending large chunks of his own time helping the Mexican team, and even travelling privately to Mexico City in order to help them sort out how best to take advantage of debt reduction.[38]

The deepening relationship described above is perhaps best illustrated by the case of agricultural reform. In 1983, Mexico stonewalled the World Bank on agricultural policy. When the idea of deepening World Bank dialogue was floated in 1983, agriculture was consensually agreed to be one of the strictly taboo areas from which the Bank was excluded. By 1989, however, the Mexican government embraced the World Bank's agenda and permitted it to train young neo-liberals to be put in charge of the Ministry of Agriculture. The change began in 1988, when at the pre-transition conference organized with the World Bank (discussed above), agricultural reform was raised. By 1989, the issue had risen to the top of the agenda of President Salinas and Minister of Finance Pedro Aspe, and a team of young neo-liberals, headed by Luis Tellez, were moved into the Ministry of Agriculture. None apparently knew anything about agriculture (in the words of one World Bank official, 'not one of them knew the difference between wheat and maize'), but they were picked out as 'heavy-hitters' in the bureaucracy, capable of implementing market-oriented reform. The training of these young neo-liberals was provided by the World Bank, with the utmost discretion, during so-called 'reverse missions' to Washington and on one occasion at the Wisconsin Land Tenure Center.[39]

Looked at more closely, the progression of agricultural policy serves closely to illustrate the mechanisms of influence depicted in this chapter. The first aspect of change was the shift in policy priorities. Mexico's *volte-face* on agriculture was greatly facilitated by incentives (loans) offered by the World Bank, along with research and evidence of the potential gains from reform. The dialogue which commenced in earnest in 1988 resulted in some seven major loans for agricultural reforms between 1987 and 1991. Additionally, two sector adjustment programme loans and five non-project loans were approved by the Bank. These loans were an important step to securing policy change. One World Bank official recalls trying to 'maximize' the leverage of the Bank by cooperating with the IADB so as to come up with as large a package as possible to offer Mexican policy-makers in return for reform.[40] So too, the quality of Bank personnel and research was important.[41]

A second mechanism of influence was reflected in the fact that the push to reform agriculture came from the Ministry of Finance and the Presidency. As these agencies accumulated power over the 1980s, so too the scope of their policy-making initiatives expanded to incorporate most areas of policy – including agriculture, where they took the lead. This factor links to a third mechanism of influence: the restructuring of ministries so as to carry out neo-liberal reforms. New 'key' personnel were appointed – as we saw in the case of agriculture – who would carry out the agenda approved by both the IFIs and Mexico's Ministry of Finance, Central Bank and Presidency. A final channel of influence was the close set of collaborative relations that emerged between officials in the IFIs and Mexican policy-makers. Bank officials talk about Mexican policy-makers providing them with more and more figures, and greater and greater access, and in return, they themselves became more prepared to be flexible in interpreting compliance and non-compliance.[42] Mexican officials speak of feeling able to trust Bank and IMF officials more than their cabinet colleagues at times – and accepting warning of political or economic events from them.[43]

Over this period, the IFIs also became involved in 'selling' the neo-liberal project to a wider community in Mexico. Just as in 1985, the World Bank sponsored a conference on trade liberalization to convert reluctant cabinet members, so too in 1989 the IMF sponsored a conference on growth, equity and external financing. This was an attempt to bring the National University (UNAM)[44] into the liberalization strategy from which its very critical economists had distanced themselves. IMF officials speak of their sense that UNAM had been 'alienated' from the reform process and needed to be brought on board.[45] Such activities highlight the role the IFIs see themselves playing. They perceive themselves as not merely setting targets for governments and ensuring policy compliance, but educating and transforming the parameters of domestic policy debate, in fact, furthering and entrenching powerful ideas.

Unsurprisingly, in 1994, when it came to the question of Salinas's succession, the four main contenders for the job were all neo-liberals: Ernesto Zedillo (as above), Pedro Aspe (as above), Luis Donaldo Colosio (as above) and Manuel Camacho (who had attended UNAM with Salinas and worked with him at the Budget Ministry from 1980).[46] All were pretty much in agreement with each other – and with IMF and World Bank officials – as to the nature of and solution to Mexico's economic problems.

The impact of the IFIs, it has been argued, was initially because of the financial incentives and rewards they offered, but over time they acquired influence through their 'knowledge', the production of authoritative accounts of the country's economy and its prospects. Such analysis required access to Mexican data and policy-makers, which in the early 1980s was granted reluctantly in return for specific incentives. By the late 1980s, however, the IFIs had virtually open access (granted secretly where necessary). The access was granted by a small number of policy-makers with powers, enhanced by the policies and support of the Fund and World Bank, to take key decisions across an ever-wider area of economic policy. This shift in power towards the Finance Ministry and Central Bank, and towards neo-liberals within these institutions, has been crucial to Mexico's foreign economic policy transformation.

The 1994–5 crisis and NAFTA

Mexico's neo-liberal transformation of foreign economic policy came to be perceived as so complete that by 1994 it had become an 'exemplary case' of reform. The IFIs and others heralded Mexico's reforms as 'spectacular, lasting, and the envy of any reform economy'.[47] Mexico became a member of NAFTA, opening up new possibilities of inward investment, as well as new vulnerabilities to shocks in international markets. In 1994, even though economic performance was handicapped by a series of shocks including the assassination of Donaldo Colosio (the man nominated as the PRI's presidential candidate), both the IMF and World Bank remained confident that the right group of policy-makers were in control in Mexico, and that the storm could be ridden out.[48]

The IFIs were both right and wrong. In December 1994, after a period of economic policy difficulties, the Mexican government widened the exchange rate band by 15 per cent, and within weeks Mexico was on the verge of default as investors withdrew. A severe economic crisis ensued.[49] The IFIs were wrong to believe that Mexico's structural reforms had insured it against such a crisis. Yet, they were right in believing that 'their men' in the Mexican cabinet – now headed by Ernesto Zedillo – would ride out the storm without wavering in their commitment to neo-liberal reform. Although mistakes were made by the new neo-liberal team under Finance Minister Jaime Serra Puche in the first few weeks of government, their overall commitment to the neo-liberal programme of their predecessors remained the same. Particularly notable is that in previous periods of policy-making in Mexico (as discussed above), economic crisis catalysed debate and brought to the fore alternative approaches to economic policy. By the mid 1990s, however, there were virtually no policy alternatives to those endorsed by the IMF and World Bank being propounded in the Mexican cabinet.

Mexico's period of economic reform was beset with contradictions. While the neo-liberals greatly strengthened their place within the existing institutions of the federal government – achieving control of all-powerful ministries, and benefiting from the hegemony of the PRI – they came to face a much broader political challenge. Economically, any 'turning back' on the liberalization project or attempt at an alternative policy (such as controlling capital or trade flows) would be heavily punished by the markets. This reality weakened the capacity of the government to use alternative policies as a bargaining strategy in negotiations with the IMF and World Bank (or other actors in the international financial community), as Mexican policy-makers did to good effect throughout the 1980s. Politically, however, the institutions within which the neo-liberals had consolidated power became greatly weakened in the period 1995–8. The power of both the central government and the PRI was significantly eroded. In 1997, the PRI lost its majority in Congress, its control of the two key states of Querétaro and Nuevo León, its constitutional majority in the Senate, its control of the Mexico City Legislative Assembly, and the first election for Mayor of Mexico City.[50] The series of political changes culminated in 2000, with the election of the first non-PRI president since the 1917 Revolution, Vincente Fox of the Partido Acción Nacional (PAN). The Fox administration has largely continued along the path established by its predecessors, but domestic support has waned since the election. With low levels of support, the neo-liberal 'technocrats' could well come to rely more than ever on the politics of the third arena – their support from (and connections to) financial institutions abroad.

The IFIs, ideas, and influence in economic policy-making

This chapter has traced the evolution of the relationship between Mexico and the IFIs. The case is presented as a heuristic one, highlighting the processes and outcomes which can be catalysed by relations with the IMF and World Bank. It must be noted that the case of Mexico is special in a number of ways which affect the strength of the mechanisms of influence detailed here. In the first place, Mexico's special relationship with the United States and that country's sensitivity to political and economic stability across its southern border have given Mexico more opportunity to push for special treatment and more capability to use 'reverse leverage'. Where the United States has been worried that Mexican policy might take a radical turn (for example, when the Mexican cabinet has seriously discussed a debt moratorium), it has ensured very speedy and reasonably favourable assistance from the IFIs. To quote a former IMF Board member, when it comes to Mexico, the United States will simply 'push and shove until it gets what it wants'.[51]

There are also domestic reasons that distinguish the case of Mexico. The country's size and, until 2000, its essentially single-party political regime – with an enormously powerful presidency and executive – greatly facilitated the rise of neo-liberal technocrats and the insulation of these policy-makers from other parts of government. Furthermore, as Graham (1990) argues, Mexico's federal structure and its process for selecting presidents has ensured a succession of candidates who have risen from within the party and the government bureaucracy, which has certainly helped to entrench and continue the neo-liberal direction of policy.

Although Mexico's peculiarities limit the extent to which this study explains the role of the IFIs in other cases of neo-liberal transformation, it nevertheless highlights several important features of relations between the

IFIs and borrowing countries which can be more generally framed so as to take into account the special features of Mexico.

First, we have seen that the initial leverage of the IMF and World Bank depends upon a government's need for external finance which it cannot obtain from international capital markets. During the 1980s, both the IMF and World Bank became crucial in filling financing 'gaps' for many countries – a role which, as a former Mexican Deputy Minister of Finance noted, gave the institutions a very strong hand.[52] On the other side of the equation, the bargaining strength of the potential recipient of IFI funds is shaped, in the words of an IMF official,[53] by four factors: the strength of the country, its policy record, its backers and the element of systemic risk involved. These are largely political calculations which highlight the possibilities of 'reverse leverage' enjoyed by some countries. A country that poses a threat to international economic stability, or to the interests of a powerful board member, will find the institutions yet keener than usual to maintain positive relations. This gives policy-makers additional room to bargain and more scope to play on fears of what their radical political opponents might do if their own position in government is not bolstered.

A second feature of relations with the IFIs is the 'linkage' that develops between staff in the IFIs and officials in governments. The two groups become linked since each depends upon the other for influence and for access (to funds or to information). A further type of linkage also emerges: that between the types of policies prescribed by the IMF and World Bank, and the government agencies that implement such policies. Just as in the 1960s, agencies such as the IADB and ECLA gave technical support which bolstered the position of planning agencies and central statistics offices,[54] so too the IMF and World Bank have enhanced the position of Finance Ministries and Central Banks. The influence of the institutions, in other words, affects not just individuals in government but also the distribution of power among government agencies.

A third and often-neglected feature of politics in the third arena is the extent to which research and knowledge become instruments of power. The IMF and World Bank enjoy an influence accruing from their status and resources as research institutions and economic monitors. They are each endowed with large resources to analyse the economies of many countries across the world, and can claim a vast technical expertise, as well as wide-ranging experience. They have access to information which few other actors have. For example, the IMF is unique in hearing all debtor/creditor negotiations in its capacity as adviser to the Secretariat of the Paris Club (the forum for negotiation of government loans to developing countries).

While some country officials argue that the middle-ranking IMF or World Bank officials offer nowhere near as good advice as the policy-makers themselves,[55] their advice must be taken seriously nonetheless, at least because each institution is closely linked to commercial banks, governments and other sources of financing. IMF approval is an important catalyst for private funds and the World Bank is a co-lender. Furthermore, the research of both institutions is accorded high status and credibility by the international financial community. Such status makes their endorsement a powerful instrument in the hands of a sympathetic policy-maker, an effect which is further heightened by the research *capacity* of the institutions.

In negotiations with member states, the technical weight of IMF and World Bank analyses puts any proponent of an alternative policy at a distinct disadvantage. In the words of one study, domestic actors simply cannot compete with the expertise and sophistication of the IFIs' technical work:

> One interesting feature of the power dispute with the international agencies is the use of technical competence and research as a strategy to negotiate policy with the local administration and the intelligentsia. The imposition of technical criteria and the heavy emphasis on detailed and quantitative research about the problems at hand put local administrators at a great disadvantage. (De Moura and Alfthan 1994:18)

Local administrators are also put at a disadvantage because in direct contrast to the clear prescriptions promulgated by the IFIs, their own alternatives look unclear, muddled and often even self-contradictory. The institutions are empowered, in other words, by the clear agenda which they have pushed since the early 1980s – offering governments in crisis an immediate policy prescription and justification.[56] The agenda is maintained by several mechanisms. Training and recruitment, for example, ensure a basic homogeneity, with most staff of the organizations recruited directly from US graduate schools in economics or finance.[57] Disputes within the institutions are managed by appeals up the hierarchy, ensuring a congruency of advice.[58]

Although the types of influence described above *can give* the IFIs influence, crucially, none are automatically operative, as evidenced by the varying degrees of 'success' enjoyed by the IMF and World Bank. Whatever the wealth of economists, data and economic knowledge, in order to exercise influence the institutions require access to a country's core economic statistics, to the policy-makers, and to the debates and range of policies being discussed. Governments can always deny them access or permission to investigate and collect data upon which to base their analyses.[59] Without access, neither the IMF nor World Bank can offer analysis or advice in key areas of economic policy-making. For this reason, access is a crucial further aspect of the relationship between the IFIs and borrowing members.

Access to data, policy discussions and groups within the government is a card in the hands of a negotiating government. Access given to IMF or World Bank officials can be altered by the government. So too, it can change over time as the elements of linkage and leverage discussed above come into play. This highlights the fact that relations between the recipient country and the

IFIs do not only affect the bargains they strike at each period in time; rather, in the longer term they affect the parameters within which bargaining is undertaken. In the Stallings framework outlined at the outset of this chapter, influence fluctuates with policy type, issue area and economic conditions. Here, it is proposed, influence can increase dramatically as relations between the IFIs and policy-makers grow, affecting the weight given domestically to information and research presented by the IMF and World Bank, and the access they are accorded to government information and discussions.

The term 'third arena' has been used to describe the forum in which senior economic policy-makers and their interlocutors within the IMF and World Bank negotiate. It has been shown that these actors, while they bargain and interact in the 'third arena', become increasingly insulated from all other politics. This occurs not just by the exigencies of neo-liberal reform (Silva 1993, 1996) but also by the *modus operandi* of the IFIs who work only with a narrow range of policy-makers, with limited consultations and under rules of strict confidentiality. This secrecy and insularity promotes not just a smooth process of bargaining, but also the formation of what might be called a community within the third arena. This chapter has charted empirically the way in which relations within this community (of Mexican policy-makers and their interlocutors in Washington) came to be marked not just by their insularity but also by regular contact, high levels of trust, and shared ideas about the nature of economic problems and their solutions.[60] Whilst the international institutions operated in part as 'agencies of restraint' (Geddes 1994), this role also permitted Mexican technocrats to use the spectre of an external restraint to strengthen their own positions. Politics within the third arena was thus enabling both of a group of Mexican policy-makers as well as of a group of IMF and World Bank officials. These relations shaped both the substance and process of Mexico's economic reforms.

Notes

1. See the work of Remmer (1986), Tussie and Botzman (1990), Kahler (1992a), Stallings (1992). A major obstacle to detailed case-studies is the high level of secrecy surrounding IMF and World Bank negotiations. Obtaining the necessary information requires relentless research and interviewing.
2. The IMF's attempts to stabilize economies in East Asia and in Russia over the past couple of years highlight some of the limits of their influence.
3. The international context in which the transformation took place is explored in Frieden (1991), Bates and Krueger (1993), Williamson (1994), Stallings (1995) and Keohane and Milner (1996). Recent accounts of Mexico's transformation include Loser and Kalter (1992), Lustig (1992), Bazdresch et al. (1993) Córdoba (1994) and Pastor and Wise (1994). This chapter focuses on changes in foreign economic policy as opposed to domestic economic policy.
4. See Note 2 above. Policy-maker accounts include Aspe (1993), Gurría (1993), Rogozinski (1993), Blanco (1994), Martínez and Fárber (1994) and Ortiz (1994).

5. Including the Finance Ministry (Secretaría de Hacienda y Crédito Público), the Ministry of Budget (Secretaría de Programación y Presupuesto), the Ministry of Foreign Affairs (Secretaría de Relaciones Exteriores), the Trade Ministry (Secretaría de Comercio y Fomento Industrial), and the Ministries of Energy, Mines, Parastatal Industry, National Heritage and Industrial Promotion. Note that in this chapter, the head (*secretario*) of each ministry will be referred to as the minister and the *sub-secretario* as the deputy minister. For the debate about trade liberalization as reflected in the minutes of economic cabinet meetings, see López-Portillo (1995).

6. See Heredia (1987). CANACINTRA is the Cámara Nacional de la Industria de Transformación and CONCAMIN is the Confederación de Cámaras Industriales de la Republica Mexicana.

7. As expressed by President Miguel de la Madrid Hurtado in launching his Economic Plan (see de la Madrid 1982).

8. This analysis draws upon IMF Country Reports on Mexico and the economists cited in note 2.

9. Interviews with senior members of the Mexican Cabinet at the time (Mexico City, 11/04/94–16/04/94). See also the analysis of cabinet and economic cabinet minutes in López Portillo (1995).

10. An excellent review is provided by Evans *et al.* (1992).

11. See Tussie and Botzman (1990).

12. This view echoes in the Global Development Plan produced by the Ministry of Budget (Secretaría de Programación y Presupuesto 1987).

13. See their National Plan for Industrial Development (Secretaría de Programación y Presupuesto 1987).

14. Rising public sector expenditure, external debt and inflation, along with a depreciation of the peso and increasing reliance on domestic bank credit led to massive capital flight. As a result, in February 1982, the Central Bank withdrew temporarily from the exchange market, leaving the peso to depreciate sharply. In August 1982, the Mexican Finance Minister made an emergency appeal to Washington (the US Treasury, the Federal Reserve and the IMF) for assistance in meeting Mexico's foreign debt repayments, while the president prepared a nationalization of commercial banks announced in September 1982.

15. The Bank Advisory Group comprised 13 banks (see Gurría 1988:73–4).

16. In discreet negotiations behind the scenes, young members of de la Madrid's incoming team were urging the IMF to take a tough line. For example, a senior IMF official who was negotiating at the time recalls that Gustavo Petricioli, one of de la Madrid's team, would meet him every morning for breakfast during the Fund's mission in Mexico City in order to urge the Fund to be tougher with the outgoing administration (Interview, Washington, DC, 15 March 1995).

17. For accounts of presidential struggles to control them, see Solís (1970) and Maxfield (1990).

18. These fears were spelt out in the Kissinger Commission Report of 1984.

19. See discussion above of their Global Development Plan.

20. Internal memorandum of the World Bank (confidential source). So too, the Director of the Latin American and Caribbean Country Department at the time, speaks of having 'picked out' Carlos Salinas in the early 1980s as a man the Bank could deal with after meeting him at a business conference (Interview, Washington, DC, World Bank, 12/04/95).

21. To put it in the words of one of the president's economic advisers (Interview, Mexico City, 14/04/94). Some of the economic functions of the Foreign Ministry

were in part shifted to the neo-liberal dominated BANCOMEXT, which by 1994 had 28 offices around the world (Interview with senior official in BANCOMEXT, Mexico City, 11/04/95).

22. From interviews conducted by Devesh Kapur in 1994 and reported in a background paper for the Brookings Institution and World Bank History Project.

23. Interviews with senior World Bank officials at the time (Washington, DC, 12/04/95 and 18/04/95 and Oxford, 1994–5). See also World Bank Development Reports 1982–92. The IMF at the time was ambivalent about trade liberalization because in the short run they could see it reducing government revenue from tariffs and thus increasing the government's deficit.

24. ITAM is the Instituto Tecnológico Autónomo de México; BANCOMEXT is the Banco Nacional de Comercio Exterior.

25. Interviews with former deputy minister of trade (Mexico City, 15/04/94) and former director of the Latin American and Caribbean Country Division (World Bank, Washington, DC, 12/04/95) and other World Bank officials. The use of this new approach to calculating and monitoring trade liberalization as of Mexico's first Trade Policy Loan is also mentioned in World Bank Reports.

26. Interview with the World Bank's then vice-president for Latin America who flew to Mexico City and lightened the conditionality on the loan.

27. *The Economist*, Mexico Survey (13 February 1993:4).

28. For example, Porfirio Muñoz Ledo, cited in López Gallo (1989:30).

29. Pablo González Casanova cited in Ramos (1987:302).

30. See *Financial Times* 18/10/88 and Lissakers (1991:228).

31. Senior World Bank officials in charge of putting together the Mexican loans of 1988 were in constant consultation with David Mulford at the US Treasury. The information in this paragraph of the chapter comes from interviews with three senior World Bank officials who were directly involved in the Mexican 'package' of 1988. (Interviews: London, LSE, 30/11/94 and Washington, DC, 17/04/95 and 18/04/95).

32. A senior World Bank official describes having his 'very best and brightest staff' prepare a series of a dozen policy papers: each based on an issue and no longer than a single-digit number of pages (Interview, World Bank, Washington, DC, 12/04/95).

33. Interviews with three senior World Bank officials (World Bank, Washington, DC, 12/04/95, 17/04/95 and 18/04/95).

34. One example of this, as a former vice president for Latin America recalls, was the case of the minister of education (Manuel Bartlett) who was replaced a couple of months after concerns were aired by neo-liberal Ernesto Zedillo (Interview, Washington, DC, 18/04/95). Other interviewees, however, noted that the circumstances were more complex than Bank staff recalled – that is, Manuel Bartlett had his own political agenda.

35. Interviews with World Bank, US Treasury and IMF officials, Washington, DC, April 1995).

36. Interviews with IMF and Mexican officials. Perhaps unbeknownst to the IMF officials at the time, the World Bank Chief Economist for Mexico was also making secret trips to Mexico City – in order to 'coach' the Mexican team for their visit from the IMF.

37. Interview with a senior Mexican finance official (Washington, DC, 24/05/94).

38. Interview (London, LSE, 30/11/94).

39. Interviews with senior World Bank officials, Washington, DC, 12/04/95, 17/04/95 and 18/04/95, and London, 30/11/94.

40. Interview with World Bank official, Washington, DC, 17/05/95.
41. The 'team' working on Mexico included the World Bank's top agricultural expert Hans Binswagen, and one of their top economists, Sweder Van Wijnbergen, whose work on the consequences of NAFTA for agriculture was particularly influential.
42. The Bank officials cited in this chapter spoke of a change in the mood and ambiance of negotiations from the early to the later 1980s. By the late 1980s, when it came to asking whether a disbursement should be withheld because the terms had not been completely fulfilled, Bank officials came to interpret compliance or non-compliance very flexibly.
43. Interview with former Minister of Finance, Mexico City, 2/06/95.
44. UNAM is the Universidad Nacional Autónoma de México.
45. Conference proceedings are published in Morales and Ruiz 1989. IMF intentions were detailed to me by the Fund officials working on Mexico at the time (Interviews, Washington, DC, 23/05/94).
46. Of course, the predominance of these neo-liberals was also a reflection of the enormous power of the president. Every one of these men was from within Salinas's own *camarilla*.
47. As quoted in Dornbusch and Werner (1994:266).
48. IMF Country Report (January 1994) following Article IV consultations with Mexico (Edwards 1995).
49. For two different interpretations see Lustig (1995) and Sachs *et al.* (1995). For the official interpretation, see IMF (1995). A good recent overview is Edwards and Naím *eds.* (1997).
50. For analyses of the broad political changes, see Morris (1995), Dominguez and McCann (1996) and Bruhn (1997).
51. Interview with Executive-Director to the IMF, Washington, DC, IMF 24/05/94.
52. Interview with former deputy minister of finance, Mexico City, 14/04/94.
53. Senior IMF Official (Interview, Washington, DC: IMF, 23/05/94). See also Haggard and Kaufman (1989).
54. I am indebted to Diana Tussie for this comparison.
55. This view is expressed by economic policy-makers throughout Latin America.
56. This agenda is clearly laid out by officials interviewed in both organizations (as given in the notes to this chapter) and by both institutions' publications. See the IMF's *World Economic Outlook* and *IMF Survey*, the Joint IMF-World Bank Publication *Finance and Development* and the World Bank's *World Development Reports*.
57. Stern and Ferreira (1993). Their survey sample of World Bank staff shows that 290 had received their highest degree from US graduate schools as compared with 175 who had received their highest degree from universities in other countries. They also found that over 50 per cent of World Bank staff had held their previous job in the United States.
58. For example, when a dispute broke out as to whether to be lenient or tough with Mexico in 1985/6, the debate rose first to the heads of the Area Department (who favoured leniency) and the Policy Development and Review Department (whose remit is to ensure that the Fund's programmes are consistent and equally tough in all countries), and was finally settled by the managing director of the Fund (Interviews with three senior officials at the IMF, Washington, DC: IMF, 23/05/94). The details of the final agreement are laid out in Gurría (1988).
59. Indeed, before 1983, the World Bank was constantly frustrated by the Mexican government, who denied it access to crucial sectors of the economy. In the

months leading up to Mexico's debt crisis in 1982, the World Bank (which had considerable exposure to Mexico) had virtually no information at all on Mexico's external public debt situation (Interviews with two former vice-presidents for Latin America, and a senior official at the World Bank, Oxford 1994/5 and World Bank, Washington, DC, 17/04/95 and 18/04/95). Apparently, the government claimed that statistics were held up owing to computer difficulties.

60. This is borne out by policy-makers who describe a network of decision-makers who were only 'a telephone call away from each other' across Latin America and who shared 'similar educations and beliefs in neo-liberal solutions to key economic problems'; they attended the same conferences, subscribed to same journals, and exchanged views in the same publications and once in government (Williamson 1994); and I am grateful to Moisés Naím, former Ministry of Industry in Venezuela – educated at MIT – and Pedro Aspe, former Mexican Finance Minister – also educated at MIT – for their accounts of this network.

References

Ascher, William, 'The World Bank and US Control', in M. Karns and K. Mingst (eds), *The United States and Multilateral Institutions: Patterns of Changing Instrumentality and Influence* (London: Routledge, 1992).

Aspe, P., *Economic Transformation the Mexican Way* (Cambridge, MA: MIT Press, 1993).

Bates, R. and A. Krueger, *Political and Economic Interactions in Economic Policy Reform: Evidence from Eight Countries* (Cambridge: Blackwell, 1993).

Bazdresch, C., N. Bucay, S. Loaeza, and N. Lustig, *México Auge, Crisis y Ajuste* (Mexico City: Fondo de Cultura Económica, 1993).

Blanco, H., *Las Negociaciones Comerciales de México con el Mundo* (Mexico City: Fondo de Cultura Económica, 1994).

Biersteker, T. J., *Dealing with Debt: International Financial Negotiations and Adjustment Bargaining* (Boulder, CO: Westview, 1993).

Bruhn, K., *Taking On Goliath: The Emergence of a New Left Party and the Struggle for Democracy in Mexico* (University Park: Pennsylvania State University Press, 1997).

Centeno, M. A., *Democracy Within Reason: Technocratic Revolution in Mexico* (University Park: Pennsylvania State University Press, 1994).

Centeno, M. and S. Maxfield, 'The Marriage of Finance and Order: Changes in the Mexican Political Elite', *Journal of Latin American Studies* 24/1 (1992) 57–85.

Córdoba, J., 'Mexico', in J. Williamson (ed.), *The Political Economy of Policy Reform* (Washington: Institute for International Economics, 1994).

De la Madrid Hurtado, M., *Plan Básico 1982–1988 y Plataforma Electoral* (Mexico City: Partido Revolucionario Institucional, 1982).

De Moura Castro, C. and T. Alfthan, *Budget Cuts in Education: Policy or Politics* (Washington, DC: Inter-American Development Bank, 1994).

Dominguez, J. and J. McCann, *Democratizing Mexico: Public Opinion and Electoral Choices* (Baltimore: Johns Hopkins University Press, 1996).

Dornbusch, R. and A. Werner, Mexico: Stabilization, Reform, and No Growth. *Brookings Papers on Economic Activity* no. 1 (1994) 253–315.

Edwards, S., *Crisis and Reform in Latin America: from Despair to Hope* (New York: Oxford University Press for World Bank, 1995).

Edwards, S. and M. Naím, *Mexico 1994: Anatomy of an Emerging-Market Crash* (Washington, DC: Carnegie Endowment for International Peace, 1997).

Evans, P., *Embedded Autonomy: States and Industrial Transformation* (Princeton University Press, 1995).

Evans, P., S. Haggard, and R. R. Kaufman, *The Politics of Economic Adjustment: International Constraints, Distributive Conflicts, and the State* (Princeton University Press, 1992).

Evans, P., H. Jacobson, and R. Putnam, *Double-Edged Diplomacy: International Bargaining and Domestic Politics* (London: University of California Press, 1993).

Frieden, J., *Debt, Development, and Democracy: Modern Political Economy and Latin America* (Princeton University Press, 1991).

Geddes, B., 'How Politicians Decide Who Bears the Costs of Liberalization', in I. T. Berend (ed.), *Transition to Market Economy at the End of the 20th Century* (Munich: Sudosteuropa, 1994).

Geddes, B., 'The Politics of Economic Liberalization', *Latin American Research Review* 30/2 (1995) 195–214.

Goodman, J. and L. Pauly, The Obsolescence of Capital Controls: Economic Management in an Age of Global Markets, *World Politics* 46/1 (1993) 50–82.

Gourevitch, Peter, 'The Second Image Reversed: The International Sources of Domestic Politics', *International Organization* 32/4 (1978) 881–911.

Graham, L., *The State and Policy Outcomes in Latin America* (New York: Praeger and Hoover Institution Press, 1990).

Griffith-Jones, S., *Managing World Debt* (Hemel Hempstead: Harvester Wheatsheaf, 1988).

Gwin, C., *US Relations with the World Bank 1945–92.* (Washington, DC: Brookings Institution Occasional Papers, 1994).

Gwin, C. and R. Feinberg, *The International Monetary Fund in a Multipolar World: Pulling Together* (Washington, DC: Overseas Development Council, 1989).

Gurría, J. A., 'Debt Restructuring: Mexico as a Case Study', in S. Griffith-Jones (ed.), *Managing World Debt* (Hemel Hempstead: Harvester Wheatsheaf, 1988).

Gurría, J. A., *La Política de la Deuda Externa* (Mexico City: Fondo de Cultura Económica, 1993).

Haas, E., *When Knowledge is Power: Three Models of Change in International Organizations* (Berkeley: University of California Press, 1990).

Haas, P., Knowledge, Power, and International Policy Coordination, *International Organization* 46/1, Special issue (1992).

Haggard, S. and R. Kaufman, 'The Politics of Stabilization and Structural Adjustment', in J. Sachs (ed.), *Developing Country Debt and Economic Performance: The International Financial System* (University of Chicago Press, 1989).

Haggard, S. and R. Kaufman, *The Political Economy of Democratic Transitions* (Princeton University Press, 1995).

Haggard, S. and S. Webb, *Voting for Reform: Democracy, Political Liberalization and Economic Adjustment* (Washington, DC: Oxford University Press for World Bank, 1994).

Heredia, B., 'Profits, Politics', in S. Maxfield and R. Anzaldua (eds), *Government and Private Sector in Contemporary Mexico* (San Diego: Center for US-Mexican Studies, 1987).

Ikenberry, J., 'The International Spread of Privatization Policies: Inducements, Learning and "Policy Bandwagonning" ', in *The Political Economy of Public Sector Reform and Privatization* (Boulder, CO: Westview, 1990).

International Monetary Fund, *International Capital Markets: Developments, Prospects, and Policy Issues* (Washington, DC: IMF, 1995).

Ize, A. I., *Trade Liberalization, Stabilization, and Growth: Some Notes on the Mexican Experience*, Working Paper no. WP/90/15 (Washington, DC: IMF, 1990).

James, H., *International Monetary Cooperation since Bretton Woods* (New York: Oxford University Press for International Monetary Fund, 1996).

Kahler, M., 'External Influence, Conditionality, and the Politics of Adjustment', in S. Haggard and R. Kaufman (eds), *The Politics of Economic Adjustment* (Princeton University Press, 1992a).

Kahler, M., 'The United States and the International Monetary Fund: Declining influence or declining interest?', in M. Karns and K. Mingst (eds) *The United States and Multilateral Institutions: Patterns of Changing Instrumentality and Influence* (London: Routledge, 1992b) 91–114.

Keohane, R. and H. Milner (eds), *Internationalization and Domestic Politics* (Cambridge University Press, 1996).

Lehman, H and J. McCoy, 'The Dynamics of the 2-Level Bargaining Game: The 1988 Brazilian Debt Negotiations', *World Politics* 44/4 (1992) 600–44.

Lissakers, K., *Banks, Borrowers and the Establishment: A Revisionist Account of the Debt Crisis* (New York: Basic, 1991).

López Gallo, M., *El Elegido* (Mexico City: Caballito, 1989).

López-Portillo, J., *Mis Tiempos* (Mexico City: Fernandez, 1988).

López-Portillo, J. R., *Economic Thought and Economic Policy-making in Contemporary Mexico: International and Domestic Components*, manuscript submitted for DPhil, (Oxford University 1995).

Loser, C. and E. Kalter, *Mexico: The Strategy to Achieve Sustained Economic Growth* (Washington, DC: IMF, 1992).

Lustig, N., *Mexico: the Remaking of an Economy* (Washington, DC: Brookings Institution, 1992).

Lustig, N., *The Mexican Peso Crisis: the Foreseeable and the Surprise*. Brookings Discussion Papers in International Economics no. 114 (Washington, DC: Brookings, 1995).

Mares, D. R., 'Explaining Choice of Development Strategies: Suggestions from Mexico, 1970–1982', *International Organization* 39/4 (1985) 667–97.

Martínez, G. and G. Fárber, *Desregulación Económica (1989–1993)* (Mexico City: Fondo de Cultura Económica, 1994).

Maxfield, S., *Governing Capital: International Finance and Mexican Politics* (Ithaca, NY: Cornell University Press, 1990).

Morales, E. and C. Ruiz., *Crecimiento, Equidad y Financiamiento Externo* (Mexico City: Fondo de Cultura Económica, 1989).

Morris, S., *Political Reformism in Mexico: An Overview of Contemporary Mexican Politics* (Boulder, Co: Rienner, 1995).

Naím, M., *Latin America's Journey to the Market: from Macroeconomic Shocks to Institutional Therapy* (San Francisco: International Center for Economic Growth, 1995).

Nelson, J. M., J. Kachanowicz, K. Mizsei and O. Muñoz, *Intricate Links: Democratization and Market Reforms in Latin America and Eastern Europe* (Washington, DC: Overseas Development Council, 1994).

Ortiz, G., *La Reforma Financiera y la Desincorporación Bancaria* (Mexico City: Fondo de Cultura Económica, 1994).

Pastor, M. and Wise, C., 'The Origins and Sustainability of Mexico's Free Trade Policy', *International Organization* 48/3 (1994) 459–90.

Putnam, R., 'Diplomacy and Domestic Politics: The Logic of Two-Level Games', *International Organization* 42:3 (Summer 1988) 427–60.

Ramos, A., J. Martinez and C. Ramirez, *Salinas de Gortari: candidato de la crisis* (Mexico: Plaza y Valdés, 1987).

Remmer, K., 'The Politics of Economic Stabilization: IMF Standby Programs in Latin America, 1954–1984', *Comparative Politics* 19/1 (1986) 1–24.

Remmer, K., 'Democracy and Economic Crisis: The Latin American Experience', *World Politics* 42/3 (1990) 315–35.

Rogozinski, J., *La Privatización de Empresas Paraestatales* (Mexico City: Fondo de Cultura Económica, 1993).

Sachs, J., A. Tornell, and A. Velasco, *The Collapse of the Mexican Peso: What Have We Learned?*, NBER Working Paper no. 5142 (Washington, DC: NBER, 1995).

Salinas de Gortari, C., *The Mexico We Want by 1994* (Mexico City: Presidency of Mexico, 1989).

Sanford, J., 'US Policy Toward the Multilateral Development Banks: the Role of Congress', in *George Washington Journal of International Law and Economics* 22 (1988) 1–115.

Secretaría de Programación y Presupuesto, *Antología de la Planeación en México, 1917–1985*, Vol. 9 (Mexico City: CFE, 1987).

Silva, E., 'Capitalist Coalitions, The State, and Neoliberal Economic Restructuring Chile, 1973–88', *World Politics* 45/4 (1993) 526–29.

Silva, E., 'From Dictatorship to Democracy: The Business–State Nexus in Chile's Economic Transformation, 1975–1994', *Comparative Politics*, 28/3 (1996) 299–320.

Solís, L., *La Realidad Económica Mexicana: Retrovisión y Panorama* (Mexico: Siglo XXI, 1970).

Stern, N. and F. Ferreira, *The World Bank as 'Intellectual Actor'* (Washington, DC: World Bank, 1993).

Stallings, B., 'International Influence on Economic Policy: Debt, Stabilization and Structural Reform', in S. Haggard and R. Kaufman (eds), *The Politics of Economic Adjustment* (Princeton University Press, 1992).

Stallings, B. (ed.), *Global Change, Regional Response: The New International Context of Development* (Cambridge University Press, 1995).

Story, D., 'Trade Politics in the Third World: A Case Study of the Mexican GATT Decision', *International Organization* 36/4 (1982) 767–94.

Szymczak, P., 'International Trade and Investment Liberalization: Mexico's Experience and Prospects', in C. Loser and E. Kalter (eds), *Mexico: The Strategy to Achieve Sustained Economic Growth* (Washington, DC: IMF, 1992).

Tussie, D. and M. Botzman, 'Sweet Entanglement: Argentina and the World Bank 1985–9', *Development Policy Review* 8 (1990) 393–409.

Williamson, J., *Latin American Adjustment: How Much Has Happened?* (Washington, DC: Institute for International Economics, 1990).

Williamson, J., *The Political Economy of Policy Reform* (Washington, DC: Institute for International Economics, 1994).

Woods, N., 'Economic Ideas and International Relations: Beyond Rational Neglect', *International Studies Quarterly* 39/2 (1995) 161–80.

11
The Shifting Foundations of Economic Liberalism in Latin American Public Policy

Laurence Whitehead

Introduction

At the close of this volume, we return to appraise the powerful resurgence of liberal economic doctrines and practices in Latin America in the 1990s. During this decade, a great deal of public policy-making in the region was rather closely governed by a prevailing matrix of liberal economic ideas (concerning fiscal and monetary discipline, state shrinking, privatization and the shift towards an increasingly outward-oriented, market-driven economic model). Ideas and practices are not always so closely harmonized, and indeed in the three years since the conference on which this volume is based, Latin America has witnessed a variety of policy retreats and setbacks that have undermined the self-confident liberal orthodoxy of the previous decade. The Argentine default of December 2001 constitutes the most spectacular reversal, but developments in Venezuela, the Partido dos Trabalhadores (PT) victory in Brazil and a variety of lesser episodes point in the same direction.

More generally, even in North America and in Europe the most prosperous market economies have pulled back from the liberal enthusiasms of the late 1990s, discouraged by financial market excesses, corporate governance failings, rising excess capacity and the broader shock to confidence arising from the successful terrorist assault on the most visible symbol of Wall Street's ascendancy, the Twin Towers in New York. But despite such bodyblows to 1990s euphoria, and mounting evidence that public policy priorities are no longer so tightly controlled by liberal economic doctrines (for example, with Homeland Security and the War on Terror threatening to trump the Doha Round or the promised new financial architecture), it is striking how little rethinking of core economic assumptions has yet occurred.

If dominant economic ideas remain largely unchallenged throughout the OECD countries, this pattern is even more striking in Latin America. A subcontinent that during the half century of import-substitution industrialization (1930–1980) was notable for its tendency to generate maverick economic analyses and dissents from liberal orthodoxy (Prebish, Furtado, Cepal, dependency theory, and so on) no longer generates intellectually significant challenges to the conventional wisdom of the 1990s. Even when first the Chilean Socialist Party and then the Brazilian Workers Party assume office through democratic elections, in conditions that might have been expected to validate some aspects of their former economic beliefs, the prevailing matrix of liberal economic ideas remains in the ascendant. Where earlier anti-market practices persist (as in Cuba) or resurface (as in Venezuela), their lack of realistic intellectual foundations is palpable and in consequence the chance of their prospects flourishing seems slight.

From this perspective, developments since September 2000 tend to bear out the assessment presented at our initial conference, which highlighted the strengths of the 1990s liberalizing movement, and drew attention to elements differentiating it from earlier episodes in Latin American intellectual history. It seems that liberal economic ideas, and indeed practices, may well persist through inertia and in the absence of effective challengers, notwithstanding the accumulation of disappointing results and the erosion of international interest. Presumably there must be some point at which adverse consequences and failed predictions could elicit a coherent intellectual alternative to prevailing economic ideas, but there is little evidence of that so far, and it may be that the legacy of the 1990s still has considerable momentum. This chapter indicates why that may prove to be the case.

The key strength identified is the extent to which 1990s economic doctrines and practices were embedded in a broader orientation toward liberalism, viewed in political and social as well as economic terms. This wider intellectual context serves to anchor the more specifically economic aspect of liberal doctrine, both reducing the risks of outright reversal and also constraining the potentially destructive and destabilizing effects of unfettered economism.[1]

The chapter begins by reflecting how new transformative policy ideas and doctrines may be assimilated over time (second section). It then discusses briefly in the third section Latin America's almost two-century long tradition of liberal social thought and practice, echoing and completing the account of Chapter 5. The fourth section then outlines further key strengths of the region's liberalizing drive of the 1990s, as compared with earlier episodes of liberal reform. The conclusion will briefly consider the implications of this argument for any assessment of the place of liberalism in Latin America's overall repertoire of social doctrines and practices.

On the diffusion and assimilation of a new doctrine

As the introduction to this volume made clear, the problem with most historical interpretations that invoke the 'power of ideas' is how to specify which ideas can be isolated, and how to demonstrate that they are responsible for their supposed effects. In much 'history of social thought', ideas unfold through the interaction of thinkers in (assumed) dialogue with each other. When outcomes are attributed to ideas, it is often simply on the basis that such-and-such a process or result was what the theory prescribed. The transmission mechanism through which a particular set of arguments or ideas were selected, adapted and pushed through to their practical conclusions is not so easy to establish. This leads to the risk that 'ideas' may become an ungrounded explanatory category.

One way to contain that risk is to focus on 'doctrines' – elaborated and internally coherent sets of ideas, buttressed by a particular academic discipline or intellectual specialism, which are championed by some network or community of practitioners. This approach is fairly close to the study of 'ideologies', which may be characterized in a similar way, except for the overtones of disapproval – an ideology is less respectable than a doctrine, its exponents may be suspected of being charlatans and its success may owe more to its dogmatism than to its coherence. What this chapter refers to as the doctrine of global economic liberalism is known elsewhere as the 'neo-liberal ideology'.

Whether we are dealing with doctrine or ideology, in the area of social theory what then requires explanation is how these ideas are converted into policies or practices. Can we identify specialized institutions which incorporate them into their objectives?[2] If so, the history of such institutions (the World Bank, the new regulatory agencies and so on) can be studied as proxies for the application of those ideas. Are there well-defined interests associated with a given doctrine (say, the interests of institutional investors in financial liberalization)? Again, the history of the ideas can then be studied through the history of their realization for those most wedded to them. Similarly, the network of specialists – the 'epistemic community' – could provide another empirically observable strand of the embodiment of the ideas. However, in line with most of the authors in this volume, we conclude that all this may be too narrow. For example, liberal economic doctrine may not be reducible to the activities of specific agencies or interests. It may exert its greatest effects on outcomes through more indirect channels – for example, altering the terms of public debate, sensitizing large diffuse audiences to new possibilities and so on In short, we may have to study liberalism as a 'discourse' – or even a *Zeitgeist* – in order to come to terms with the full range of its historical effects.

For the purposes of this volume, we need a more specific picture of how global economic liberalism may have been diffused and assimilated in contemporary Latin America over the past generation.[3] As Gourevitch sets out in Chapter 2, our starting-point is a period of crisis or policy paralysis in which hitherto prevailing ideas, doctrines and ideologies no longer carry conviction as sources of guidance for the future. Alternative social doctrines therefore find a more receptive audience than in the past. Such doctrines may be entirely new or could just be straight restatements of old ideas that had passed out of fashion. However, most probably they will be somewhat renovated, through claiming a respected pedigree. That would give them some initial credibility, together with the flexibility to cope with the specific requirements of the crisis. A good social doctrine needs to be pitched at a high level of generality. It should not be too obviously tailored to an imme-diate 'conjuncture' that could quickly be superseded. Nonetheless, it also needs to highlight underlying regularities that serve to explain what alterna-tive doctrines cannot account for and that point to relevant remedies. A good doctrine does not need to embrace any 'silver bullet' remedy to the situation it confronts. It is perfectly possible to argue that the rootedness of existing errors makes it extremely difficult to introduce the appropriate remedies, let alone to enjoy their benefits, any time soon. A robust social doctrine can envisage a better world that is very distant and costly to attain. However, the more visionary the doctrine, the more penetrating must be its critique of the existing situation.

Let us assume, then, that these initial ideas are articulated into a coherent and far-reaching doctrine that wins the necessary assent and begins to be converted into action. As the old assumptions crumble, and failed practices are swept aside, the doctrine will become identified with more specific inno-vations, and with conflicts through which its protagonists and antagonists acquire well-defined identities. This is the point at which doctrine can be said to generate ideology. The success or failure of specific innovations carries implications not just for the coherence of the theoretical ideas that may inspire them, but also for the power and success of the authors of these policies. Even so, if the initial doctrine is sufficiently coherent and gen-eralizable, it may not easily be damaged by the failure of any particular inno-vation it has generated. Usually such failures can be accounted for within the original belief system. If the crisis which started the whole process was sufficiently severe, as with the Latin American crisis of the inward-looking development model in the 1980s, then successive failures of reform may merely pave the way for further, more ambitious, root-and-branch proposals from within the same doctrinal school. Thus, the process of feedback from policy outcome to questioning of the doctrine may be long delayed and deflected.[4]

Eventually, however, any social doctrine will face increasing pressure to answer for its results, rather than solely to rely on its promises. With the passage of time, the initiating crises will gradually fade from memory, and the next generation of policy-makers, however steeped in the assumptions of the newly hegemonic doctrine, will be expected to explain when their initiatives generate undesired consequences.[5] Particularly in the case of liberalism, ideology cannot indefinitely cover up an inability to achieve promised goals, because the foundational doctrine provides not only principles of freedom and criticism but also practices of accountability (for example through democratic processes) that will eventually expose failure and incoherence to criticism. On this basis, we may hypothesize that in due course, the current liberalizing wave in Latin America will become more subject to effective critical feedback, to the extent that it proves incapable of fulfilling the expectations it has raised. But 'in due course' could be some considerable time in the future, bearing in mind the severity of the 1980s crises and the continuing disarray of neo-liberalism's Latin American critics. Indeed, on these grounds, one could also hypothesize that the most effective sources of criticism may well be generated broadly from *within* the liberal framework of analysis, rather than from outside and against it.

The long liberal tradition in Latin America

For almost two centuries, the formal written principles governing public policy life in the Latin American republics have been explicitly liberal. Popular sovereignty, the division of powers, federalism, press freedom, independence of the judiciary, citizen rights and the foundations of a market economy have all been enshrined in the successive constitutional documents enacted since independence. Although independent Brazil began life as a monarchy, it too adopted a liberal constitution.[6] In general, the liberal tradition is clearer and more longstanding in Latin America than in any other large world region, apart from the United States.[7]

Of course, these constitutional principles were more often suspended or disregarded than they were enforced. Until fairly recently in many countries they were a loose regulatory framework that was honoured only in the breach, and not allowed to regulate very much of social life. It was after all thought possible for several generations in the United States and elsewhere to espouse liberal doctrines at the intellectual level, while relying on slavery or other forms of coerced labour in the realm of production. However, for the most part these constitutional principles remained in place as the nominal aspirations or long-term objectives of these societies. Liberal ideas and ideals may have been neglected or downgraded, but they were seldom explicitly repudiated and replaced by clearly articulated alternative principles. The Cuban socialist constitution of 1975 is a clear exception to this rule, but otherwise the displacement of liberal principles has taken the form of states of exception, institutional acts justified in the name of national security and other temporary provisions that have left the underlying liberal framework of regulatory principles on the statute books. This foundational doctrine was therefore readily available to be revived and reinvigorated when more-ambitious and assertive variants of liberal practice came into fashion after the 1982 debt crisis.

Of course, this is a large generalization which requires numerous qualifications and footnotes. The term 'liberal regulatory principles' is capacious enough to accommodate a considerable range of variation. However, what is excluded should not be underestimated either – in particular given the legacy of three centuries of Iberian colonial rule. Monarchy, hereditary rights, *castas* and, by the late nineteenth century, slavery, were precluded. The temporal claims of the church were dethroned. The principle of self-government – implying a periodic selection of officeholders endorsed by popular suffrage – was enshrined. If the courts were no longer to be an instrument of colonial rule, then, at least in legal principle, their function would become to uphold the law of the republic, and ultimately to protect the rights of its citizens (whoever they may be). Press freedom was also pregnant with social implications. Given the context in which they were introduced, these liberal ideas and principles were powerful and transformative. If they were often weakly applied, this was not because they were irrelevant or insignificant, but rather because if fully applied their effects would be too strong to cope with.

This volume is about economic ideas and practices, rather than social doctrines in their entirety. Economic liberalism can clearly be analysed in isolation from the rest of liberal thought. However, this chapter chooses to discuss Latin American liberalism conceived very broadly. The economic elements are viewed as embedded in a set of ideas that were originally political in inspiration, and that have strong legal, social and even cultural implications. So it may be useful to situate the recent upsurge of economic liberalism in the subcontinent in the context of the region's broader engagement with western liberalism, conceived not just as a set of ideas or an ideology, but as a *Zeitgeist*. This is perhaps particularly relevant if we are trying to understand the momentum behind what is often termed the current wave of 'neo-liberalism' in Latin America. More than just an economic doctrine, ideology or set of reforming practices, it may be viewed as the unfolding of a more broadly based and deeply rooted potential in the region's formative experiences.

If political liberalism in Latin America was often only honoured in the breach, economic liberalism was more explicitly challenged and downgraded. Between about 1930 and 1980, liberal economic doctrines were on the defensive and in retreat throughout most of the region, and public policies were frequently oriented in an explicitly anti-liberal direction. There were restrictions on international payments, state-directed interest rates and price controls, corporatist forms of compulsory economic association, the nationalization of foreign investments and the expansion of public enterprises – in summary, a trend towards statist and inward-looking economic strategies. Economic nationalism can even be identified at the constitutional level, for example, in the Bolivian constitution of 1938 (following the expropriation of Standard Oil) or the Cuban constitution of 1940. As recently as 1988, the Brazilian constitution was rewritten in terms at variance with current principles of economic liberalism (making commitments which the authors of that document have subsequently had to invest much energy and political capital in attempting to circumvent).[8]

This long liberal tradition *persisted* during the last century. Without belittling the scale of the nationalist populist and socialist challenges to economic liberalism that arose in Latin America in the middle decades of the twentieth century, it requires restatement that – with the exception of Cuba – the basis of the market economy remained in place. Economic liberalism may have been challenged, and indeed driven back both as doctrine and as practice, but it retained crucial reservoirs of strength, both internationally (especially following the US-led victory over the Axis powers) and internally (for example in the financial sector, in the traditional press, and in key professions, notably the law). These internal sources of support for economic liberalism were not infrequently thrown onto the defensive by the new challengers, being forced into an embattled defence of unfashionable positions, and perhaps even in some cases became isolated and even demoralized. However, in a faithful reflection of both the heterogeneity and the resilience of elite structures in most Latin American societies, they were seldom uprooted or destroyed.[9] Moreover, they preserved their business and social connections with their counterparts in the 'developed' world.

These supporters possessed the material and cultural resources to keep abreast of the debate between economic liberalism and the more collectivist alternatives that were also underway in the OECD countries. Therefore, they knew that however adverse conditions might seem for them at home, all was far from lost for their positions in the international arena. Throughout the 1960s and 1970s, there was no shortage of foreign educational establishments or career paths available to form a self-confident next generation of Latin American economic liberals, ready to reconquer their own societies when local conditions became more propitious for them. Following the 1982 debt crisis, they were readily available throughout the subcontinent (as they were not in say, most of sub-Saharan Africa) to reverse the tide of policies and ideas that had for so long seemed to flow against them. In the Southern Cone, as is well known, this reversal began almost a decade earlier with the Pinochet coup.[10]

The strengths of the current drive for liberalization

Its increasing rootedness with time is already a strength of the current version of liberalism. This section identifies five further key sources of strength in contemporary global liberalism, each of which marks a contrast with the pre-1929 version of the same tradition, as it was experienced in Latin America. The emphasis is on economic liberalism, but similar points could be made about liberalism conceived more broadly, as a social and political doctrine, and indeed as a total 'world view'. The strength of economic liberalism as a doctrine cannot be divorced from this broader context, which is evident from the accompanying rise of liberal democratic political practices and institutional norms. Without these protections, economic liberalism on its own would be much more vulnerable to backlash and reversal.

The five strengths identified here are (1) the robust intellectual foundations of the current doctrine; (2) its wide practical application; (3) its relative pluralism; (4) the impressive range of sources of social support that it can still mobilize; and (5) the continuing disarray of its opponents. Each point is considered in turn.

Intellectual foundations

The intellectual foundations of contemporary 'global' liberalism are both narrower and more tightly constructed than was true of the earlier variants present in Latin America since the independence period. These earlier variants were often richly textured, with multiple sources of inspiration, but they contained inconsistencies of doctrine and practice, and they did not constitute an all-encompassing system. Thus, nineteenth-century liberalism might have to coexist with slavery, or with aristocracy, or with imperialism or suffrage restrictions. The contest between religious faith and secular liberalism was still hard fought, and on the other side of the spectrum, socialism and Marxism were also serious challengers to liberalism.[11] In contrast, the global liberalism of the 1990s can take secular assumptions for granted, can treat socialism as a defeated alternative, and can project both democracy and markets as values of universal applicability. Liberal doctrines are no longer constrained by the need to defer to any inherited source of tradition or institutional authority. Even such key institutions of global liberalization as the IMF or the World Bank may find themselves subjected to the same critique from liberal first principles as can be directed at all other collective agencies and authorities.

The first principles in question are now more rigorously and parsimoniously articulated. The intellectual foundations of contemporary liberalism are uncompromisingly radical. Individualism provides the building blocks for all understanding of both values and behaviour. Thus, the old divide between political and economic liberalism is superseded, and collectivist concepts such as solidarity or altruism are deconstructed. Working from such postulates, the underlying 'rationality of the market' can be put beyond question (at least at the level of theory and the ideal, 'really existing' markets being subject to 'imperfections'). Political and social critiques of this radical variant of liberalism can be delegitimized as manifestations of 'rent-seeking' and constituency-building by self-seeking brokers and intermediaries.

This system of thought is doctrinally solid and all-encompassing. Although most fully developed in neo-classical economics, it is far more than an economic doctrine. It is also a general research programme based on a coherent philosophical outlook, albeit one not often fully articulated.[12] Thus, it penetrates and reformulates the social sciences: in general, it proposes a strategy for the interpretation of history and it prescribes its own canons of method. It focuses on individual self-regarding behaviour and relies heavily on observable outcomes and indicators, to the neglect of discourse, intentions, collective memories, traditions, cultures and values. Within this framework, it is possible to derive many 'liberalizing' prescriptions, and to generate a wide range of public policy conclusions validated by 'objective' research findings. It thus has greater transformative power than the earlier more tentative and contextually restricted variants of liberalism. In contemporary Latin America, as elsewhere, its intellectual elegance continues to win new converts (especially in the younger generations).[13]

Practical applications

Not only is contemporary liberalism intellectually well grounded, it also has very wide practical applications. The central proposition is that all forms of monopoly – economic, political and even social concentrations of power – can be presumed collusions against the interests of outsiders, unless proved otherwise. From this, one can derive 'liberalizing' prescriptions that apply as much to the professions or the arts, as to trade, finance and political representation. The implications for 'the state' are particularly wide-ranging in Latin America, where so much hope and expectation had been invested in an institution that had fallen so far short of its pretensions. The subtlety and sophistication of some of these practical applications merit considerable elaboration, but here we are only concerned with the basics.

In practice, of course, not all the prescriptions that can be logically derived from first principles are taken up with equal enthusiasm, however well structured and comprehensive such principles may be. That is as true of global liberalism as it is of all other social doctrines. Thus, if the liberal case for liberalization of trade and financial exchanges across international boundaries is so powerful that it has become an almost unquestionable mantra, on grounds of doctrine one could conclude that the liberal case for dismantling immigration controls or for legalizing the sale of narcotics is almost as compelling.

In practice, however, the analysis becomes inarticulate when challenged to explain why the doctrine applies so well to capital flows, but not to labour flows; or why alcohol and tobacco markets should be legal and competitive, but marijuana should be criminalized and cartelized.[14] However, it is not necessary to adopt the view that contemporary liberal prescriptions are meant to apply equally to *all* social relations.[15] All that is claimed here is that the doctrine has *very wide* practical applications, and that it is a major source of strength that these essentially quite simple principles can be elaborated and refined to address such a large array of policy issues, both large and small. In Latin America during the 1990s, the principles were widely disseminated, and a considerable variety of important policy problems were tackled from within this perspective. But many areas of social life remain to be liberalized. The full potential of this doctrine as an instrument for transforming social relations in the subcontinent is as yet far from being fully revealed. This is a powerful reason for concluding that the current cycle of reforms, (inspired as always 'from above and without') still has a considerable distance to run. Global liberalism has by no means yet exhausted its impact on contemporary Latin America.

Relative pluralism

Third, while the model is dominant and deeply rooted historically, it is also somewhat more pluralist than one might expect and than has been true in the past. For example, there is a NAFTA model promoted by the United States, but also a MERCOSUR variant closer to the European approach. Throughout the 1990s there was the Argentine fixed exchange rate, and there still survive various other instances of dollarization (recently in Ecuador and El Salvador), but there are also many experiments with floating currencies. Brazilian gradualist strategies of liberalization contrast with the root-and-branch approach adopted by Fujimori and Menem. An important consequence is that when external models are invoked as guidelines for economic reform, these are now more detailed, more closely evaluated, and more likely to include other Latin American experiences, and not just an idealized account of a distant United States or Europe. Thus, for example, in the mid 1990s Bolivian pension reformers borrowed some specific proposals from Chile, and then passed on their experience and advice to Honduras and Haiti. In general the models being debated are more problem-oriented than in the past, and the region is displaying more pragmatism and greater reciprocity, although as some of these examples suggest, diversity can also arise from the failure to devise consistently viable solutions to key economic problems.

This limited pluralism within a broadly liberal consensus reflects the emergence of a denser and more internationally integrated network of policy advisers, specialists and intermediaries. Latin American economic thought has long been heavily influenced by the development of the discipline (and also the course of economic experimentation) in the 'core' countries of Europe and North America. This is especially true of liberal economic analysis, renovated over the past 20 years by 'neo-liberal' economic influences (derived especially from the United States). This is not to deny that there is always a process of local adaptation, filtering or even 'distortion' of external influences.[16] Nonetheless, frequent and intense exchange between local and global practitioners of the 'dismal science' has ensured that most major international ideas arrive quickly in the region and are now quite fully assimilated.

The 'epistemic community' of Latin American economists who circulate through such international institutions as the World Bank and IADB constitutes a vigorous and to some extent autonomous intellectual resource capable of diffusing doctrines throughout the whole of the subcontinent. Again, the range of doctrinal possibilities is narrower than before. For example, Mexico used to dispatch PEMEX officials and land reform experts to Bolivia to advise on the creation of state oil companies and the enactment of sweeping land redistributions. Nonetheless, within the broadly liberal democratic and market-oriented framework of current policy-making, the region is developing a much larger community of well-trained, competent and versatile professional experts and advisers. There is less scope than before for the isolated Renaissance man empowered to implement his transformative vision. Today's reformers are more dependent upon teamwork, mutual monitoring and comparative evaluation. Thus plurality broadens the sources of support, our third source of strength, to which we now turn.

Sources of social support

Although the patterns of popular resistance and incomprehension that used to block successive waves of liberalizing reform have by no means disappeared, some of the key impediments have been durably weakened. Greater political freedom, press criticism and institutional accountability may lead to more consensual strategies of reform, with greater diffusion of responsibility and more sense of local ownership. Of course, where transformative initiatives threaten to harm sectional interests, greater democracy and a more autonomous civil society can produce intensified resistance. Recent episodes such as the urban protest movement against water privatization that brought the process to a halt in Cochabamba, Bolivia, the mass movement against dollarization in Ecuador, or more general indications of an 'anti-globalization' backlash in many parts of Latin America all indicate a continuing social demand for alternatives to what is viewed as the prevailing neo-liberal orthodoxy. But such countervailing pressures represent only a relative and uneven process.

The key point is that contemporary liberalism can present itself as highly inclusionary. Critics of neo-liberalism may be right to assert that the material benefits of liberalization are often very unequally distributed. From this standpoint it may seem as though only a narrow stratum – financial operators, managers and large shareholders of international corporations, and associated consultants and media types – have strong reasons to back contemporary neo-liberalism. However, such a reductionist perspective overlooks two other sources of attraction that generate support from much wider constituencies.

The first is that in its present more robust and parsimonious form, liberal doctrine is seen as occupying the intellectual high ground. It appeals to the bright and the ambitious in many societies, whether or not they stand to gain any immediate material advantage, because it seems to provide convincing and practical answers to a great range of questions that are not so adequately addressed by alternative doctrines. It has high academic prestige, a strong pedigree, a succession of unexpectedly convincing successes to its credit, and its analysis is bold and unmistakable. Small wonder, then, that recent cohorts of the 'best and the brightest' in Latin America and around the world have often rallied to liberal positions, rather than to the nationalist or socialist doctrines that exerted so much pull over earlier generations.

The second feature making contemporary liberalism appear so inclusionary is that it has demonstrable appeal, not only to business elites and to yuppies, but also to much broader sections of the populace at large. This is often dismissed as 'middle-class' support, but that is quite misleading. The key point is that liberalization, conceived as the challenging of 'insider' privileges, and the extension of access through broadened competition, strikes a chord with all sorts of (real or imagined) outsiders. Public ownership provides one good example of the kind of target that can mobilize consumers, competitors, and indeed all non-participants against a cosy-looking monopoly. Even well run and socially responsible public enterprises find it difficult to defend themselves against this reflex, since it is so broadly based. Trade unions offer a similar target, especially in those parts of Latin America where corporatist privileges really have been enjoyed at the expense, not only of society as a whole, but of much union membership as well.

Throughout the 1990s Menem's Argentina provided a vivid illustration of the broad social appeal of contemporary liberal arguments in a society which, since the 1930s, had invested so much hope in anti-liberal doctrines to so little avail. The collapse of 2001/2 brought great discredit to Menem and his entourage, and briefly awakened illusions that the people of Argentina would henceforth spurn the illusions of economic liberalism, but in the absence of a coherent economic alternative such rhetoric is likely to prove ungrounded. More generally, it is often the votes of the lower-income deciles that have sustained recent liberalizing initiatives in Latin America in the face of opposition from organized challengers. If anything, critiques of liberalism may strike more of a chord with the middle classes, however that vague term is defined, than with other social strata.

Here it may be worth briefly noting a contrast between the broad inclusionary potential and intellectual self-confidence of contemporary liberalism in Latin America, as compared to the doctrine's late-nineteenth and early-twentieth-century forerunners. At that time, as already noted, liberal theory was more complex, more compromised and less focused. In addition, its sources of social support within Latin America were considerably more constrained. In still heavily agrarian societies, its appeal was mainly urban. In cities where conservatives and socialists might both seek lower-class support, the educated middle classes were most likely to pick up liberal ideas. However, the main sources of liberal doctrine were foreign – France, the United States and Britain – at a time when nationalism was stirring. Merchants and those in export enclaves might claim allegiance to liberal ideas, but their ways of pursuing self-interest would not necessarily win them converts in other sectors of society.

The disarray of opponents

This brings us to what is probably the most important source of liberal resilience in the 1990s, as contrasted to previous episodes: the weakness of resistance to contemporary liberalism, in contrast to earlier times. First, the Catholic Church no longer combats either democracy or the market with anything like the militancy of the past, and in any case, its capacity for influencing social thought has plummeted. To a large extent, it, and the other sources of religious influence that carry increasing weight in various parts of Latin America, have come to terms with a secular liberal worldly order, except on a narrow range of 'moral' topics. Within the church Opus Dei probably has more influence in promoting liberal doctrines than liberation theology in resisting them.

Second, the collapse of the Soviet bloc not only discredited Bolshevism, but also destabilized western social democracy, leaving the main ideological initiative to a resurgent liberalism. Admittedly, large parts of the Latin American left still manifest considerable nostalgia for these fading nostrums. Castro, Chávez and 'Tirofijo' all continue in their different ways to declare defiance, but all these examples can be taken as confirmation of the weakness of resistance to contemporary liberalism, rather than evidence to the contrary. The evolution of the Chilean Socialist Party is more telling about the power of liberal doctrine, and the difficulty of resisting it, rather than seeking to tame it from within.

Third, we should note that contemporary liberalism is a *global* doctrine, and derives much strength from the apparently inexorable advance of what is loosely known as 'globalization'. The key point here is that whatever else it involves, this process signifies the shrinkage and wholesale restructuring of the Latin American state. As noted, state expansion, and the associated doctrines of political and economic nationalism, constituted the most formidable sources of resistance to liberalism in Latin America from the 1929 depression to the 1982 debt crisis. If statism and nationalism are no longer seen as viable options, this removes the most serious obstacle to the advance of contemporary global liberalism.

Moreover, the absence of an intellectually coherent alternative continues to undercut all such episodes of resistance. In this respect, ideas really *do* matter. It is evident that after any particular setback or disappointment the public authorities will need to rethink and reformulate their tactics. Shocks like the 'contagion' from East Asia in 1998, and disappointments like the persistence of slow growth and acute inequality despite the implementation of sweeping reforms (for example, in Argentina), may create a public demand for more far-reaching shifts in economic doctrine and practice. But the absence of a credible strategic alternative to the central assumptions of economic liberalism, and given the range of possibilities that can be accommodated within that broad intellectual position, most replacement tactics consist essentially of different ways of packaging and timing policies that remain embedded within a univocally liberalizing frame of reference. The Chávez administration in Venezuela no longer offers much prospect of an exception to this generalization, but even if it had, Venezuela's oil resources would be needed to underpin the deviation.

In view of the robust intellectual foundations, varied practical applications, relative pluralism, broad basis of support, and weakened sources of resistance to global liberalism, it is hard to avoid the conclusion that the 1990s represented at least a fairly substantial break with the past. Contemporary liberalism offers a series of ambitious and wide-ranging projects of transformation, catch-up and 'modernity', which even if they have originated 'from above and without' may be carried through to fulfilment and anchored in the collective institutions and memories of the subcontinent, to a far greater extent then earlier initiatives.[17] It may define the context of 'modernity' in a more precise, specific and operational form than ever before, and it converts its vision of the future into a realizable present. That, at least, is what the liberal *Zeitgeist* presumes. The twentieth century witnessed several major setbacks to the liberal view of progress (1914, 1929, 1939 and so on) and it would be rash to assume that such discontinuities are only a thing of the past. However, barring some rather drastic interruption of this kind, the current process in Latin America seems likely to continue more or less on course for a considerable period still to come. It is therefore too soon to judge the full effects of the liberalizing reforms undertaken in the 1990s.

Conclusion

This chapter has sketched an interpretation of the resilience of the global liberal economic doctrines and practices currently being applied in contemporary Latin America. It has argued that the region's long liberal traditions, not confined to economic liberalism, help explain the strong take-up of recent prescriptions, and may help to limit the prospect of eventual reversals. For reasons of brevity, 'doctrines' and 'practices' have been bracketed together, since they were closely connected during the 1990s, although less so since 2000. In a more extended exposition it would be desirable to separate them. The guiding doctrine may be labelled a variant of liberalism, but the prevailing practices have been something rather different – namely liberalization. The difference arises from the fact that liberalism theorizes about an equilibrium outcome, whereas liberalization concerns the transformative processes required to liquidate obstacles to that outcome, and to put in place the conditions for its entrenchment.[18]

The distinction between liberal doctrine and the far from obviously liberal practices undertaken in its name was very pronounced in Latin America during the nineteenth century, when the doctrine in question was as much constitutional, legal and political as it was economic. At that time a broad array of theoretical positions traceable to French, Spanish, British, and American debates over liberal social theory were taken up by the new governing elites of the subcontinent, and came to occupy foundational roles in the official discourse and public policy outlook of the new republics. Although much of this discourse has been characterized as misleading rhetoric, it did in fact generate some practical consequences, both in the short term – the way in which elite interests were articulated and serviced – and as a long-run resource for structuring public policy when illiberal practices had failed. For example, the Argentine constitution of 1853 embodies a complex structure of liberal doctrines that were still available to be reactivated after 1982. These domestic foundational resources were also nourished and reinforced by a periodic replenishment of liberal contacts and influences from Europe and North America, external sources of orientation that never ceased to exercise influence over substantial sectors of Latin American elite opinion. This long and loose liberal tradition serves to differentiate the subcontinent from most other 'third-wave' democracies, and 'emerging markets', and may help account for its receptivity to the latest global resurgence of liberal doctrines.

As acknowledged in the third section of this chapter, the balance and content of liberal doctrines and practices has of course varied greatly over time and space. Initial liberal orientations were broad, varied and inspired by a range of partially conflicting external models. They also ran up against severe obstacles, both in terms of opposition from alternative doctrines, and in terms of social incomprehension and resistance. So even during the most favourable periods (for example, 1870–1914) and in the most receptive settings, there was a great deal of mixing and matching. Liberal doctrines (both economic and political – the two not necessarily well differentiated) were applied selectively and unevenly. Enforcement was usually fairly incomplete. Even so, a long, loose, chain of liberal debates, examples, doctrines, ideologies, practices and critiques has constituted a continuous and influential strand of Latin American historical experimentation over the past two centuries. Between about 1930 and 1980, this current was on the defensive or even driven underground, but it never dried up. It remained embedded in a variety of institutions, interests, professional associations and international networks. After the 1980s, all this could be reactivated and given renewed impetus and self-confidence. The transformative effects it has achieved over the past 20 years, and the continued strength of the consensus behind it even now, can hardly be explained without taking into account these deep-rooted antecedents.

So the recent surge of economic and political liberalization across the region clearly builds on its old liberal traditions. But, particularly on the economic front, contemporary liberalism is also distinctively new. This chapter has argued that the current doctrine is narrower then before, but also better focused. It rests on robust intellectual foundations. It also generates rather precise prescriptions for liberalization which weaken the organizational and social bases for alternative projects (for example, trade unions), and which thereby create 'facts on the ground' that successive governments will have to live with, whether they endorse liberal economic doctrines or not. The prestige of economic reasoning is now so great that that component of liberal doctrine comes to the fore even in analysis concerned with politics or with social policy. Much of the 'republican' resonance (anticlericalism, secularism, state-building) of traditional liberalism have faded from view. Global liberalism need no longer defer to inherited privilege or compromise in the face of a challenge from socialism. There is now a powerful and unifying external stimulus and source of orientation transmitted from the United States (on economic matters from the 'east coast establishment' – Washington, Wall Street, Ivy League universities, and the Bretton Wood twins). But all this is reinforced by the presence of a broader liberal *Zeitgeist* generated from Europe and from within Latin America, as well as from the United States. Economic doctrines gain reinforcement from the propagation of a related official consensus about democratisation, human rights and 'good governance'. Within Latin America, social support comes not only from elite circles, but also from substantial sections of the society at large.[19]

In the five years since the Oxford conference there have been many adverse developments affecting the Latin American economies. The December 2001 collapse of Argentina's convertibility plan, and the country's subsequent default on its international liabilities, was probably the most pivotal event, but it should not be viewed in isolation. Brazil and Uruguay were similarly affected and required emergency IMF assistance. For different reasons, both Venezuela and Colombia have also faced severe economic emergencies. More generally, world trade prospects deteriorated abruptly and sharply, and capital inflows (apart from direct foreign investment) dried up, leaving the entire regional economy adrift. Indeed, despite a decade of pro-market and outward-oriented reforms, Latin America finds itself once again facing the prospect of a possibly extensive period of economic underperformance, with a consequent upsurge of discontent and social protest against 'failed neo-liberal' policies. This downturn was followed by an abrupt and unexpected commodity boom, which has tended to reinvigorate an old image of Latin America as a primary product exporter. The durability of this upswing remains uncertain, however. Defenders of the new economic model can draw little comfort from the developed world, with Washington itself no longer practising 'Washington consensus' virtues of fiscal and monetary discipline, and with Europe and Japan also facing underperformance and disorientation. The main impetus for further economic reform must still be provided by the Doha Round of world trade negotiations, but in current conditions these face severe protectionist obstacles, and following 11 September 2001 most policy-making is now focused more on issues of security than on the previous agenda of economic liberalization. However, this volume is concerned only indirectly with such adverse economic developments. The focus is on economic ideas, and one striking feature of the present situation is that these have changed surprisingly little, despite the challenge to them posed by recent instabilities. Admittedly there has been some fresh discussion of the role and functions of the international financial institutions, stirred up in particular by the critique launched by Joseph Stiglitz. Whereas some optimists in the 1990s had begun to suggest that the result of improved techniques of economic management might be to abolish the business cycle, a more pessimistic alternative view now suggests that pre-Keynesian cycles of overinvestment followed by protracted restructuring may characterize the present market-based system of economic coordination. As the financial excesses of the late 1990s are exposed, there is some renewed interest in certain aspects of economic re-regulation. But, at least so far, such shifts of focus of economic debate constitute minor adjustments within a still dominant (and indeed unchallenged) framework of economic analysis. Whereas economic liberalism faced major rival doctrinal and policy contenders during earlier "hard times", no such ideational alternatives are visible on this occasion.

In Latin America, at least, the opponents of what they term neo-liberalism now rest their case on moral exhortations, rather than on economic arguments or some analytical framework that aims to contest dominant ideas on their own terrain. The new PT administration in Brazil is eloquent in this sense. While ideologically and emotionally out of sympathy with economic liberalism, it starts out with an expressed intention to achieve its goals while reassuring the markets of its reliability and its commitment to 'responsible' economic policies. Whatever the eventual outcome of the Lula experiment, this initial stance represents a remarkable victory for liberal economic ideas in an apparently unpromising setting. Whether or not one considers present economic ideas to be either correct or durable, it is important to examine how they came to prevail and from whence they draw their strength.

Notes

1. Karl Polanyi famously highlighted the way market-economy assumptions and practices have become artificially differentiated from the social and political context in which they are embedded. He traced this from the mid-eighteenth to the mid-twentieth century in *The Great Transformation* (1944). Since then, a vast literature has grown up analysing the social embeddedness of the market, and how it acquired its appearance of naturalness. Two good recent collections are Haskell and Teichgraeber (1993), and Mirowski (1994).
2. For an illuminating comparative analysis of 'developmental' ideas and institutions in Argentina and Brazil, see Sikkink (1991).

3. A useful guide is provided by Biersteker (1995), and more recently, by Biersteker and Kearney (2000).

4. Who, for example, would have foreseen in 1990 that despite the collapse of the Russian economy and the disintegration of Russian society under the impact of liberalizing reforms in the ensuing decade, there would still be a nucleus of western liberals who would persist in claiming that their doctrine could be vindicated by this experience? Ten years later income per head in the Former Soviet Union was half its previous level. How much further would it have to fall, and for how long, before the custodians of liberal doctrine would admit to any fundamental error? For an early doctrinal critique that now reads rather well, see Murrell (1992).

5. A case I have attempted to make in Whitehead (2000).

6. In the words of Bradford Burns (1993:127), 'liberal ideology seemed dominant among the elite, particularly those segments associated with the cities and with exports ... They favoured free trade; they argued the advantages of free navigation of rivers ... However, removed from is original context ... The liberalism of the Brazilian elite had the ultimate effect of deepening Brazil's dependency.' For the ambivalence of Brazilian elites regarding the political aspects of the liberal tradition, see Sérgio Adorno (1988).

7. For a recent re-evaluation of Mexican liberalism, which makes a good case for reintegrating it more fully into the mainstream of the western liberal tradition, and thus for reassessing that tradition as a whole, see Aguilar Rivera (2000).

8. The recent Venezuelan constitution could also prove an impediment to economic liberalism at the doctrinal level, although the practical economic content of the new charter is still to be revealed.

9. This tug-of-war between liberal and nationalist economic doctrines in the postwar years is well documented in Lourdes Sola, *Idéias Econômicas, Decisões Políticas* (USP press, Sao Paulo, 1998). See also the unpublished Oxford DPhil thesis by Oscar Landerretche, 'Inflation and Socio-Political Conflicts in Chile, 1955–1970' (1983).

10. See, for example, Whitehead (1997).

11. Jose Guilherme Merquior wrote a powerful synthesis of the western liberal tradition while serving as Brazilian ambassador to Mexico. See his *O Liberalizmo: Antigo e Moderno* (1991).

12. As with all philosophical positions its coherence is no guarantee of its correctness. But this chapter is concerned only with explaining its resilience. Philip Mirowski's recent genealogical critique exposes the underlying vulnerabilities; for example, 'It is a prerequisite for understanding the vicissitudes of the constrained optimization in the twentieth century to keep in mind that the paradigm of the constrained optimization of utility split off from its physics inspiration just prior to the elaboration of the Second Law of Thermodynamics ... this goes some distance in explaining its persistent blindness to problems of dissipation, the fragile nature of knowledge, and problems of temporal orientation' (2002:30).

13. As with any hegemonic doctrine, these are of course very important internal tensions, and the associated research programme is far from static. On the contrary, for all its parsimony, contemporary liberalism remains remarkably dynamic, and has proved capable of generating coherent responses to successive waves of criticism. For example, in answer to the charge that it neglected political institutions it responded with the 'new institutionalism', which relies on its theory of incentive structures. Charged with neglecting history, it recast historical investigations in terms of the emergence of individual property rights. Part of its appeal to the next generation may be that it dispenses with the need to assimilate the

knowledge acquired by prior generations, disqualifying all previous work both on theoretical and methodological grounds.

14. At the theoretical level, this incoherence can be disguised (but not overcome) by resort to a dichotomous distinction between 'the right' and 'the good'. So long as these two components of 'ought' are kept rigorously separated, it is possible to segregate technique (trade liberalization becomes the technically right and necessary way to organize trade) from preference (individual voters do not consider it good to be 'swamped by immigrants'). However, if the social appeal of liberalism rests ultimately on its identification with the value of liberty, the realm of freedom lies precisely in between technical necessity and revealed preference, both of which become in a strict sense illiberal when reified.

15. It is interesting to observe that even the IMF and World Bank have recently come under scrutiny as questionable monopolies, although as far as I am aware, this line of reasoning has yet to be extended to the US Supreme Court, the Internal Revenue Service, or the Federal Reserve Board.

16. For the most celebrated recent example of Latin American adaptation and feedback, see Hodara (1987). For a much earlier instance of feedback, see Brand (1987).

17. For an overview of two centuries of successive, partial, and incomplete efforts to implant 'modernity' in Latin America, driven 'from above and without', see Whitehead (2002), which also explores how far the 1990s represented a fundamental break with the past.

18. In his 1979 lectures at the Collège de France, Foucault attempted to generate a dynamic account of liberalism, as a governmental practice that both produces and consumes liberty. This conveys the idea that 'liberalism is not something that accepts freedom, it is that which seeks to manufacture it at each moment', thus enabling him to direct attention to the costs of liberalization, its limits, and the need to prevent economic freedom from becoming a social danger. (So far so good, but from this starting-point he moves too eagerly to the controlling and repressive aspects of liberalism, downplaying its creative 'liberating' potential).

19. The recent election campaign in Peru illustrates this point. The rival contenders were both competing for the votes of the poor. However, they were also both seeking the endorsement of Hernando de Soto, whose latest volume *The Mystery of Capital: Why Capitalism Triumphs in the West and Fails Everywhere Else* (2000) restates his influential liberal polemic in favour of popular capitalism in Latin America.

References

Adorno, S., *Os Apredizes do Poder: O Bacharelismo Liberal na Política Brasileira* (Rio de Janeiro: Paz e Terra, 1988).
Aguilar Rivera, J. A., *En Pos de la Quimera: Reflexiones sobre el Experimento Constitutional Atlántico* (Mexico City: Fondo de Cultura Económica, 2000).
Biersteker, T. J., 'The Triumph of Liberal Economic Ideas in the Developing World', in B. Stallings (ed.), *Global Change, Regional Response: The New International Context of Development* (Cambridge University Press, 1995).
Biersteker, T. J. and C. Kearney, 'Global Economic Doctrines: Still the Triumph of Liberal Orthodoxy?', paper presented to conference on Economic Doctrines in Latin America (Oxford University Latin American Centre, September 2000).
Brand, Salvador Osvaldo, *El Origen Latinoamericano de las Teorías de la Moneda y de la Inflación* (Bogota: Plaza y Janés, 1987).

Burns, E. B., *A History of Brazil* (New York: Columbia University Press, 1993).

De Soto, H., *The Mystery of Capital: Why Capital Triumphs in the West and Fails Everywhere Else* (New York: Basic, 2000).

Hall, P., *The Political Power of Economic Ideas* (Princeton University Press, 1989).

Haskell, T. L. and R. F. Teichgraeber (eds), *The Culture of the Market: Historical Essays* (Cambridge University Press, 1993).

Hodara, J., *Prebisch y la CEPAL* (Mexico City: Colegio de Mexico, 1987).

Merquior, J. G., *O Liberalismo: Antigo e Moderno* (Rio de Janeiro: Nova Fronteira, 1991).

Mirowski, P. (ed.), *Natural Images in Economic Thought* (Cambridge University Press, 1994).

Mirowski, P. *Machine Dreams: Economics Becomes a Cyberg Science* (Cambridge University Press, 2002).

Murrell, P., 'Conservative Political Philosophy and the Strategy of Economic Transition', *East European Politics and Societies*, 6/1 (Winter 1992) 3–16.

Polanyi, K., *The Great Transformation* (New York: Reinhart, 1994).

Sikkink, K., *Ideas and Institutions: Developmentalism in Brazil and Argentina* (Ithaca, NY: Cornell University Press, 1991).

Whitehead, L., 'La Economía en México: El Poder de las Ideas e Ideas de Poder', in A. Hernández Chávez and M. Carmagnani (eds), *Europa en México: Por una Colaboración en Ciencias Sociales* (Torino: Centro Universitario di Storia dell'America Latina, Centro de Estudios de México en Italia, 1997).

Whitehead, L., 'Privatization and the Public Interest in Latin America: Partial Theories, Lopsided Outcomes', in W. Baer and J. L. Love (eds), *Liberalization and its Consequences: A Comparative Perspective on Latin America and Eastern Europe* (Northampton: Elgar, 2000).

Whitehead, L., 'Latin America as a Mausoleum of Modernities', in L. Roniger and C. H. Waisman (eds), *Globality and Multiple Modernities: Comparative North American and Latin American Perspectives* (Brighton: Sussex Academic, 2002).

Yee, A., 'The Causal Effect of Ideas on Policies', *International Organization*, 50/1 (Winter 1996) 69–108.

Index